ENGLISH ILLUMINATI

Including the History of the Order of the Illuminati and the Mysteries of the Illuminati.

Plus the revived Illuminati Rituals and Ordinances.

ENGLISH ILLUMINATI

Including the History of the Order of the Illuminati and the Mysteries of the Illuminati.

Plus the revived Illuminati Rituals and Ordinances.

Alistair McGawn Lees

Lewis Masonic

First published 2019

ISBN 978 0 85318 545 1

Published by Lewis Masonic

an imprint of Ian Allan Publishing Ltd, Shepperton, Middx TW17 8AS
Printed in India.

Visit the Lewis Masonic website at www.lewismasonic.co.uk

Frontispice - Ceiling in the Illuminati Hall Bavaria, - Leopold Engel, 1906

Plaster Ceiling from the Illuminati Hall

Illuminati College, Ingolstadt, Bavaria
By
Leopold Engel 1906
(History of the Illuminati Order)

Illuminati Hall was restored in 1903 and 1904 to its present condition. The room is unique because of its artistic baroque ceiling of historical art significance and because of the historical scenes that occurred in this room.

In 1900, Professor Joseph Hartmann gave the following description of the location of Illuminati Hall.

The domestic room in which the Illuminati in Ingolstadt were accustomed to hold their meetings, still exists today and is commonly called the Illuminati Hall. He finds himself in a small back building of the house no. 23 on Theresienstrasse, which was used as number 298 on the Wine Market in the possession of university professors. Thus, it was owned in 1719 by Professor Dr. Johann Adam Morasch, and in 1762, by Professor Georg Christoph Emanuel Härtel. Around 1777, during the period of Weishaupt, it was already owned by a citizen Franz Riedmaier, the so-called Augsburg messenger.

This room was suitable for holding meetings of lodges and the minutes record that the meetings could be held unobserved.

The decoration was mainly executed in the richly appointed stucco ceiling, the four large and four smaller medallions in stucco have paintings and a three metre by almost two metre wide centre painting (p. 120/21). In the blunt fashion of that age, a medallion showing the punishment of curiosity, the goose is a symbol of stupidity. This compares the priest before higher Illuminati in the upper medallion; the three dogs represent loyalty, obedience, vigilance. Above him floats an eagle, representing divine inspiration. The two major side medallions describe spring as a time of sowing and autumn a time of harvesting. The smaller medallions are symbols of security, justice, love and peace.

When the Order was abolished in 1785, and the lodges had to be closed, this space was soon forgotten. It decayed, and served the most profane purposes for storage, printing, and finally as a shoemaker's workshop. The patina and the dirt of 118 years had to be removed, so that the clean lines of the stucco work could be visible, and now be enjoyed by the eye. The hall is shown to foreign visitors of Ingolstadt, by a plaque indicating, where one has to go. The prominent building in the urban high school is essentially characterized by three construction projects: the building from 1434 was rebuilt as Pfündnerhaus, alteration to the first Bavarian university from 1472, and the historical reconstruction in the 1930s by the Ingolstadt-based city planner Franz Schwäbl. After further alterations that affected the staircases and the library, the university was finally moved in 1800 to Landshut. In 1942 the late-Baroque plaster ceiling from the Illuminati Hall (formerly Theresienstraße 23) was installed on the first floor.

From 'Geschichte des Illuminaten-Ordens' 1906 written by Leopold Engel, 1858-1931

CONTENTS

Contents	*9*
List of Figures	*11*
Foreword	*13*
Preface	*15*
Acknowledgements	*17*
Introduction	*19*
The revived Illuminati	*20*

Chapter I
Finding the English Illuminati *21*

Westcott's transcription	23
Illuminati rituals	25
Illuminati images	26
Images of the ordinances	27
Reuss' pamphlet	28
Chance spotting of the words Illuminati	30
Papus illuminati letters to Westcott	30
Transcription of first Illuminati letter	31
Scan of the first Illuminati letter to Westcott	32
Second Illuminati letter	36
Transcription of second Illuminati letter	37
Scan of second Illuminati letter to Westcott	38
The Prussian Illuminati & the French Martinist	40
Wrong history, wrong Order	40
To summarise 1901	42
Illuminati letterheads	45
First Illuminati letterhead	45
Illuminati Minerval certificate	47
First wax seal	49
Second wax seal	52
Second letterhead	53
Third letterhead	56
Irregular Freemasonry	57
New material	60
Illuminati rituals date	60
Illuminati Regent warrant (Dresden) 1902	62
The seals on the Dresden Regent's warrant	64
Accept the position of Regent	66
Unsubstantiated note (postcard)	66
New regent warrant from Hamburg	66
Illuminati regent warrant (Hamburg) 1902	67
The seals on the regent warrant (Hamburg)	69
College minutes	70
October 1902	70
The end of the English Illuminati	73
Last English Illuminati letter	74
But I could not work the Illuminati here	75
Transcription of 16 October 1902 letter	77

Chapter II
History of the Order of Illuminati *81*

Introduction to the 'History'	83
Original document	84
History of the Order of the Illuminati	86
Antiquity	86
Moses	87
Greece	87
Initiation	88
Egypt	88
Feasts	89
Not the only knowledge	89
Rosicrucians	89
Theosophists	90
Rosenkreuz	90
Brahmins	91
Rosicrucian degrees	92
Weishaupt	92
Alombrados	93
Secret society	93
Knigge	94
Teachings	95
America	96
Impending First World War	97

Chapter III
Mysteries of the Illuminati *99*

Introduction	101
Original document	101
Translation and original document	106

Chapter IV
Revived Illuminati regulations and rituals *113*

Introduction	115
Why are the rituals so different?	115
Dating of the Bavarian Illuminati rituals, 1786?	116
Weishaupt twelve German Illuminati books	116
Illuminati Rose-Croix warrant	117
Supreme council 33° disapproval	118
Dating of the Prussian Illuminati rituals, 1896?	118
Dating of the English rituals 1902?	118
German ritual & translations	119
German printed material timeline	120
English translations	120
Innere Ordens-Ordnung	121
Constitutions and regulations Minerval Lodges	123
Introduction	124
Women members	125
Name and purpose of the Minerval Lodges	125
Situation	126
Foundation of lodges	126
Membership and admission	126
Officials	127
Fees	127
Work	127
General meeting	128
Inspection	128
Free entry and departure	129
Dissolution of a lodge	129
Ritual Minerval grade	131
Introduction	133
Opening of the lodge of the Minerval	135
Admission in the lodge of the Minerval	135
Closing of the lodge of the Minerval.	136
Ritual Schotten grade	137
Introduction	139
Ritual Schotten grade/Andreas Knight grade	140

Chapter IV (continued)

Ritual Rosenkreuzer grade   143
    Introduction   144
    The number of words in each   146
    A side by side comparison   146
    Opening of the Rose-Croix grade   147
    Ceremony of initiation into Rose-Croix   148
    Closing of the Rose-Croix grade   150
Ritual de Synoden   151
    Introduction   153
    Opening of the Ritual de Synoden   155
    Closing Ritual de Synoden   156

Chapter V
Heckethorn's Bavarian Illuminati   157

    The term Illuminati   159
    Foundation   159
    Organisation   159
    Initiation into the grade of Epopt or priest   160
    Initiation grade of Regent   161
    The greater mysteries   161
    Magus grade   161
    Homo Rex   162
    Nomenclature   162
    Cipher   162
    Higher mysteries cipher   162
    Secret papers and correspondence   163
    Refutation of charges   163
    Suppression   163
    Illuminati in France   164
    La Secte des Illumines ceremonies of initiation   164
    Oath of la Secte des Illumines   164
    Credibility of above account   165
    Heckethorn oath of an Illuminati   165
    The Jesuits oath   165
    The proposed English Illuminati ritual oaths   166
    English Illuminati - Minerval oath   166
    English Illuminati - Andreas knight grade oath   166
    English Illuminati - Rose-Croix grade oath   166
    English Illuminati - Opening and closing Synods   166
    English Illuminati - Word of the Regent's grade   166

Chapter VI
Characters in the revived Illuminati story   167

DR WILLIAM WYNN WESTCOTT   169
    Capable of setting up the Illuminati   171
    Westcott and the S.R.I.A.   172
    The family man   172
    Family   174
    Freemasonry   175
    Non-masonic   178
    Publishing   181
    Westcott box of numbered papers: 182

THEODOR (ALBERT) KARL REUSS   183
    Freemasonry   183
    Munich   185
    London   185
    Berlin   185
    Revived Ludwig Lodge 1895   186
    Grand Lodge of Germany   188
    Non-masonic memberships   189
    Oriflamme magazine   189
    Oriflamme lodge calendar   190
    The meeting dates   190
    Translation   190
    A list of Reuss' writings: 191

DR GÉRARD ENCAUSSE - PAPUS   193
    Personal life   194
    Freemasonry   194
    Non-masonic memberships   195
    After Papus   200
    Papus meets Westcott for the first time   200
    Le libre Examen   203
    Russia   206
    Protocols of the Elders of Zion   207
    Was Papus losing control?   207
    Pierre Deullin   209
    Edouard blitz   209
    A list of Papus' writings: 211

JOHN YARKER   213
    Non-masonic memberships   214
    Freemasonry   217
    Conclusion   221
    Yarker's articles for Quatuor Coronati Lodge   223
    A list of Yarker's writings   224

Bibliography   225

Index   227

LIST OF FIGURES

Figure	Page
Frontispiece. Ceiling in the Illuminati Hall, Bavaria	6
1. Front page of Westcott's ACTA	15
2. Front cover of History & Mysteries	19
3. Revived Illuminati logo	20

Chapter I
Finding the English Illuminati

Figure	Page
4. Westcott's first page of the 'History'	23
5. Book number 55.	24
6. High Council library	25
7. Dresden Illuminati Ordinances 1901, (a) (b) (c)	26
8. Prussian Illuminati Ludwig logo	26
9. Enlarged Z.O.Ɫ.O.M rune letters.	27
10. Dresden Illuminati J.G.	28
11. Illuminati R.M. and J.G.	28
12. Die Mysterien der Illuminati	29
13. High Council Minutes 10 October 1901	30
14. Papus' 1st Illuminati letter to Westcott	31
15. Scan pf Papus' 1st Illuminati letter to Westcott	32
16. Mathers lives 600 yards from Papus 1899	35
17. Papus' 2nd Illuminati letter to Westcott	37
18. Scan of Papus' 2nd Illuminati letter to Westcott	38
19. Lodge and Temple of Perfection No. 14 in 1900	39
20. Oriflamme with the Harry Seymour error	40
21. Alliance with Kabbalistic de la Rose-Croix	43
22. The direction of the flow of Order s in 1901	44
23. Scan of 'Illuminati Lawful letter'	46
24. Minerval Warrant sent on 29 July 1901	48
25. Red wax seal and Illuminati motto	50
26. French masonic tracing board using S.O.M.O.	51
27. Second wax seal. Eye of Horus	52
28. Transcription of Reuss' letter to Westcott	53
29. List of 'Swedenborg Rite' Grand Officers	54
30. Scan of List of S.R.I.G. High Council Officers	55
31. Illuminati Grand Mother Ludwig image	56
32. W.Bro. Gotthelf Greiner	58
33. German Freemasonry in the Present Era'	59
34. Pledge from Reuss to Westcott	61
35. Illuminati Order Regent's Warrant Dresden	63
36. Beige paper seal	64
37. Enlarged red wax seal of Dresden	64
38. Rubber stamp mark	64
39. Religious character stamp 'L'	65
40. Hereby accept the position of Regent	65
41. Hamburg 'New Regent Warrant'	68
42. Enlarged red wax 'Great Seal' of Hamburg	69
43. Enlarged red ink authentication stamp	69
44. Enlarged blue rubber stamp mark	69
45. Westcott letter to Reuss on 12 October 1902	71
46. The direction of the flow of Order s in 1902	72
47. Last Illuminati letter from Westcott to Reuss	74
48. Transcription of Westcott's last Illuminati letter	77

Chapter II
History of the Illuminati

Figure	Page
49. Westcott's notebook	83
50. Title page of History of the Illuminati	84
51. Front Geschichte des Illuminaten-Ordens	85
52. Inside cover of History of the Illuminati	85
53. Two Kings and Architect	86
54. Moses by Loutherbourg	87
55. Man praying, Jacobs ladder	87
56. Ancient pyramids and cave, by Kircher	88
57. Nature crowning man in Temple,	89
58. Three kneeling & praying	89
59. Rosicrucian silence	90
60. St. Jerome by Q. Matsys	90
61. Rebus Materia Prima	91
62. Book of Law, world and learning	91
63. Man being led by nature to the Temple	92
64. Jesuit I.H.S.	92
65. King Altar & Fire, Emblazoned Delta	93
66. Hermits/Adepts following Sophia	93
67. Man summoning Hermes and Nature.	94
68. Baron von Knigge	94
69. Ark, mountain, King, cow, Pillar, Pyramid	95
70. Let there be light, and there was light	95
71. The Trinity, Universe, Spirit of Man	96
72. Benjamin Franklin, Paris, 1778	96
73. The World by Kircher	97

Chapter III
Mysteries of the Order of Illuminati

Figure	Page
74. Westcott's transcription of 'The Mysteries'	101
75. Back page of Ellic Howe's book	102
76. 'Die Mysterien der Illuminaten' original	102
77. 'Die Mysterien der Illuminaten' inside cover	105
78. 'Die Mysterien der Illuminaten' last page	111

Chapter IV
Revived Illuminati regulations and rituals

Figure	Page
79. 'Lord Engagist Bazeilles' Castle near Sedan	117
80a. Handwriting Rose-Croix Ritual 1902	119
80b. Handwriting History of the Illuminati	119
80c. Handwriting Zelator Ritual 1905	119
81. Front page of 'Innere Ordens-Ordnung'	121
82. Cover page for the Minerval Lodges	123
83. Last page for the Minerval Lodges	124
84a. Inside dedication Reuss J.G	125
84b. Dresden blue stamp mark	125
85. Front page of Minerval = Grad	131
86. Minerval Owl with P.C.M.V.	133
87. Front page of Ritual Schotten Grad	137
88. Front page of Rosenkreuzer	143
89. Front page of Synods Ritual	151

Chapter V
Heckethorn's Bavarian Illuminati

Figure	Page
90. Cross Bottony of the Dresden Illuminati	161
91. Heckethorn, Cipher 1897	162
92. Abbe Barruel, Cipher 1799	162
93. Heckethorn, Scottish Knight Cipher	162

Chapter VI
Main characters in the story

Figure	Page
94. Portrait of Westcott, 1906	169
95. Westcott's personal bookplate	169
96. William Wynn Westcott, 1894	170
97. Annie Kenney and Christabel Pankhurst	170
98. Westcott, Supreme Magus S.R.I.A., 1903	171
99. Home and H.Q., 396 Camden Road	172
100. Extra Pharmacopoeia, 1884	173
101. Last known picture in South Africa, 1924	174
102. Banner of the Parret and Axe Lodge	175
103a. Westcott admitted into Stella Matutina	178
103b. Secret Stella Matutina College	179

Figure	Page
104. Westcott's Martinist Certificate, 1899	180
105. Westcott drawing from scrap book	181
106. Theodore Reuss as young man	183
107. Reuss wearing Royal & Select Masters	184
108. Reuss wearing W.M. apron and a top hat	184
109. Letter to Wilhelm Hübbe-Schleiden 1893	186
110. Reuss' Illuminati Ludwig Lodge address.	188
111. Prussian Illuminati magazine *Oriflamme*	188
112. Meeting dates in *Oriflamme* magazine	190
113. Gerard Encausse signature	193
114. Dr Gerard Encausse or Papus	193
115. The Papus signature	194
116. Martinez de Pasqually	194
117. Henri Viscount Delaage	195
118. Suprême Conseil 1900	196
119 Ordre Kabbalistique De La Rose Concordat	197
120. Westcott's Martinist Warrant	198
121. Dr Gérard Encausse portrait	199
122. Papus writes letter of introduction	187
123. 'Inspector Principal & Dr en Hermetisim'	201
124. Detail of Westcott's Breast Jewel	203
125. Le Libre Examen	204
126. Brochure INRI Paris Temple & Lodge	205
127. Papus sister marriage to Deullin	206
128. Encausse in Russia	206
129. Scan of letter dated 9 March 1902	207
130. Transcription of Deullin & Blitz letter 1902	208
131. Number 4 Rue de Savoie	209
132. Dr Gerard Encausse in his office	210
133. Yarker's work address	213
134. Imperial Constantine Order of St George	214
135. Three Martinist Degrees 1 May 1895	215
136. John Yarker, Ancient & Primitive Rite	216
137. S.R.I.A. Lancashire College, 1882	218
138. Eri Knight's Star Jewel	218
139. Much older portrait of John Yarker	219
140. The Kneph, publication 1881 sent in 1900	220
141. John Yarker's AQC Articles	224

FOREWORD

By Derek Bain

John
Enjoy the Light.
LUX
Derek

You hold in your hand a unique work. This remarkable book at its core, represents the author's passion, not only for the subject matter itself, but his desire to give the reader every ounce of value that his extraordinary research has yielded. Over the years, the subject of the Illuminati has had the power to stir the imagination and has given birth too many fanciful and ridiculous theories. However, books that are based on primary source material and written to inform rather than fan flames of speculation are comparatively rare. So, it is a pleasure to welcome a new work dealing in facts.

In considering how to approach writing this Foreword, it seemed to me that something akin to a user guide was needed as this work can be approached from several directions, all of which reward careful reading.

For those who like a rollercoaster detective story, the author narrates the highs and lows of the researcher and documents both the dead ends and spectacular finds; therefore simply start at Chapter One! For those who prefer to dip into volumes to extract specific information on an 'as needed' basis, this book is written in discrete chapters, each with its own index and bibliography thereby providing the owner with a wonderful source book. For those who seek the truth behind some of the wild speculation that whirls around everything connected with the Illuminati, this book delivers hard facts. The actual rituals of the Illuminati, translated into English are presented here along with images never published in the public domain. But there is more. Alistair Lees, delves into the personalities and motivations of the key players who were striving to control and promote the Illuminati at the turn of the twentieth century. He provides us with intimate biographies of these truly colourful characters setting them in the social and political milieu of the day. Their intertwined stories take a fascinating twist as the unfolding saga of the Illuminati morphs into an epic adventure tale about those who were ultimately seeking to dominate and control what is sometimes known as 'fringe' or High Grade Freemasonry across much of Europe. Indeed, what is revealed here for the first time is what could truly be called 'Grand Lodge Wars'. Therefore this book, whilst delivering revelations about the Illuminati at its centre, is also a holistic snapshot into the fascinating world of semi-secret societies.

PREFACE

Allow me to introduce myself, my name is Alistair McGawn Lees. I have long been fascinated by esotericism. I am a longstanding Freemason but my real passion is for Rosicrucianism, its history, philosophy and practices. My interests led me eventually to join the Societas Rosicruciana in Anglia, who are the Rosicrucian Freemasons, henceforth designated the S.R.I.A. I currently hold the position of Right Worthy Director General of Studies and a member of High Council, the S.R.I.A's governing body. In 2010, I assisted a professional archivist who listed the contents of the society's headquarters and library in Hampstead, London on behalf of the society. In a completely separate project, I also assisted in the cataloguing and valuation of the High Council Library. Both these projects unearthed a treasure trove of previously unknown and forgotten material, in the form of books, correspondence and artefacts. One particular moment set me on a quest that may never end, but as of this moment has resulted in the book you hold in your hands. This was the unearthing of an old notebook.

The noble aims and objectives of the original Bavarian Illuminati, leapt off the pages of William Wynn Westcott's hand written translation of the *History of the Order of the Illuminati* and its companion *The Mysteries of the Illuminati,* unseen for a hundred years, shedding a completely new positive light on the 'Bavarian Illuminati.' The Illuminati rituals, rules and regulations were found elsewhere and there were plans by the 'Revived Illuminati of Prussia' to introduce them into England and the British Empire in 1902.

From new, original source material, found in official diaries, books, photographs, images, letters, certificates, ordinances and rituals a completely fresh story emerged. It revealed what really went on behind the scenes, during a period in history, when ancient and new esoteric and masonic orders were being traded between England, France and Prussia by the heads of these Orders, William Wynn Westcott, John Yarker, Gérard Encausse (Papus) and Theodore Reuss. This story perhaps changes perceptions and repairs tarnished reputations of some of the players involved.

A story that started with the Illuminati and then ended up being about Grand Masters and 'Grand Lodges' of Europe and 'Magus of the World,' encompassing some of the leading personalities and esotericists at the end of the Victorian era and involving many esoteric side Orders and masonic degrees.

Above all, it is about practical masonic type rituals that would seek to inculcate and promote the theoretical and academic system developed by Adam Weishaupt. Rituals that were actually used in Illuminati lodges in both France and Prussia in 1901 and what happened when they were introduced to England in 1902.

This book is really three new stories in one. Firstly, a record of my personal voyage of discovery in investigating Westcott's 'History and Mysteries,' found in the S.R.I.A. archives and where they originally came from. Secondly, the discovery of the revived 'Illuminati rituals' found in the Library and Museum of Freemasonry, along with the rules and ordinances that went with them, which lead to the previously hidden story of the power struggle for leadership of the Illuminati .

Thirdly, the discovery of Westcott's official diary known as ACTA provides, on occasions, detailed proof of the story you are about to read. An ACTA is a bit more than a posh word for a diary. It is Latin for 'Acts' and means 'official records' or 'official acts' or 'official deeds'. In this case, it is the official diary of the Secretary Generals of the S.R.I.A. between 1881 and 1891, and then Westcott's ACTA as Supreme Magus of the S.R.I.A. from 1892 to 1925. It corroborated the evidence and correspondence that were lost for eighty years and provided a snapshot into the collection of rites, orders and degrees that were being exchanged between different countries.

This roller-coaster tale can now be fully told and some of the Illuminati's secrets can be understood because of the discovery of this new, original and largely unpublished primary source material. I have emphasised the names of orders rites and degrees to make it easier to read, in my opinion.

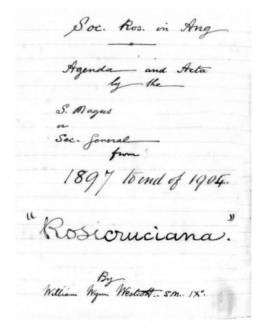

Figure 1 - Front page of Westcott's ACTA

ACKNOWLEDGEMENTS

The author would like to expresses his gratitude to everyone who assisted in the creation of this book, especially the support of my wife Bea.

More specifically:

John Paternoster, Supreme Magus IX°, head of the S.R.I.A.'s for access to the library and archives.

Mark Peters, an independent film maker and former member of the S.R.I.A., for his invaluable help in transcribing from the original, the *History of the Order of Illuminati,* and *The Mysteries of the Illuminati.* Also for transcribing three of the four English Illuminati rituals, the Minerval Grade, Andreas Knight Grade and Synode Grade.

Derek Bain for re-reading, correcting the text and co-editing the book. His great interest and patients in listening and talking to me about the project and for finally helping me bring this book to fruition.

Philip Dawson, antiquarian book seller and valuator, inspiration and early proof reader and co-editor.

Evan Sepion, proof reader extraordinaire, I only hope I managed to keep in all his punctuation, during the final stages.

For two French speaking members of the S.R.I.A., who wish to remain anonymous, who translated the letters written by Papus into English. Also the German member and his mother who also wish to remain anonymous, who translated the earliest Reuss letter from Munich.

Robert Gordon, for listing the S.R.I.A's study groups' papers in a separate project, which proved that there were no pervious papers written on the Illuminati.

Trevor Dutt, for taking the time to transcribe one of the many library lists, which proved, that there were no other Illuminati books. The list unfortunately did not have enough detail to help with the valuation or the location or existence of the books on the list.

Alexi Petrou and **Bonislav Radev** for proof reading the very first draft and their kind comments.

Lucy Shepherd, professional archivist for the S.R.I.A. and co-finder of some of these treasures in the archives

All the staff at the Library and Museum of Freemasonry in Great Queen Street, especially:

Diane Clements, Director, for her support and help in securing the loan of the S.R.I.A's library, which will give better access to all researches and the public.

Martin Cherry, Librarian, who has always helpful and interested, for his help in finding the Illuminati rituals and the ordinances original documents and much more.

Susan Snell, Archive manager, for her subtle training in the art and her interest in the project and support.

Peter Aitkenhead, Assistant Librarian, who helped track down the information on the Pilgrim Lodge.

.

INTRODUCTION

A new century had turned the pages of history as the revived Illuminati were introduced into France and then into the UK from Germany, in 1900. This is a real story about real people and real events and how different people from different organisations impacted on each other. Some people would go as far as to call these people quite well known colourful characters of the Victorian esoteric tradition.

What I like so much about this story is that it fills in some of the gaps in our understanding of those times and what has been written by some authors in the past was not necessarily wrong, just that they came to their conclusions based on the only information available at the time. I hope they would have changed what they wrote if they had known about some of this new first-hand evidence. I have had access to a fabulous store of information from the S.R.I.A. archives that I now lay before you to decide for yourself what conclusions to come to, on the formation of this new Order.

The views expressed here are my own and in no way have any official sanction or approval by any of the organisations mentioned.

This story essentially centres on a little known attempt to found the 'English Illuminati' in 1901. This was following two earlier revivals, the first in Munich in 1880 and the second in Berlin in 1895, the capital city of the Prussian Empire and this is the reason why I have called them the 'Prussian Illuminati.'

There was every chance and every reason to believe that the 'English Illuminati' would succeed in Great Britain, because the job of introducing it was placed in the hands of someone who had set up one of the most infamous modern Rosicrucian Orders of all time the 'Hermetic Order of the Golden Dawn.' It had attracted a small pool of enlightened men and women as candidates. William Wynn Westcott[1] had also breathed new life into another Rosicrucian Order eight years before that and he later headed up as their Supreme Magus and was already expanding its membership throughout the British Empire.

It was the case that huge political global events dramatically overtook these plans in the shape of what was called the Great War. Additionally, it did not matter what all encompassing, extremely rational, hugely grandiose plans lay behind the revival of the Illuminati. As these plans were also on a collision course with probably all the established 'Grand Lodges of Europe.' However, there were several other reasons why it failed, as we will discover.

This, then, is the story of the revival of a non-religious secret society, whose only aim originally was the further enlightenment and education of ordinary men, women and children, at a time when women and children had no access to any public or formal education, and even then severely limited to only a few church schools and universities. It was only then, once established, that it was grafted onto Freemasonry; a delivery mechanism for the initiated and then in time, they became the initiators of these ordinary men and women.

The colourful image of the Illuminati continues to this day, perpetuated by recent fictional films with ridiculous premises and also on the internet by

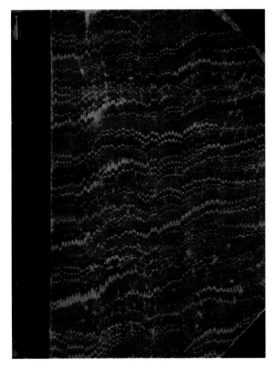

Figure 2 - Front cover of History & Mysteries

the constant re-quoting from the same two books, both written after the original Illuminati had been proscribed, around 1785. One was written before the French Revolution, the other after it had ended, by two different types of detractor with two different takes on the original movement.[2] Strangely, this was after the Illuminati had already been officially crushed by Bavarian and Prussian politics so it must have carried on behind the scenes. Perhaps their reason was to encourage those who wanted to spread fear and hatred of all secret societies to the popular world and also to minimise the spread and some of the effect of the French Revolution, a people's revolution that could have so easily spread to the rest of Europe. But this was

---

1 See Chapter VI for a brief biography of William Wynn Westcott.

2 The Illuminati detractors were Barruel 1799, *Memoirs* and Robinson, 1789, *Proofs of a Conspiracy*.

also at a time when Rosicrucians, Freemasons, Jesuits and the Illuminati were all unjustly painted with the same black brush. The Illuminati's detractors seem to have failed in their attempt to wipe out the Bavarian Illuminati as all these organisations seem to have continued to flourish to this day, the Illuminati mainly in America, as is stated in the Westcott MSS, *History of the Illuminati Order,* and the starting point of this story.

THE REVIVED ILLUMINATI

As a quick guide, let me briefly tell you what the 'Revived Illuminati' were offering to introduce into Great Britain. The original 'Illuminati Order' was an organisation whose name tells you what was inside the tin; a method of shedding light on the mysteries of life.' The 'Revived Illuminati' was only one of many different 'Orders of Light' that had the same aim in view and that are mentioned in this book at the appropriate juncture.

The 'English Illuminati,' Minerval Grade was designed to be an introduction into new educational methods and their particular Illuminati wisdom school for those groping in the darkness. Their secret word was 'Through me let the blind see' and the Minervals were given the sign of blind obedience.

Once you had become qualified as a Minerval, to progress you were ennobled in the Illuminati's 'Scottish Knight of St. Andrew.' This introduced the legend of the 'Scottish Knights Templar' and the word 'Novice Notuma' an anagram of 'Aumont,' (Pierre d' Aumont) the Grand Master of the Knights Templar after their fall from grace in 1313 and his lessons on vengeance and obedience. They give the 'Scottish Knight' 'light' during the ceremony on his journey from the words of God to Moses 'I am that I am.' It also explains the revived Illuminati initial letters J.G. and the flaming star that is found on their 'Revived Illuminati' Logos.

The Illuminati 'Rose-Croix Grade' or as they called it their 'Rosenkreuzer Grade' was an older more alchemical version of the '18° of the Ancient & Accepted Rite.' The three moral virtues on their ladder were Faith, Hope and Love, not Charity as in the former 18°. Their shibboleth was the word I.N.R.I. found on the last four steps, but the Illuminati gave two further alchemical and cabalistic explanations of these initial letters. The overall message given to the 'Knights Rose-Croix'

is to travel many years to find the Logos and realise that the journey starts and ends with Love.

The 'Synod Grade' or Priests Grade, introduces the importance of a covenant or profound promise. They use the word 'Mizpah,' meaning a 'watchtower' or 'stone pillar' set up in Gilead, marking a covenant between Jacob and Laban, his father in law, to honour his daughter and all women. This is reinforced by the sad lesson of Jephthah from Gilead who made a covenant with God which cost him his daughter Adah's life, who gave herself up to her Father to be offered as a burnt sacrifice.

All very profound moral lessons I hope you will agree? The 'Minerval Grade' a lesson for 'Light,' the 'Scottish Knight & Rose-Croix Grades' for 'Love' and finally the moral lesson of 'Life' in the 'Synod Grade' to keep the promises you make and, above all, help others to keep their covenants.

Figure 3 - Revived Illuminati Logo

Summed up for us in the last line that can be found in the pamphlet written by Reuss and is called by him *The Mysteries of the Illuminati* see below and (see fig 78).

Love, Light, Life.

Liebe, Licht, Leben

Chapter I

Finding the English illuminati

FINDING THE ENGLISH ILLUMINATI

The beginnings of a very personal journey

WESTCOTT'S TRANSCRIPTION

This story really begins in January 2010 in the library of the S.R.I.A. in Hampstead, London. Philip Dawson an antiquarian book seller and valuer, picked up from the pile he had created, a very interesting one hundred year old black, half marbled note book. He opened it to the title page and said:

> *History of the Order of the Illuminati, no author, no date, it looks like William Wynn Westcott's handwriting!*

I quickly typed those details into the spread sheet on my laptop computer and immediately grabbed the book out of Philip's hands, before he could put it back on the pile of books ready to go back on to the library shelves.

> *Yes* I said*, it is definitely Westcott's handwriting, but what is so interesting is that this book is not on the list we made last year of the 220 titles of books and papers that he has written and which were found in the recently discovered wooden 'Westcott Box' of papers.[1]*

And so it began. My interest was immediately aroused by the relatively large size of what was essentially a hardback, posh notebook, which had lined pages, about A5 paper size (Crown octavo). It was the same kind of book stock that had been used in other instances for recording important information in the society like the High Council or College minutes, which in itself was very interesting. I had not seen it used for writing an historical paper in like this before.

What immediately struck me was that this was his very neatest handwriting, on what was very expensive paper. Westcott's other master manuscripts and papers were written on single pages of paper by hand or typed and then bound together inside a brown leather effect cover, probably the height of fashion in Victorian England, with a brass hole punched in the top left hand corner. There were of course several other printed and published pamphlets of his other papers. But this was something quite different on a subject I had never seen any of our members write about, a volume on the *History of the Order of the Illuminati*, at this point we had not noticed there was a second section to Westcott's book. Another very distinctive feature, as I have mentioned, was that it was written in William Wynn Westcott's[2] distinctive best handwriting, (see fig 4). It is neatly laid out and as you can see with no illustrations or sub headings. He had several different writing styles as he was a doctor by profession, we all know how difficult it is to read a prescription and one of his styles of writing is truly unreadable!

Figure 4 - Westcott's first page of the 'History'

What was Westcott's source for this material? Why had he lavished so much time and attention on this book? Was this simply an unknown, unpublished very long college paper that, significantly, he did not deliver to an S.R.I.A. college or study group?

It had already taken me about the best part of a year to list all the different versions of Westcott's papers in spare moments, while it had only taken a month or two for a willing volunteer, Robert Gordon, to concentrate on listing all the study groups' papers over the last one hundred years and their authors, many of them written by Westcott but none of them on the Illuminati.

---

1 Locked wooden trunk with over 220 Westcott papers, drafts, pamphlets and printed material, was found in the High Council Library, Hampstead, in 2010 unopened for at least 80 years because the keys were lost.

2 See Chapter VI - William Wynn Westcott.

So many questions! Philip gave me one of those quizzical looks that a teacher gives you when they want answers you do not have. I had none to offer even though I was there as the so called expert trying to assist in the valuation, for insurance purposes, of the S.R.I.A.'s extraordinary collection of over 4,000 books and papers, most of them telling the story of the Rosicrucian Enlightenment, some of them over 400 years old. All of which belong to the High Council Library and are in the special care of the Supreme Magus, who at this time was John Paternoster.

Figure 5 - Book number 55.

Philip's second job as valuer, was to highlight any books that needed repairing and putting to one side if they were quite special and valuable. The society had agreed to repair any distressed books so that they would not get damaged any further. I was there because it was a two handed job, one to open and read the title page of each book and gauge its value, based on the condition and the providence of the book, the other to note down the different entries on computer. This arrangement halved the time taken and therefore the cost to the society. The old High Council Library list was woefully out of date and all the previous lists did not have enough detail for a valuation and none of them could tell us

what was on the shelves or what needed repairing or restoring.

You might consider that the *History of the Order of the Illuminati* was just another High Council library book, but it was not. Inside the front cover it had the distinctive High Council bookplate (see fig 5), featuring St. Jerome, an image that had been used in the past by the S.R.I.A., as a kind of representation of Christian Rosenkreuz. When I checked further, book No. 55 was not listed in the library card system or in any of the previous library lists, which was very strange as virtually everything else we found was listed somewhere.

From the dedication on the front page (see fig 15), it would seem that Westcott also thought it so important and valuable enough not to take with him to South Africa when he retired.

One clue as to how important and how different this book was compared to all the other valuable books in the library was in the simple handwritten dedication inside the first page, saying:

> *This was amongst the papers given to me by Dr Wynn Westcott when he went to South Africa, W.E.C.D.*

I had no idea to the identity of the initials, but the handwriting was confirmed in 2016, when I showed the book to the author and collector of Rosicrucian material in his own right, Tony Fuller, who both recognised the handwriting and the initials as belonging to another Doctor of medicine Dr William Elliot Carnegie Dickson.[3] Just how he came into possession of Westcott's private material is yet another story.

The *History of the Order of the Illuminati* was clearly something special. It was not, for example stored, on the open shelves in the valuable library. It was found by Philip Dawson and me in the fireproof black steel trunk bought by the society to protect and house its most valuable records. The box was found locked among twenty other trunks, listed by Lucy Shepherd in the summer of 2010 as part of her very valuable and completely separate archive project, undertaken on behalf of the society. This steel archive trunk was still locked and almost certainly had been unopened for approximately 80 years. It contained the very first Minute book, the first signature book, the first Golden Book (a book containing the names of members and their Latin mottos), the first rituals and many more irreplaceable documents. So, the *History of the Order of the Illuminati* was clearly seen as something to be protected by whoever filled

---

3 Dr William Elliot Carnegie Dickson (1878-1954). M.D. of Abercorn, F.R.C.S. Edinburgh. His address at the time was: 11, St. George Road, St. Margret's, Twickenham, Middlesex.

the truck and locked the contents away from easy access.

Indeed, so important was it that it was found alongside the most precious original rituals that had been found in Freemasons' Hall, London circa 1863 by Robert Wentworth Little (1838-78) the founder of a branch of the Scottish Rosicrucians in London on the 1 June 1867 and he became the first Supreme Magus of the S.R.I.A. in 1869, until his death in 1877.

I decided to take Westcott's handwritten book home. I eagerly began reading it on the tube and by train from Hampstead. The *History of the Order of the Illuminati* proved a very interesting and enlightening read. By the time I arrived at Twickenham, my final destination, I was convinced this book was as important as it seemed, but for some reason I could not yet work out why. As far as I knew in 2010 this was the only Illuminati material in the possession of the S.R.I.A. This was absolutely the first item I found and there was absolutely no indication at the time that this book was part of an attempt to revive the Illuminati in England.

My first impression was that it was a completely different account of the Illuminati from any of the stories I had heard about them previously. This was a refreshing history of the Illuminati, with a very positive 'take' on its aims and objectives. An organisation that I knew only a little about at that time and like so many other people around the world, had only recently been introduced to Dan Brown's Illuminati, portrayed by him as an evil murderous organisation, working to bring down the Pope and the Vatican at any cost, in the purely fictional account in his book and film *Angels and Demons.*

The *History of the Order of the Illuminati* was put aside once again, so it could be transcribed and perhaps published for the members of the society at some future time as an interesting paper written by Westcott. It was nothing more than a very interesting subject, written by a famous member of the S.R.I.A., little appreciating then the journey I was about to embark on!

The other items found in the archives and the High Council library (see fig 6), were far more distracting and far more interesting at the time, than a simple paper on the Illuminati in a note book.

Towards the end of 2011, Mark Peters, an independent film maker and a member of the S.R.I.A., approached me and offered to help with any worthwhile project with regards to the newly re-discovered material in the S.R.I.A. archive. He agreed to proceed with two major transcription projects for the society. The first project was the *History of the Order of the Illuminati* transcription, which was completed on 21 December 2011. During the transcription, Mark realised that there was a second part to the book, which was called the

Mysteries of the Illuminati, something that did not seem out of place, but we had no idea of the significance of the second part. Mark had preserved the pagination, lining, punctuation and in some cases grammatical and spelling errors, which made double-checking the work easier for me. He also highlighted the words he wanted checking or was unsure of due to the Latin or German words used; which I subsequently researched and added my comments.

ILLUMINATI RITUALS

Then Mark casually mentioned that he had seen during his researches in the Library and Museum of Freemasonry,[4] some Illuminati rituals. I looked up

Figure 6 - High Council Library

the entries in the online archive catalogue, booked ahead by email quoting the references with the Librarian Martin Cherry and went along and had a look at the English translations myself. A spectacular find! I was told that there were four German originals, but not being able to understand German I did not look at them. However, it would also seem from their catalogue entries, that William Wynn Westcott had actually paid to translate and transcribe the four German rituals into English. Why was that?

It was about this time that the idea of conducting more research on the Illuminati began to form in my mind, and if this proved fruitful, documenting my findings in a book.

---

4 Freemasons Hall, Great Queen Street, London WC2B 5AZ.

7(a)   7(b)   7(c)

Figure 7 - Dresden Illuminati Ordinances 1901

The primary source material I had read thus far was leading me to think that the Illuminati had received, perhaps unfairly, bad press. Maybe the aim of restoring some sort of balance, based on fact rather than hearsay, with regard to the image of the Illuminati was in order.

I knew that the newfound, undated Illuminati rituals needed to be included in the book I had in mind, along with the *History and Mysteries* of the Illuminati. Intriguingly, at this stage there was no obvious direct link between the Illuminati rituals and the Westcott transcription. Mark kindly volunteered to transcribe the rituals and managed to get three out of four finished before his work dragged him away from the project.

ILLUMINATI IMAGES

Figure 8 - Prussian Illuminati Ludwig Logo

Although I now had plenty of new original unpublished primary source material, I had not found any images at all and I could hear the voice of the potential publisher in my head saying:

What, no images, it is pictures that sell books!

The very first Illuminati images were found in an unexpected location on the 1 October 2012. I had gone back to conduct more research on the Illuminati rituals at the Library and Museum of Freemasonry, when Martin Cherry, the librarian, of his own volition and knowing my interest in the Illuminati, showed me some of the other Illuminati material he had in his possession. Another spectacular find, although at the time I did not fully appreciate just how important this new material was to be. The *Innere Ordens-Ordnung* or *Inside the Order*, written in German were the constitutions and regulations of the *Illuminati Order* and had been printed in Dresden. These ordinances contained my first Illuminati images. Not only were there three Illuminati logos on the front and inside the back cover, but also two Illuminati signatures.

Was Westcott a member of the Illuminati? I did start to wonder if the *History and Mysteries* notebook was something that a newly admitted member of the Illuminati was asked to write out after their admission, as a way of illuminate's learning more about the ceremony they had just passed through. Had Westcott after his admission been asked to do the same? Many esoteric Orders at the time asked their candidates to copy out the rituals, for example after the grade meeting in their own handwriting, hoping it would remind them of the ceremony through which they had just passed and make it easier for them to read the ceremonies in the future.

Perhaps another reason why the *History and Mysteries* was handwritten was because esoteric rituals were not generally printed or published at the time, to avoid duplication by its enemies or detractors.

The finding of the *Innere Ordens-Ordnung* booklet, (see fig 7), seemed at the time to fit that conclusion very well, as during admission into masonic type Orders, you are usually given the by-laws of the lodge and a set of rules or constitutions of the society you have just joined. Was that what the *Inner Ordens* document was for?

I had the ordinances of the society, their rituals and their history and now some images. Surely that must be enough to write my book. From the dedication on the front page of *Innere Ordens-Ordnung* the document must have been sent to Westcott by Theodore Reuss. *Issued to Brother Dr W. Wynn Westcott S.M. IX° by Theodore Reuss, Berlin, 17/X/01.* The handwritten initial letters after, Westcott's name that look like *'Ill.'* are in fact the letters 'S.M.' which stands for Supreme Magus and have been erroneously interpreted by previous archivists. The date is not in cipher, Reuss has simply used the letter 'X' for the tenth month of October and '01.' followed by a full stop and the abbreviated version of the year, making the date 17/10/1901.

The last page of the *Innere Ordens-Ordnung* is signed by Leopold Engel. Printed above his signature is 'Der Geheime Areopag.' This translates as 'The Secret Areopagus' and is equivalent to the 'Grand Lodge of the Illuminati' in their terms, (see fig 7c.) Engel was directed by the Custos-Office or 'Grand Lodge'. This consists of three people and a council, which are called the Custos, the Vice-Custos and the Archivist. They are assisted by a supervisory board of five members of the Order elected by the ordinary voting members. The Office of the Custodian and the Supervisory Board are the 'Secret Areopag.' They organise all current Illuminati (religious) Orders and manage the Order and supervised the entire organisation.

Now Dresden, where it was printed and published, is quite a distance from Berlin where the previous owner Reuss lived at the time. Historically, Dresden was a significantly different Province of Germania. It was from this point on I realised there might in fact be two different, separate and distinct resurrected 'Illuminati Orders' in 1901. One Order operating from Berlin and another operating out of Dresden. In my mind I started calling them for my own clarity of thought, the 'Prussian Illuminati' from Berlin and this new found organisation the 'Dresden Illuminati.' Without realising that this was going to be a self-fulfilling prophesy and a significant part of the unfolding story. At the time I knew nothing about Theodore Reuss or Leopold Engel, or what the rituals were for. I had a vague recollection that Reuss had something to do with the *'Ordo Templi Orientis,'* known as the 'O.T.O.,' which became better known and infamous when Aleister Crowley became the head of the order in 1916.

IMAGES OF THE ORDINANCES

The first image I found (see fig 8) was in the top right hand corner of the document and was a distinctive rubber stamp mark in blue ink from the 'Prussian Illuminati.' It consists of a double circle around the outside, with a double equilateral triangle or sacred delta touching the inside, on which is overlaid the rune letters spelling ᚼ ⋄ ᛁ ⋄ ᛘ or Z.O.Ɪ.O.M. not Z.O.T.O.M., also (see fig 9), for a close up of the image. The blazing Sun is superimposed over the triangle. Inside the glory is a circle with several rows of what looks like petals and in the very centre is the image of the flaming (sacred) heart.

Figure 9 - Z.O.Ɪ.O.M rune letters

The second image can also be found on the front page and is printed in black ink. I would find out later that this image was exclusively used by the 'Dresden Illuminati.' It consisted of a 'flaming star' with a five pointed star or pentagram superimposed on top. Inside the pentagram is a bottony cross in the very centre. The bottony cross exhibits four trinities at the points of the cross and is the cross symbol used in both the *'Epopt Grade'* rituals used in the 'Bavarian Illuminati' rituals and the 'Synod Grade' of the 'English Illuminati' rituals. According to the Illuminati ritual this is the pentagram symbol of the Illuminated man, the son crucified,[5] it has the initials J. and G. either side,[6] (see fig 10). I speculate in the introduction of this chapter that these letters stand for Japheth and Gomer, son and grandson of Noah from Biblical times.

The third Illuminati image, (see fig 11), can be found on the last page of the regulations in the form

---

5 See Chapter IV - Oath of an Illuminati, footnote.
6 See Chapter III - Andreas Knight Grade ritual, *I know the J.G. and the flaming star.*

Figure 10 - Dresden Illuminati J.G.

of a red ink stamp mark under the words written in German 'Der Geheime Areopag' meaning 'The Secret Areopagus' of the 'Illuminati Order.' At the top of the red stamp mark are the initials R.M. which probably stand for 'Ritter Meister' or 'Cavalry Captain' or 'Master Knight,' (see fig 11), underneath that is a 'flaming star' or Sun with a pentagram imposed on it, but this time with the initial letter 'L' in the very centre of the pentagram and the initials 'J' and 'G' underneath.

The 'Dresden Illuminati' logo comes in several forms and is different to Reuss' 'Prussian Illuminati' logo, in that it does not display the rune letters, the sacred delta, rose petals or the sacred heart. All three logos have something different in the centre of the image, the first the flaming heart, the second the bottony cross of the trinity and the third the initial letter 'L.' The letter 'L' could stand for the German words *Liebe, Licht* or *Leben* or 'Living.' It may perhaps represent all three as can be found on the last line in the 'Mysteries,' see the last line in Chapter III (see fig 76) and later in this chapter.

The images on the front cover of each of the German rituals are similar to (fig 10), with this difference, the initial letters 'J.G.' are under the 'flaming sun' with the letter 'L' in the centre.

On the front page of the *Innere Ordens-Ordnung* was the signature of Theodore Reuss of Berlin and on the last page of the ordinances I saw for the first time, another signature of a member of the resurrected Illuminati in Dresden. It belonged to one of the Illuminati's Principles, Leopold Engel. On further investigation I found that he was a Russian, born in St. Petersburg, and was both an occultist and a writer.

Six months later, imagine my disappointment having found the first three images of the Illuminati, when a second-hand paperback contained the same.[7] It was a biography of Theodore Reuss and when it finally arrived in the post. It contained two of what I had thought were exclusive Iluminati images. There on the back page

was a rather wonky version of the second image mentioned above (see fig 12), but without the initial letters 'J.G.'

Inside that book I found on page 155, (see fig 8), the first image described above. These images may be new to you but at least two of them have been published before and appear on several Internet pages. Such are the ups and downs of a researcher. This book is only available in the German language and I had hoped it would have a description and some kind of explanation of the 'Prussian Illuminati' logo (see fig 8) above. The book said nothing about the meaning of the ᚺ ᛟ ᛁ ᛟ ᛗ rune letters or the logo worth writing about here, a big fat nothing, which is the way it goes sometimes.

Merlin Peregrinus is an interesting name for Theodore Reuss. Why would he choose to use it, perhaps it meant 'magical crusader?' Presently it remains a mystery but *Peregrinus* is Latin for 'the crusader.' But we must remember that Theodore Reuss was originally a member of the Pilgrim Lodge No. 238 in London and it conducts its rituals in German, so there may have been a sentimental reason for his choice of pseudonym.

Figure 11 - Illuminati R.M. and J.G.

REUSS' PAMPHLET

Suddenly I realised that the image on the back page of the Möller & Howe book[8] was in fact the front page of a pamphlet by 'Caratheodoro' an alias of Theodore Reuss, published in Berlin, Germany: by Druck von Trowitsch & Sohn, 1894, called *Die Mysterien der Illuminati* which translates to *The Mysteries of the Illuminati.*

When I checked the online archive of the Library and Museum of Freemasonry, there it was, (see fig 12). This meant buying that book was not such a waste of time after all, because it led to the answer to many of my questions about who wrote the *History and Mysteries of the Illuminati.*

---

7 Helmut Möller and Ellic Howe, 1986, *Merlin Peregrinus: Vom Untergrund Des Abendlandes.*

8 See the back page mentioned in fig 75.

No wonder we did not find the author's name for the second section of Westcott's transcription *The Mysteries of the Illuminati*, it was spelt incorrectly as 'Garatheodoro.' I now knew for sure that the *'Mysteries'* section was originally written by an active member of the resurrected 'Bavarian Illuminati,' namely Theodore Reuss. The pace was picking up!

I then discovered from the recently published book on the 'Bavarian Illuminati' called *The Secret School of Wisdom*[9] that the original *The Mysteries of the Illuminati* was in fact another book, this time written by Adam Weishaupt and was going to be used as part of something he wrote called, *The Magi ritual* of the 'Bavarian Illuminati.'

Figure 12 - Die Mysterien der Illuminati

But before this ritual could be established in Bavaria and the ritual published, the society was proscribed and presumably that is the reason why the revived 'Prussian Illuminati' did not include 'The Magi grade' in their set of rituals. In fact it was one of the last degrees ever written by Adam Weishaupt during the last days of the original Bavarian Illuminati existence, in 1781. Weishaupt called it the 'Docetists degree.' However, it was never disseminated because at that time the 'Bavarian Illuminati,' it was assumed, had faded away. Or so it was thought.[10]

The online archive record showed that the *Die Mysterien der Illuminati* also had a dedication on it, which states:

Reuss, Theodor, 1855-1923, Former owner, and *with compliments to Frater Dr. Westcott (Wynn) S.M. IX° Berlin 17/ X/ 01.* (There is a typo in the original; *G. Ill* is in fact S.M.)

This is the same dedication that appears in the *Innere Ordens-Ordnung* ordinances, meaning they must have all been sent together by post to Westcott by Reuss on the 17 October 1901.

At last the *Mysteries* could be linked to the Dresden ordinances and hopefully the undated rituals. It did not take long to find out that Westcott's *History of the Order of the Illuminati* was in fact an anonymous work written by Theodore Reuss. The online archive at the 'Library and Museum of Freemasonry' did not help me, as their copy of *Geschichte des Illuminaten-Ordens* was not correctly accredited to Reuss, but to Leopold Engel. He wrote his own 500 page version in 1906 and the 'Library and Museum of Freemasonry' do in fact hold a copy of both books.

Leopold's history contains just one page about the 'Revived Illuminati' and is almost exclusively about the 'Bavarian Illuminati,' with some very interesting pictures of Weishaupt. It is in much more detail than the 28 pages written by Theodore Reuss and published in Bitterfeld, Germany: by Druck von F. E. Baumann in1896. The dedication inside the front cover of the 'Library and Museum of Freemasonry' copy has a different date, but is the same dedication:

With compliments to Illustrious Frater Dr. William. Wynn Westcott S.M. IX° from Theodor Reuss 12/X. /01

Meaning it was dedicated on 12 October 1901, not the 17th for some reason. It has three former owners, Reuss, Theodor, 1855-1923, former owner. Westcott, W. Wynn 1848-1925 as the former owner and lastly Quatuor Coronati Lodge, No. 2076, London, donor. Significantly, the author ascribed to the book is Theodore Reuss, no confusion there.

I now knew at last, that the two booklets supplied to Westcott to produce his handwritten English version were also actually written by Reuss and that Westcott had had them translated by some unknown person after October 1901, the date of the inscription. Subsequently, Westcott then transcribed these two translations into one notebook. The reason it had taken so long to work this out was that the *History* was anonymous and the *Mysteries* author was transcribed or translated wrongly as 'Garatheodoro.'

There would be still more amazing finds of original Illuminati primary source material, but the next part of my journey was more about picking up on a single reference in a letter that I did not understand when I first came across it.

---

9 Wages, Markner & Singh-Anand, 2015.
10 See Chapter V - Heckethorn for more details.

CHANCE SPOTTING OF THE WORD 'ILLUMINATI'

It was a chance spotting on the 21 April 2011, of the word 'Illuminati' in a 1901 letter to Westcott from the Frenchman, Gérard Anaclet Vincent Encausse (1865-1916) or Papus as he was better known that galvanised me into action. I knew Papus was the founder and inspiration of the Ordre *Martinist*. I had several of his books at home and knew that a member of the S.R.I.A. John Yarker had a warrant to make their qualifying members, Martinist. How did that come to pass?

I had found in a large brown envelope in the S.R.I.A. archives, twenty or so personal letters, warrants and certificates of the first English Martinists under John Yarker from 1895. There were also some letters sent to Westcott in 1901 that I thought were very interesting.

I approached the correspondence mentioning the Illuminati with trepidation, armed only with my schoolboy French. The letter from Papus to Westcott transformed my initial project of publishing the *History'* and *'Mysteries'* of the Illuminati, from a very interesting story, into something else entirely.

For example, I did not know that Papus had ever been a member of the Illuminati. Now I half remembered something I had read somewhere, that Westcott had also been a member and that the Illuminati were mentioned in the High Council minutes of the S.R.I.A. (see fig 13). I went back through the minutes and found this reference.

High Council Minutes 10 October 1901:

It was notified that a friendly correspondence had been carried on with Brother Theodore Reuss of Berlin, who had been initiated in the Pilgrim Lodge London, No.238 in regard to an alliance between the Society and the Order of the Illuminati of Germany, which Brother Reuss had been instrumental in restoring to active existence, and the establishment of an offshoot of the Rosicrucians Society in Germany. The Supreme Magus has conferred the rank of Honorary Associate of the Soc. Rosi. Upon Brother Reuss; while Brother Reuss has conferred the grades of the Illuminati Order upon the Supreme Magus; and this amicable procedure was approved by the High Council, as well as a scheme for the establishment of a German Rosicrucian Society by the Societas Rosicruciana in Anglia.

Figure 13 - High Council Minutes 10 October 1901

These minutes confirm that Theodore Reuss made Westcott a member of the 'Illuminati Order' and that the S.R.I.A. was happy about this relationship between the two and had formed an alliance.

It also proves that the person who sent the Illuminati material to Westcott was well respected and had been honoured with S.R.I.A. Grand Rank. It also shows Westcott's motive behind what happens next; he wanted an S.R.I.A. college in Berlin that would later be called the S.R.I.G. 'Societas Rosicruciana in Germania.' This letter from Papus must have been the start of this process.

PAPUS ILLUMINATI LETTERS TO WESTCOTT

I called in a favour and turned to a Belgian member of the S.R.I.A., who wishes to remain anonymous, who kindly agreed to make the translation of the Papus letter for me. Let me tell you they were two anxious days waiting for his reply to my email and to read what it said. It turned out that, yes, Papus had been made an 'Illuminati' in 1901 and was writing to Westcott to say that the Illuminati were interested in forming an alliance with the S.R.I.A. and to create an S.R.I.A. college in Berlin. The letter also asked Westcott if he would write to Theodore Reuss in Berlin, (see fig 14). The letter was indeed the beginning of that relationship between the S.R.I.A. and the Illuminati and it perhaps explains for the first time how Westcott became a member of the Illuminati. More importantly it explains how Reuss was first introduced to Westcott, by Papus. This letter is also the beginning of the process of the exchanging of degrees, orders and rites, between England, France and Germany and that the 'English Illuminati' was just one Order in this mix and how this process set off a chain of events which resulted many years later in Aleister Crowley's O.T.O. but that is another story.

In fact there were two letters from Papus to Westcott in 1901, one in June and the other ten days later in July. Why? They are virtually on the same subject, certainly with the same aim in view. The first contained Theodore Reuss' home address in Berlin, not the lodge address. The second letter revealed a new Illuminati name, a new head of the 'Revived Illuminati' and a new address in Dresden, one I already knew. This new information matched up with the people and places in the *Inner Ordens* document. Papus wrote his first letter about the Illuminati to Westcott in London, from Paris on the 27 June 1901. The letter was written on 'Rite Primitif et Originel de la Franc-Maconnerie, Paris' or in English 'Original & Primitive Rite of Freemasonry' (Swedenborg Rite) letterhead, asking Westcott to write to Reuss at his home address in Berlin, (see fig 14) and the transcription and translation of the scanned letter (see fig 15).

TRANSCRIPTION OF FIRST ILLUMINATI LETTER
Look, I have my own Swedenborgian Order in France.

T∴ T∴ G∴ O∴ T∴ G∴ A∴ O ∴T ∴ U∴

Original & Primitive Rite of Freemasonry
(Swedenborg Rite)

Lodge & Temple   Secretariat
I.N.R.I. (No. 14).   Hermetic School
Paris.   4, Savoie Street

June 27th 1901

Very Illuminated Master [W.W.Westcott]

Travelling to Berlin, I had the opportunity to engage in fraternal relationships with the German Illuminati.

They have just nominated me as representative of their Order in France.

But I promised them that I would make sure to get them in contact with you, as they have the highest desire to see established in Berlin a representation of the Rite that you are chairing.

This is why I kindly ask you to write on my behalf to the following address while sending your own address (you can write it in English as M. Reuss runs [heads/manages] an English newspaper in Berlin).

M. Theodor Reuss

Bellealliancestrasse 86 Berlin

I managed to get your excellent article on Ramsay translated, I am going to publish it in

L'Initiation.

Fraternally yours.

G. Encausse

Figure 14 - Papus' 1st Illuminati letter to Westcott

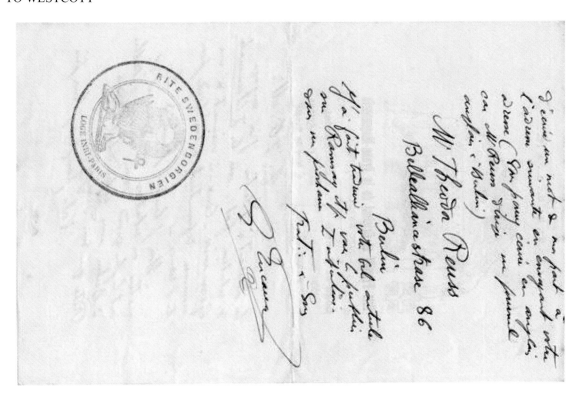

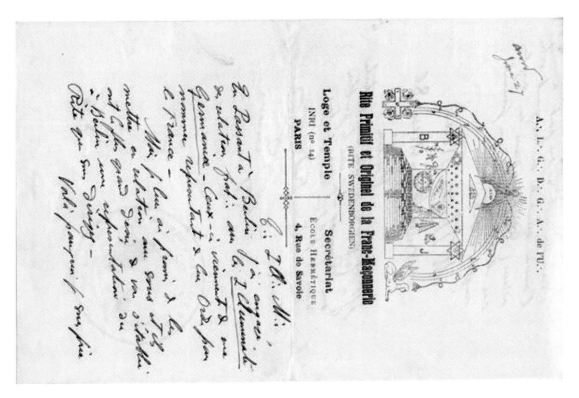

Figure 15 - Scan of Papus' 1st Illuminati letter to Westcott

There are several other early letters from Papus in the S.R.I.A. archives on many different types of letterhead, including those from his home and the hospital in which he worked. But these two letters were something brand new and from a different address for Papus (see fig 15 and fig 18). The new Swedenborg Rite Lodge in Paris letterhead was probably used to add a little more credibility and authority to his letter.

I now think that he was showing off to the Grand Secretary of the 'Swedenborg Rite' in England, that he had gone to the trouble to produce a letterhead, for the proposed 'Swedenborg Lodge and Temple' It was sent from a new work address for Papus at number 4, Savoie Street, where we will find out later that all his organisations in Paris were based at this time. It represented a 'Swedenborg Lodge and Temple' that was in a 'start -up phase' and was only meant to be working under a dispensation from John Yarker, which is clarified in a letter dated 1899.[11] The dispensation allowed Papus to admit members, before the lodge and temple was fully chartered at some later date, which actually took place in 1906, when there were enough members to conduct proper ceremonies.

Papus' first letter about the Illuminati went unanswered and after only some ten days, without a reply, Papus wrote again. Was this because Papus felt guilty that he may have over played his hand in the first letter or perhaps he felt that Westcott had already become disillusioned with him before? Westcott had already turned down or rejected running two of Papus' French Orders in Great Britain.[12] I say this because Westcott's communications with Papus were to cease altogether in early 1902, very soon after this 'Swedenborg Rite' saga ended.

I can think of three other reasons for Westcott breaking off communications with Papus. It may have been the anti-Jewish and fascist beliefs that Papus wrote about in the Paris press. Or, his visits to Russia to meet with Martinists and to see the Tsar Nicholas II, that may have irked him. Or, perhaps it was Papus and his family's involvement with setting up a woman's only 'Adoption Lodge' in Paris, working under the 'Grande Loge de France,' something else that was found in the S.R.I.A. archives.

It was not the traditional French type 'Rite of Adoption' of the eighteenth century *tenue blanche* or 'White Table Lodge,' where women joined the men after their meeting. This was a set of degrees specially designed for women, with moral lessons about women from the Bible. It was not a mixed lodge as it conferred degrees on woman only. Papus' sister Louise Deullin was the founding Grand Junior Warden in 1901 and it started life being attached to her husband Pierre Deullin's lodge that was called Le Libre Examine No. 217. It was a famous lodge during the 'Paris Commune.'

Papus, allegedly, was never a Freemason and the reason for mentioning this here, is that it is strange, but the office address used by Pierre Deullin for Le Libre Examine No. 217 lodge business in the letter he already wrote to Westcott in the archives,[13] is the same address as that used by the 'French Illuminati' and all Papus' other Paris based Orders like the 'Swedenborg Lodge.' This Paris 'Adoption Lodge' brought the condemnation of all the established 'Grand Lodges' of the world in 1902, something to which A.E. Waite alluded to many years later.[14]

Do I think that Westcott simply ignored Papus' first letter? I feel this is very unlikely, especially after considering the speedy reactions to the letter that took place later. I began to think it must have been something else, something which Westcott felt he did not need to explain to anyone or express in his diary. Then I thought maybe Westcott was simply away on summer holiday and did not receive the first letter until his return.

After I took another look at Westcott's official diary,[15] it confirmed this, but in a negative way. What I mean by this is that there were no entries at all between 25 June 1901 and 10 July 1901. When I checked backwards and forwards in the diary over a seven year span, I found the same absence of entries in the diary, over the same two weeks, usually over the same dates each year. Westcott after all was a civil servant, working for the Home Office and probably took his family on summer holiday at the same time every year. However, as a general rule Westcott never mentions his family or domestic events at all in his official diary so we may never know for sure.

I originally knew very little about Papus when I started writing this book. Why was he travelling to Berlin? My first thought was that he was actively involved in spreading the 'Martinist Order' in Europe as its head. There were after all, forty five numbered Martinist Lodges in 1893, the very last one on their archive list was called the 'Ancient & Primitive Rite of Masonry' Lodge No. 45 (Withington, England). There were many active European Lodges, but absolutely no active Martinist Lodge s in Germany at that time.

---

11 Letter from Yarker to Westcott 11 November 1899 in the S.R.I.A. archives.
12 The 'Ordre Martinist' and the 'Ordre Kabbalistic de la Rose-Croix.'
13 Letter dated 5 May 1900 - Pierre Deullin to Westcott, about the Swedenborg Rite Lodge and Temple.
14 Gilbert R.A. 1987, *A.E. Waite; Magician of Many Parts.*
15 ACTA for 1897-1904.

Was Papus going to make Reuss the 'Ordre Martinist' Sovereign Delegate in Germania as he had made John Yarker in 1895 and then attempted to make Westcott in 1899? The answer was no!

Papus was not the only person to spread Martinisim in Europe. The emphasis in the Martinist Order is on personal initiation between two people. It is interesting to note that John Yarker claims to been initiated into Martinisim not by Papus, but by a non-mason, the Baron Adolf Franz Leonhardi von Platz (1856-1908) probably in 1893. The pedigree and lineage of your initiation are very important to Martinists. According to the Martinist Archives, in 1895 for example, Baron Leonhardi started a Martinist circle, which turned into the 'Martinist Lodge No. 12,' called *U modré hvězdy* (ob gurney) with the vaguest of addresses in Austria, which then later moved to Prague. This is exactly how Martinisim works, you start a circle of a few members, when it gets big enough it become a Martinist lodge. This, however, is not how Freemasonry works, to form a new lodge you have to have the members first before you can obtain a warrant to establish the lodge. I wondered if Papus, who was not a Freemason, had been trying to form a 'Swedenborg Lodge' along those Martinist lines.

What stands out for me in the first letter from Papus to Westcott, which is not mentioned at all in the second, is the emphasis on the 'German Illuminati' wanting to have an S.R.I.A. College established in Berlin.

Highest desire to see established in Berlin a representation of the Rite that you are chairing.

Was this first letter a hook to catch Westcott, the 'sprat to catch a mackerel?' The first letter to Westcott only mentions 'Reuss' and the city of 'Berlin.' It is Reuss, who Papus suggests that Westcott should write to and no other person. There is absolutely no mention of Leopold Engel in the first letter. You may speculate that Reuss and Papus may have been trying to deliberately cut out Engel in June. Why was that? Was it because Papus thought that Engel's attempt to takeover Reuss' (Prussian) 'Illuminati Order' over the last four years was unfair?

If you read Engel's, *History of the Illuminati*, 1906, you will see that he had a very low opinion of Reuss and of the way that he ran the Order and was probably jealous that Reuss had resurrected the 'Illuminati Order' sixteen years before he had ever been involved with it. They were both Freemasons, Engel allegedly a member of a Russian Lodge in the 'Orient of Petersburg' where he was born. Reuss had been regularly initiated

into a London lodge with very strong connections with Germany.

In the 1914 edition of the *Oriflamme*, Reuss claimed that he had actually revived the 'Illuminati Order' at Munich in 1880 in the 'Ludwig Lodge.' The full name of the 'Illuminati Order' lodge in Munich appears on a letterhead that was used by Reuss in a note to the editor of the Sphinx Magazine and the head of the original 'Theosophical Society,' Wilhelm Hübbe - Schleiden (1846-1916) on 30 October 1893.

It was called 'Die Unterrichtsloge des alten und angenommenen freimaurer genannt Ludwig im orient Munchen' which translates as 'The Lodge of Instruction of the Ancient and Accepted Masons,' (Illuminati Chapter) called 'Ludwig' in the 'Orient of Munich.' If I were to guess from the title, it could have been an Illuminati study group working under an 'Ancient & Accepted Rite Lodge' called 'Ludwig.' I suggest that the members of the 'Ludwig Lodge' studied the 'Bavarian Illuminati' and their revived 'Masonic Illuminati rituals.'

Reuss went on to resurrect the 'Munich Illuminati' Lodge of Instruction 'Ludwig' in Berlin sometime in 1893, which we may deduce from the letter to Hübbe-Schleiden above. There was obviously enough interest the next year for Reuss to go ahead and publish under a pseudonym von Caratheodoro, *Die Mysterien der Illuminaten* 1894 and then revived the 'Illuminati Order,' as he mentioned later in 1914. It gathered momentum the next year and it was then in 1895 allegedly, that he first met Engle, who shared the same passion for the Illuminati.

Where and how did Reuss and Engel meet? We know that Reuss was elected vice president of the new German section of the 'Theosophical Society' on 29 Aug 1896 in Berlin and that Engel was elected the treasurer at the same meeting, under the leadership of Franz Hartmann. So the German section of the 'Theosophical Society' seems a good fit for both to meet. They were both writers, Reuss a journalist and Engel was the editor of a spiritual magazine called 'Wahrheit-Sucher' (1896-1897), which mentioned Reuss by name in the September 1896 edition. After only one year, the magazine changed its name to *Das Wort* (1897).

What is very interesting is that Reuss' *History of the Illuminati, 1896* or *Geschichte des Illuminaten-Ordens* was printed in Bitterfeld, Germany by Publisher, Lehrstatt-Verlag; F.E. Baumann. This is the same printer and publisher of Engel's *Wahrheit-Sucher* magazine, the title translates as a *Monthly scrap-book*.

This timeline fits with Engel then being admitted an Illuminate in the 'Prussian Illuminati' in Berlin on 9 November 1896. Reuss was still traveling around Europe for his job and Engel probably found it easy to persuade Reus that his publishers could print all the material for the 'Ludwig Lodge' and this led to more control. This fits with what previous authors have already said:

Engels in 1897 founded his own Order of the Illuminati at Dresden, but it was united with Reuss' Order in 1899.

From that last statement it would appear that Engel set up his own Illuminati in Dresden first in parallel with Reuss's in 1897 and set up his own headquarters based in his home town. They then came to a compromise in 1899, when Engel found a way to wrestle complete control of the 'Prussian Illuminati Order' from Reuss. This accommodation lasted for two years.

On the 12 March 1901, both Reuss and Leopold Engel had agreed to warrant a Berlin, 'Die Grosse Freimaurerloge für Deutschland.' In English the 'Grand Freemasons Lodge of Germany,' (see fig 23). However, Reuss stupidly back dated this warrant to the beginning of 1900, probably to add more credibility to his new Order. Engel did not like this deception and they fell out again in March 1901. Did this argument somehow leave Reuss free to deal directly with Papus in June and offer him fraternal relationships with the 'German Illuminati' and then later with Westcott? Reuss must have contacted Papus after March and before June to invite him to Berlin. How did Engel feel about that? Were Papus and Reuss trying to out-manoeuvre Engel as head of the 'Dresden Illuminati,' either before or after Papus' visit in June? Was Engel jealous of Reuss' proposed preferment in the 'Ordre Martinist?'

From the first Papus letter, we know that he travelled to Berlin sometime in June. He sent the letter to Westcott on his return on the 27th June with no mention of Engle. You can imagine that during the Berlin meeting they probably discussed a 'Swedenborg Rite' warrant for Reuss. Whatever the reason in June, Papus ensures that he includes Engel's details in the second letter to Westcott in July, perhaps to try and mend fences already broken. The first Papus letter comes from someone who is already designated the Berlin 'Illuminati representative' in Paris. Was it meant to be a kind of 'what is good for me (Illuminati) may be of interest to you?' (Westcott) and was it likely designed to be a second hook, for Reuss to catch Westcott and the 'Swedenborg Rite?'

I did not know why, specifically, Papus decided to write to Westcott in the month of June, unless it was simply after he returned from his trip to Berlin. It took a little time to work out the actual date of his trip to Berlin and what led up to it. The author Tau Apiryon[16] may shed some light here on both issues, by putting a possible date to that visit in Berlin. Apiryon says:

That Gérard Encausse (Papus) provided him (Reuss) with a charter dated June 24, 1901 designating him (Reuss) Special Inspector for the Martinist Order in Germany.

To me this means that Papus went to Berlin with a charter to make Reuss the 'Special Inspector' for the 'Martinist' in Germany and that it was Monday 24th June that was probably the date of the meeting. Papus wrote the letter to Westcott three days later. This is the same rank that Papus had proposed to make Westcott in the letter sent to him by Yarker in 1899 and not the higher office or rank of 'Sovereign Delegate for Great Britain,' which Papus, had already made Yarker. Which begs a question that I cannot answer, did Papus intend making Leopold Engel the higher rank of 'Sovereign Delegate' of the 'Ordre Martinist' in Germania? I have found no evidence to suggest that he did. So, it is entirely possible at the June meeting in Berlin that Papus was made an Illuminate by full ceremony and then became the representative of the Illuminati in Paris. Papus must have made Reuss 'Special Inspector for the Martinist Order' in Germany at the same time.

I had to go back eighteen months in the ACTA to find out what led up to these events in the correspondence in the archives and it was all wrapped up in the politics of the leaders of the 'Ordre Martinist,' an organisation of which all three were members. It all perhaps centred on the way that Papus had obtained his membership of the 'Swedenborg Rite' in Britain, which was by going behind Westcott's back and approaching Yarker directly, as he was also the head of the 'Martinist Lodge No. 45' in England. Papus had also gone back on his word to pay all backdated fees to Westcott and to add insult to injury, had not paid Westcott for new candidates either and their certificates that he had issued over the previous eighteen months.

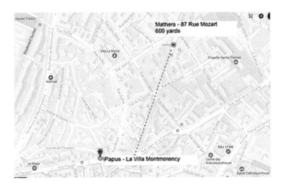

Figure 16 - Mathers lives 600 yards from Papus in 1899. (Google Maps)

---

16 *Doctor (Albert Karl) Theodor Reuss, 33° 90° 96° X°, 1995.*

The 'Swedenborg Rite' letterhead would only serve to remind Westcott of Papus' previous errors. What changed in late June and early July? That might have persuaded Papus to add Engel's details to his second letter to Westcott? Papus' letter to Westcott starts with:

Travelling to Berlin, I had the opportunity to engage in fraternal relationships with the German Illuminati. They have just nominated me as representative of their Order in France.

Had Papus been invited to Berlin by Reuss to become their French representative of the 'Illuminati Order' in Paris or was it the other way around? The impression here is that the Iluminati instigated the meeting and had chosen Papus to represent them in the French Empire.

Two facts emerge which makes me think that this June meeting in many ways actually 'broke' the combined Illuminati of Berlin and Dresden. From the second letter, we must assume that Papus was appointed the representative of the joint-Illuminati based in Dresden, with Leopold Engel as the head. 'Mr Reuss' in the letter was only the 'General Delegate to Masonry.' Why would Reuss be made the Martinist representative in Berlin and not Engel? Why should Papus ask Westcott to write to Reuss?

The first letter is signed G. Encausse and the second using Papus. Finally, the 'P.S.' after the signature in the first letter;

I managed to get your excellent article on Ramsay translated,

I think this would have further irritated Westcott. It was not Westcott's article! It is featured in Papus' magazine *L'Initiation* in June 1901 on page 247. Its full title was *L'ancienne Maconnerie et le chevalier Ramsay* and it was written by John Yarker!

Curiously in 1899 Yarker had warned Westcott that the reason Frederick Holland, the founder of the 'Hermetic Society of Eight' and the Grand Secretary of the 'English Martinists 1895,' had nothing more to do with Papus, was because of a case of plagiarism in the *L'Initiation*, perhaps this was another nail in Papus coffin as far as Westcott was concerned.

SECOND ILLUMINATI LETTER
Transcription of the second letter

Papus had not had a reply to his letter of 27 June, because as we have established Westcott was probably on holiday and so he wrote to Westcott

again on the 6 July 1901, (see fig 17 and 18). It is again written on the brand new letterhead of the 'Original & Primitive Rite of The Freemasonry' ('Swedenborg Rite'). Had Papus been in touch with Reuss and found out that he and Engel both wanted to mend fences after the back dating of the 'Die Grosse Freimaurerloge für Deutschland' Warrant incident? Had Papus then modified the second letter and added Engel's name accordingly?

German Illuminati

Who were these 'German Illuminati' from Berlin that are mentioned in the second letter? Westcott must have known that the 'Bavarian Illuminati' had only officially lasted for eleven years 1776-1787 and were thought to have completely ceased to exist in Europe before the French Revolution.[17]

Westcott must also have known that they were found in Ingolstadt, north of Munich, in the Southern German State of the Prussian Empire, which was only created in 1871. Before that it had been the independent Kingdom of Bavaria from 1805 to 1914. The letter goes on to say:

They are High Masons.

More properly they were 'High Grade Masons,' which means members of an organisation or 'Grand Lodge' of grades, degrees, orders or rites, higher than the established three degrees of craft masonry. Implying, I believe, that they thought Westcott was also of a similar high grade status and regularity as the high grade German Illuminati members.

What the second Papus letter on 6 July proves for the first time is that the head of the revived 'German Illuminati in 1901 was based in Dresden[18] and not in fact Reuss in Berlin. They were not the 'Bavarian Illuminati,' or Reuss' 'Prussian Illuminati' of Berlin, but the 'Dresden Illuminati.' I have had to make this distinction between the two revived organisations to distinguish between them.

I was also beginning to realise that the 'English Illuminati' translations of the rituals of the 'Prussian Illuminati' to be found in England today are probably completely different rituals to the original 'Bavarian Illuminati,' they are more 'Masonic type Illuminati Rituals.' They have opening and closing sections and a familiar masonic structure to the ceremony. In fact, they are 'newer rituals' of a much later date than those to be found in previous exposés of the 'Bavarian Illuminati', and what can be found in the new book, *The Secret School of Wisdom.* [19]

---

17 See Chapter II History of the Illuminati.
18 S.R.I.A. archives Papus, Second letter, 1901.
19 Wages, Markner & Singh-Anand, 2015.

TRANSCRIPTION OF SECOND ILLUMINATI LETTER
Similar but not the same as the first letter.

T∴ T∴ G∴ O∴ T∴ G∴ A∴ O ∴T ∴ U∴

Original & Primitive Rite of Freemasonry
(Swedenborg Rite)

Lodge & Temple   Secretariat
I.N.R.I. (No 14).   Hermetic School
Paris.   4, Savoie Street

July 6th 1901

Dearest

I think that Master (Most Worthy Master?) you might have an interest in officially getting in touch with the 'German Illuminati'.

Consider the combination (the approach) that might be the most favourable (suitable/workable) for you. They are all 'High Masons'.

The Head is Mr Engel (Leopold) Augsburgerstrasse 82 in Dresden & the General Delegate to the Masonry is Mr Theodor Reuss, Bellealliancestrasse 86 Berlin.

I think that in exchange they might grant you the high representation in England.

You can write in English as they both understand it very well and Mr Reuss runs (heads) the English-American Register in Berlin.

I have not met anymore Mr Mac Gregor Mathers for almost one year. He left my neighbourhood (area) in the sad state of his business, and he went to live in Montmartre.

Frat∴ to you, Dearest Master (Most Worthy Master?)

      Yours

        Papus

Figure 17 - Papus' 2nd Illuminati letter to Westcott

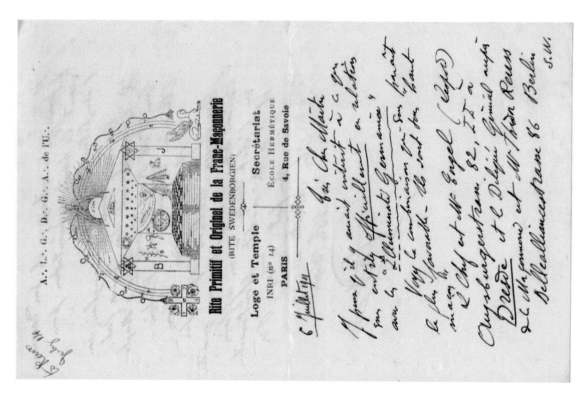

Figure 18 - Scan of Papus' 2nd Illuminati letter to Westcott

SECOND ILLUMINATI LETTER (continued)

What does Papus mean by?

General Delegate of the Illuminati to Freemasonry.

This phrase, Delegate of the Illuminati to Freemasonry, would have different meanings in all three countries of the people involved here. It would also be different depending on whose perspective Papus is talking about. Does he mean from his perspective from Reuss' or Westcott's?

In France at that time it would be a very confused term. The French had several 'Grand Lodges' that were not on good terms or in amity with any of the established 'Grand Lodges' of the world. The French were outside the masonic family for several different reasons. Mainly, due to changes they had made to Freemasonry themselves. For example, in the 'Grand Orient' members could express no belief in 'The Supreme Being' and other changes that were made by Napoleon Bonaparte's brother Joseph, who was their Grand Master in France after the Revolution.

By 1901 in Germania the situation was no better, with seven or eight different 'Grand Lodges' in Prussia, three or four in Berlin at different times. However, most of them were generally recognised by each other and in 1901 generally by the established 'Grand Lodges,' but not Reuss' own new 'Grand Lodge.'

In London there was technically only one 'High Grade' system recognised by the 'United Grand Lodge of England' and that was the 'Holy Royal Arch.' However, the 'Ancient & Accepted Rite,' 'Supreme Council 33°' was a quite separate Rite and yet was also in amity. I am only using this as an example, to illustrate the point. What did Papus really mean by to Freemasonry?

I noticed in the second letter to Westcott that Papus used a different correspondence address for Leopold Engel. This address is 82 Augsburger Strasse in Dresden, which is completely different to the correspondence address I found when I had a look at a copy of his magazine *Das Wort*, which was the official spiritual newspaper or magazine of Engel's followers.[20] In the magazine the address given is, Leopold Engel, Dresden 'Striesen, Augsburgerstrasse 77.' It is just down the road from his home address. This is similar in many ways to Reuss, who lived very close to his lodge.

Please note also that the address in this letter is the home address of Reuss at 86 Bellealliancestrasse, which is a now a modern residential block. The address of Reuss' 'Die Grosse Freimaurerloge für Deutschland' and the 'Ludwig Mother Lodge' are both at number 74

Bellealliancestrasse less than 100 yards down the same road. This building has completely disappeared off the map today, probably due to Second World War damage, caused by the Red Army that staged a major battle in this important thoroughfare in Berlin.

The final paragraph of Papus' second letter may help highlight some of Westcott's distrust of Papus at this time, concerning his relationship with 'Mr Mac Gregor Mathers.' It is a very interesting story but it is too long a story to go into here; however it is a tale spread across the pages of the ACTA. I believe that Papus felt that one of the reasons Westcott might not have replied to his first letter

Figure 19 - Lodge and Temple of Perfection No. 14 in Paris 1900

was because of Papus closeness to Mathers. In fact Mathers had indeed been living in Paris since 1892 and was now living at 87 Rue Mozart, Auteuil, in Paris.[21]

Papus had several different addresses but in 1899 he lived 600 yards away, see fig 16, from Mathers in the Villa Montmorency, 10 Avenue des Peupliers, Auteuil Paris. Papus had also joined Mathers' 'Golden Dawn' Ahathoor Temple, at 1 Avenue Duquesne Paris in 1895, which was only about five kilometres away, (see fig 16).

20 The Library and Museum of Freemasonry, London.

21 Westcott's, letter to T.W. Lemon, 1899.

MacGregor Mathers was one of the co-founders of the 'Golden Dawn' in 1888 with Westcott and had, allegedly, engineered the resignation of Westcott in 1897 to gain overall control of the 'Golden Dawn'.

In 1900, Mathers had launched a further attack on Westcott's credibility from Paris. It was concerning the forging of letters and the cipher MSS on which the 'Golden Dawn' was founded, the accusations proved groundless in the end. It is therefore understandable that Westcott may have found this all very troubling.

There is no further exchange of letters between Papus and Westcott recorded in the ACTA, after Papus introduces Westcott to Reuss in 1901, which seems to me very significant.

Figure 20 - Oriflamme, the Harry Seymour error

THE PRUSSIAN ILLUMINATI & THE FRENCH MARTINIST

What is so significant about all this and its relevance to the revived 'English Illuminati?' These two letters prove for the first time that Papus became a member of Reuss' revived 'Prussian Illuminati' in Berlin first, but it was under the authority of Leopold Engel's Dresden Head Quarters, a fact implied in the second Papus letter.

It proves that Papus was the first 'Revived Illuminati' representative outside Germany in Paris in 1901 and that as a reward Reuss had become the 'Sovereign Delegate' of the 'Ordre Martinist' in Berlin. It also suggests that Papus, while in Berlin had discussed with Reuss the fact that he had directly obtained a dispensation from John Yarker in 1899, a fellow Martinist and head of the 'English Martinist' and that Yarker had given his permission to form a 'Swedenborg Rite Lodge' in Paris. This fact was reinforced by Papus writing to Westcott with the letterhead of his new 'Lodge and Temple' of the 'Swedenborg Rite.'

I imagine the Illuminati letters from Papus certainly caught Westcott's attention on many levels and probably only annoyed him. The letterhead contained many non 'Swedenborg Rite' lodge symbols such as the Egyptian Sphinx from Yarker's 'Ancient & Primitive Rite of Masonry' and featured his own 'Order Kabbalistic Rose-Croix' emblem, (see fig 19 and 21), neither of which were anything to do with the 'Swedenborg Rite.'

The new name given to the 'Swedenborg Lodge and Temple' was 'I.N.R.I.' This would have not pleased the Rosicrucian in Westcott or Yarker, as 'I.N.R.I.' is a significant word in the 'S.R.I.A.' and in many other Order s too, including the 'Ancient & Accepted Rite' and the 'Revived Illuminati,' but this was not all, the pamphlet that launched the new Order, contained serval serious mistakes.

WRONG HISTORY WRONG ORDER

What happened next in 1901 was glossed over by the parties involved in 1902 and no other researchers seem to have picked up on this until now. It can be corroborated in the guarded correspondence held in the S.R.I.A. archives. The reason Papus and Reuss probably thought they had all got away with their mistake was by quickly introducing yet another high grade Order into France and Germany to cover it up.

The new Order was namely the *Rite of Memphis & Mizraim* (Yarker's 'Ancient & Primitive Rite'). They had to do this to placate their new members who had been unintentionally deceived. This mistake, as we shall see, was a direct consequence of information, which was probably supplied to Reuss by Papus, a situation I think that would ultimately lead, to Westcott abandoning the 'Swedenborg Rite' altogether and Papus completely.

What Reuss did was to launch his new 'Swedenborg Lodge and Temple,' to his German audience, in the January edition of the 'Oriflamme Magazine' 1902, (see fig 20).

He did this, apparently, without checking any of the details with either Yarker or Westcott.

WRONG HISTORY & ORDER (continued)

Some of these inaccuracies were introduced by Papus in 1900 and duplicated by Reuss in 1901. Had he checked with Westcott and Yarker, he would not have called his new 'order' by the wrong name and published the wrong higher grades.

Reuss announced his new Order as the 'Ancient & Primitive Rite (Swedenborg Rite),' the brackets being added by Reuss. The 'Ancient and Primitive Rite of Masonry' is not the 'Swedenborg Rite.' They are two separate Orders but both belonging to Yarker at that time. Just so we are all clear on this point their full names are:

The Ancient and Primitive Rite of Masonry
.(The Rite of Memphis and Mizraim) 96°

The Swedenborg Rite of Primitive and
Original Freemasonry
(Swedenborg Rite from the balustrade) 6°

Paris 1900,' (see fig 19), Papus slipped up and mixed up certain facts concerning the two 'Yarker Orders' named above.[22]

I have every reason to suppose that Papus also did not check any of the details with either Yarker or Westcott before publishing them.

It alludes to being given permission to hold lodges under the constitutions of Yarker.

John Yarker's, 33° (Scottish) 90° (Mizraim) 96° (Memphis) Supreme Grand Master of the Grand Lodge and Temple Swedenborgian for Great Britain and Ireland.

However, Papus had only been given a dispensation to recruit members and it does not mention a warrant or charter at all. But the big mistake that Papus made was not quoting Yarker's true rank. His real grade in that Order was 6° as 'Supreme Grand Master' of the 'Swedenborg Rite.'

French and German Translations

PRIMITIVE AND ORIGINAL FREEMASONRY (SWEDENBORG RITE 6°)

(French) - La franc-maçonnerie Primitive et Originale
(German) - Die Primitive und Ursprüngliche Freimaurerei
(German to English) Primitive and Original Freemasonry

ANCIENT & PRIMITIVE RITE OF MASONRY (RITE OF MEMPHIS & MIZRAIM 33°, 90°, 96°)

(French) - Rite Ancien et Primitif de la maçonnerie
(German) - Alte und Primitive Ritus der Freimaurerei
(German to English) 'Old and Primitive Rite of Freemasonry'

Crucially, the 'Swedenborg Rite' contains only 6° whilst The 'Ancient & Primitive Rite of Masonry' confers 96°. Reuss' errors were further compounded by supplying the wrong history for the founding of the English 'Swedenborg Rite.' Reuss said it was founded by an American warrant in 1872 by its 'Sovereign Grand Master,' Harry Seymour. The Rite had in fact been founded in 1876 by a warrant from its 'Supreme Grand Master,' Colonel McLeod Moore in Canada, who had received it from its original founder Samuel Beswick.

This new piece of the jigsaw puzzle I was gradually putting together came from a Papus promotional pamphlet that he published in February 1900 to launch his own 'French Swedenborg Rite Lodge and Temple.' In the brochure called the 'General Information about the Lodge and Temple of Perfection in the East of

Papus only reproduced his loftier ranks of 96°, in the 'Ancient & Primitive Rite of Masonry'. This Rite does contain 'Scottish Rite Freemasonry' as Papus claimed within the first 33° of the 96°, but this was as part of the 'Cerneau Rite' system, a direct competitor in America to the 33° of the 'Ancient and Accepted Rite.'

There is, however in my limited knowledge, no 'Scottish Rite Masonry' worked as such, in the 'Swedenborg Rite' as Papus stated. Papus, in the same document goes on to say quite wrongly that:

The INRI Lodge and Temple delivers the Swedenborgian Grades corresponding to the 4°, 18°, and 30° of the Scottish Rite.

---

22 He may have received this 'brochure' on 29 May 1900, see Chapter VI – Papus biography.

I now believe that Papus supplied Reuss with his erroneous pamphlet the 'General Information of the Temple of Perfection INRI' in Berlin at the June 1901 meeting.

This was when Papus was made the 'Illuminate' representative in Paris and Reuss the head of the 'Martinist Order' in Germany. I speculate that Papus showed Reuss the erroneous pamphlet sometime during the course of their discussion on obtaining a 'Swedenborg Rite' warrant for Germany.

Papus may also have supplied Reuss with a copy of a 1900 *Kneph Magazine* article on the history of the 'Ancient & Primitive Rite of Masonry. It was 'ironically written to help correct errors and explained the founding of the 'Ancient & Primitive Rite' of masonry.[23] The culprit, yes I believe was Papus!

It is almost word for word what Reuss wrote in the *Swedenborg Rite Constitutions* published in the *Oriflamme*, (see fig 20).

I say this because Yarker wrote to Westcott in 1902 enclosing a copy of this very same *Kneph* edition,[24] writing at the top of the page found in the archives:

Is this to which Brother Reuss alludes to in his letter?

The original Reuss letter to Yarker is not in the S.R.I.A. archives. Once this mistake of confusing the two Orders was discovered in March 1902, what on earth could Papus and Reuss do about it? They both needed to obtain the 'Ancient & Primitive Rite of Masonry' from Yarker to ensure that their recruited members were not disappointed in only receiving the 6° as conferred by the 'Swedenborg Rite,' when they had both promised so much more. Could this be why the 'Ancient & Primitive Rite of Masonry' was so quickly introduced into both countries at the end of 1902? By the way, Westcott had absolutely nothing to do with either introduction. In the Appendix, I explain why I believe it was important that both the 'Illuminati' and the 'Order Martinists' have the 'Swedenborg Rite' as part of their own collection of Orders as well as each other's prime Orders.

It is also worth saying that Yarker is not blameless in this mistake on several counts and probably why he aided the quick introduction. He nearly always used 'Ancient & Primitive Rite of Masonry' letterhead paper even when corresponding about the business of other Orders.

As proof of that there are no letters in the S.R.I.A. archives bearing 'Swedenborg Rite' letterheads.

He also signed himself YARKER, 33°, 90°, 96° and only very rarely appends the 6° as 'Supreme Grand Master' of the 'Swedenborg Rite.'

The names or titles of the Yarker Orders were too alike, especially when translated from English to French and then to German, see below.

As a senior member of the 'Swedenborg Rite' but not the 'Ancient & Primitive Rite of Masonry,' what did Westcott think of all three people involved with this enormous mistake? As a coroner, someone used to dealing in fine detail, it is interesting to speculate on what impression this essentially sloppy writing by Papus in 1900 had on him. This revelation served to make me wonder just how much Papus and Reuss actually knew about these two rites they were hoping to get involved with.

What happened next is that Westcott tried to resign from the 'Swedenborg Rite' in March 1902. To plicate Westcott, Yarker then promoted Westcott in the 'Swedenborg Rite' to 'Grand Senior Warden,' second only in rank to himself and asked Westcott to stay on for just one more year. Westcott did, and finally resigned on 8 March 1903. Westcott's last ever letter to Papus was on 10th February and received a reply on the 9th March *Heard from Papus re Rosics & Swed. Rite*, but no other details. Westcott probably stuck with Reuss because he was going to open an S.R.I.A. college in Berlin. However, as we will see later, Westcott also had finished with Reuss and the 'Illuminati Order' by 10 October 1902.

TO SUMMARISE 1901

Therefore, to summarise 1901, I speculate that Papus suggested that Reuss should approach Westcott, the Grand Secretary of the 'Swedenborg Rite' so that Reuss could acquire the 'Swedenborg Rite' directly from him, as this was the correct masonic way of going about this kind of thing.

However, Papus thought the six degrees of the 'Swedenborg Rite' was the Yarker Order with ninety six degrees, namely the 'Ancient & Primitive Rite of Masonry.' When Papus and Reuss found out later in March 1902 that they had mixed up the Orders and what they actually contained, they both wanted the 96° Rite as well.

This had to be directly obtained from Yarker as Westcott was not a member of the 'Ancient & Primitive Rite.' Papus may also have suggested to Reuss that to facilitate acquiring the 'Swedenborg Rite' he might like to ask Westcott to become an

---

23 It said quite ironically it says: *Misrepresentations are constantly being made in regard to this valuable Rite (Ancient & Primitive Rite) by error or design and that John Yarker wanted to put certain facts to his audience.*
24 Letter from Yarker to Westcott 20 February 1902.

Illuminate and also petition for a German S.R.I.A. Warrant for a College in Berlin.

This might help sweeten the arrangement because that would give Reuss more power and give him more grades and be something that his nemesis, Leopold Engel could no longer have any control over.

Perhaps mistakenly, Papus thought that he may still persuade Westcott to take on both the 'Ordre Martinist' and the 'Kabbalistic de la Rose-Croix' thereby extending his power and his control of Orders in England, after the failed alliance in 1899, (see fig 21).

What did Reuss want? He wanted it all! Under his 'Grand Freemasons Lodge for Germany' he already had the three craft German language degrees of the 'Schroder Rite,'[25] and the 'Mother Ludwig Lodge' of the Illuminati with its 'Minerval, Knight of St. Andrew, Rose-Croix and Synod Grades.'

From Papus, he had obtained the French 'Ordre Martinist,' and potentially to follow, the 'Kabbalistic Rose-Croix,' the Gnostic Church or 'Eglise Gnostic' and from Yarker the American 'Adoptive Rite.' Reuss was also looking to acquire the English 'Rosicrucian Society' (Westcott) for Berlin, also the (Beswick/Yarker) 'Swedenborg Rite' and the (Yarker) 'Ancient & Primitive Rite.' In short, Reuss was trying to build a 'Grand Lodge of the Prussian Empire' of all degrees.

What may not have been appreciated before now, was that Reuss could, legally under the Prussian Clubs and Societies Law, warrant Lodges and societies underneath the umbrella of his own 'Grand Lodge' in Berlin. Carl Kellner a close of friend of Reuss called this aspiration by another name, the 'Academia Masonica.'

This probably goes a long way towards explaining why Reuss was motivated to 'collect' and acquire as many degrees as possible to form a powerbase in Europe of which he could be the head or Grand Master.

I hope I have shown that introducing the revived Illuminati into England involved more than just one Order, it was conditional on a number of Orders being traded between three countries.

It might help show the movement of rites, orders and degrees between each country at this time, by putting them in a flow chart (see fig 22).

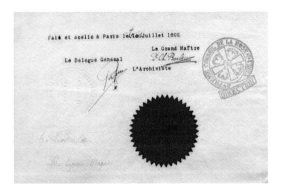

Figure 21 - Alliance between S.R.I.A. and Kabbalistic de la Rose-Croix 13 July 1899

---

25 Friedrich Ludwig Schroder (1744–1816) restored in 1801 the true ancient Craft Freemasonry. It was the ritual used by Reuss' Mother (Pilgrim) Lodge in London.

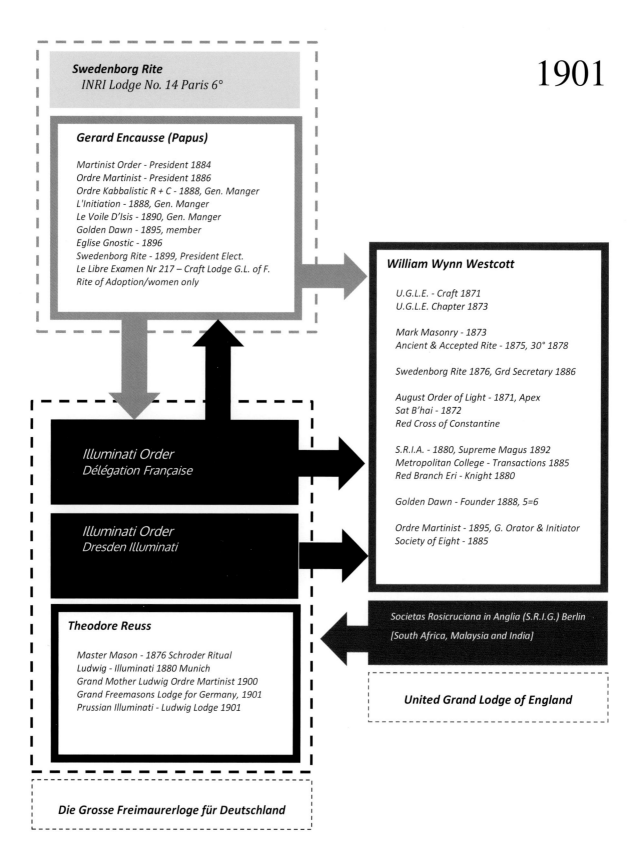

1901

Swedenborg Rite
INRI Lodge No. 14 Paris 6°

Gerard Encausse (Papus)

Martinist Order - President 1884
Ordre Martinist - President 1886
Ordre Kabbalistic R + C - 1888, Gen. Manger
L'Initiation - 1888, Gen. Manger
Le Voile D'Isis - 1890, Gen. Manger
Golden Dawn - 1895, member
Eglise Gnostic - 1896
Swedenborg Rite - 1899, President Elect.
Le Libre Examen Nr 217 – Craft Lodge G.L. of F.
Rite of Adoption/women only

William Wynn Westcott

U.G.L.E. - Craft 1871
U.G.L.E. Chapter 1873

Mark Masonry - 1873
Ancient & Accepted Rite - 1875, 30° 1878

Swedenborg Rite 1876, Grd Secretary 1886

August Order of Light - 1871, Apex
Sat B'hai - 1872
Red Cross of Constantine

S.R.I.A. - 1880, Supreme Magus 1892
Metropolitan College - Transactions 1885
Red Branch Eri - Knight 1880

Golden Dawn - Founder 1888, 5=6

Ordre Martinist - 1895, G. Orator & Initiator
Society of Eight - 1885

Illuminati Order
Délégation Française

Illuminati Order
Dresden Illuminati

Theodore Reuss

Master Mason - 1876 Schroder Ritual
Ludwig - Illuminati 1880 Munich
Grand Mother Ludwig Ordre Martinist 1900
Grand Freemasons Lodge for Germany, 1901
Prussian Illuminati - Ludwig Lodge 1901

Societas Rosicruciana in Anglia (S.R.I.G.) Berlin
[South Africa, Malaysia and India]

United Grand Lodge of England

Die Grosse Freimaurerloge für Deutschland

Figure 22 - The direction of the flow of orders in 1901

ILLUMINATI LETTERHEADS

The three genuine Illuminati images I discovered, completely by chance was on 28 July 2013. They were the first genuine Illuminati images from Berlin and were on three different letters on different subjects all written to Westcott.

They were stored in a beaten up old cardboard file box, in a corner of the High Council Library which was filled with a number of other filing boxes. I was drawn to the obscure name 'Swedenborg Rite,' an organisation from the past, that I had vaguely heard of and as far as I knew had nothing to do with the S.R.I.A. let alone the Illuminati.

The Westcott Illuminati letters had been mistakenly filed away in the archives, with many other John Yarker letters and correspondence relating to the 'Swedenborg Rite.' I believe this was because the archivist at the time probably did not know about these Illuminati organisations at all and filed them there, for good reason because two of the three letters mention the 'Swedenborg Rite.'

I immediately recognised the 'Prussian Illuminati' Logo of Reuss on all three, an image that up to that point, I had only found as a 'stamp mark' on the 'Dresden Illuminati,' printed documents. What are significant about the letterheads are the names of the three organisations they represent.

FIRST ILLUMINATI LETTERHEAD

The first letterhead I found had not been seen for at least one hundred years. It use Gothic type and was 'Die Grosse Freimaurerloge für Deutschland' or the 'The Grand Freemasons Lodge of Germany,' (see fig 23).

In it Reuss declares for the first time that I am the lawful and recognised Grand Master of all Masonic Lodges constituted under a warrant of the said Order of the Illuminati, 29 July 1901. He explains that the Illuminati are legal and operates under a 'Grand Lodge', of which he is head. It also confirms in plain writing that the '(Mother) Ludwig Lodge of Illuminati,' is a subordinate Illuminati lodge not a masonic lodge, working under this 'Grand Lodge' and this implies that by 29 July 1901 the Illuminati was no longer under the leadership of Leopold Engel but Reuss, as the second Papus letter had implied on 6 July 1901.

I then looked in the ACTA to corroborate the date and it turned out to be the actual letter that Westcott received from Theodor Reuss in reply to Westcott's query, concerning the legality of the Illuminati in Germania.

This letter confirms that Reuss was the legitimate 'German Grand Master' of this 'Grand Lodge for Freemasons in Germany.' This 'Grand Lodge' was created in March 1901 because of the alleged confusion among the eight other 'Grand Lodges' of Germany at that time. It was the same 'Grand Lodge' mentioned earlier, that had its warrant backdated by Reuss to January 1900, which so upset Leopold Engel.

I believe that Westcott received two other items in the post from Reuss that day. One of which is the 'Diploma as an Illuminate' or 'Minerval Certificate,' (see fig 24). The second was the undated document, *Bestimmungen für die Minerval-Logen des Ordens der Illuminaten.* This translates as the *Provisions for Minerval Lodges of the Order of the Illuminati.* There is, however a dedication inside the front page in Reuss' handwriting, (see fig 82):

> The constitutions and regulations of the Minerval Lodges of the Order of the Illuminati, Great Britain, William Wynn Westcott, Regent of Britain for the Order of the Iluminati of Dresden, Germany.

All three documents were signed by Theodor Reuss as the Grand Master of the 'Freemasons Lodge of the Illuminati Order,' none of them mention Engel at all.

The only reason I believe that these three documents were sent together is because they refer to the same 'Grade,' as can be found in the letter on Westcott's Certificate, 'legitimately Minerval in the Order of the Illuminati,' and in the 'Provisions for Minerval Lodges.'

Westcott seems to have accepted this letter as proof of the legal status of Reuss in 1901 and of the Illuminati in Germany, without any kind of further checking at this stage.

It is very interesting that Reuss thought that the:

> Order of Illuminati is a lawful and a recognised body.

My first thought when I started writing this book in 2011, was recognised by whom? The 'Bavarian Illuminati,' which was at first banned and then collapsed as a central organisation, was always a separate independent Order from Freemasonry and had always competed for members with other masonic lodges and orders in Germany. The *History of the Order of Illuminati* would have already explained all this to Westcott.

Die Große Freimaurerloge für Deutschland

im Orient zu Berlin.

Berlin S.W., den 29. July 1901 190

Belfealliance-Straße 74.

Care Frater :.,

You are quite right, the Order of Illuminati is a lawful and recognised body and organisation of Masonic High Grades. I am the lawful and recognised Grand Master of all Masonic Lodges constituted under a warrant of the said Order of Illuminati. The Supreme Council of the Order which issues these warrants is called : Die Grosse Freimaurerloge für Deutschland - (see above), - Great Freemasonslodge for Germany-, and is an absolutely independent Body

The Lodge "Ludwig" is a subordinate Lodge working under a warrant from the above named GrandLodge, and I am Pastmaster of the Lodge Ludwig.

There never existed in Germany the equivalent for what in England is the Grand Lodge of Freemasons of England, from which I hold my Masters Certificate, for there existed only a "Federation of German Grand Lodges", but even this "Federation" has now dissolved itself into hostile Camps of which one holds no friendly intercourse with the other. Our "Grosse Freimaurerloge für Deutschland" is therefore an absolute independent Body, but in Amity with all Masonic Lodges.

What I want from you is a regular Warrant to establish in Germany Lodges or a lodge of the Swedenborg Rite. This Warrant I would like to have before August 5 as I must leave the next day for my holiday and we have a meeting thatday. The Ritual you can send at your leisure, in course of September.

I enclose your Diploma as Illuminat, the Document as "Grand Representative" will follow with the Treaty of Friendship for the Rosi*soc* later on.

Yours Fraternally

Theodr Reuss. G.M.

Figure 23 - Scan of 'Illuminati Lawful letter'

The 'Bavarian Illuminati' was unrecognised by all the established 'Grand Lodge' of Freemasons in the world. But it turned out that Reuss was correct, his 'Revived Illuminati' was lawful in Prussia at this time as we will see later and therefore he was a legitimate Grand Master in Berlin.

To understand what Reuss meant in the letter by *organisation of Masonic High Grades,* in the first paragraph, you need to have an understanding of how masonry was organised in Prussia at the time and in Berlin specifically, as it was completely different to that in England and France.

I believe that it was very naïve of Reuss to ever think that other 'Grand Lodges' in any country would consider using his Illuminati degrees as a form of 'High Grade Freemasonry' as part of their own existing systems. This is what happened in France before the French Revolution, but times had changed.

There is no real indication in his diary of when Westcott received this letter, which was dated 29 July. There are only four entries in the ACTA up to and including 27 August, then a gap of 15 days, but he had already been on annual summer holiday.

The only reason I can think of for Westcott's second, prolonged absence is very tragic. His son Edmund William Westcott was born in 1874 and died in 1907. This was after six years of illness following the amputation of his leg sometime in 1901. It may certainly explain why the next entry is uncharacteristically two months later in the ACTA and as a result Westcott had not been able to hit Reuss' requested deadline:

> *What I want from you is a regular Warrant to establish in Germany Lodges (or a lodge) of the Swedenborg Rite. This Warrant I would like to have before August 5th as I must leave the next day for my holiday, and we have a meeting that day.*

Whatever happened to Westcott, Reuss did not get his warrant by 5 August. In my opinion, it was also very short notice to give Westcott to enable him to produce such a warrant.

As it happens, it was also an impossible deadline to meet, because Westcott had not yet heard back from John Yarker to confirm his agreement as the Grand Master of the 'Swedenborg Rite.'

The next entry in the ACTA is only an ambiguous note, two months later on 30 September:

> *Theodor Reuss from………*

As the Illuminati Minerval Certificate was issued on 29 July 1901, I can only assume this was received by Westcott in September, (see fig 24).

ILLUMINATI MINERVAL CERTIFICATE

Westcott was made a Minerval of the Prussian Illuminati of Berlin according to the certificate he received in July 1901, (see fig 24). The transcription and translation of the Certificate reads:

On Behalf

of the

Secret Areopagus

of the

Illuminati Order,

J. G.

We hereby confirm that on this day, the owner. *Right Worshipful Brother W.W. Westcott S.M. IX°* be as legitimately Minerval in the Order of the Illuminati has been taken.

Given on the 29th day of the month, Thirmeh 1271.

A.D. 700, 70 Jezdegerd

Theodor Reuss

Grand Master of Freemasons Lodge of the Illuminati

Order.

The date on the certificate is not as much a mystery as it at first seems if you have read the Illuminati's own works on the subject of dating letters and documents.[26] Specifically the section at the end of 'Heckethorn's Illuminati,' where their ancient Persian dating system is mentioned:

> *The brethren dated their letters according to the Persian era, called after the king who began to rule in Persia in 632 before Christ, (Jezdegerd). The year began with them on the 21st March.*

---

26 See Chapter V - Heckethorn's Illuminati – Nomenclature.

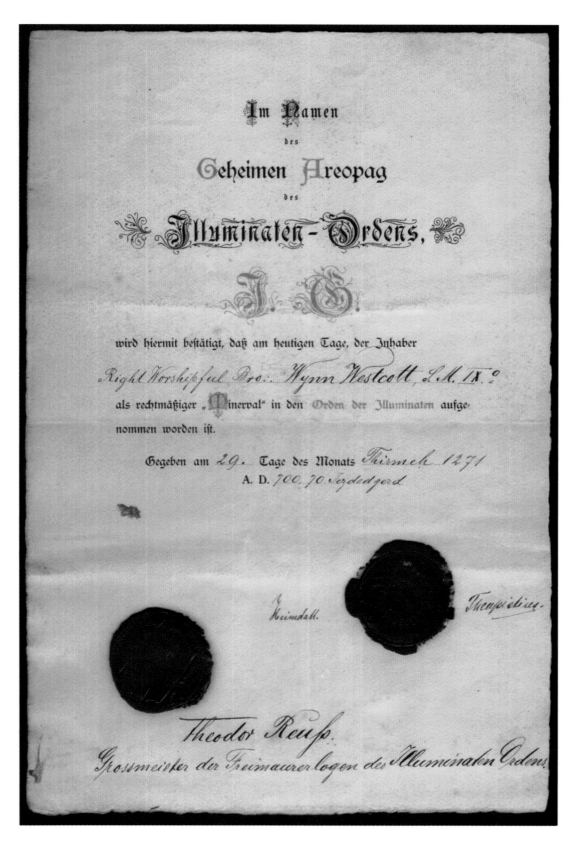

Figure 24 - Minerval Warrant sent on 29 July 1901

If you subtract 1271 on the Certificate from the year 1901 you get 630. This is the date modern Persian calendars are dated from, which was the coronation of King Jezdegerd III, not 632 as Heckethorn quotes.

I believe, therefore, the year of the certificate is 1901. It is also clearly spelt out on the diploma:

Given on the 29th day of the month, Thirmeh 1271. A.D. 700, 70 Jezdegerd.

If the Illuminati also used Persian calendar months, so the month of 'Thirmeh' is July, which corresponds to the date the certificate was posted. The other names of the Persian calendar months are:

Pharavardin	(April)
Adarpahascht	(May)
Chardad	(June)
Thirmeh	(July)
Merdedmeh	(August)
Schaharimeh	(September)
Meharmeh	(October)
Abenmeh	(November)
Adarmeh	(December)
Dimeh	(January)
Benmeh	(February)
Asphandar	(March)

The date of the certificate also seems to corroborate Reuss' letter of 29 July 1901, it states:

I enclose your Diploma as Illuminate.

The wax seals on the Minerval Illuminati Certificate and the general layout and lettering are completely different from those on the other two Illuminati certificates.

They were found in the S.R.I.A. archives, including the ones that are issued from the 'Dresden Illuminati' and the 'Hamburg Illuminati.'

The impression in the wax made by the 'stamp' of the 'Prussian Illuminati' seal are fainter and therefore seem to me to be much older and perhaps have had more use. Where did Reuss obtain the old stamps?

FIRST WAX SEAL

The first, older Minerval red wax seal, (see fig 24), on the left of the certificate consists of a double circle with a motto around the outside, a triangle with Runes across the top, a blazing Sun and a blurred centre, which looks like a heart, (see fig 25) for enlarged detail. The Latin motto around the outside circle of the older seal is:

FRATERNITATIS ILLUMINATI MAGNUM SIGILLUM

This translates as:

Great Seal of the Brotherhood of the Illuminati.

After a great deal of research I can find no mention of this motto or Great Seal anywhere else. This particular seal does not feature the 'Eye of Horus,' the symbol that so many people have assumed was the symbol of the Illuminati, as reported on in so many publications and as seen on the American dollar bill for example.

What is very interesting about the rune letters to be found in the apex of the triangle is that they are much more distinctive than anywhere else, such as for example, on the letterheads of the Illuminati. This was probably caused because the top part of the metal-stamp does not have as much applied pressure as the centre of the stamp mark and it produced a very interesting surprise.

The five rune letters featured[27] read as:

ᚼ ᛜ ᚱ ᛜ ᛗ.

I had, for several years, thought that the letters on the 'Dresden Ordinances,' read as S.O.T.O.M. This was mainly because Ellic Howe tentatively suggested that the middle three characters may be the origin of the initial letters of the O.T.O., although even he admitted this was pure conjecture, (see fig 9 and 25).[28]

I had, for several years, thought that the letters on the 'Dresden Ordinances,' read as S.O.T.O.M. This was mainly because Ellic Howe tentatively suggested that the middle three characters may be the origin of the initial letters of the O.T.O., although even he admitted this was pure conjecture.

---

27 The Rune letters can be found as a Microsoft Office default fonts: Segoe UI Symbol.
28 See the image Ellic Howe & Helmut Möller, 1986, *Merlin Peregrinus: Vom Untergrund des Abendlandes*, page 155.

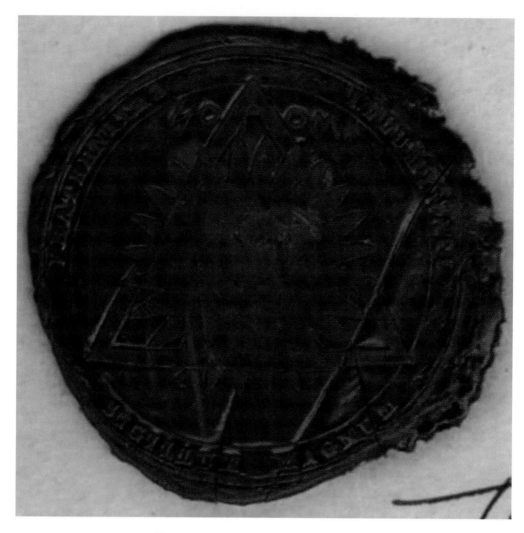

Figure 25 - Red wax seal and Illuminati motto

However, it would take me several more years to work out what S.O.T.O.M. really meant.

ᛌ ◇ ᚱ ◇ ᛗ.

The letter 'L' is not 'T', as I had first thought. The middle Rune letter is 'ᚱ' this is the rune letter 'L' it can also stand for Laukaz / Lagu / Logr / Laf. The rune letter 'L' could stand for 'Licht' or 'Light' (the irradiated Sun) or 'Liebe' 'Love,' (the blazing heart) or 'Leben' Life. All would be equally applicable to the Illuminati and their proposed enlightenment as we have seen previously.

The big question is, what does the Rune letter 'ᚱ' or 'L' stand for in the middle? When you look closer at the seal (see fig 25), you see that the four other letters all fall outside the sacred delta in the Illuminati Logo. Only the Rune letter 'ᚱ' or 'L' falls inside the sacred delta, is this significant?

There are three excellent Illuminati examples of the use of the letter 'L' from the last lines in Reuss' pamphlet *Die Mysterien der Illuminati,* which I have already mentioned several times and they are the last lines in Chapter II and they read:

Love, Light, Life.

(Liebe, Licht, Leben)

Taken as a whole, I believe that perhaps the meaning of the five Runes is God's 'Love' or 'Light' or 'Life,' or all three, is spread across the four quarters of the world.

However, the 'Bavarian Illuminati' did use the plain letters S.O.M.O. somewhere else, which was on their lodge tracing boards to mark the four points of the compasses. In England it is very much the same but we would use the letters N.E.S.W.

These tracing boards were used to illustrate the Illuminati lodge symbols just like in all other masonic lodges, during their meetings in the first to third degree ceremonies.[29]

The Illuminati tracing boards were also orientated like those in the old French lodges, East or Orient at the top. I give an example of a French tracing board (see fig 26). It starts on the left with S. Septentrion for North at the top is O. Orient for East. On the right is M. for Midi or South and O. for Occident or West at the bottom.

Figure 26 - French masonic tracing board using S. O. M. O.

These four letters stand for:

	LATIN	FRENCH	ENGLISH	LODGE ROOM
S.	Septentrion	Nord	North	Darkness/Night
O.	Orient	Est	East	Rising Sun
M.	Midi	Sud	South	Midday Sun
O.	Occident	Ouest	West	Setting Sun

---

29 Wages, Markner & Singh-Anand, 2015 in their book on page 26 and on pages 121 and 147.

SECOND WAX SEAL

The second Minerval red wax seal (see fig 24), on the right of the certificate consists of a circle, triangle, blazing Sun, pentagram inside the triangle, the 'All Seeing Eye' or 'Eye of Horus' and with an engrailed or bottony cross in the centre. See fig 27 below for the enlarged details.

There is no motto around the outside edge of the circle and very significantly, no Rune letters on the top of the triangle where the wax is breaking off.

This wax seal is newer, less used and very similar to the beige paper seal on the 'Dresden Illuminati' seal because of the 'engrailed cross in the centre.' The bottony cross or engrailed cross is mentioned as part of the revived 'Illuminati Priests' or 'Epopt Illuminati Degree.' There are three symbols in the sections of the pentagram, two as yet unidentified.

This seal mark is the only appearance of the symbol that so many people in general, associate with the 'Bavarian Illuminati' the irradiated eye.

I have seen the irradiated eye more used, in other masonic orders, especially on ordinary lodge banners as the 'All Seeing Eye.'

This, I believe, is where the Illuminati may have obtained this symbol, Freemasonry! Not the other way round, as Grand Lodge Masonry started sixty years previously in 1717 and the Illuminati only in 1776. The 'Ludwig Lodge' started as an 'Ancient & Accepted Rite' study group or 'Lodge of Instruction' and it is not surprising that Albert Pike in his Magnum Opus 1857 writing about the 'Ancient & Accepted Rite' mentions the 'eye' fifty eight times, especially in his 4° Degree, Chapter IV page 7:

The Eye upon the blue flap of the apron is a symbol of the sun in the sky, eye of the universe, and to the Ancients an emblem and image of the Deity, the great Archetype of Light. Light and darkness, said Zoroaster, are the world's eternal ways. An Eye, the Egyptian hieroglyphic for the WORD 'Iri', [to perform religious ceremonies], was the second syllable of Osiris, [Osu-Iri], the Sun deified, Personification of the Principle of Good.

This leads me to think the Illuminati use of this image has more to do with ancient Egypt and symbolises sacrifice, healing, restoration, and protection. This seal is called in the *Illuminati Ordinances* the 'recognition stamp mark.'

Figure 27 - Second wax seal - Eye of Horus

Berlin S.W., den *25. Jany* 1902
Bellealliance-Straße 74.

My Dear Bro. Westcott

Having safely returned to Berlin I desire to thank you once more for the brotherly kindness and hospitality you extended to me while I was in London. By arrangements I sent out from London the Lodge next today and received my report. I have requested to ask you the favour to be the Grand Representative of our Grand Lodge for Germany (Swedenborgian Rite) at the Supreme Grand Lodge and Supreme Grand Council for Great Britain & Ireland (Swedenborgian Rite). I enclose a printed notice we are sending out to all German Lodges and I added a list of our Grand Officers, begging you to reply post haste at your very earliest convenience a leaflet or notice (like the one you showed me) on which are given our Grand Lodge for Germany, which constitutes the Grand Lodge for Germany (Swedenborgian Rite). We are willing to pay for the printing of these leaflets and beg you to send us about 50 to 60 copies of it.

Please have the warrant for the Soc. Ros. in Germania written on the same piece of paper as the Swedenborgian Rite was on, and not on the Parchment used for the Honorary members. The names of the subordinate Lodges [Berlin, Dresden & Hamburg] are given correctly on enclosed leaflet in Germany. I made some mistakes in my note given to you in London.

We are obviously looking forward to your earliest communications. Pray remind me to Mrs Westcott her kindness, to your Fratres and with most pleasant greetings I am

> *My dear Brother*
> *Yours most fraternally*
> *Theodor Reuss*

Care Frater:

> *Your Registered Packet arrived and the books first class. I send due acknowledgment with my best thanks. We regard now that Lavender's Warrant is the Warrant for the Grand Lodge of Germany. Soc. Ros. and your publishing above leaflets will be your confirmation of the Grand Lodge. Most fraternally, always yours T. R.*

Figure 28 - Transcription of Reuss' letter to Westcott

There is a second modified version of the 'Die Grosse Freimaurerloge für Deutschland' letterhead with the 'Prussian Illuminati' logo (see fig 28).

It is what I believe to be a mock-up of what the proposed new 'Swedenborg Rite' letterhead would look like. With the details of the proposed, 'Grand Lodge' of the 'Swedenborg Rite' written by hand over the letterhead, dated 25 January 1902.

The proposed list of 'Swedenborg Rite' officers in Berlin was written on this letter. On the back of this page is also written the proposed list of officers for the S.R.I.A. College in Berlin or the S.R.I.G. The implication here is that at the beginning of January 1902, Reuss was going to use 'Die Grosse Freimaurerloge für Deutschland' as the over-arching 'Grand Lodge' for all his 'units' the 'Swedenborg Rite,' the 'Iluminati Order' and the 'S.R.I.G.' In the bottom right hand corner can be found the full address in Berlin used for all three letterheads, number 74 Bellalliance Strass.

This particular letter is probably the very reason why the Illuminati letters were filed away in the 'Swedenborg Rite' folder, as no-one realised that was what they were.

The fact is that very few S.R.I.A. members knew Westcott had been admitted into the Illuminati, even less that Papus had been too and even fewer members would have heard of Theodore Reuss, or that there was an attempt to found the Illuminati in England.

There was an additional piece of plain paper with a list on each side, sent with the letter, on 25th both handwritten manuscripts by Reuss, (see fig 29 and Fig 30). One I believe is a list of the proposed Grand Officers of the 'Grand Lodge for Germany,' for the 'Swedenborgian Rite.' It was sent to Westcott as the Grand Secretary of the 'Swedenborg Rite,' so he could include all the names in the warrant he needed to produce for the 'Supreme Grand Master' John Yarker to sign.

As they were nearly all members of Reuss' Illuminati organisation, it was worth reproducing them here in full. It is interesting to note that Leopold Engel's name has been crossed out as Deputy Grand Master and demoted to Grand Senior Warden on the second line. No doubt due to a quarrel at this time between the two. The officers are written as Grand Officers of Germany, but as far as Yarker and Westcott were concerned they were only a Provincial Grand Lodge in Germany.

See the transcription below and scan fig 29:

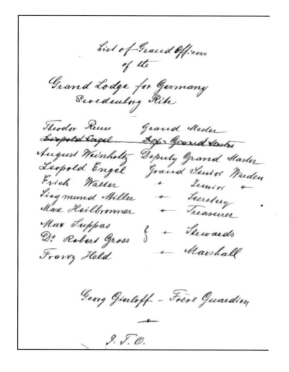

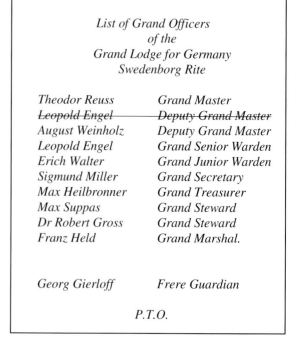

List of Grand Officers
of the
Grand Lodge for Germany
Swedenborg Rite

Theodor Reuss	*Grand Master*
~~*Leopold Engel*~~	~~*Deputy Grand Master*~~
August Weinholz	*Deputy Grand Master*
Leopold Engel	*Grand Senior Warden*
Erich Walter	*Grand Junior Warden*
Sigmund Miller	*Grand Secretary*
Max Heilbronner	*Grand Treasurer*
Max Suppas	*Grand Steward*
Dr Robert Gross	*Grand Steward*
Franz Held	*Grand Marshal.*
Georg Gierloff	*Frere Guardian*

P.T.O.

Figure 29 - List of 'Swedenborg Rite' Grand Officers 25/09/1902

On the back of the same hand written manuscript[30] is a list of officers sent to Westcott by Reuss, of the proposed members of the new college of the S.R.I.G. This is the abbreviation used to designate the, 'Societas Rosicrucian in Germania' which Reuss called the 'Rosenkreuzer Order in Deutschland' (see fig 30).

Note that the list only has seven names on it at this early stage, later on only five of these would make the official list of the nine names in six months' time.

At the bottom of the page it lists the three proposed S.R.I.G. colleges, in Berlin, Dresden and Hamburg. These two new colleges must have been discussed with Westcott in London in early January and were later approved by the S.R.I.A. High Council. It is essentially the proposed list of High Council members for Germany, which was urgently required by Westcott to print in the next High Council meeting notice, so the names could be entered in the Minutes, to officially announce its formation.

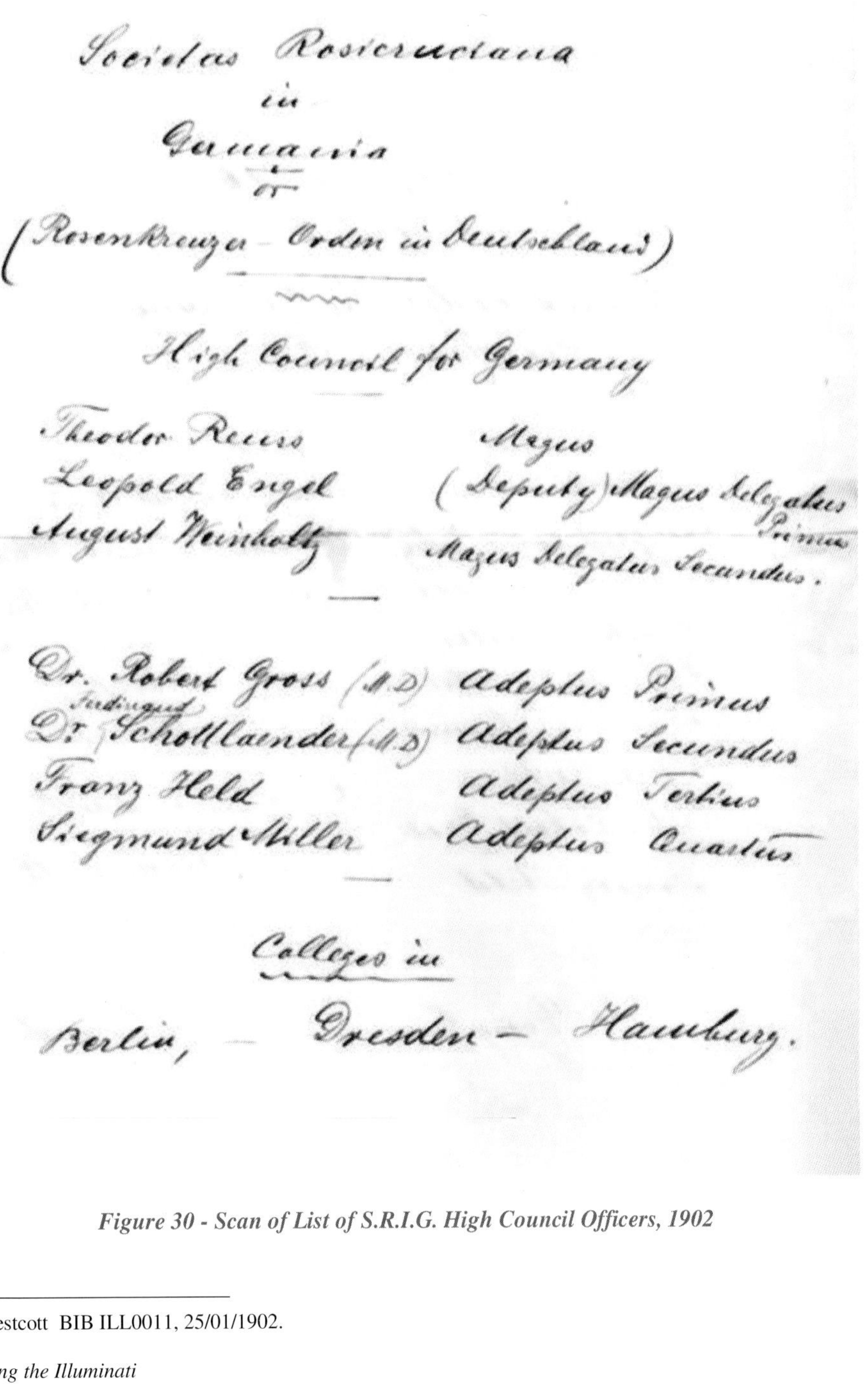

Societas Rosicruciana
in
Germania
or
(Rosenkreuzer Orden in Deutschland)

High Council for Germany

Theodor Reuss — Magus
Leopold Engel — (Deputy) Magus Delegatus Primus
August Weinholtz — Magus Delegatus Secundus.

Dr. Robert Gross (M.D) — Adeptus Primus
Dr Ferdinand Schottlaender (M.D) — Adeptus Secundus
Franz Held — Adeptus Tertius
Siegmund Miller — Adeptus Quartus

Colleges in

Berlin, — Dresden — Hamburg.

Figure 30 - Scan of List of S.R.I.G. High Council Officers, 1902

30 Letter Reuss to Westcott BIB ILL0011, 25/01/1902.

THIRD LETTERHEAD

The third new image is again on a letterhead with Gothic type and has the 'Prussian Illuminati' logo above the title of 𝕲𝖗𝖔𝖘𝖘𝖊 𝕸𝖚𝖙𝖙𝖊𝖗𝖑𝖔𝖉𝖌𝖊 "𝕷𝖚𝖉𝖜𝖎𝖌" or Grand Mother Lodge "Ludwig" (see fig 31). You could almost miss it if you are not looking, but Reuss further recognised his 'Ludwig Lodge' as 'Grand Lodge' on the letterhead as he also states underneath its name, 'Im Orient zu Berlin.' This translates as 'In the Orient to Berlin.' In Germany, for example, the 'Interior Orient' is designated a Grand Chapter or the principle body in the higher degrees. In America, the 'Grand East' is the location where a 'Grand Lodge' holds its communications or meetings. In France, the 'Grand Orient de France' is their oldest 'Grand Lodge', the examples are endless.

Meaning, I believe, that this was the first organisation or lodge of Illuminati set up in Berlin and therefore the 'Mother Lodge' of the revived Illuminati lodges in Prussia, called Ludwig. To use other terminology, this was the logo of the founding lodge of the Illuminati in Berlin, which only later operated legally under the umbrella organisation the 'Die Grosse Freimaurerloge für Deutschland.' The letter is dated 14 October 1902, which would imply that the lodge had not ceased operating in Berlin, as many previous authors like Engel have stated.

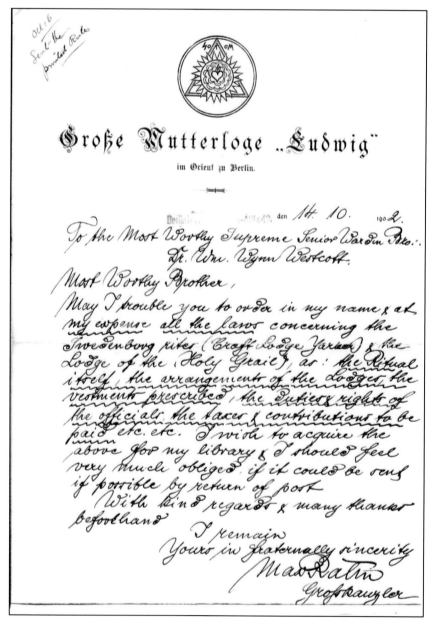

Figure 31 - Illuminati Grand Mother Ludwig Image

Chapter I - Finding the Illuminati

The letter itself only concerns the 'Swedenborg Rite' and is from the secretary of the 'Holy Grail Swedenborg Lodge No. 15' in Berlin, requesting that Westcott send him the actual Swedenborg ritual and layout of the lodge room for his library. Max Rahn who signed the letter was an Illuminate in March 1901 and was the second Celebrant of the S.R.I.G. in November 1902. We know that on 16 October, Westcott sent him the rituals, as the handwritten note by Westcott in the top left hand corner proves, (see fig 31).

All three letterheads use Reuss' 'Prussian Illuminati' (Ludwig Lodge) Symbol exclusively, (see fig 8). This is the only logo that features the five rune letters ᚺ ◊ ᚱ ◊ ᛗ and has none of the 'Dresden Illuminati' symbols. However, there was at least one letter to Westcott from Leopold Engel accompanying the Dresden Warrant issued on 24 February 1902, but it has not survived or been found as yet in the archives. The letters are all reproduced here as they help tell the chronological story of the 'English Illuminati.' They also prove, perhaps for the first time, that there was something called the 'Grand Mother Ludwig Lodge' and that there was a real 'Grand Lodge of the Illuminati' started by Reuss in Berlin.

It proves that these were not just fanciful names Reuss plucked out of thin air, as some authors have accused him of doing. That these organisations had been set up, with their own stationary, something that cost more to do then, than it does now. It shows good intent and meaningful purpose. The names of the people documented in the letters also go to show that real people were involved. Some of the same people were still involved with Reuss many years later and not just names to be found on paper alone as Engel accused Reuss of in his 1906 History of the 'Illuminati Order.' These people, therefore, cannot have minded having their names associated with Reuss in 1901.

It was not until 13 September 2013, that I found the time to scan these letterheads which contain the so called mythical names of Reuss' organisations and lodges of the 'Prussian Illuminati' with its Logos. They enabled me to get the first high resolution images of real Illuminati organisations in Prussia.

On 5 November 2013, I found, on the internet, a text copy of the 'Dresden Illuminati' logo on a Swiss website,[31] research conducted on behalf of 'The Ordo Templi Orientis' O.T.O. by Peter-Robert Koenig. When translated from the German, this research answered some of the technical questions I had about words like, 'Custos', 'Areopag' and those mysterious initial letters J.G.

and R.M.,[32] which can be found in the correspondence and on the certificates.

IRREGULAR FREEMASONRY

Who is going to help solve this charge of making 'Irregular Masons?' There is no doubt at all that the original 'Bavarian 'Illuminati' Order 1776 was an irregular masonic organisation, because it belonged to no recognised 'Grand Lodge' in any country, it conferred the three craft degrees in its system, it was quasi-masonic and it allegedly made women and children masons. However, this was not the case with the revised Illuminati. So what is irregular Freemasonry and why is it so important? I here quote the whole of item number 176 of the U.G.L.E. *Book of Constitutions.*[33]

You cannot be a member of a quasi-masonic or other organisation..... Imitative of masonry, or regarded by the Grand Lodge as irregular...... or as incompatible with the Craft, may not be initiated into the Craft. ......A Brother who subsequent to his initiation has in any way been or is connected with any such organisation as above mentioned shall be bound to disclaim and finally to sever such connection, or on failure so to do when called upon to do so by any proper Masonic authority shall be liable to suspension or expulsion and shall not thereafter be entitled to a resumption of his Masonic privileges...

I was already aware, that in 1978, that Ellic Howe had written a paper that was called *Theodor Reuss: Irregular Freemasonry in Germany, 1900-1923.* Implying that Reuss and the (Bavarian) Illuminati and his 'Grand Lodge' were irregular and that Reuss was, therefore, also an irregular Freemason. In the paper Howe refers to a letter from Westcott to Reuss:

Some of your German Masons are hostile: some German Masonic journalist is trying to attack you and suggests that you want to 'make Masons clandestinely' - that is underhand - he has written to an Official of the Grand Lodge of England for information.

This letter was not about the 'Prussian Illuminati' at all, or Craft Masonry, but another Order, the 'Swedenborg Rite' in Germany. Although a member of the S.R.I.A. briefly, the author Ellic Howe never had access to the original source material used in this book and it is this material that explains what happened next. He also had not

---

found out about the legality of what Reuss did under Prussian Law in his research. Reuss could only be classed as unattached, but not an irregular Freemason, because he was not a subscribing member of a lodge in amity with the U.G.L.E. All that he can be accused of is letting his lodge membership lapse when he left England for Berlin.

Around October 2015 I was working on a hunch that the Pilgrim Lodge No. 238 in London met on the same day as the S.R.I.A. Metropolitan College. With the help of some of the staff searching all the United Grand Lodge of England *Year Books for the 1900-1902* periods, it turns out that the lodge did meet on the 9 January 1902. However, both the Library and Museum of Freemasonry and the Pilgrim Lodge secretary could not find the minutes for those meetings, as they have been lost. So, it is entirely possible that Reuss attended that day and would later returned to the status of a full paid up member and attached to a lodge operating under the constitutions of the U.G.L.E.

Now, some of my earlier cul-de-sacs started turning into highways, mainly because of a single mention of the name 'G. Greiner' in Westcott's ACTA on the 29 January 1902 it says:

Heard from G. Greiner that a German journalist charged Swedenborgian Rite with making masons clandestinely. Answered him registered letter. Copied.

On further investigation, I realised that Johann Freidrich Amandus Gotthelf Greiner (1850 - 1921), (see fig 32), was the 'Official of the U.G.L.E., the actual person to investigate Reuss' so called masonic irregularity, mentioned by both Ellic Howe and Westcott, something, I do not think anyone else was aware. I found that Greiner held the position of Assistant Grand Secretary of German Affairs, which started at the same time as he was asked to investigate Reuss in 1901.

A British naturalised German, Greiner plays three important roles in our story, that other writers may have missed, concerning Reuss' masonic membership and the regularity of the 'Swedenborg Rite' in Prussia. This is probably because Greiner's name does not appear in any of the letters previously available to other authors, but his name is in Westcott's diary.

Greiner was very able to appreciate Reuss' position, as he was not only a fellow German but also a former member of Reuss' Pilgrim Lodge. Not only that, but there had been a special 'Lodge of Mourning' held for his predecessor in the 'Grand Lodge' role who had also been German and a member of the same lodge. This meeting was held on 9 January 1902, the day I allege Reuss may have attended to regularise his membership of 'Grand Lodge' by again simply requesting to become a

subscribing member of his Mother Lodge. My research also proves to my satisfaction, that on legal grounds Reuss was not an irregular Freemason in England or Germany. He, therefore, did not conduct irregular activity between 1895 and 1902 as Ellic Howe alleges in his otherwise excellent and informative paper, Quatuor Coronati Lodge (AQC).[34]

The first role Greiner plays is when he writes to Westcott on the 29th January 1902 on behalf of the U.G.L.E. that a German journalist has charged the 'Swedenborg Rite' in Berlin with making clandestine masons, a charge that is satisfactorily answered by Westcott in a registered letter the next day and during several meetings with Greiner. Although never recognised by the U.G.L.E., the 'Swedenborg Rite' had never admitted non-masons

Figure 32 - W.Bro. Gotthelf Greiner

in to the first three degrees of their system. They only conferred the 4° to 6° on Master Masons and therefore they were no more irregular than the 'Supreme Council 33°.' All Westcott had to do was supply a set of 'Swedenborg Rite' constitutions and an official list of their 'Swedenborg Rite' Grand Lodge Officers, which was called a 'Baluster,' a 'Swedenborg Rite Grand Lodge communication.'

This complaint was from an unidentified journalist in Germany writing to U.G.L.E. and would have, therefore, been directed to Greiner. Yarker later speculated that it could have been the famous German writer and historian J.G. Findel, but the name was never revealed. The charge of

---

34 Howe E. 1978, *Theodor Reuss: Irregular Freemasonry in Germany, 1900-1923.*

making clandestine masons in the 'Swedenborg Rite' in Germany had, therefore, potentially serious consequences for Westcott and Yarker, as Greiner knew they were the heads of the 'Swedenborg Rite' in England. If upheld, it would scupper all their grandiose plans including a German S.R.I.A. college in Berlin. Westcott was probably particularly concerned not to rock the boat, because he knew he was about to get his first Grand Rank in U.G.L.E. in a couple of months' time.[35]

The second role was as a witness to Reuss' presence at the 'Pilgrims Lodge No. 283' in London on 9 January 1902. Westcott would have explained to Greiner why Reuss was in London in early January, to be admitted in to the S.R.I.A. and what the qualifications for membership were and that Reuss was to be not only the first 'Provincial Grand Master' for the 'Swedenborg Rite' but also the first Celebrant and Chief Adept of a new S.R.I.A. college in Berlin. All we know is Greiner was satisfied, so too was the U.G.L.E. So were the members of the 'S.R.I.A. High Council' and what transpired was published for all the members to read in the High Council minutes.

Lastly, Greiner's scholarship also helps prove that Reuss and Westcott were not conducting irregular masonic activity in their respective home countries and that Reuss' 'Die Grosse Freimaurerloge für Deutschland' was a legal entity in Prussia and its ability under Prussian Law to warrant lodges and to also operate the 'Swedenborg Rite,' the 'S.R.I.A.,' the 'Order Martinist 'and the 'Revived Illuminati.'

Six years previously, Greiner had delivered a paper to Quatuor Coronati Lodge[36] (see fig 33), which appeared in their 'Ars Quatuor Coronatorum' (AQC), or the transactions in 1896. The paper clearly stated that it was legal for anyone to set up a 'Grand Lodge' in Prussia (Germany) at that time. Thereby making Reuss a regular Freemason in Prussia and so too his masonic and non-masonic activity. Both Westcott as a Past Master and John Yarker as a correspondence member of Quatuor Coronati Lodge would have read this paper, because they were both regular contributors to the AQC transactions. In fact, John Yarker went on in 1906 to defended Reuss in the Masonic Press in Germany and France and quotes that very same Greiner paper, describing how the new 'Prussian Clubs Act 1892' had made it legal for someone to set up a 'Grand Lodge' in Prussia (see fig 33).

---

35 Past Junior Grand Deacon by the United Grand Lodge of England on 4 June 1902. He was appointed Past Grand Standard Bearer by the Supreme Grand Chapter of Royal Arch Masons.

36 Greiner, G. *German Freemasonry in the Present Era* Quatuor Coronati Lodge No. 2076, London, 1896. It starts on page 55Volume IX and continues on page 60.

The three Berlin Grand Lodges enjoyed until quite recently the exclusive privilege of warranting Daughter Lodges in Prussia. But in 1892 the erection of a fourth Grand Lodge at Berlin by Dr. Hermann Settegast, Professor, Geheimrath, and Past Grand Master of the Royal York, under circumstances which have already, to some extent, been related in our Transactions (A.Q.C., v., p. 193; vi., p. 154), brought in question the validity of the Royal Edict of 1798. The Three Globes, Grand National Lodge, and Royal York, fully believing that they possessed the monopoly of erecting Lodges in Old Prussia, relied on that circumstance to defeat the design of Dr.

Figure 33 - 'German Freemasonry in the Present Era' by Greiner AQC transactions 1896

Settegast. The President of Police objecting to Dr. Settegast's proceedings, the latter appealed successfully to the Verwaltungsgericht, (Court of the Inner Administration at Berlin,) and on further appeal, the O Server waltungsgericht on April 23rd, 1892, delivered judgment.

The decision was, that the Edict of 1798 is now practically inoperative, and that all Lodges in Prussia stand under the same general laws regulating clubs and other societies. Since then all the German Grand Lodges have been free to warrant Lodges in Prussia, and some have already done so. For example, of the 19 regular Lodges in Berlin, the Three Globes possesses five, the Grand National Lodge eight, the Royal

York four, and the Grand Lodges of Frankfurt (Eclectic) and Hamburg, one in each.[37]

It is very true that the 'Grand Lodges' of the world would have never condoned what Reuss did in Berlin. This was not 'Masonically' a correct thing to do, but as a German by birth living in Germany, by the strict letter of the law in Prussia he was entitled to form a 'Grand Lodge' and have different societies, orders, rites and degrees working under its name. The eight existing 'Grand Lodges' of Germany had many different versions of Freemasonry working under their banners and they were at that time, in amity with the U.G.L.E. It had been Greiner's predecessor, Bro. Gustavus Adolphus Caesar Kupferschmidt (1840-1901), while acting as the first Assistant Grand Secretary German Correspondence that had achieved this concordat of the eight German 'Grand Lodges.'

How important was Greiner's opinion in the role of Assistant Grand Secretary German Correspondence? He was second only to the Grand Secretary of the U.G.L.E. in responsibility and power. In his new position he was very unlikely, as the new incumbent, not to have done anything other than a thorough job over Reuss' alleged irregularity and membership. Greiner was the Worshipful Master of the Quatuor Coronati Lodge, No. 2076 from 1901 to 1902, so his paper had added gravitas over this Prussian Law. Finally, in a strange way, it might help explain why Reuss' attendance may not have been recorded as a visitor and petitioner on 9 January 1902. On that day, the Pilgrims Lodge No. 238 held a special 'Lodge of Mourning' meeting for the late Bro. Kupferschmidt and two other lodge members meaning that a re-joining member would be a minor consideration.

NEW MATERIAL

I had actually finished writing this book and had produced a draft copy for proof reading and editing when I received an email from Susan Snell the archive manager from the Library and Museum of Freemasonry. It said that some 200 items of S.R.I.A. property was being returned to their ownership and that she had produced a box list of the contents and asked if I would like to come and collect it and return it to the society.

When I opened the grey archive box, there on the top of several assorted documents, were three A3 sized Illuminati certificates, with bright red wax seals along with several other certificates belonging to Westcott from other Orders and a photograph of Westcott taken towards the end of his life in South Africa. Thank you Saint Anthony, I did not even know that I had l lost them!

Specifically, there were two letters written by Reuss which I do not believe anyone has seen in print before. The first is written on an 'English and American Register' letterhead from Reuss' Illuminati office address at 74 Bell Alliance Strass, Berlin. It is the name of the organisation that Reuss wrote seven or eight pamphlets for, under various pseudonyms between 1901 and 1904 and were published by Hugo Steinitz of Berlin.

They include *Reiseführer von Berlin und Potsdam* (a travel guide to Berlin and Potsdam*)* by Br. Peregrinus, (Brother Pilgrim); *Was muss man von der Freimauerei wissen?* (What you need to know about the Freemasonry?) The subtitle was *And a general representation of the Order of the Freemasons; Illuminati and Rosicrucians,* it was written by von Peregrinus 1901.

In the February letter (see fig 34), Reuss reveals when he sent the undated Illuminati rituals to Westcott. He also pledges himself, not to dispense the 'Swedenborg Rite' to any person that is not a Master Mason. This pledge means he will not confer the first three degrees of Freemasonry in the 'Swedenborg Lodges' in Germany and thereby not make irregular masons.

This demonstrates to me, the lengths that they were prepared to go to ensure nothing irregular is going to transpire. It would seem that Reuss is also under attack at home by the latest Latomia, who claim that, the 'Swedenborg Rite' was not recognised by U.G.L.E. That was absolutely correct then, as it is today. U.G.L.E. does not recognise any other rite or order other than the three craft degrees and the Order of the 'Holy Royal Arch.'

ILLUMINATI RITUALS DATE

We now know from this letter, for definite (see fig 34), that the original German Rituals for the Illuminati rituals 'Minerval, Scottish Knight, Knight Rose Croix, Synods,' were all sent to Westcott by Reuss via book post on the 3 February 1902.

The priest degree he mentions in this letter is the 'Synod degree' and Reuss confirms that he gave Westcott the secret 'Word' while in London in January 1902.

The scribbled note in the top left hand corner is in Westcott's handwriting, and is part of his method of keeping track of correspondence and replies, saying that he had sent a copy to John Yarker and a new issue of the 'Swedenborg Rite' Balustrade on the 5 February 1902.

---

37 Ibid. This paragraph is found (AQC) (see fig 33) above.

In the handwritten note at the end of the letter, Reuss says:

What is the name of the scoundrel that wrote to United Grand Lodge of England!?
Please try!

I do not think Westcott knew the answer to that question, as the original letter was written to 'Grand Lodge' directly and probably Greiner knew the answer. If I was to guess, it was written anonymously and Greiner did not know the name of the writer either.

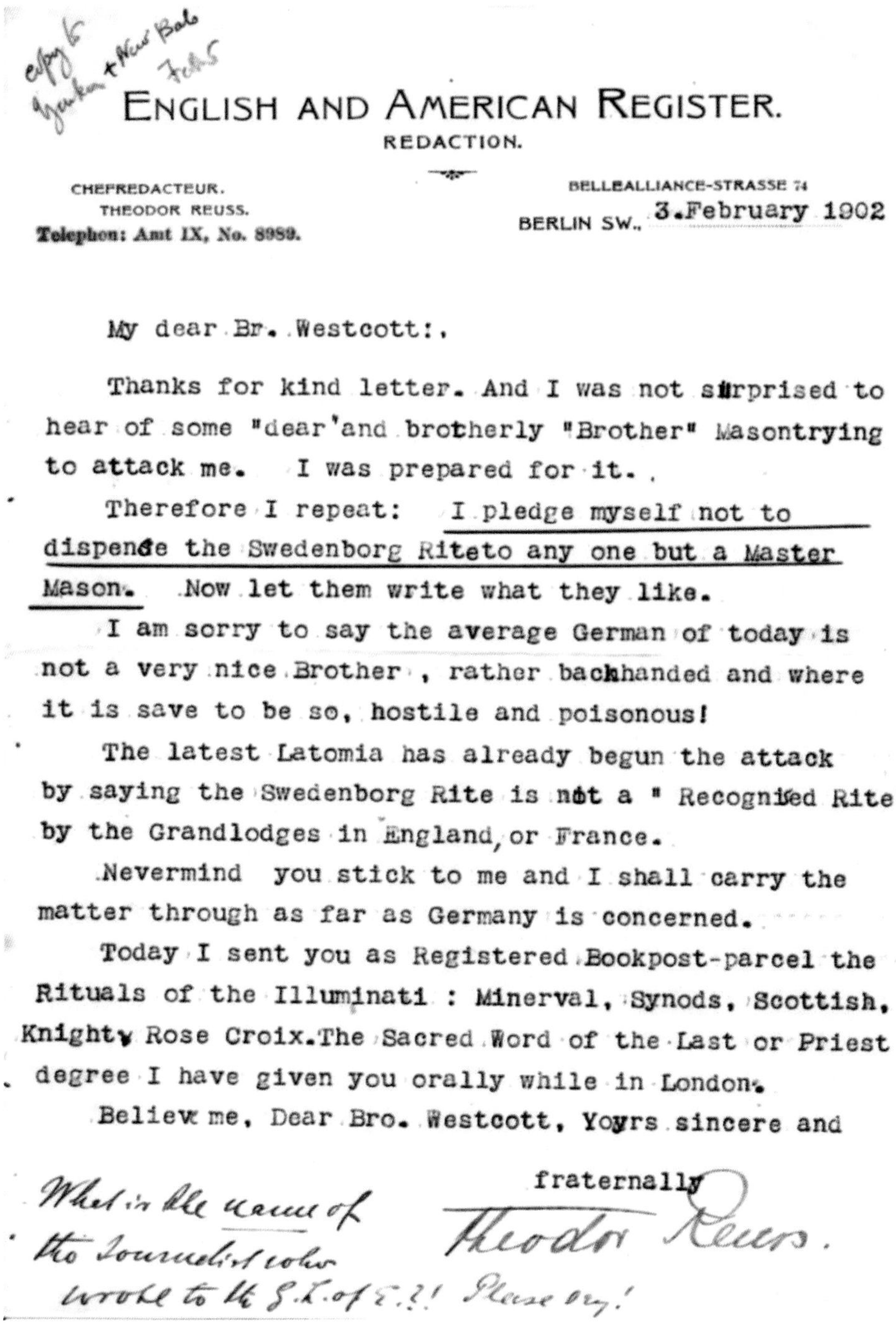

ENGLISH AND AMERICAN REGISTER.
REDACTION.

CHEFREDACTEUR.
THEODOR REUSS.
Telephon: Amt IX, No. 8989.

BELLEALLIANCE-STRASSE 74
BERLIN SW., 3.February 1902

My dear Br. Westcott:,

Thanks for kind letter. And I was not surprised to hear of some "dear'and brotherly "Brother" Masontrying to attack me. I was prepared for it. ,

Therefore I repeat: I pledge myself not to dispense the Swedenborg Riteto any one but a Master Mason. Now let them write what they like.

I am sorry to say the average German of today is not a very nice Brother , rather backhanded and where it is save to be so, hostile and poisonous!

The latest Latomia has already begun the attack by saying the Swedenborg Rite is not a " Recognised Rite" by the Grandlodges in England, or France.

Nevermind you stick to me and I shall carry the matter through as far as Germany is concerned.

Today I sent you as Registered Bookpost-parcel the Rituals of the Illuminati : Minerval, Synods, Scottish, Knighty Rose Croix.The Sacred Word of the Last or Priest degree I have given you orally while in London.

Believe me, Dear Bro. Westcott, Yours sincere and

fraternally
Theodor Reuss.

What is the name of the Journalist who wrote to the G.L.of E.?! Please try!

Figure 34 - Pledge from Reuss to Westcott

ILLUMINATI REGENT WARRANT (DRESDEN) 1902
A Spanner in the works from Engel

The translation of Certificate reads:

On Behalf of the Secret Areopagus

of the Illuminati-Order,

J. G.

Situated in Dresden

It confirms the undersigned officers of the Head office, by virtue of their right as the Order's Acting Board, that *Dr. William W. Westcott* is entitled in *London*, to represent the Order of the Illuminati in the districts as Religious-Regent of the Province of-*Great Britain*, to represent the Order of the Illuminati in fine districts that accord the *Kingdom of England and Ireland* and extrajudicial court, according to the Ordinances and Statutes of the Order. As a mark of respect of the Head Office it is hereby provided the power accorded to supply to it by the existing Head Office, to manufacture according to, existing and future Order decisions made when no important reason according to No. 27 of Members Code exists to recant them.

So authenticated for the Illuminati = Order.

Dresden, the *24th February 1902*

Signed: Leopold Engel (Custos)

Signed: Max Larberg (Deputy Custos)

Signed: Carl Engel (Archivist):

There is no indication in the ACTA when Westcott received this certificate from Leopold Engel (see fig 35). Westcott does mention to Reuss later in June that he had heard from Leopold Engel and that:

> *I must consider myself as an "Illuminatus," under the Dresden Head centre.*

Did Engel write to John Yarker directly in February and then later forward the certificate to Westcott? The whole thing seems very political as Reuss and Engel are just about to argue about the back dating of a warrant in March as has been previously mentioned and they would split up irrevocably over the next couple of months!

Was the breakup specifically about Westcott and the proposed 'English Illuminati?' There is no clue that it was, but Reuss had issued Westcott with a Minerval Certificate on the 29th July 1901 and now seven months later Leopold Engel issued his own Certificate on 24 February 1902 from the Head Office in Dresden.

I do not know if it is significant but Theodor Reuss alone signed the 1901 Minerval certificate, which has no city or territory associated with it. Whereas three members sign the 'Dresden Illuminati' certificate above, Leopold Engel, Max Larberg (Deputy Custos) and his father Carl Engel (Archivist) without asking for Reuss' name.

However, it does mention a territory, 'The Province of Great Britain' administered from Dresden unlike the Minerval certificate that does not mention where it was administered.

By February 1902, Reuss had Westcott's agreement to go ahead with five 'Swedenborg Rite' Temple & Lodges and three 'S.R.I.A. / S.R.I.G.' colleges in Germany. Engel was not involved with running any of them, was this why he issued Westcott with a 'Regent's Warrant' in London for Great Britain, with no mention of Reuss on the certificate thereby attempting to undermine Reuss before the March bust up?

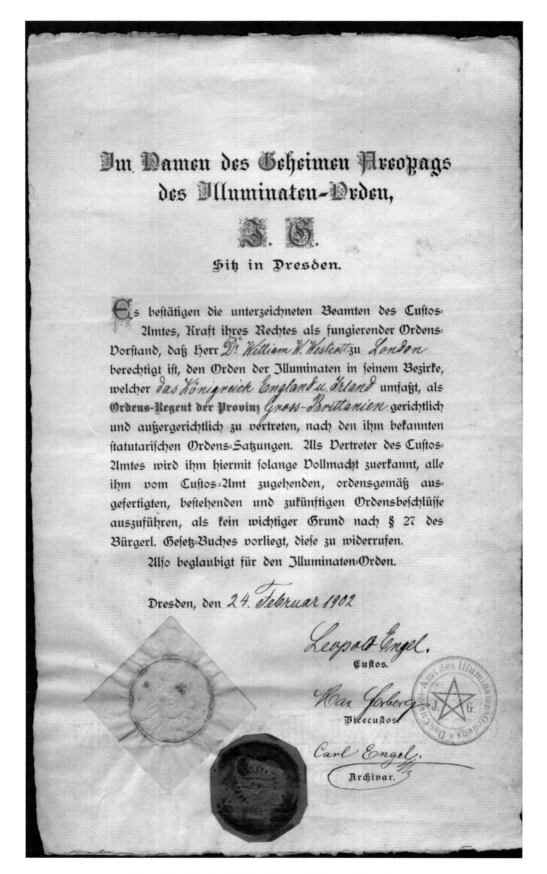

Figure 35 - Illuminati Order Regent's Warrant from Dresden

THE SEALS ON THE DRESDEN REGENT'S WARRANT

The first **Beige Paper Seal** (see fig 36) on the left of the warrant consists of a circle, triangle, blazing sun and a pentagram with a bottony cross inside. It seems to be the same 'stamp' that was used in the red wax seal, (see fig 27). It is possible to use the same metal stamp on wax or paper. It also features the 'All seeing Eye' or 'Eye of Horus' in the top part of the pentagram with the same two unidentified symbols in the two lower sections of the pentagram as in the wax seal. This seal is called in the 'Illuminati Ordinances' the 'recognition stamp mark.'

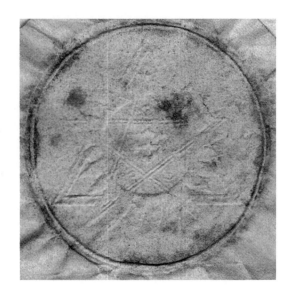

Figure 36 - Beige paper seal

The second **Red Paper or Great Seal** (see fig 37) in the middle of the warrant is blotchy and worn and the 'stamp' impression is very faint. It consists of a double circle with a motto around the outside; a triangle with the rune letters ᚺ ᛜ ᛁ ᛜ ᛗ across the top; a blazing Sun and a very blurred centre.

The Latin motto around the outside circle of the older seal is*:*

FRATERNITATIS ILLUMINATI MAGNUM SIGILLUM

This translates as Great Seal of the Brotherhood of the Illuminati and is the same type of seal that is on the Minerval Certificate, (see also fig 25).

Figure 37 - Rubber stamp mark

The third seal is a **Rubber Stamp Authentication Mark** (see fig 38). It is a blue ink stamp placed directly on to the paper. The motto inside the concentric circles is:

Das Custos - Amt des Illuminaten - Ordens.

This translates as:

Given by the High Areopagus of the Illuminati.

On each side of the pentagram are the initial letters 'J. G.' short for Jehovah (or Japheth) used by the Illuminati for the secret inner word and perhaps 'G' for Gomer the outward word.

Figure 38 - Rubber stamp mark

Figure 39 - Religious character stamp 'L'

12. 2. Authentication stamp showing the general **religious character** with an 'L' in the middle.

    b. The general religious character of all the certificates that are sent out from the Illuminati, as a sign of their origin.

    c. The Custos/Head Office performs a recognition stamp which is printed on beige paper hereof.

    d. Productions of the alleged Order certificates, which were provided with counterfeit stamps or counterfeit seals issued incorrectly by unauthorized person for the purpose of deception will be considered as a criminal forgery.

From this insight we can assume that the Red paper seal is the 'Great Seal' of the 'Custos-Office' or the 'Head Office's recognition stamp mark. The square beige seal or stamp mark and the rubber stamp are the 'Authentication stamps.'

On this occasion, the Authentication stamp mark does not have the letter 'L' in the centre, but an 'engrailed cross.' There are examples of both of these in the archives. The one on the right, (see fig 39), you will remember from the ordinances of the 'Dresden Illuminati.'

The original 'Dresden Illuminati' Statutes and Ordinances that were given to Westcott in 1901 help explain the seals in a little more detail:

Section copied from the Dresden Ordinances:

    12. Seals and stamps.
        a. The Secret Areopagus gives.

    12. 1. A Great Seal, for all new documents of the admitted are sealed.

Soc. Ros. in Anglia.

Dr. Wynn Westcott, S.M. IX°   F. Leigh Gardner, VIII° Sec. Gen.

Office of the High Council. 396, CAMDEN ROAD, LONDON, N.

August 26th, 1902

Care Frater,

    I have duly read, your card & letter & Report, for all which best thanks. I hope you are well again. I am sorry you missed seeing my Bro. Gardner. I note what you say about the Illuminati and hereby accept the position of Regent, and must find a good man to work it up. Do I understand that Engel is now out of the order? I have not heard any more from him.

Re - Rosics.

    Your Fratres must each choose a Latin motto; mine is "Quod scis, nescis." — Even what you know — you don't really know — is a free translation — I will read your Report on Second Thursday in October to the High Council and Metropolitan College.

    There must be a lot of Rosic M.S.S. lying hid in your country, make every effort to find some. We have copies of two here. I will ask the High Council about the use of Library.

    I propose to keep German contributions for buying further Books for it, and for that alone. You might look out to buy any German Rosic books for us.

    Yours sincerely,

    W. Wynn Westcott.

Figure 40 - Westcott accepts the position of Regent

ACCEPT THE POSITION OF REGENT

Westcott ignores Leopold Engel's offer to be the Illuminati Regent for Great Britain, which was issued by the Dresden Headquarters. We must assume that he heard about the argument between Reuss and Engel in March and that Engel was now out of the 'Illuminati Order.'

Instead Westcott replies to Reuss on 26 August 1902, (see fig 40) accepting the position of Illuminati Regent, the equivalent position as 'Provincial Grand Master' for Great Britain:

> *I note what you say about the Illuminati and hereby accept the position of Regent.*

Fortunately, one of the letters in the book *Occult Theocracy*[38] fills in the gap for us and supports the ACTA entries and confirms that Westcott had received both a (post)-card and letter containing the report from Reuss of the founding of the S.R.I.G. College in Berlin on 8 July, neither are in the S.R.I.A. archive.

The second half of the letter is not relevant to the Illuminati and is about choosing suitable mottos for members of the S.R.I.G. and obtaining Rosicrucian books.

UNSUBSTANTIATED NOTE (POSTCARD)

I believe the postcard mentioned above was an unsubstantiated note I found and transcribed, confirming that Westcott controversially had found a way of attending the consecration of the S.R.I.G. College in Berlin without telling a soul in England, nor writing it in his ACTA. The only clue is that the postcard gives the impression that Westcott had now been through an Illuminati ceremony and was returning home and it was sent to him under a separate cover and not with the official report of the S.R.I.G. and Illuminati meeting.

> *It is my hope that you will like the ceremony and will consider setting up an 'English Illuminati' Order when you return home. I will send you the German Rituals, which it's best you translate into English and will confer on you a warrant to found other Illuminati Lodges in England and more much more. What do you say?*

I am still intrigued as to what 'German Rituals' Reuss refers to in this note, as he sent four in February 1902.

NEW REGENT WARRANT FROM HAMBURG

The third new certificate was in fact the 'Regent Warrant' issued on 17 September 1902, (see fig 41) and there is absolutely no mention in the ACTA of Westcott receiving anything like the 'New Regent Warrant' in the post.

I did not know of its existence nor did anyone else, until I found it among the new material returned to the S.R.I.A. archives in 2015. It is effectively a 'Provincial Grand Masters' warrant for Dr. William W. Westcott in London, to represent the Order of the Illuminati in the districts of Great Britain and Ireland:

> *Dr. William W. Westcott is entitled in London, to represent the Order of the Illuminati in the districts of Great Britain and Ireland as, Religious-Regent of the Province to represent the Order of the Illuminati in fine districts that accord in Britain... according to No. 27 of Members Code exists to recant them. [HAMBURG]*

The Illuminati Religious Regent of a Province, reports directly to Secret Areopagus or High Council of the 'Illuminati Order,' which is now situated in Hamburg. This Hamburg warrant is nothing like the Minerval certificate 29 July 1901 but is exactly similar to the wording of Dresden warrant (see fig 35) dated 24 February 1902:

> *Dr. William W. Westcott is entitled in London, to represent the Order of the Illuminati in the districts as Religious-Regent of the Province of - Great Britain, to represent the Order of the Illuminati in fine districts that accord the Kingdom of England and Ireland... according to No. 27 of Members Code exists to recant them. [Dresden]*

I speculate later that the revived Illuminati rituals may have included, the more detailed lectures and also the questioning of a Minerval, requested by Westcott and this is mentioned in Chapter IV.

---

38 Lady Queenborough, (Edith Starr Miller), 1933,
　　Occult Theocracy, p 511.

ILLUMINATI REGENT WARRANT (HAMBURG) 1902
Finally a warrant to make Illuminati in England

The translation of the Certificate reads:-

On Behalf of the Secret Areopagus

of the Illuminati-Order

I. O.

Situated in Hamburg.

It confirms the undersigned officers of the Head office, by virtue of their right as the Order's Acting Board, that

Dr. William W. Westcott is entitled in *London*, to represent the Order of the Illuminati in the districts of *Great Britain and Ireland* as, Religious-Regent of the Province to represent the Order of the Illuminati in fine districts that accord in *Britain* and extrajudicial court, according to the Ordinances and Statutes of the Order. As a mark of respect of the Head Office it is hereby provided the power accorded to supply to it by the existing Head Office, to manufacture according to, existing and future Order decisions made when no important reason according to No. 27 of Members Code exists to recant them.

So authenticated for the Illuminati=Order.

Hamburg, the *17th September A.D. 1902*

Theodor Reuss
  Termasliucs
    Regens

Signed: *Otto Hermes*
(Custos)

Signed: *Max Leichnitz*
(Vice-custos)

Signed: *Mardim Lupochewik*
(Archivist)

Franz Held

The stamp mark consists of a pentagram, with the initial letters I. O. either side that mean 'Illuminati Order.'

There is a difference between the Hamburg warrant stamp mark and the Dresden stamp. On either side of the pentagram are the initial letters 'I. O.' short for the 'Illuminati Order.' While earlier we saw that on the Dresden stamp mark were the initial letters 'J. G' short for Jehovah (or Japheth) used by the Illuminati for the secret inner word and 'G' for Gomer the outward word.

The warrant is signed by Theodor Reuss and his friend Franz Held, who lived and worked in Hamburg and was made the Provincial Grand Adeptus Tertius of the German High Council, of the S.R.I.G. on 9 July 1902 and was one of the founder members attending the meeting. In Freemasonry, Held was the Worshipful Master of the 'Phoenix zur Wahrheit,' masonic lodge that worked the Schroeder ritual. The Hamburg organization, with Franz Held as its Grand Commander General, had two subsidiary Grand Councils. There was one at Hamburg under Held and another at Munich under Maximilian Dotzler. Held and Dotzler fell out in 1905 over a financial affair that was reported in the masonic press at the time.

Another signatory, Mardim Lupochewik was the Hamburg Archivist of the 'Prussian Illuminati' and was also one of the founders of the S.R.I.G. I can find no mention of the Vice-Custos Max Leichnitz, except in the list of members. But Otto Hermes, the Custos, was the 'Junior Warden' of the 'Swedenborg Lodge' in May 1902 at Berlin. Hamburg is also 'Masonically' significant for Germans as this city hosted the first ever English warranted lodge of Freemasons and is where the Grand Orient of the 'Ancient and Accepted Scottish Rite' had its headquarters. However, the Symbolical 'Grand Lodge' of the 'Scottish Rite' for Germany was at Leipzig.

Westcott last wrote to Reuss on 26 August and there was no record of a reply. It was too early to be a letter thanking Reuss for the new warrant, was this letter something else?

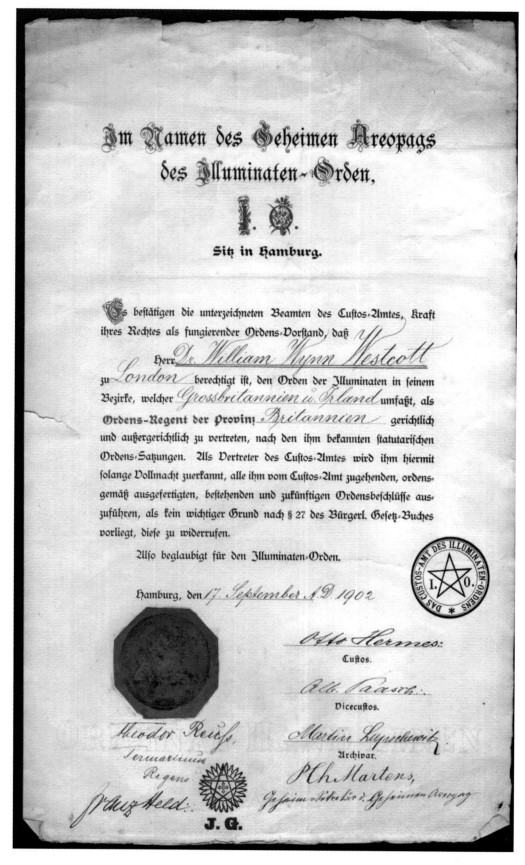

Figure 41 - Hamburg 'New Regent Warrant'

THE SEALS ON THE REGENT WARRANT (HAMBURG)

The first **Red Wax Seal** or 'Great Seal' on the left of the warrant (see fig 42) is the same impression mark as the very faint Dresden red paper seal, (see fig 37), except that it only has eight sides. It consists of a double circle with a motto around the outside; a triangle with the rune letters ᚼ ◇ ᛁ ◇ ᛗ across the top; a blazing Sun on top of the triangle, with a faint flaming heart in the very centre. Around the outside of the seal are the letters spelling the following:

FRATERNITATIS ILLUMINATI MAGNUM SIGILLUM

This translates as 'Great Seal of the Brotherhood of the Illuminati' and is the same type of seal as that used on the first Minerval Certificate and then the Dresden Warrant. It would seem that when Engel and Reuss split up, Reuss kept possession of the 'Great Seal' as it is used on all three documents, the Minerval certificate and the two warrants.

In his history of the Illuminati in 1906, Engel gives a new name to the Illuminati Ludwig Lodge and that is the Adam Weishaupt zu Pyramide Lodge in the 'Orient Berlin-Schöneberg.' This is in a different part of Berlin to Reuss' home and office. He said it was founded in Munich1880, revived in 1896 in Berlin and then moved to Dresden in 1902 and back to Schöneberg Strauss 139, Berlin in 1905. Allegedly the lodge had 40 members in 1914.[39]

The second **Red Ink J.G. seal**, (see fig 43), which can be found below the wax seal and to the right on the warrant, is the 'authentication stamp mark.' It consists of a pentagram superimposed on a blazing star, with the general religious character or bottony cross in the centre, exactly the same as Inner Ordens 1901, (see fig 7) from the Dresden Ordinances, except it has the letters J.G. underneath, instead of the letters R.M.

The third **Blue Rubber stamp mark,** (see fig 44), which can be found on the far right of the warrant is a blue ink stamp placed directly on to the paper. The motto inside the concentric circles is:

Das Custos - Amt des Illuminaten - Ordens.

This translates as 'Given by the High Areopagus of the Illuminati.'

---

39 Eberhardt A.P. 1914, *From the angle lodges Germany-Masonic lodges recent-in the last quarter of a century,* Leipzig, printed and published by Bruno Zechel.

Figure 42 - Enlarged red wax 'Great Seal' of Illuminati Order Hamburg

Figure 43 - Enlarged red ink authentication stamp

Figure 44 - Enlarged blue rubber stamp mark

COLLEGE MINUTES
Was Westcott there?

Before going into the details concerning the most important Illuminati letter sent from Westcott to Reuss in October 1902, it might be worth setting the scene, with the minutes relating to the founding of the S.R.I.G. and a letter on a more personal note, to show that there everything seems quite normal and pleasant, before Westcott drops a bomb shell on proceedings.

The next relevant entry can be found in the minutes of Metropolitan College for 9 October, which can be found in the 'Metropolitan College Transaction for 1902.'

> *The Supreme Magus said the new province of Germania which he had formed, and the new College of Berlin were consecrated on July 8 with much success. R. W. Frater Theodor Reuss, Hon. 8°, of Berlin, who was initiated in the Pilgrim's Lodge, 238, London, being the first Magus, and Celebrant of the College.*
>
> *The S.M. said he had designed a small certificate of membership of the Society, suitable for carrying in a pocket book; these will be issued to all new Fratres in addition to the large certificate already in use, and any present member could have one on application. These small certificates will be honoured by the German Fratres when presented by any English Frater travelling in that country and he requested all English Fratres to receive with fraternal greeting any German frater visiting this country.*

I have underlined two sections of the College minutes above, because I note, with continued interest that the words used are, *Which he had formed* and *the new College of Berlin was consecrated*. Both statements could imply that Westcott was indeed present at the consecration and that he could have taken part.

The High Council of the S.R.I.A., also met that same day on the 9 October at the Frascati restaurant in London. There were only four members of High Council present and the first official report of the Province of Germania was adopted and ordered to be entered on the minutes.

There are also two additional pages, titled the SOCIETAS ROSICRUCIANA IN GERMANIA, first Report to the Most Wise Supreme Magus in Anglia. This special report appeared on page 7 in the printed High Council reports.

OCTOBER 1902
Lillian Westcott's Marriage

For the whole month of September and October there is only one entry in the ACTA that mentions Reuss, the Illuminati or any other of the Orders or Rites that I have written about. There was the usual amount of entries you would expect in a month as head of the S.R.I.A.

Two days after the S.R.I.A. meetings, on 12 October, it simply says in the ACTA, *wrote to Reuss* with no other details, with no idea what this letter was about, other than perhaps sending Reuss a copy of the minutes of the meetings. However years later I found a reproduction of that letter to Reuss in a book,[40] (see fig 45) with the transcript below.

The first paragraph is all about a wedding. Westcott is thanking Reuss for his letter of congratulation on a wedding. Who's wedding and who was Gee? But more significantly there had obviously been an exchange of correspondence, a gap in the recorded story. Did Westcott invite Reuss to the wedding? Perhaps during this exchange of personal letters, the Hamburg warrant dated in September was sent to Westcott around the time of the wedding.

There was indeed another reason for the relative lull in communications over the last two months. It was to do with Westcott's personal life, something that generally does not appear in his entries in the ACTA. I soon found out from September to October he and his wife must have had other things on their mind.

On 25 September at Lewisham Albert Fredrick Gee (1863-1934) married Lilian Margret Westcott (1880-1924) Westcott's 22 year old daughter and the loving couple subsequently both left, to return to his native Natal, in South Africa, where Gee was very involved with the building of the Natal railway.

But I was also to find that Albert Gee was admitted on 9 October into the Metropolitan College S.R.I.A. something which is not mentioned in the minutes above and he was made a Zelator only three weeks after getting married.

In October, Westcott is still very cautious about Mather's potential involvement, as the last 'private' paragraph attests.

See (fig 46), for the flow of Orders between countries in 1902.

---

40 Lady Queenborough, (Edith Starr Miller), 1933, *Occult Theocracy*, (Appendix IV page 24 and 25)

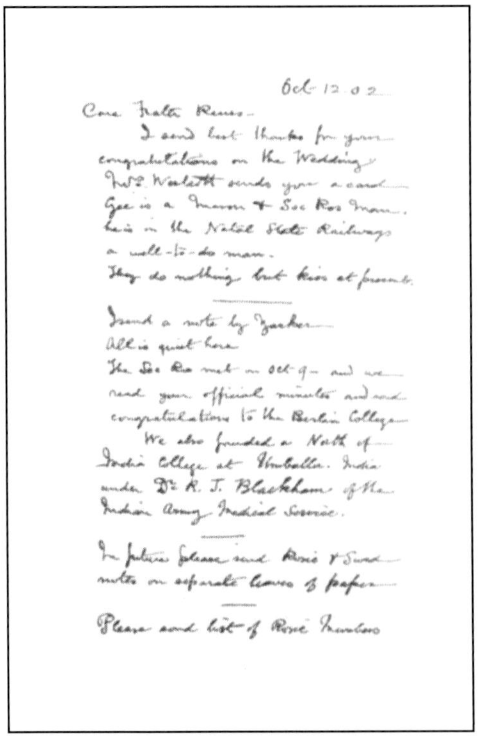

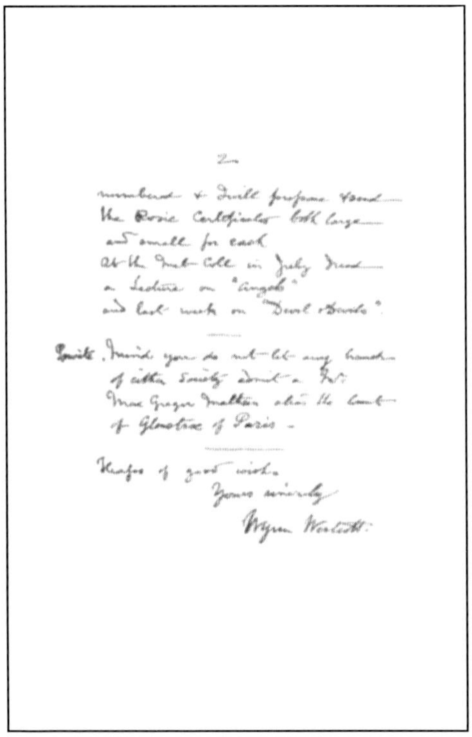

Figure 45 - Scan & Transcription Westcott letter to Reuss on 12 October 1902

Oct 12 - 1902

Care Frater Reuss

I can but thank you for your congratulation on the Wedding. Mrs Westcott sends you a card. Gee is a Mason & Soc. Ros. Member, he is in the Natal State Railways a well to do man.

They do nothing but kiss at present.

I send a note by Yarker. All is well here.

The Soc. Ros. met on Oct 9th and we read your official minutes and send congratulations to the Berlin College.

We have founded a North of India College at Umballa. Under Dr R.J. Blackham of the Indian Army Medical Service.

In future please send Rosi & Swed notes on separate leaves of paper.

Please

Private: *send a list of Rosic members. Numbered & I will propose & send the Rosic Certificates both large and small for each.*

At the Met. Coll. in July I read a lecture on Angels and last week on Devil and Devils.

Mind you do not let my branch of either society admit a Mr Mac Gregor Mathers alias the Count of Glenstrae of Paris. -

Good wishes

Yours sincerely

Wynn Westcott

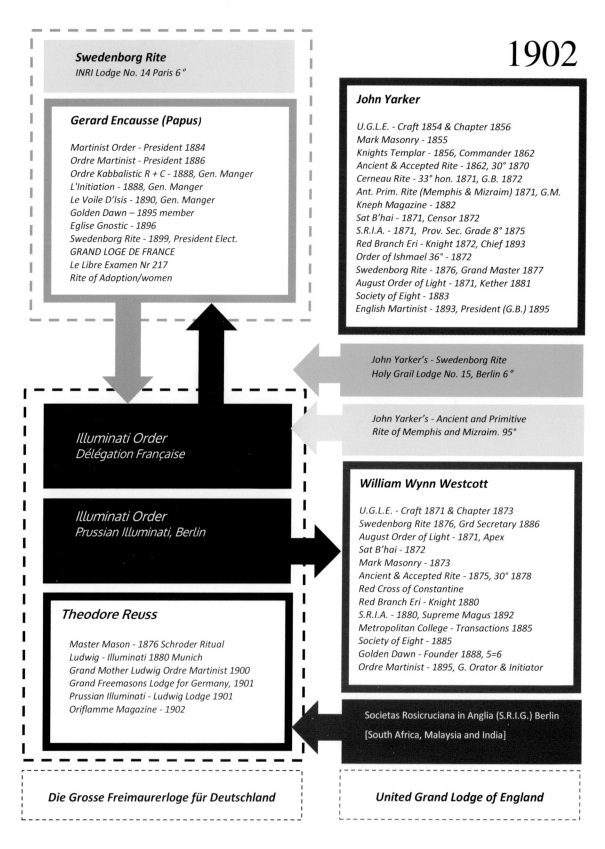

Swedenborg Rite
INRI Lodge No. 14 Paris 6°

Gerard Encausse (Papus)

Martinist Order - President 1884
Ordre Martinist - President 1886
Ordre Kabbalistic R + C - 1888, Gen. Manger
L'Initiation - 1888, Gen. Manger
Le Voile D'Isis - 1890, Gen. Manger
Golden Dawn – 1895 member
Eglise Gnostic - 1896
Swedenborg Rite - 1899, President Elect.
GRAND LOGE DE FRANCE
Le Libre Examen Nr 217
Rite of Adoption/women

John Yarker

U.G.L.E. - Craft 1854 & Chapter 1856
Mark Masonry - 1855
Knights Templar - 1856, Commander 1862
Ancient & Accepted Rite - 1862, 30° 1870
Cerneau Rite - 33° hon. 1871, G.B. 1872
Ant. Prim. Rite (Memphis & Mizraim) 1871, G.M.
Kneph Magazine - 1882
Sat B'hai - 1871, Censor 1872
S.R.I.A. - 1871, Prov. Sec. Grade 8° 1875
Red Branch Eri - Knight 1872, Chief 1893
Order of Ishmael 36° - 1872
Swedenborg Rite - 1876, Grand Master 1877
August Order of Light - 1871, Kether 1881
Society of Eight - 1883
English Martinist - 1893, President (G.B.) 1895

John Yarker's - Swedenborg Rite
Holy Grail Lodge No. 15, Berlin 6°

John Yarker's - Ancient and Primitive
Rite of Memphis and Mizraim. 95°

Illuminati Order
Délégation Française

Illuminati Order
Prussian Illuminati, Berlin

William Wynn Westcott

U.G.L.E. - Craft 1871 & Chapter 1873
Swedenborg Rite 1876, Grd Secretary 1886
August Order of Light - 1871, Apex
Sat B'hai - 1872
Mark Masonry - 1873
Ancient & Accepted Rite - 1875, 30° 1878
Red Cross of Constantine
Red Branch Eri - Knight 1880
S.R.I.A. - 1880, Supreme Magus 1892
Metropolitan College - Transactions 1885
Society of Eight - 1885
Golden Dawn - Founder 1888, 5=6
Ordre Martinist - 1895, G. Orator & Initiator

Theodore Reuss

Master Mason - 1876 Schroder Ritual
Ludwig - Illuminati 1880 Munich
Grand Mother Ludwig Ordre Martinist 1900
Grand Freemasons Lodge for Germany, 1901
Prussian Illuminati - Ludwig Lodge 1901
Oriflamme Magazine - 1902

Societas Rosicruciana in Anglia (S.R.I.G.) Berlin

[South Africa, Malaysia and India]

Die Grosse Freimaurerloge für Deutschland

United Grand Lodge of England

Figure 46 - The direction of the flow of orders in 1902

THE END OF THE ENGLISH ILLUMINATI

The ACTA once again simply says:

Wrote to Reuss.

It is down to us to piece together what happens next! But the formal official end of the roller-coaster ride was in fact a four page letter from Westcott to Reuss on 16 October 1902 (see fig 47) and the transcript (see fig 48). These pages appear in the Appendix at the back of Edith Starr Miller's book 1933, *Occult Theocracy*.

The letter was written after the High Council meeting of the S.R.I.A. on 9 October, where Westcott probably talked to his colleagues about his next steps.

What were the other possible reasons for the 'English Illuminati's' demise?

1. The threat of Westcott losing his two new Past Grand Ranks from U.G.L.E.
2. Possible expulsion from the 'Ancient & Accepted Rite, Supreme Council 33°.'
3. Conferring of any sublime or symbolic degrees in a clandestine or irregular manner.
4. Both Reuss and Papus going behind Westcott's back for the 'Swedenborg Rite' and now the 'Ancient & Primitive Rite of Memphis and Mizraim' in 1902.
5. Foreign language access to written material and associated translation costs.
6. Papus mistakes with grade numbers and involvement with MacGregor Mathers.
7. Prussian war aggression and Reuss' alleged spying activities.
8. Rejecting Westcott's compromise of only taking 50% of the Illuminati grades.
9. Reuss' over ambition and alienation of 'European Grand Lodges.'
10. Reuss' lack of real commitment to the S.R.I.A. and the S.R.I.G.

However, I believe that the real reason behind Westcott's pulling out of the Illuminati was that this was the year he had received his first major Past Grand Ranks. They were in the United Grand Lodge of England, where he became a Past Junior Grand Deacon, and in the Supreme Grand Chapter of Royal Arch, where he became Past Grand Standard Bearer, on 4 June 1902. These are significant first appointments and it had taken him thirty one years to get to this significant point in his masonic career. He was, therefore, unlikely to jeopardise these honours.

The reason that Westcott gave in the letter, was that the Illuminati's, 'Rosenkreuzer-Grade' or 'Rose-Croix Grade' could not be used in England

as it was too much like the 18° 'Ancient & Accepted Rite, Supreme Council 33° Prince Rose-Croix degree.'

It was! It might have been an earlier and therefore older version, but it was the same. It is worth noting that the original 'Bavarian Illuminati' rituals did not have a Rose-Croix Grade.

He told Reuss he was a grade 30° in that Rite and therefore this means he had gone through the chair of his Rose-Croix Chapter and had received his first Provincial Rank.

What he failed to say, is that many of the potential members of the 'English Illuminati' would also have been similarly compromised if they joined the Illuminati, as this quote from the 'Rules and Regulations of the 'Supreme Council 33°' for England and Wales of the 'Ancient and Accepted Rite,' state in items:

47) Except as herein provided a Brother, other than one affiliated from another jurisdiction, having sworn allegiance to this Supreme Council shall not receive any other of the Thirty-three Degrees of the Ancient and Accepted Rite from any other masonic body.

49c) The Supreme Council alone has power to expel Brethren or erase Chapters provided that a Brother expelled by the United Grand Lodge of England shall deemed to have been expelled at the same time from this Order.

50) If a member of the Order within this jurisdiction aid, assist or be present at the conferring of any sublime or symbolic degrees in a clandestine or irregular manner, contrary to the true intent of these Rules and Regulations or of any directions of the Supreme Council, he may be suspended or expelled from the Order.

69) Any matter not specifically dealt with in these rules and regulations shall be governed by the Book of Constitutions of Free and Accepted Masons under the United Grand Lodge of England.

Also, Westcott did not mention to Reuss that the 'Schotten' or 'Andreas Knight of the High Illuminati Order' was too similar but not the same as part of the 'Rite of Strict Observance' and parts of the '29° of the Knight of St. Andrews' belonging to the 'Supreme Council 33°' and this would have caused the same potential problems for candidates that were members of the Supreme Council.

I am pretty sure that Westcott was not aware of the C.B.C.S. growing power in Europe from their base in Switzerland, (see page 76). The Illuminati 'Andreas Knight' is very similar to its 'Squire Novice grade.' The Sovereign Sanctuary as we will see, had already made Blitz its head in America and was trying to get Papus to head up their order in France and the pre-requisite was to drop the Ordre Martinist, which Papus was not prepared to do, but I feel those Grand Lodge politics must have been working behind the scenes.

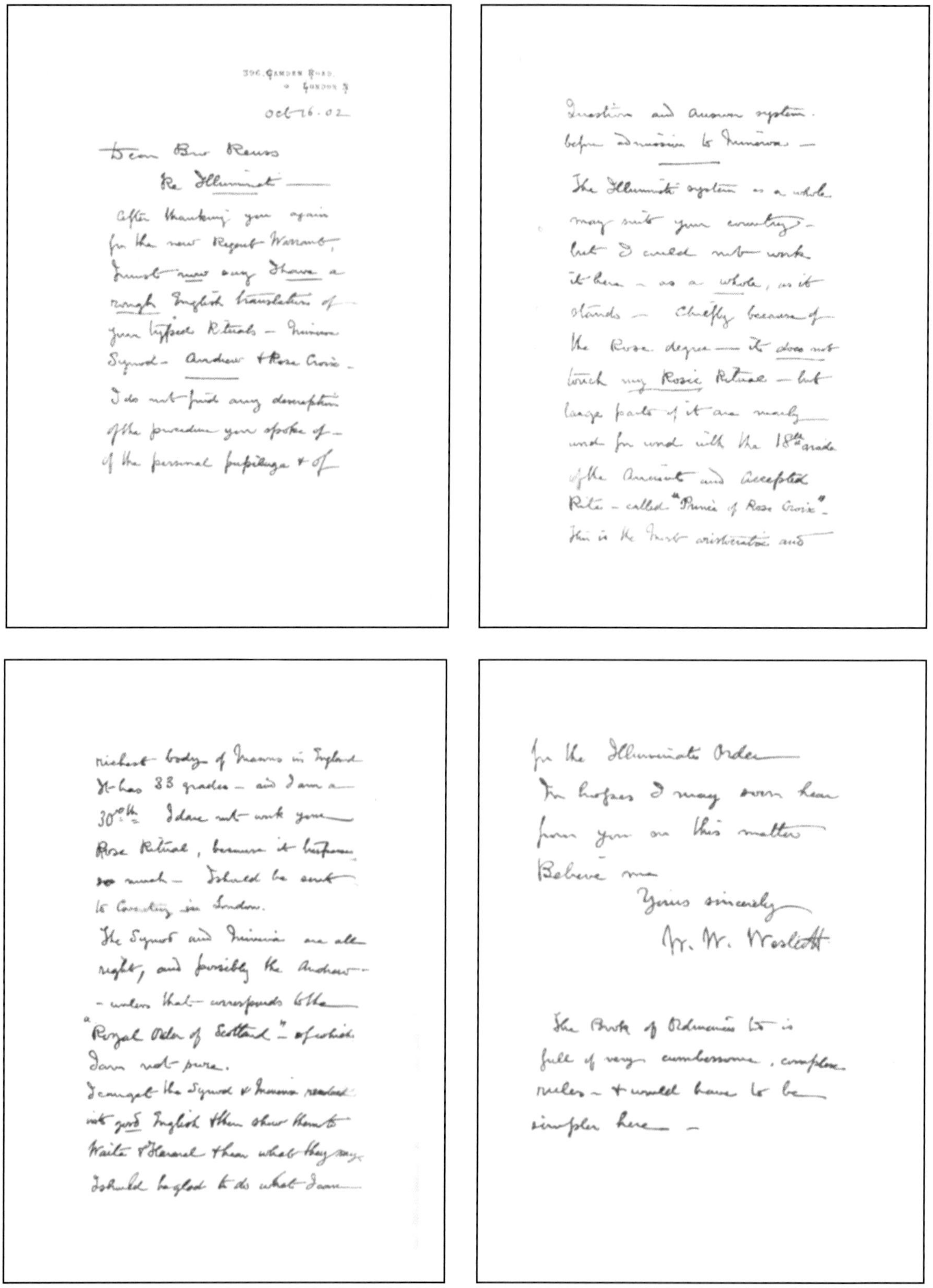

Figure 47 - Last Illuminati letter from Westcott to Reuss

BUT I COULD NOT WORK THE ILLUMINATI HERE

In the first paragraph of 16 October letter Westcott thanked Reuss for the 'New Regent Warrant,' of Hamburg. It had been issued on the 17 September 1902 (see fig 41).

For quite a while I thought the Hamburg Warrant, might have been a separate warrant from a separate third Illuminati Province of the resurrected Illuminati, like those of Berlin and Dresden. Hamburg must have been, presumably, where Reuss re-located the headquarters of his Illuminati after his falling out with Engel in Dresden.

Reuss also probably felt the need to issue a 'New Regent Warrant' to Westcott, because Leopold Engel had issued one back in February.

I was not surprised to see the signature of Franz Held on the warrant underneath that of Theodore Reuss as Held lived and worked in Hamburg. But it just goes to show how people quickly change. In 1905-6 Franz Held, resigned and turned on Reuss quite savagely and pursued him in the German Masonic Press over the high fees he charged for warrants.

In the second paragraph of the letter it confirms that Westcott had had only a rough translation of all four Revived Illuminati rituals and had made his decision based on these. However for the sake of accuracy, the originals were all typed as he wrote, except the 'Rose-Croix Degree' which was handwritten.

The first ritual, the 'English Illuminati' 'Minerval Ritual' as you will see' seems to be quite special, even unique. It is not to be found in the John Robson or Abbe Barrel exposes or in C.W. Heckethorn's Illuminati rituals. Neither is there quite like it in the original 'Bavarian Illuminati' rituals of Adam Weishaupt that have been reproduced in *The Secret School of Wisdom*. [41]

With regard to the 'Minerval Grade,' Westcott specifically mentions the 'personal pupillage,' in paragraph two of the transcription (see fig 48), which was the Bavarian Illuminati's question and answer system, before admission to 'Minerval Grade.' I believe it is also quite an important part of the Illuminati's system, something which is an improvement on Craft Masonry, as it is so specific and tailored to each candidate. I can find no record of the 'personal pupillage' ever being sent by Reuss or received by Westcott. However, the 'questioning' can be found in the Addendum in the new book *The Secret School of Wisdom*.

What Westcott said in paragraph three of his letter, (see fig 48).

The Illuminati system as a whole may suit your country.

England did not traditionally have such a rich tapestry of *haut-grade* or high grade orders and rites as Europe had enjoyed for the previous three hundred years. Most of these 'high grades' had died out during the French Revolution and Napoleon's invasion of Europe. They were now, at this time, slowly starting up again and seem to becoming more prevalent and attached to the older 'Ancient Lodges' in both France and Germany.

But I could not work it here - as a whole, as it stands.

England only really traditionally worked the three 'Craft Degrees' and the Order of the 'Holy Royal Arch,' as agreed at the Union of 'Grand Lodges' in 1813. Some, more adventurous masons had joined the 1845 American version of the 'Supreme Council 33°.'

These were masons that had taken a pledge to join a Christian only Order and enjoyed the more Christian ceremonial. John Yarker with his several different Rites were an oddity and appealed to the few 'Ancients' type Freemasons who were anti the 1813 Union of the 'Grand Lodges.' They were for those masons who were interested in historical history of the older rituals, rites and orders from antiquity.

Chiefly because of the Rose (Croix) degree.

Westcott was absolutely right, the 'English Illuminati' Rose-Croix degree is a cut down version of the '18° Knights of the Pelican and Eagle and Sovereign Prince Rose Croix of Heredom' of the American Northern Jurisdiction version of the 'Supreme Council 33°.' As can be seen from the side by side comparison you will find in Chapter IV.

It claims descendancy from Stephen Morin's 1761 warrant from France and it travelled via the Caribbean, back to France and then to Frederick the Great's Prussian charter in 1786. In fact the Illuminati ceremony has only one quarter of the words and does not have the extended lectures and explanations and little of the rubric to help you understand what is going on, or how to move around the rooms.

---

41 Wages, Markner & Singh-Anand 2015. *The Secret School of Wisdom.*

BUT I COULD NOT WORK THE ILLUMINATI HERE (continued)

But large parts of it are nearly - word for word with the 18th grade of the Ancient and Accepted Rite called the Prince of Rose-Croix.

Yes I completely agree, much of the Illuminati ritual is word for word the same but, the signs of recognition in the degree are very different. Where it differs significantly is that it does not confer any intermediate or previous degrees 1° to 17°, nor does it confer masonic knighthood and there is no sharing of the 'agápē.' The Illuminati qualification for admission is that you have already received your masonic knighthood in the 'Andreas Knight' degree of the 'Strict Observance' of the 'Scottish Rectified Rite.' So you do not receive your masonic accolade in this 'Illuminati Rose-Croix degree.' The Holy 'Word' is the same, but with 'Revived Illuminati' ritual has added two additional cabalistic and alchemical significations to the ceremony.

It does not touch my Rosic Rituals.

His English Rosicrucian system has been around since at least 1857. In fact Jean Marie Ragon mentions a (The Rosicrucian) *Rose-Croix Anglais* ritual on page 373 of *Tuileur général de la franc-maçonnerie au Manuel de L'Initie* written in 1833.

The English S.R.I.A. ceremony since 1865 and it is completely different from any of the 'Rose-Croix' ceremonies in many ways. Some parts of its ritual can be found in un-worked degrees of Albert Pike's 33° of the 'Ancient & Accepted Rite.'[42] The nine grades of the S.R.I.A. confer different types of physical, experiential and philosophical secrets in the first S.R.I.A. Order. In the second S.R.I.A. Order, there are spiritual and experiential secrets. In the third S.R.I.A. Order, it physically in my opinion communicates the genuine secrets of the philosopher's stone to those ready to receive them and has absolutely nothing to do with any form of knighthood. Westcott said:

This is the most autocratic and richest body of Masons in England. It has 33 grades - and I am a 30th, I dare not work your Rose Ritual, because it trespasses so much - I should be sent to Coventry in London.

Yes, the 'Supreme Council 33°' is the most autocratic and richest body of Masons in England. Many senior members of 'Supreme Council 33°' are very senior and influential members of the United Grand Lodge of England. If a member of the 'Ancient & Accepted Rite of the Supreme Council 33°' is excluded from the United Grand Lodge of England, they are automatically excluded from membership of 'Supreme Council 33°.' In the UK it only works the 18°, 30°, 31°, 32° and 33° degree ceremonies. These 33° are made up of a collection of ancient ceremonies from different groups of Rites in use before 1786.

There is also absolutely no mention of the contents of this letter in Westcott's ACTA and it was several years until I came across this copy in the back of the book *Occult Theocracy*[43]

Westcott was right when he said in the third paragraph:

The Synod and Minerval are all right,

The Synod, or priest degree, has no equivalent in any Order that I am aware, but I do not know them all. We have already discussed the Minerval.

Westcott was not a member of the 'Royal Order of Scotland' as far as we know, which he mentions in the last paragraph.

This Order has nothing whatsoever to do with the 'Andreas Knight grade' or the 'St. Andrews degree' nor of the '29° Knight of St. Andrew' of the 'Ancient & Accepted Scottish Rite.' The 'Royal Order of Scotland' is a standalone complete system of collected masonic degrees from antiquity, exceptionally well crafted to correct the errors introduced into Freemasonry in modern times.

However, the 'Andreas Knight degree' is something completely different. It was a pre-requisite for the 'Theoricus Grade II' of the German 'Gold und Rosicrucians' and was also part of the 'Scottish Rectified Rite' or 'Rite of Strict Observance.' Created by Jean-Baptiste Willermoz (1730-1824) before the French Revolution, he promulgated the system in Paris, from his home in Lyon.

Much later Willermoz system established itself in Zurich and was renamed the *C.B.C.S.* they are the initial letters of the 'Chevalier Beneficent de la Cité Sainte' or 'Knights of the Holy City.'

Some modern 'Martinist Orders,' work the 'C.B.C.S.' from warrants that were allegedly issued by Papus. But Papus turned down the office of Great Prior of France of the C.B.C.S., rather than give up the 'Ordre Martinist,' which was a condition of the offer, according to Edouard Blitz the C.B.C.S.' Great Prior of America.

One of the people mentioned in the letter is Fergus Edward Hamel, who was married to one of Westcott's daughters Elsie Bridget Westcott and he also became a member of the S.R.I.A. but not until the 8 January 1903.

---

42 A small but significant part of the S.R.I.A. Zelator grade can be found in Albert Pike's 1867 *Rituals* and in his *Magnum Opus*, in both 1° and in the 24° Prince of the Tabernacle.

43 Lady Queenborough, (Edith Starr Miller), 1933, *Occult Theocracy*, (Appendix IV).

396, Camden Road,
London N.

October 16*th* 1902

Dear Bro. Reuss.

Re - Illuminati.

*After thanking you again for the new **Regent Warrant**, I must now say I have a rough English translation of your typed Rituals - Minerval, Synod - Andrew and Rose Croix.*

———————

I do not find any description of the procedure you spoke of - of the personal pupillage and of question and answer system, before admission to Minerval -

———————

*The Illuminati system as a whole may suit your country - but I could not work it here - as a whole, as it stands - Chiefly because of the Rose (Croix) degree - it does not touch my Rosic Rituals - but large parts of it are nearly - word for word with the 18*th* grade of the Ancient and Accepted Rite called the Prince of Rose Croix - This is the most autocratic and richest body of Masons in England. It has 33 grades - and I am a 30*th*, I dare not work your Rose Ritual, because it trespasses so much - I should be sent to Coventry in London.*

The Synod and Minerval are all right, and possibly the Andrew - unless that corresponds to the Royal Order of Scotland - of which I am not part.

I can get the Synod and Minerval rendered into good English and then show them to (A.E.) Waite and Hamel and hear what they have to say.

I should be glad to do what I can for the Illuminati Order. In hopes I may soon hear from you on this matter.

Believe me.

Yours sincerely.

W.W. Westcott.

The book of Ordinance is full of very cumbersome, complex rules and they would have to be simpler here.

Figure 48 - Transcription of Westcott's last Illuminati letter

BUT I COULD NOT WORK THE ILLUMINATI HERE (continued)

The other name mentioned in the same paragraph is, very significantly, Arthur Edward Waite (1857-1942) who was a well-known author, at the time, albeit a relative novice in all the masonic orders, but not for much longer. However what is significant is that Westcott did as we will see, lend Waite the 'Revived Illuminati rituals,' I can see why, but Waite actually did not seem to do anything with them in the end.

Why in this letter did Westcott approach Waite of all people? Waite was 43 years old before he was initiated into Freemasonry, a year before on 19 September 1901, he was raised a Master Mason on 10 February 1902. Only then could he have been admitted into the S.R.I.A. earlier that year with Blackden on 10 April 1902.

He then rapidly proceeded to be exalted in the 'Holy Royal Arch,' on 1 May, followed one week later with his Installation as a 'Knights Templar' at the Consecration of the King Edward VII Preceptory. It is during this very active year that Waite broke completely with 'Papus' who he had known for a few years and from the 'Ordre Martinist,' when he learned of the bad odour in which the latter was held by orthodox masonic bodies in France.

Waite had not finished being admitted to new Orders and he entered the 'Swedenborgian Rite' in Hermes Lodge and Temple No. 8 in London on 1 September, with no doubt with Westcott's help and guidance.

It is at the end of 1902 that Waite started work on creating his own collection of degrees, rites and orders, with his 'Golden Dawn' associates, Marcus Worsley Blackden and Robert Palmer-Thomas.

They created a 'Secret Council of Rites' on 2 December 1902 that was finally constituted in April 1903. The qualification was a 'Royal Arch Mason' they included, Martinisim (Malkuth), reformed 'Golden Dawn' (Jesod), Rectified Rite of Swedenborg (Hod), Order of the Eastern Star (Netzach), Rectified R.R. et A.C. (Tiphereth), Order of Illuminati (Chesed), the new Reformed Adoptive Masonry (Geburah) the C.B.C.S. (Chokmah) and he then added the Daughters of Zion (Binah) Rite of 7..16 intermediate (Daath) and finally Supreme Crown or 3rd Order R.R. et A.C. (Kether).[44]

Coming back to our story briefly, Westcott sent Waite the revived Illuminati rituals on the 26th January 1903 and a further set of manuscripts by registered post on the 5th February. You can see why now.

In 1903, Waite travelled to Kilmarnock, Scotland to receive the 'Early Grand Rite of Scotland 47°' on 8 February 1903 from Colonel Spencer. This is a little known Order, but gave Waite legitimate access to a number of degrees. He was admitted first to the '41st Degree' called the 'Priestly Order or White Mason.' This is otherwise known of today as the 'Royal Arch Knight Templar Priest'. He then purchased all the remaining degrees from the '4th to the 44th Degrees.' By chance he found that he was also in possession of the 'Order of the Temple for Scotland.' It was regard by some to be affiliated with the 'Mark Degrees of Masonry,' it was therefore allegedly a rival of the 'Royal Arch Knights of Malta,' 'Red Cross of Rome and Constantine' and even the 'Royal Ark Mariners.'

All very confusing I am sure but does show how Waite was beginning to collect a number of degrees and orders and why the Illuminati would have been of interest to him.

Waite was introduced to the 'C.B.C.S.' by Eduard Blitz the head of the 'Ordre Martinist' in America, and completed his application forms in late February. He was admitted into the 'Helvetian Priory' in Geneva, Switzerland on 28 February 1903. The 'C.B.C.S.' system of masonry includes the 'St. Andrews degrees.' On 16 April that same year he was given a warrant by the 'Helvetian Priory' for England. It was this warrant that was eventually picked up by the members of the S.R.I.A. and it is the A.E. Waite warrant that is used to this day, only for selected members of the higher grades of the S.R.I.A. In 1907, Waite was admitted into the degrees of the 'Profess' and 'Grand Profess' by correspondence only.

The 'Helvetian Priory' of the 'C.B.C.S.' thinking that the English Order was in abeyance, 34 years later in 1937, issued a second English warrant to the 'Great Priory of the United Military Religious and Masonic Order of the Temple' and today this Order is restricted to only the most senior members of 'Great Priory of the Temple' in England.

The reality was that A.E. Waite set up his equivalent of a 'Grand Lodge' of all Grades and Rituals and called it the 'Secret Council of Rites' and its Constitutions are dated from April 1903. He did not actually take up the Illuminati Grades and his Council went nowhere.

From the briefest sketch of A.E. Waite's activities you can see that Reuss, Papus, Yarker and Westcott were not alone in 1902-3 in creating collections of degrees, rites and orders. They would also not be the last.

---

44 Gilbert R.A. 1978, A.E. Waite *Magician of Many Parts*. Appendix B, page 175.The names in brackets above are the ten Sephiroth on the Kabbalistic 'Tree of Life.'

There is no record of a reply from Reuss to that 16 October 1902 letter; in fact, the next entry in Westcott's diary is asking Reuss:

That he must send a Report on German Progress.

This was more than a month later. There were Christmas cards from Reuss to Westcott but no other formal contact.

The last entry in the ACTA mentioning the Illuminati is when Westcott:

Sent a packet of Illuminati [Reuss] manuscripts to Waite by registered post.

This was on 5 February 1903.

The *History and Mysteries* of the Illuminati were an impressive find in the S.R.I.A. High Council Library. The Illuminati rituals and ordinances found in the Library and Museum of Freemasonry were a providential find with help from some friends. Papus' letters in the S.R.I.A. archives gave fresh impetuous to my amazing voyage of discovery and from which I learnt so much. So much new information was found in the ACTA and it provided me with a day by day account of the whole story as it unfolds. I was very lucky to have access to the S.R.I.A. and U.G.L.E. archives and they gave me the ability to corroborate my new story with the correspondence in the archives and some of the undated material. Finally, the Illuminati certificates and warrants were the images of the Illuminati that I did not have at the beginning and were the icing on the cake.

Chapter II

History of the Order of the Illuminati

HISTORY OF THE ORDER OF THE ILLUMINATI
Westcott's handwritten copy 1902

INTRODUCTION TO THE 'HISTORY'

I now present William Wynn Westcott's 1902 handwritten *History of the Order of the Illuminati,* which has never been published before and was found in the S.R.I.A. archives in 2010, (see fig 49). It reveals a refreshing, unbiased look at the original Illuminati Order founded in 1776.

It was located in a locked steel trunk with the most precious archive material of the S.R.I.A. This included rituals and documents that would be used for reference and only then by the select few members with a key and so not readily available to the other members. This is unusual in itself. The key had been lost for at least eighty years and it was one of many tried, from amongst many old rusty keys in a beaten up King Edward cigar box, which had been recorded on the archive property list.

The box it was rediscovered in, was one of twenty found when all the S.R.I.A. documents, papers, rituals and minute books were professionally archived in 2010 by Lucy Shepherd. This volume was not considered part of the archive but a book and therefore part of the High Council Library. Therefore, it was not until six months later during the listing and valuing of the library that this very handsome copy of the *History of the Order of the Illuminati* was recorded. Because of its very interesting subject matter, it was put to one side and its discovery led to an amazing and interesting voyage of discovery.

Upon inspection, I found that it was not signed by anyone, making me first think that Westcott had simply researched the subject and wrote a paper on the Illuminati, which for some reason was never published or delivered in a college study group meeting. The second chapter was attributed to a 'von Garatheodoro,' Berlin 1894, which meant nothing to me at the time.

What was strange is that it was obviously written by Dr William Wynn Westcott in his very best and distinctive handwriting. This indicated that he had spent a great deal of time on this book. Nearly two hundred papers of his had been found in another archive box, some typed, but others in his less legible handwriting and much more difficult to read. So, identifying his handwriting was easy enough.

The black leather quarter (Quarto) bound, marble-fronted lined note book, contains two chapters. Both written in ink and it would seem with a quill pen as the ink fades as the ink runs out along each line.

Apart from his distinctive writing, the only other reason we know it belonged to Westcott, is from a handwritten dedication in the top right corner inside the front cover, (see fig 50), which says:

This was amongst the papers given to me by W. Wynn Westcott when he went to South Africa Signed W.E.C.D.

On further investigation, the initials turn out to be those of Dr William Elliot Carnegie Dickson (1878 – 1954) M.D. a well-respected senior member of the S.R.I.A. The handwriting was confirmed as belonging to Dr W.E. Carnegie Dickson by Anthony Fuller, who has several letters and documents belonging to Carnegie Dickson, given to him in New Zealand, that are now part of his collection of papers. So, this valuable document was given to Carnegie Dickson by Westcott before he left England to live in Natal, South Africa. This does not concretely confirm when he was given it, as Westcott made several journeys to Natal. He visited Natal in 1906 to consecrate the Ladysmith College. Westcott retired from public office in 1918 and then gave notice to leave England in

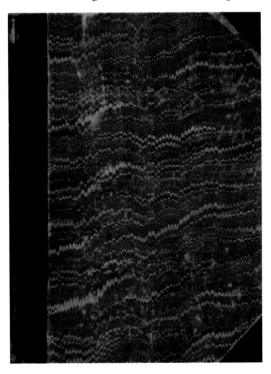

Figure 49 - Westcott's notebook

1919, eventually leaving in 1920. This is probably when Carnegie Dickson was given Westcott's property. He did return the next year for a short visit with his wife, who tragically fell to her death in Tunbridge Wells during the visit and so he left alone for good in 1921 and died in 1925. Carnegie Dickson had twenty nine years to deposit the *History of the Illuminati* in the secure box before he died in 1954.

Why had Westcott taken such care in writing this book or document? And, why wasn't it among the list of well-known papers that he had written and delivered in S.R.I.A. colleges? What was its purpose?

I just wanted to share with future generations this completely refreshing description and unbiased history of the 'Illuminati Order.'

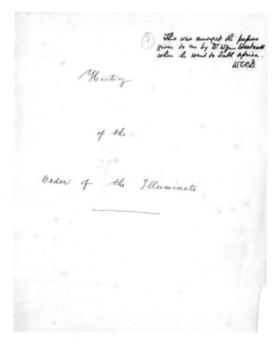

Figure 50 - Title page of History of the Illuminati

The Illuminati has so often been painted as an evil organisation and repeatedly accused of being the centre of so many conspiracy theories. I believe they were neither evil, nor a group planning to bring down religions, governments or countries. Their ideals and aspirations were lofty and all inclusive, so why were they ridiculed? Was it something to do with the times they lived in, or perhaps only the suspicious minds of those afraid of change? Hopefully, we all recognise that times have changed now and I hope that some people will change their minds about the Illuminati.

Only much later after it was written was the original source and the author revealed. I had no idea when the original text was supplied to Westcott in German, by Theodore Reuss, the original author of the documents. I would only find out exactly when they were sent to Westcott, by

referring to his own official diary or ACTA and seeing the original documents,[47] four years after I began work on the book. On further research, the *History of the Order of the Illuminati,* is in fact Westcott's English translation of Theodore Reuss' pamphlet written in German *Geschichte des Illuminaten Orden 1896,* which has also, as far as I know, never been published in English. This English transcription was made on my behalf by Mark Peters in 2011.

Finally, to make the plain text in the original manuscript more interesting, I have added section breaks and titles from the text to make it easier to refer to later. I have also added some images, which I hope, are relevant to each part of the first chapter of the history. They are included here only to help highlight certain parts of the text. The twelve numbered line drawings were taken from a book in the High Council Library called *Freymäurerische Versammlungsreden der Gold- und Rosenkreutzer des alten Systems* by Ecker von Eckhoffen H. 1779, and each numbered drawing illustrates text from the Bible, but which I think help highlights the text and are contemporary with the age of the manuscript. The original German document written by Theodor Reuss and the Westcott's translations, only contain text and have no images.

We know now that Reuss sent the original pamphlets to Westcott on Thursday 17 October 1901 from the signed dedication to Westcott, on the original pamphlets inside front cover, (see Fig 52). Westcott received the history from Reuss two days later, on Saturday the 19th October 1901, with three other documents one of which was the *Mysteries of the Illuminati.* I still have no idea who translated them for Westcott, or when they had been copied by Westcott from those translations.

ORIGINAL DOCUMENT

I only identified the original source material for the first chapter in Westcott's handwritten note book in 2015, having first established that the *Mysteries of the Illuminati* was from Reuss' pamphlet *Die Mysterien der Illuminaten* (1894).[48] There was no corresponding entry for the *History of the Illuminati* in the online archive search engine for the Library and Museum of Freemasonry. This is a good example of trusting and believing in yourself and not being afraid to ask for help. It transpires out that it been incorrectly listed sometime in the past as *Geschichte des Illuminaten-Ordens, (History of the Illuminati Order)* by Leopold Engel, who did write his own voluminous 500 page history of the Illuminati.

---

47 Library and Museum of Freemasonry.
48 *Geschichte des Illuminaten-Ordens*-UGLE Code: YG 699 (ILL) GES-Item ID No. L3306; 28 pages; 19.5 x 13.5 cm.

In a book with the same title as Reuss, but it was published in Berlin, by H. Bermühler Verlag in 1906. Reuss' 1894version was anonymous and only 28 pages long.

There is only one illuminati logo printed in the document, but two different Iluminati logos used on rubber stamps (see figs 51 and 52).

On the front cover is the blue stamp mark of the Prussian Illuminati Ludwig Lodge logo. With a sun superimposed on a triangle in a double circle, with a flaming heart inside several rows of petals and rune letters across the top, see the Prussian Illuminati Ludwig Lodge Logo, (see fig 8).

Printed as part of the pamphlet, on the cover page is the sun in splendour with a pentagram superimposed and with a bottony cross in the centre.

In the top right hand corner is the 'Quatuor Coronati Lodge' ownership stamp.

On the inside front cover is a dedication:

With compliments to Illustrious Frater Dr. Wm. Wynn Westcott S.M. IX° from Theodor Reuss 12/X.01.

Underneath that, a stamp mark of the Dresden Illuminati with the initial letters J.G. underneath a sun in splendour with a pentagram superimposed, with a bottony cross in the centre. The same image can be found in fig 7 on the *Dresden Ordinances* and on the Hamburg Regents Warrant (see fig 45).

Printed on the inside front page is the sun in splendour with a pentagram superimposed, with a bottony cross in the centre, that appears on the front cover. At the bottom of the page is the same blue stamp mark as on the front page of the 'Prussian Illuminati Ludwig Lodge logo (see fig 8).

Figure 51 - Front Geschichte des Illuminaten-Ordens

Figure 52 - Inside cover of History of the Illuminati

HISTORY OF THE ORDER OF THE ILLUMINATI

Translated and transcribed by William Wynn Westcott 1902.[49]

The following explanations are intending to make it clear that the origin of the Order of Illuminati, on account of the revival and re-organisation of the same by Weishaupt, is not to be regarded as a new creation of this man, but rather as an institution which we can trace back to the oldest time, so that, in this Order, as well as in the lap of all societies known to us, those teachings have been preserved to us which were understood by the mysteries of antiquity, and were lost to the generality.

First of all, we must cast a glance over the mysteries of antiquity; to be enrolled amongst their number (namely with the Greeks and Egyptians) was regarded by every educated person of that time, as quite as important as nowadays every thoughtful person considers it necessary to enter into the subject of the reason and object of creation. Truth and elucidation, contrary to the naive belief of the lowly superstitious people, could only be obtained by initiation, for only in this manner could the seeking and spiritually active person discover the way to the self-thinking and self-conclusion of the inner man, a purpose which is generally followed in theosophy, whilst every mystery can only enclose within itself one tested and practically proved way.

ANTIQUITY

The *Mysteries of the Illuminati*, which we do not intend to investigate here, encloses within itself firstly its course of instruction and then its ritual, both of which are derived from the traditions of antiquity, that period which is so often regarded as a time of dark heathendom, whereas in reality it was more Christianly inclined than the present time, which is only covered with the patched mantle which is hardly able to cover the sad nakedness of the miserable body. The wisdom of the old mysteries was based entirely on spiritual knowledge and therefore the initiation into the mysteries is as old as civilization.

Pausanias (110-180AD), who was himself initiated, declares that initiation lead men to greater piety. Aristotle's describes it is the most beautiful of all religious institutions.

Isocrates states that the initiated leave the world filled with the most beautiful hopes. Diodorus relates that Jason, Castor, Polluk, Hercules and Orpheus were all initiated into the mysteries of the Samothraki, and adds:

Ideoque vetusti heroes ac Semidei, qui praeclari fuerunt, initiari summopere cupieruat. [50]

Cicero laid down the moral of the initiation in his *Somnium Scipionis*[51] it is the respect and awe of the deity and the conviction of the immortality of the soul.

Figure 53 - Two Kings and Architect, looking at plans of Temple No. 1

The holy fathers, several of whom were also initiated, hold different views on the subject. However, as the adherents of the religion were persecuted, the true teachings of the initiation were in every respect kept a mystery, not only for the initiated but also from the initiators; with the exception of the teachings of virtue and piety in connection with it, the meaning of the same had been entirely forgotten and only the real form had been preserved, for which reason it was despised by some apostolic fathers. Later on these apostolic fathers grew to know less and less about the mysteries, and therefore regarded the old forms of initiation as godless and absurd.

---

49 Written Anonymously by Theodore Reuss, 1896, to which I have added headings and some illustrations, keeping his punctuation. A.M. Lees 2015.

50 Translation (and therefore with an ancient heroes and demi-gods, who are the famous, to be initiated into the greatest cupieruat).

51 *The dream of Scipio.* written by Cicero, is the sixth book of De re publica.

MOSES

The history of Moses as it is told in the book of Exodus seems to prove that the Jews had accepted the teachings of the Egyptians, as well as the initiation of the same. It is strange, that so many expounders of holy writ have taken no notice of this fact. In the eyes of the Egyptians all foreigners were unclean; before they could be received into the Order, and be initiated, they had to subject themselves to many tests which should place them on the same level as the citizens. But Joseph married Asenath, the daughter of Potiphar the priest of ON, and we believe that initiation alone helped him thereto. The sons he begat by this wife, Ephraim and Manassa, became the fathers of a race in Israel. Now if Asenath was one of the initiated, and priestess for the daughters of the high priest had to be so then it was natural that the children of Ephraim and Manassa should also be initiated into the mystic forms at Heliopolis; that is to say to the Solar service. A good part of the customary ceremonies were taken over by the Christians of the first century.

Figure 54 – 'Moses' by Loutherbourg

GREECE

According to Homer the initiation of Ulysses was a solar mystery. Ulysses dwells for a whole year in the Palace of Circe, who is a high priestess of the sun. Homer places exalted teachings on her lips that she communicates to Ulysses; she persuades him to become initiated and compels him to descend into the infernal regions to the abode of the

Figure 55 - Man praying, Jacobs ladder Delta, Sun, Moon & Star No. 2

dead for whom she professes the deepest reverence. Ulysses immediately sets sail with his companions. The old historians generally wrongly described the infernal regions as caves where the mystic rights were celebrated, and where the dead appeared. We would remark here, that the Hebrews, during their stay in Egypt anyhow accepted the use of these phantasmagoria otherwise how could Moses have made a law forbidding the questioning of the dead? See here Deuteronomy, Chapter 18, V. II. Ulysses prepared himself for the initiation.

The warrior becomes pious, he makes sacrifices, he turns his attention to relics, and praise before deaths heads (from this it will be seen, that the worshipping of human remains was known at least ten centuries earlier in Greece than with the Christians). Here he perceives shadows, which appear to emanate from the bowels of the earth; namely the shades of his friends and of his parents. Three times he tries to embrace his mother's soul, and three-times she slips from his arms like a shadow. But neither Circe, the Egyptian high priest, nor the priests of Eleusis may be regarded as conjurers and wizards.

As soon as one thinks, what the tests the nightly festivals of the mysteries must cause these results, and what they bring about, then every thought as regards a deception will vanish. The Hierophants made use of a comedy which was quite harmless in itself, in order to instil into the soul of the neophytes the belief of the immortality of the soul, of reward and punishment after death.

The originators of these mysteries were convinced, that the representation of a god who punished and rewarded, lay deep down in the soul of every person, and that by such spiritual illustrations it could be awakened. The person to be initiated, in their opinion, should see the punishment of Sisyphus and Tantalus, he must be a witness of the joy of the worthy and of the heroes, in order to be able to grasp the fact that he must live honestly in order at some future time to share their honour and happiness, who by practising honesty and reverence for the deity, had become saints.

Dupuis, Lenoir, Pigault-Lebrun, Voltaire[52] and others have found that great similarity occurs amongst the different religions on earth. And the explorer can easily convince himself how easily this declaration can be attributed to the mysteries of the old Greeks, the Roman Christians and the Illuminati. Refer to *Le Monde Ancien* by Grave, Volume III in the article "initiations aux mysteries". In the different religions in the world many

Abuses crept in. This made reforms necessary, and caused them to take place. Researches of every kind after truth and after means of improving mankind; these are the real purposes after which the Illuminati strive, and whoever followed these was a true member of the Illuminati or Theosophy.

INITIATION

We therefore consider that Theosophy could and should form a firm and single band which must embrace all men. Those who are to be initiated must be carefully prepared, and great attention must be paid to their position and character, and the questions which are to be put to them and the tests to which they are to be subjected should be based accordingly.

The Illuminati admitted people from every land and of every religious sect; for this reason the questions must be so put that they do not offend the various religions the examiner must go to work in such a manner as to compel those to be initiated to feel respect for the Illuminati. Only bodily tests have many inconveniences.

In the first place they retract from the seriousness of the rites, and secondly they do not lead to any real proof regarding the worthiness of the candidate. But on the other hand, moral tests were a necessity; these had reference to the:

1) Acknowledgement of God
2) Knowledge of himself
3) And of his behaviour towards his fellowmen.

It is left to the judgment of the examiner as to what methods he will adopt in order to discover the views of the candidate with regard to the deity, the spirit world, the creation etc. Only he must pay great attention to the differences in the various beliefs of different people, and he must not neglect to take into account the fact that civilization, climate and modes of government have their influence to a certain extent, and further to collect together and test the rights of man, as he is taught, as it is taught elsewhere and as it was taught formerly.

EGYPT

From the contents of the foregoing representations, we already begin to see that the system of the Illuminati was derived from the ancient Egyptians. The initiation rites are the same as those of the ancient Egyptians, whose only purpose was the remembrance and origin of the world, the theory of good and bad principles, the astronomical system and the old moral teachings. Our mysteries were handed down by the Egyptians to the Indians by these two to the Greeks, and by these again to the first Christians and finally to the Crusaders and Illuminati of the last century. Christ himself denotes the illuminated One, therefore Illuminatus.

Figure 56 - Ancient Pyramids and cave, by Kircher

---

52 Charles François Dupuis (1742-1809) developed the Christ myth theory that the cult of Christ is merely a cult of the Sun. Lenoir A. (1761-1839) – Book *La Franche-Maçonnerie rendue à sa véritable origine*, 1814. Curator of the Museum of French Monuments. Egypt, the first civilization, is constantly invoked by Lenoir to interpret the French monuments. Pigault-Lebrun, (1753 - 1835). His *Citateur* (2 vols. 1803), was a collection of quotations against Christianity, that was forbidden and yet several times reprinted. François-Marie Arouet (1694 – 1778) who known as Voltaire, with his attacks on the established Catholic Church, and his advocacy of freedom of religion, freedom of expression, and separation of church and state.

Figure 57 - Nature crowning man in Temple, working tools and cross No. 3

FEASTS

The Illuminati are therefore a very old religious association, who for their origin have to thank the Egyptian, the Greek and Christian mysteries. Their Emblems, their customs and the virtues which they practice, and which were those of the first Christian's faith, hope and love, would place this beyond a doubt, if the ceremonies did not do so. Neither should these be allowed to go by unnoticed, nor we will therefore say something about various feasts which are still celebrated in the society of the 'Freies illumines.' There are four of these, which have to be celebrated according to instructions, namely, the first on spring day and night equinox; the second at the period of Summer solstice; the third on autumn day and night equinox and the fourth at the period of Winter solstice.

1) The feast of the awakening of nature. This feast is celebrated on the first Sunday after spring day and night equinox.

2) The second is: The feast of the triumph of light. This is to be celebrated on the day on which the sun enters the sign of the crab, or upon the following Sunday. The ancients called this constellation the crab because the sun when it reaches its highest northern point makes a backward movement towards the equator, that is to say, it goes like a crab. Therefore at about this time the sun is at its meridian, and is the brightest. The sages of olden times who practised the culture of nature always designated this by festivities, and the attention to these proceedings of nature raises the spirit to its originator. The allegory of this feast is a pyramid over which the sun shines.

3) The third is: "The feast of nature". This feast is celebrated on the autumn day and night equinox, or that Sunday directly following it. The chief purpose of this feast is to thank the everlasting one for the benefits bestowed during the finer Seasons. And finally the fourth is "The feast of the re-birth of life."

4) This feast, which is generally, celebrated on the day of St John the Evangelist, takes place some days after the sun enters the sign of the Ram. This is to remind one of the new strength of the sun and the hopes are raised for a new and happy year. The ceremony starts with the search for light. As soon as the new sun is discovered breaking through, the party of illuminated rise to give up a prayer of Thanksgiving.

NOT THE ONLY KNOWLEDGE

The Illuminati in no way assert that they are the only people who have any knowledge, and who had secured this knowledge for themselves, but on the other hand they are always willing to admit that outside of their order wise people are found, whether they belong to similar societies or not.

ROSICRUCIANS

Amongst these closely related societies we may mention the Rosicrucians, who stood and still stand in most intimate relationship with the Illuminati.

Various writings exist about these, which are very likely not unknown to our Illuminati members.

Figure 58 - Three kneeling & praying No. 4

Several writings of this kind were brought to light, which deal with the teaching and partly with the leading of these secret societies, which were formerly much thought of, and which refer to the discovery of the secrets of nature and the studies of a more sensible theology than that of the Romans. These societies of the German Rosicrucians are to be found bearing various appellations, borrowed from the sciences which they preferably practice. The most important amongst them are:

THEOSOPHISTS

The Mystics or Theosophists, who rose up in arms against the intolerable dogmas of Roman spiritualism. They created their teachings from the "Fama Fraternitatis". This system existed in Germany already a long time ago, and it was believed that it was founded by Christian Rosenkreuz himself, whose birth is supposed to have taken place in the year 1389, and who journeyed to the Holy Land with a view of studying Christianity in its cradle.

ROSENKREUZ

Many people going by the name of Rosenkreuz (Rosicrucian) believed that he was an allegorical being who had never existed.

It is quite certain that in olden times the Rose was regarded as a symbol of secrecy; Mythus says,

Figure 59 - Rosicrucian silence

Figure 60 - St. Jerome – by Q. Matsys

Amor[53] presented a rose to Harpocrates in order to persuade him to keep silent respecting certain secrets.

There are also traces that with some mysteries the initiated were presented with a rose to remind them of the duty of silence they had taken upon themselves. According to this we can explain the origin of the expression: "to tell anything to someone "sub Rosa".

Without pausing here to give an opinion regarding this matter, we will simply relate his legend. Rosenkreuz lived for a long time in Damascus[54] where he held conferences with Chaldean sages.

From these he is said to have learned secret sciences, magic and cabala, in which mystic arts he afterwards perfected himself in Egypt and later on in Lydia, where he furthermore, by means of the most learned researches, was instructed regarding the true life of Christ.

Upon his return to Germany, after he had thought out a double reform, that of science as well as of religion, he founded a secret society in order to gain these ends, in which the members were admitted after the same fashion as were the ancient Christian initiated members. It was also his wish to hand down his science and theosophy to posterity.

The first Society of these Rosicrucians, from whom later on all the other brunches descended, had the greatest number of members. The studies of Rosicrucians comprised alchemy, chemistry, magic and phantasmagoria.

---

53 'Amor' should read 'Eros.'
54 Also in 'Damcar' which can be found in old maps of Yemen, N.W. of Aden [A.M. Lees 2015].

Figure 61 - Rebus – Materia Prima

His decoration was a wide white band round the neck; on the other hand his emblems were the sun, the moon and the double triangle, (see below) in the middle was a point of the Hebrew letter Yod which, as we have seen above, designated the name of God written with one letter, and which is the root of the other two names for God, Jao and Jehovah.

We would remark that these earliest Rosicrucians, and those of whom we shall speak later on, had not more than three degrees, in which they explained their scientific symbols, although as time went on these became increased, without materially altering the teachings which rested on two bases, one of which was the study of nature and its hidden powers, the other, researches in supernatural matters.

A portion of these studies had the effect that these Rosicrucians often fell into grave errors, for they asserted, like the cabala, that the knowledge of the holy name of God placed people in a position to work wonders, and that the science of the cabala was drawn from this reverend name and from the name of the angels, as well as the elements of the seven planets, the explanation and use of which was found in the Bible.

The mysteries themselves and their reception had a great resemblance to the purifying and the tests which took place in the Eleusinian mysteries. As regards the symbols, it was these which are nowadays in use with the Rosicrucians; nearly all of them agnostic.

They served, and still serve to explain the General harmony in which man is united with mankind and man with the entire world and the whole world with the great master builder of the world. On account of this teaching and science

these German Rosicrucians were often called the Brahmins of the north.

BRAHMINS

They have always asserted themselves to be the depositors and guarders of the Masonic dogmas. The medical philosophers (les philosophes medicines) were Rosicrucians whose systems were drawn from the agnostics and from the cabala. With them the teachings of Jesus and of mankind went hand in hand.

They believed, amongst other things, that the creation of the world was caused by powers of attraction. They only recognized matter and motion, and tried to found their ideas from the Bible. They did not translate the beginning where it tells the story of the creation: "God created heaven and earth out of nothing" but "in the beginning God arranged heaven and earth". They try to give weight to this meaning by adding the corresponding Hebrew word in Latin *formavit* according to the meaning which the ancient Rosicrucian attributed to this passage, they must have accepted the eternity of matter, a meaning which amongst the scientists of Europe, Asia and America seems likely to predominate. With regard to the science of medicine, these Rosicrucians believe in Paracelsus.

We have found these doctrines also in England, where they were spread by Robert Fludd. Amongst the Germans there were many who believe that this system came to them from England. They placed its origin about the time of King Arthur. This meaning is, like the origin of many masonic systems, thickly shrouded in darkness, although the grandmaster of these rights was always called Johann I, Johann II and Johann III.

The Theosophical alchemists, like Nicolai, believe that they existed already before 1616. This

Figure 62 - Book of Law, world and learning No. 5

Figure 63 - Man being led by nature to the Temple No. 6

system was, so it is said, at this time fairly widespread under the name of Rosicrucians of the Orient. Their decorations amongst others, was a ring bearing the letters I.A.A.T., which might refer to the four elements: Ignis, Aqua, Aer, Terra, and which are connected to the teachings of the Egyptians.

ROSICRUCIAN DEGREES

These Rosicrucians had the following degrees:

1. Adeptus
2. Adeptus Junior
3. Adeptus Practicus
4. Adeptus Theocritus
5. Adeptus Minor
6. Adeptus Major
7. Adeptus Exemptus
8. Magister Templi
9. Magus

WEISHAUPT

We have made nearer reference to these matters, because only with such knowledge can a clear representation of the history of the Illuminati be obtained, and thus we see that Weishaupt is by no means regarded as the founder of our Order, but only as the reorganiser of the same. He himself only regarded himself as such, and therefore in his first instructions he recommends the study of the old Egyptian mysteries as a necessity to the knowledge of the secrets of the Illuminati. It is a historical fact that no founder of an Order ever set to work in such an open manner as Weishaupt.

It must therefore seem strange that even nowadays so much that is false is said about the Illuminati is believed, and is spread further. We will now give a brief description of the fate and solution at that time of the Order under Weishaupt.

Adam Weishaupt was born in Ingolstadt in the year 1748, studied law there, became Doctor in 1768, soon after repeater of legal faculty, in 1772 extraordinary and in 1775 ordinary professor; not only of canonical law but of the law of nature. He also obtained the attribute of the Bavarian counsellor of the court. But it was just this position which drew upon him enmity and persecution.

Because, as the position of teacher of Canonical rights at this university had always been filled by a man of the spiritual order, it was natural, that these same, who considered themselves ousted by him, should try to harm him in every way; although he, a protégé of the Jesuits, after their order had been raised, had become their bitterest enemy. As he had a clean head, he did not fail to become acquainted with other enlightened people, whom he strove to win over and succeeded in winning over to his cosmopolitan system. But he went to work in such an open way, as stated above, that his enemies had no hold over him. They therefore tried in secret to make suspicion fall upon him, the clergy in especial strove to overthrow him.

But with the students he was very highly considered who always congregated in large numbers in his lecture room and it was not difficult to win them over to the cosmopolitanism of their teacher. This encouraged the members to extend their Illuminati order wider afield, and its only object was to teach the art of governing in which the welfare of the whole should be no longer doubtful. He added on the teachings of Pythagoras. The renown of Weishaupt only stirred up the enmity of the clergy against him still more, and so it came to pass that chiefly on account of their testimony he was deposed from his position, and in 1786 sentence of death was passed upon him. But he escaped, before the sentence could be carried out, where he fled to Nuremberg, then to Gotha, where he lived as a Private teacher.

Figure 64 - Jesuit I.H.S.

Figure 65 - King Altar & Fire, Emblazoned Delta No. 7

With the title of a ducal councillor of legation of Saxe-Gotha, he received a small pension from the Duke, and increased his fame by publishing various writings. Amongst these latter was:

> *Pythagoras or views on the secret art of governing,* Frankfort and Leipzig 1790.

Is without a doubt that, which represents the most clearly, the spirit of Illumination. Goethe & Duke Karl Augustus became here members of the order, which in spite of the persecution of the State of Bavaria and Thuringia, continued to exist.

ALOMBRADOS

But when there is a question about the Illuminati, it must not be forgotten that the Alombrados in Spain towards the end of the XVI Century; the Guérinets in the middle of the XVII Century, who were a Society of mystics in Belgium in the latter half of the XVIII century, were also of the Illuminati out of whose writings and teachings Weishaupt borrowed his material.

Weishaupt, inspired with the desire to benefit mankind, had nothing to help him but the moral perfection of his contemporaries, which he hoped to arrive at by working in unison with all stations of life.

SECRET SOCIETY

For this purpose he created a secret society which he, a pupil of the Jesuits, founded according to Jesuitical laws and customs, because these appeared to him feasible as a method of becoming intimately acquainted with the members. In the year 1776 he was made a Freemason in Munich in the Strict Observance Lodge called *Theodor zum guten Rath* (Theodore for good Advice) but at the very beginning several mistakes were made in his plan, which were harmful to the whole idea; for not only did the speedy increase in the number of members cause great inconveniences, but to a much greater extent was harm done by the impatient eagerness with which some of the members tried to obtain influence on public business and thus gave themselves into the hands of their enemies. Weishaupt relates that already in years 1765 and 1766 he had made out written plans for a secret society,

> *In which the society is strengthened by mankind and their scattered energies collecting together.*

As in the year 1773, immediately after the Order of Jesuits had been abolished, he had obtained the teacher's chair for spiritual law in Ingolstadt which for the past 90 years had been filled uninterruptedly by Jesuits, these Jesuits the following year made a most shameful plot with a view to ousting him again, and as they were not successful in doing this, they tried to slander him in every way, and to persecute him. He on his past hoped to obtain the support of a band of free thinking and enlightened men, and this thought awakened in him the desire to found a new society. Another cause was, that at about this time there fell into his hands the writings of the famous abbot *Vom Verdienst*. He himself admits that this book exercised a great influence on his will and on his character, and states that the following passage contained the whole spirit of the Illuminati system the Abbott said:

> *Many people who desired present and eternal good fortune or well-being, so arranged their life and doings that they became ever happier and more perfect; the preparation "causes that similar rules were just as easy to them as they were appreciated; to contrive such position; therein they must lead all that is stubborn to a common good; therefore all complicated matters, and most cases must be thought over; they must set to work even before anyone else*

Figure 66 - Hermits/Adepts following Sophia No.8

Figure 67 - Man summoning Hermes and Nature No. 9

can see the possibility; they must work for years, sometimes without reaping the fruit; they must comfort, support and even spur themselves on; they must disregards all obstacles and every danger; they must not submit to indifference and luke warmness, and all this simply because it is necessary for the good and peace of the dearly loved fellowmen, that is to say, all those who are created after the same image as ourselves. Oh, where are we to find the man who will do this? If he no longer exists, where is his statue? Where is his marble bust? Tell me, so that I may go and clasp the cold stone in my arms, and wet the image with the scalding tears of thankfulness.

This passage contained exactly the idea which Weishaupt himself had striven to realize, by all the degrees and arrangements with regard to the order of Illuminati, as well as by his letters. Immediately after reading the same, he set to work and composed the statutes. On 1 May 1776, the foundation was started.

Regarding the purpose of the order he expresses himself as follows:

Self-thinking people from every part of the world and of every denomination, and free to think whatever they like, in spite of all the different ideas and feelings were to be bound together in one band by their higher interests; to make them impassioned and sensitive to such a degree, that at the greatest distance they are present an equal, that many should work as one man and have one desire, and do by their own energy and from their own conviction, what could never be done by force ever since the world began. The society which can do this, and quite alone, is the masterpiece of human sense: in it and through it the art of governing has attained its highest state of perfection.

KNIGGE

In the year 1780, Weishaupt explained his views to the Adolph Franz Friedrich Ludwig Knigge (1752-1796). It was to be a society which attained its ends by the finest and safest means, which were to create virtue and wisdom in the world instead of wickedness and stupidity, to make the most important discoveries in all branches of science, and to make its members great and noble men, and then to assure to them the reward of their virtue already in this world, to protect them against persecution and oppression, and in every way to bind the hands of despotism.

To all of this Knigge gave his full approval, showed great energy for the society, and took up a great number of educated, learned and good men. But these were not in a position to make good again the harm which had been done to the society by the earlier admission of so many young and in many cases incompetent and uneducated, and in some cases unworthy men.

As Weishaupt wished to educate young people to the spirit of the society, a hurried increase of members was almost impossible. But these young men, when they had attained to one or other of the higher degrees, saw themselves ousted by those who came in after them, became annoyed, and this quarrelling amongst the members, of course lead to no good or else they tried to arrive at their ends by their own means, and tried to influence business for their own good and thus were to a great extent the cause of the state officials finding them out. Weishaupt himself complained about those who hindered the few worthiest members in their work, and brought shame upon the Society. Whilst these highly suspicious circumstances continued, and

Figure 68 - Baron von Knigge

Figure 69 - Ark, mountain, King, cow, Pillar, Trismegistus, the Tribes and a Pyramid No. 10

grew worse Von Knigge separated himself from Weishaupt and continued Illuminatism in eclecticism by himself. At this critical state of the affairs of the society, suddenly open complaints were raised against the same. The book dealer Strobel, the Canon Danzer and the Professor Westenrieder were his accusers.

But at the same time they raised objections to the Freemasons, and so it came to pass that by order of the Kurfürst (Elector of Bavaria) on 22nd of January 1784, all secret brotherhoods were forbidden. Illuminati and Freemasons suspended their gatherings. But in spite of this, warnings appeared in print, in which both these societies were subjected to suspicion and contumely. Those who were seized asked for a legal examination and offered to lay bare all their papers.

But in vain, the Fratres Franck and Krettmayr issued on the 2 March 1785 a second order in the name of the master of the land, forbidding all secret gatherings, and in spite of the fact that the Illuminati could not be convinced that they had disobey these state orders, and it was just the best men who were persecuted and punished, and Weishaupt himself was banished. Now three former members of the society Utzschneider Cosandey and Grünberger, formerly secret informers of the society, were had up before a commission.

They were to write down and swear to everything that they knew regarding the society. From this time forth the persecution became general. Zwack fled, after his papers had been taken away from him, which papers later on appeared in print. People of standing and influential men were considered in every way in this process. That Weishaupt himself had the very best intentions when founding this society is very clearly proved by his writings. But blame must be given, that by no means were suitable methods employed to disband the society in Bavaria.

In States outside of Bavaria, such as the states of Thüringen and Saxony in Germany, in France where it was started by Mirabeau, and in America, it continued to flourish.

TEACHINGS

The teaching of Weishaupt is founded on the fact that it is only our passions and emotions which make government necessary; if everyone knew and fulfilled his duty then no power on earth could have the right to force him.

This teaching finally stated that all people, simply by examining their duty, would be very sensitive of perfection. It is impossible to decide from this teaching that the Illuminati hated princes: nobles and priests; because as there were a great number of these in the society, the result would have been that they hated themselves: it should be stated that the members of the first class of this society, consisted to a great extent of people in exalted positions, and of government officials from the different states, and even of imperial ministers.

It is quite true that Weishaupt desired to attain in his society the equality of mankind but this had to be, in order to be able to teach the purist morals, and in order to overthrow the vices, and the fulfilment of such a scheme could scarcely be hoped for centuries to come: that which can be said about this society is this, that it strove to bring to light the faults of the different methods of government, without making the slightest attempt to overthrow the same. As regards the doctrines which obtained in the Weishaupt order of Illuminati, these had long been familiar to him, as he has himself stated, and these were near akin to the ancient mysteries.

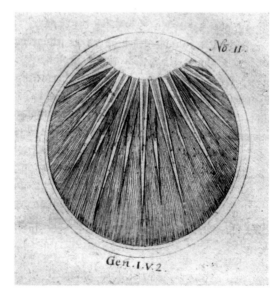

Figure 70 - Let there be light and there was light No. 11

After the denunciations Illuminatism was dissolved, not only because of the disclosure of the doctrines but also on account of the government commands.

The Roman priests, who regarded the society as being highly dangerous to their power, went to any amount of trouble to prevent its recreation, in which, however, they were not successful. Mirabeau, who in his writing always expressed himself against every kind of secret order, and freemasons of every kind, describes the Illuminati in his *De la Monarchie Prussienne* (Mirabeau, 1788, p. 96) as enlightened people and as virtuous philosophers who were eagerly striving to keep mankind, and who were being wrongly persecuted.

The writings of the society, not all of which had come before the public, did not have any effect and for the most part were published by innovators in connection. After what has been said above, it is easy to believe that the writers, who wrote against the Illuminati, hardly had a full knowledge of the institutions of that society. Of course it is quite impossible that in a small work, like this, which is given over to the profane printer, newer details regarding the organisation and spread of the order of Illuminati should be disclosed.

But the following can always be mentioned. In Thuringia Lodges are still to be found. In the same way the burgomaster Fischer, banished from Ingolstadt, founded amongst the circle of his nearest friends and relatives a band of Illuminati. This burgomaster Fischer was one of Weishaupt's most devoted followers, and after his banishment fled to a Swabian town, where his descendants flourish to this day. A genuine member of the Illuminati was the Royal Bavarian staff-Captain Anton von Fager in Regensburg, who, on 6 August 1870, fell in the battle at Wörth. Furthermore in the Swabia-Bavarian Lichrain the mysteries of the Illuminati were faithfully observed in the family of the merchant Caspar Reuss from Friedberg and his

Figure 71 - The Trinity, Universe, Spirit of Man, and flaming Earth No. 12

Figure 72 - Benjamin Franklin Paris 1778

offspring. Goethe worked to the end of his life in the interest of the order of Illuminati. In Nurnberg, whence Weishaupt first fled after his banishment a society of Illuminati still existed in the year 1860, that of the engineer Richter since dead.

In Zurich, in London, in Paris, in Egypt and South America societies of Illuminati still exist. In the year 1880 various Illuminati met together in Munich, revived the old statues and altered them to suit the new period. A few new members were also admitted. A commemoration article was also worked up three of the most important men of the order, which was handed to H.M. King Ludwig II of Bavaria in Castleberg, in August 1880.

AMERICA

King Ludwig had his approval of the efforts made by the society expressed by a cabinet writing. Also in places outside of Europe the order flourished, for in May 1776 the Order of Illuminati was planted in America. Burke initiated Thomas Jefferson,[55] and the later started a society of Illuminati or Lodge at the William and Mary University in Virginia. When in the great revolutionary war this university went down, the students and professors who constituted the major portion of the members of the Society of Illuminati continued it at the Yale University.

55 NOTE - I do not believe that Thomas Jefferson was a Freemason. However Benjamin Franklin was dispatched to France as commissioner for the United States 1776-1785. During his stay in France, Benjamin Franklin was active as a freemason, serving as Grand Master of the Lodge 'Les Neuf Sœurs No. 24' from 1779 until 1781. He was a Past Grand Master of Pennsylvania. On 2 April 1756 William & Mary College, Virginia. The first honorary degree from the College, a Master of Arts, was conferred upon Benjamin Franklin [A.M. Lees 2015].

Edmund Burke, 1765-1795 born Dublin Ireland. Entered the House of Commons in 1765. As a Member of Parliament he became known as a Political thinker and important in the history of political theory and he was a confirmed Mason [A.M. Lees 2015].

Chapter II – History of the Illuminati

The Lodge at the Yale University made an alteration in the name of the order, in as much as they gave it to the name of the Phi – Beta – Kappa Society. This designation came from the Greek initial letters of the leading foundations of the Illuminati that is to say:

May Philosophy guide your life?

Phi = Φ, Beta = B and K = Kappa

The "Phibetians" as they called themselves for short, however, are in no way connected with the Order of Illuminati of today.

On account of circumstances, the Order in the last years has again been brought to light by various members. It is his endeavour, in this dreadful time of war of all against all to throw the spiritual hand of love round all who are still not quite strangers to the love of their fellowmen.

END

Here ends the History of the Illuminati Order from Westcott's transcription. The original was written anonymously and on investigation proved to be written by Theodor Reuss in 1896. It was translated and transcribed by W.W. Westcott sometime in 1902. Interestingly this was twelve years before the First World War actually started [A.M. Lees 2015].

Figure 73 - The World by Kircher

Chapter III

Mysteries of the Order of the Illuminati

MYSTERIES OF THE ILLUMINATI
Westcott's handwritten copy 1902

INTRODUCTION TO THE 'MYSTERIES'

The *Mysteries of the Illuminati* forms the second section in Westcott's handwritten notebook and it has its own front page, (see fig 74). It was copied by him from an unknown translator of the original document, which means this was not researched or written by Westcott. During the process of associating the English transcription with the German text of the original German pamphlet for this chapter, it is quite clear to me that there could be a completely different interpretation of this translation, because when you reverse translate from English to German there are many different words used. This is, however, a reproduction of Westcott's 1901 transcription that was found amongst his possessions in the S.R.I.A. archives in 2010, side by side with the original source material from the Library and Museum of Freemasonry.

It was transcribed for me, with grateful thanks to Mark Peters, in 2011. It continues the explanation of the Illuminati and their Mysteries. In Westcott's notebook it is just hand-written line upon line and has no illustrations or pictures.

ORIGINAL DOCUMENT

I only identified the original source material for this second chapter in Westcott's handwritten note book in 2015, when I purchased a copy of Ellic Howe's book called *Merlin Peregrinus* about the life of Reuss. My only problem with this wonderful source book is that it is written in the German language. On the back page of Reuss' paperback book I was later to discover, was the image of the front cover *of Die Mysterien der Illuminaten,* the answer had been staring me in the face all the time, (see fig 75).

Could this, therefore, be the first English translation of the first pamphlet that Theodore Reuss wrote on the Illuminati? It was published in Berlin 1894, two years before he published the *History of the Order of Illuminati* in 1896.

On closer inspection you can see on the title page (see fig 74), that the pseudonym for the author of the second part *Mysteries of the Illuminati* was translated as 'Garatheodoro.' The name made no sense as I could not find such an author. However, I found the correct spelling of the author four years later and it would seem that the translator mistook the Gothic type 'ℭ' for 'ℭ' an easy mistake to

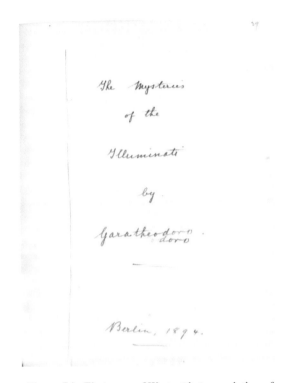

Figure 74 - First page of Westcott's transcription of 'The Mysteries of the Illuminati'

make. So the name was 'Caratheodoro,' one of many pseudonyms of Theodore Reuss.[56]

Armed with this new information I was able to go online and find that the Library and Museum of Freemasonry had a copy of the original pamphlet of sixteen pages, which was called, in German, *Die Mysterien der Illuminaten* (1894) printed in Berlin, Germany.[57] Published by Druck von Trowitsch & Sohn, it is reasonable to assume that it must have been in the possession of the S.R.I.A. at some time, as it has written inside on the first page:

With compliments to Frater Dr. Westcott (Wynn) Supreme Magus IX° Berlin 17/X/01 (17th October 1901) Reuss, Theodor, 1855-1923.

This helps with dating of the undated Westcott manuscript, as the translation and transcription by Westcott could not have been started before October.

In fact, it turns out that Reuss posted five documents to Westcott on that date. When I looked at the entries in his official diary, Westcott received

---

56 Other pseudonyms-Caratheodoro, Merlin Peregrinus, Charles Theodore, Hans Merlin, Theodor Regens.
57 Its U.G.L.E. reference number is YG 699 (ILL) MYS.

all five on 19 October 1901, two days later which fits in with all the other activity that month and the dedication dates. The *History* and the *Mysteries* and two other documents can now be identified as part of that delivery of five documents.

When I took the time to look at the copy to be found in the Library and Museum of Freemasonry, I saw that Westcott had written between the German printed text the following in English on the front cover:

The Constitutions and Regulations

BESTIMMUNGEN FUR

of the

DIE MINERVAL-LOGEN

Minerva Lodges

DES

of the

ORDENS DER ILLUMINATEN

Order of Illuminati, Great Britain.
Wm. Wynn Westcott, Regent of Britain, for the
Order of Illuminati of Dresden, Germany.

The German translation Westcott used of *BESTIMMUNGEN FUR* is not exact, the document should be called *Provisions for the Minerval Lodges,* but I have used Westcott's description for the purposes of this book as *The Constitutions and Regulations.*

The online catalogue entry of the Library and Museum of Freemasonry simply states:

Die Mysterien der Illuminaten / von Caratheodoro. Published: Berlin, Germany: Druck von Trowitsch & Sohn, 1894.

The Mysteries of the Illuminati by Caratheodoro, which translates as 'Dear Theodor.' This was one of several pseudonyms of Theodor Reuss. It was published in Berlin, Germany: by Druck von Trowitsch & Sohn, 1894, (see fig 76).

The inside front page (see fig 77), features the rubber stamp mark of a five pointed star with a bottony cross and sun inside with the sun's rays and underneath the letter J. G. on this title page:

With compliments to Frater Dr. Westcott (Wynn) S.M. IX° Berlin 17/ X 01

The date of the inscription is not such a mystery as it seems, it is 17 October 1901.

Figure 75 - Found on the back page of Ellic Howe's book

Figure 76 - 'Die Mysterien der Illuminaten,' front cover

Having found the authorship of the *Mysteries,* it then took a little longer to find out and prove that Reuss also wrote the anonymous pamphlet on the *History.*

What was the purpose of producing these two pamphlets? First in German by Reuss and then later translated into English by Westcott?

They were posted to Westcott at the same time as the constitutions of the Illuminati, meaning that they were official documents. I believe that the *History* would be given to Minervals as part of the resurrected Illuminati first ritual and admission into the Illuminati Order.

While I started to believe that the *Mysteries* would have been issued much later to those, that passed into one of the higher degrees of the resurrected Illuminati as printed text books.

It would seem reasonable to assume that Westcott translated them both to use as part of the support material for the English Illuminati aspirants.

The Library and Museum of Freemasonry copy of the original document is titled:

Die

Mysterien

der

Illuminaten

von

Caratheodoro.

Berlin, 1894

I now present a transcription of *The Mysteries of the Illuminati* which was made by Mark Peters and the scans by permission of Library and Museum of Freemasonry.

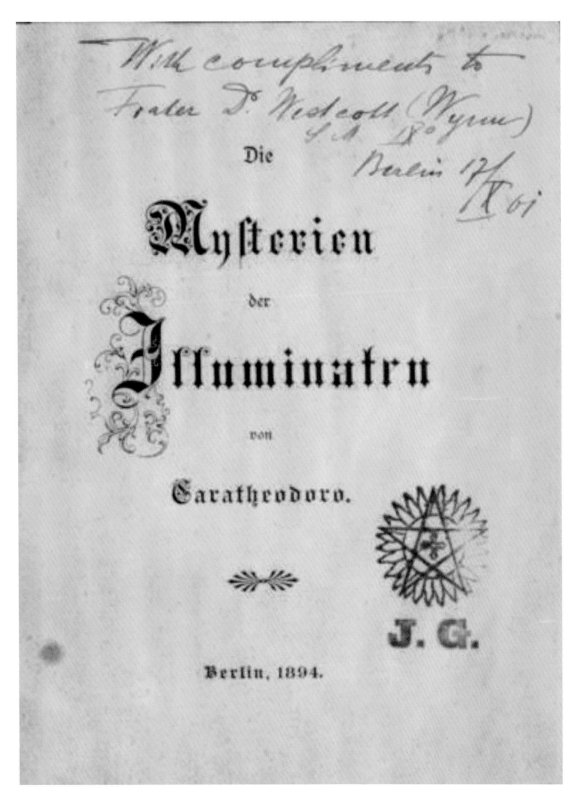

Figure 77 - 'Die Mysterien der Illuminaten,' inside cover

The

Mysteries of the Illuminati

♋ ♐ ♉

There are truths, certain holy truths, which give to mankind some explanation regarding their former, present and future existence.

Such truths certainly exist; call them revelations or what you will. Anyhow they are the results of detailed and deep researches, or even the disclosures of highly nervous, aesthetic people!

Every comparatively thoughtful and clever person must feel that he needs certain explanations, because he is in doubt regarding such numerous things in nature.

[4]

Can he see these doubts removed, or can he not do so?

Are the explanations which have been preserved by different people by priests, philosophers or explorers, true, or are they not so?

To do this, it is more than just a matter of common sense.

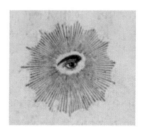

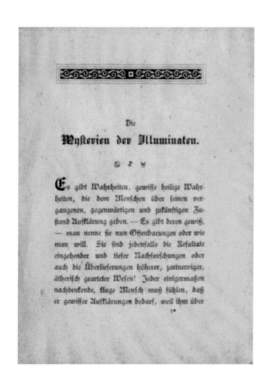

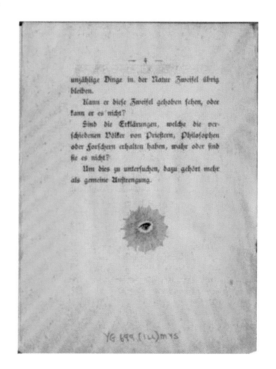

City business, business relations, official positions, human passions of every kind, and a great many other hindrances, make it difficult for the majority of people to devote themselves to the study of these questions and knowledge of these things.

In former times this was not so much the case, at that time our wants were not so numerous and varied, our connections and pursuits not so interwoven, our passions not so intense and exaggerated. When mankind did not regard their business and business relations as the chief point of their existence, then the first object of man was the fulfilment of his decisions.

First he saw himself as a member of the chain of creatures and further as a citizen of the earth.

But later on true wisdom, real insight behind the veil of the hidden picture of Sais became more and more rare ever more and more interwoven and falsified with human statutes, in the direction of the age, and finally only the monopoly of a small number of people who, far removed from disturbing elements, continued to plant the seeds of truth and to hand them down to their descendants.

But as these people never forgot that they were at the same time citizens of the earth, so that they always kept before their eyes, the great pile, which was torn away by the stream of culture, and to give it such a direction, that the same, as far as circumstances permitted, did not make too deep inroads into the shore.

With this object of view they clothed their teachings; the genuine, only true basis of truth, in every century, in such a covering as would suit the age.

They never forgot that they were not only in the world to philosophise, and perhaps to be in them peaceful and happy; but that it was their duty to give help and comfort to their fellowmen.

Amongst these various wisdom schools, which teach such holy matters, and which work for the good of all men, the most important is the Order of the Illuminati.

Now is the time when such a school of wisdom is the most necessary. The world has attained such a false spiritual direction, that one must really start again from the beginning, before one can instruct mankind in the higher wisdom. They must be made sensitive for the wisdom again.

The members of the Order of Illuminati are in a position to do this. But they do not desire that their word should be taken for this, but only that they should be judged according to their works.

They have secrets, but they use them only for the good of mankind.

The <u>Illuminati Order possesses a threefold secret</u>:

Which it must preserve; an outer one the purpose, operations and personalities of which are to be kept secret from the profane; an inner one in which just so much of the arrangements of the Order are to be disclosed to the members, as may be justified by the reliability, the extent of his circle of work, and his faith and zeal; and finally <u>a sensual one</u>, which <u>warrants to every initiated person the understanding of the end of all things, the highest personal happiness, for all eternity</u>!

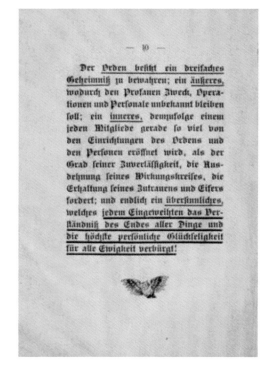

11

The Order teaches:

God can only be worshipped in spirit, in quiet, without words and outward signs. To grow like him is the greatest service you can render him. A silent, earnest prayer is the kind of worship most agreeable to him.

God appears to and discloses himself also to chosen people.

The Order teaches:

> The secret power of Theurgy, which makes those who have knowledge of it the masters of nature.

> Theurgy is a real science, which connects the earthly with the supernatural.

> All creatures attract or repel one another.

12

Whoever knows these laws, can prophecy and is the master of the past and of the future.

The Attracting and repelling powers are to be found in animals, stones, herbs, in various signs, words and formulae.

The Order teaches:

> How to heal sickness naturally.

> How to prolong life.

> How to conquer finiteness.

The Order embraces horticultural schools, schools for wisdom, and the esoteric circle of chosen enlightened ones.

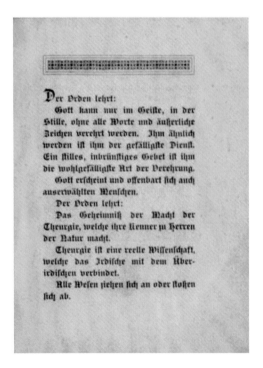

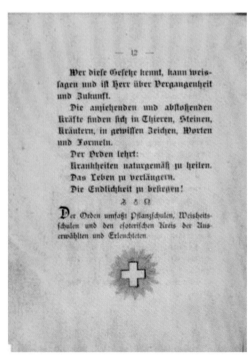

[13]

♃ ♂ ♎

The Initiated do not partake of any meat food, no beer, no spirits, only fruit, bread and wine, which, however, must be mixed with water. (Exceptions are only made in special cases).

They adhere to strict moderation and seemliness. Each member is shown a point of view according to which he must act. He must be prepared to work there, where the fruits will only be reaped by his descendants. His private affairs must only be of use to him in as much as they are of benefit to all men.

Such a man or such a woman would be welcomed by the Order. The same does not labour to benefit himself, for the members themselves decide their contribution. Entry into the Order must be sought with longing and with unbounded faith.

[14]

Truth

Love, Light, Life.

(Liebe, Licht, Leben)

Patience - Fervour

Discretion.

(Secrecy)

FINIS

"Every Sin reaps its own reward."

☿ ♐ ☉

Seekers bask in contact with the editors of the Sphinx

Figure 78 – Die Mysterien der Illuminaten last page

Chapter IV

Revived Illuminati Regulations and Rituals

REVIVED ILLUMINATI REGULATIONS AND RITUALS

INTRODUCTION

My hope is that these new English Illuminati Rituals and Constitutions will add to the growing store of Illuminati material that is now becoming available.

What I believe is extraordinary about the four 'Revived English Illuminati Order' rituals is that they were similar but not the same as those rituals of Adam Weishaupt 1778, that appear in the books by Robison, 1789, Barruel, 1799, Heckethorn, 1875 and the modern day book *Secret School of Wisdom*[58] They seem to be much newer Illuminati rituals, but how could that be?

In fact, what strangely seems to corroborate the newness of these rituals is that the 'English Illuminati Rose-Croix ritual' is exclusive to this set of Illuminati rituals. It has never before been published but does, historically, have a link to both the Illuminati Order and Weishaupt. It would also seem to be a very early version of the 'Rite of Perfection' or 'Scottish Rite' and also the more modern '18° Prince Rose-Croix' of the 'Ancient & Accepted Rite of Scottish Rite Freemasons.'

The ritual with the biggest difference is the one that would have been used the most and that is the 'Minerval Ritual.' In the 'Revived English Illuminati' series, it has both an 'opening' and 'closing' that are not found in Weishaupt's rituals and a bit more of a ceremony for the admission of candidates. It is more of a masonic type ritual that could be used in a Lodge of Freemasons. Not just a series of talks and lectures and an oath taking, that you might expect from the pen of the University professor Adam Weishaupt. In fact, the lengthy lectures are completely missing from this 'Revived English Illuminati Minerval Ritual,' making it much easier to use in practise.

At first I was disappointed that the final degree in the 'English Illuminati' series, the Priest or Epopt or Synod grade consisted only of an 'opening' and a 'closing.' However, I cannot find an 'opening' and 'closing' in any of the previous books on the Illuminati rituals and these two short parts seem to fit exactly around the lectures that can be found in the Weishaupt ceremonies, which involve the reading of long passages, some in Latin.[59]

As has been mentioned, what is very noticeable by their absence in all four English Illuminati rituals and their translations are the very lengthy lectures written by Adam Weishaupt for the 'Bavarian Illuminati' 1778.

Is this because Reuss had not supplied them to Westcott at this early stage of introducing the Order into England? Was he going to supply them later? Or, had the members of the 'Revived Illuminati' realised that this lecture material proved to be too long and that what we find is that they had adapted the rituals to make them shorter and more appealing for Freemasons to use?

All the rituals are very basic in the sense that they only contain the barest minimum of instructions or rubric on regalia, furniture and movement. This is to be expected in older degrees or systems, in my experience, as you were expected to know the important words and the movement around the Lodge room, having attended meetings before. Today, the rubric is printed in the rituals and I believe is a modern innovation.

WHY ARE THE RITUALS SO DIFFERENT?

It would seem that the 'Bavarian Illuminati' rituals evolved and changed several times during their short eleven year life. Adam Weishaupt, for example, started writing his 'Minerval Illuminati' rituals on his own in 1776.

His concept or basic idea was to deliver some esoteric knowledge, University style, to his new Illuminati members. This would not have changed much once he became a freemason, as Freemasons generally learn from the symbols and ceremonies, rather than being taught or lectured on the subject.

He was admitted to the 'Theodor zum guten Rath', 'Scottish Rectified Rite' or 'Rite of Strict Observance' Lodge at Munich in 1777. However the next change came, when the experienced Freemason, Baron Adolph Franz Friedrich Ludwig von Knigge was made an Illuminate. He was also of a member of the 'Rite of Strict Observance,' and was asked by Weishaupt to help create new masonic versions of the Illuminati rituals in 1780. He must have added the 'Masonic Three Degrees' and the 'Andreas Knight' section of the 'Rite of Strict Observance.' Only later did Knigge attempt to change the higher grades.

Weishaupt did not like all of these suggestions and there was probably at some time a compromise, because we learn that the last two grades Magi/Magus and Rex was never quite finished.

---

58 Wages, Markner & Singh-Anand, 2015, *Secret School of Wisdom*, London: Ian Allan.
59 See Chapter V, 'Heckethorn's, Bavarian Illuminati the Epopt Grade.'

DATING OF THE BAVARIAN ILLUMINATI RITUALS 1786?

There were other influences during the eleven year Bavarian phase that could have developed these rituals further. By the time of the Wilhelmsbad Congress in 1782, both Weishaupt and Baron von Knigge presented quite an enticing promise of the secrets, which the Illuminati had to offer, to the over one hundred and twenty masonic delegates from around Europe. The delegates went back to their Lodges so impressed that they then became *Illumined,* to use a common phrase of the time, by adding these higher grades to their original systems and creating new collections of grades. This phase, however, is too soon historically to be the date of the English *'Revived English Illuminati'* rituals.

Then, one day in 1783, not very happy with one of these Knigge modified rituals, Weishaupt asked him to re-write the Priest or Epopt (Synod) ritual. This was all too much for Knigge and they fell out. This might be one of the reasons why the *'English Illuminati Synod'* ritual is so different from the *'Bavarian Illuminati'* series.

Weishaupt then rewrote that ritual, which represents a second change back to his previous solo efforts, a return no doubt to long tracts of text, which is the kind of teaching you would expect from an academic, rather than masonic type of ritual written by Knigge.

However Knigge left the Order completely on 1 July 1784 and his guidance and different style of teaching was greatly missed by the Order, so we are told.

There was further calamity in 1784, when the Illuminati Order's secret correspondence was discovered in Bavaria and then published. Their political detractors did not like women and children being esoterically educated. While their jealous masonic enemies in the mostly Protestant 'Golden und Rosicrucians' from Prussia, interpreted this organisation as seditious and against the state and eventually the 'Bavarian Illuminati' was officially banned in several different edicts between1784-86.

As mentioned in the *History of the Order of the Illuminati.* Adam Weishaupt was deprived of his (Bavarian University) chair and was banished with a pension from the independent country Bavaria in 1785. Weishaupt refused the pension and moved to Regensburg, subsequently finding asylum with Ernst II, Duke of Saxe-Gotha-Altenburg (1745-1804).

It is not perhaps such a coincidence that in 1787 Adam Weishaupt then wrote his book *The Improved System of the Illuminati* or *Das Verbesserte System der Illuminaten* followed by an *Addendum to justify his intentions* or *Nachtrag zur Rechtfertigung meiner Absichten.*

Does this mean he was still promoting his ideas to a wider audience even at this latter date? How successful was he? He lived in Gotha until his death and wrote at least twelve books on the Illuminati while in exile.

Weishaupt's twelve German Illuminati books:

(1786) *Apologie der Illuminaten.* - Apology of Illuminaten

(1786) *Vollständige Geschichte der Verfolgung der Illuminaten in Bayern.* - Complete History

(1786) *Schilderung der Illuminaten.* - Description of the Illuminati

(1787) *Einleitung zu meiner Apologie.* - Introduction to my apology.

(1787) *Einige Originalschriften des Illuminatenordens.* - Some original documents

(1787) *Nachtrage von weitern Originalschriften.* - Extracts from other original documents

(1787) *Kurze Rechtfertigung meiner Absichten.* - Short justification of my intentions.

(1787) *Nachtrag zur Rechtfertigung meiner Absichten.* - Supplement to justify my intentions

(1787) *Apologie des Mißvergnügens und des Übels.* - Apology of discomfort and evil

(1787) *Das Verbesserte System der Illuminaten.* - The Improved System of the Illuminati

(1788) *Der ächte Illuminat, oder die wahren, unverbesserten Rituale der Illuminaten.*

The true Illuminat, or the true, unencumbered rituals of the Illuminati.

(1795) *Pythagoras, oder Betrachtungen über die geheime Welt- und Regierungs-Kunst.* Pythagoras, or

reflections on the secret world and government art.

ILLUMINATI ROSE-CROIX
WARRANT

There were perhaps two other influences on the Illuminati rituals that happened towards the end of Weishaupt's life in exile, which may help explain the significant differences between the original Weishaupt rituals and the 'Revived English Illuminati' rituals. This was on 1 May 1786, when Frederick II, the Great of Prussia, allegedly signed the constitutions of a nine grade system that would be later called the 'Ancient and Accepted Rite' in Berlin, he unfortunately died months later on the 17th August, the same year. One of these nine grades was the 'Rose-Croix' ceremony; another was the 'Knight of St. Andrew.' The Illuminati called them the 'Rosenkreuzer' which translates as 'Rose-Croix' and the 'Andreas Knight' grade. However the 'Knight of St Andrew' is also part of the 'Rite of Strict Observance,' which both Knigge and Weishaupt were members. How did the 'Rose-Croix' ritual become part of the Illuminati?

At this time in history there were some European Freemasons, who were jealous of this new Illuminati system. They were mainly members of a Protestant Order called the 'Golden Und Rosicrucians.' They were based in Prussia like Frederick II and wanted to continue their system in direct competition with the mainly Catholic, Illuminati system. But I think Ellic Howe has the answer:

> *There was yet another (Illuminati) warrant or its equivalent. According to Leopold Engel, it had been given to Adam Weishaupt when he was at Regensburg on 19 November 1786 by 'the Prince of Rose-Croix Bro. Louis Gabriel Lebauche of Bazeille, near Sedan. It had always been in the possession of Illuminati and is now in the custody of the Ludwig Lodge.*

To add credibility to this account, on further investigation I found that Louis Gabriel Lebauche of Bazeille, near Sedan was a real person. Before the French Revolution (1789-1799), his father Louis (1698-1780) was knighted in April 1769 and became Lord Engagist Bazeilles, (see fig 79). This means that Louis Gabriel Lebauche of Bazeille was of French nobility and inherited his father's titles before 1780. They lived at Avenue Graveyron in Staint Bazeille in an old bourgeois house. He may have fled to Regensburg a few years before the French Revolution had started and this is when and where he probably met Weishaupt. So Ellic Howe's warrant has some credence.

The Ellic Howe warrant claim does not appear in Leopold Engel's copious *History of the Illuminati*, 1906, but can be found in Engel's own magazine *Das Wort* in 1902. Here, Engel says that the warrant had always been in the possession of

Figure 79 - 'Lord Engagiste Bazeilles' Castle near Sedan

Illuminati and that it was now in the custody of the Ludwig Lodge, but not which Ludwig Lodge? There is no suggestion that it was Reuss' 'Ludwig Lodge of improvement,' that reopened in Bavaria 1880 or the 'Ludwig Lodge' that was revived again in Berlin in 1893-1895? Did Theodore Reuss possess this warrant of the 'Rose-Croix' personally, if not who did? It would however explain why the 'Rose-Croix Grade' is included in the 'Revived English Illuminati' series. However, the 'original source material' in this book does prove, and for the first time, that the 'Ludwig Lodge' did exist in 1900.

The biggest difference between the Illuminati system and the '18° Rose-Croix degree' is that you received your Illuminati masonic knighthood in their grade of 'St. Andrew Knight' or the 'Andreas Knight Grade,' which in their case comes from the 'Rite of Strict Observance.' While in the 'Supreme Council 33°,' of the 'Ancient and Accepted Scottish Rite,' you currently receive your masonic knighthood in their 18th Rose-Croix degree.' In the Illuminati system, the 'St. Andrew Knight' comes before the 'Illuminati Rose-Croix grade.' Therefore, the conferral of masonic knighthood has either been removed from the Illuminati 'Rose-Croix Grade,' or it was never in it from the beginning, why was that?

There are other systems that follow the Revived Illuminati System, one is the Paris based 'Philalèthes System' operated by the 1778 'Loge Les Amis Réunis.' Another for example, is the Swedish System of today that has masonic Knighthood in their first or 'St. Andrews Grades IV and V' before their highest grade IX the 'Red Cross.' The Swedish rituals were finally formulated in 1800 by the then Duke Karl of Södermanland (1748-1818), later Charles XIII of Sweden (1809-1818).

The date 1786 is, therefore, the very earliest possible date that an Illuminati Order could have added the 'Rose-Croix Grade.' Just because the Order was supressed in Bavaria does not mean that the degrees may not have carried on being worked around Europe, after the success at the Wilhelmsbad Congress. This is because Weishaupt could have carried on developing and supervising the Illuminati in Europe as he did not die until 1830, long after the French Revolution. This is the best I can do in trying to explain the development of the 'Rose-Croix' Grade.

SUPREME COUNCIL 33° DISAPPROVAL

Westcott feared he would be sent to 'Coventry' for working the 'Rose-Croix' Grade in England. Would the 'Supreme Council 33°' disapprove of anything else in the English 'Revived English Illuminati' grades? Well yes! For example the Illuminati 'Scottish Knight of Saint Andrew' is similar to their 29°. To be fair, the ceremony is no longer worked in the 'Ancient & Accepted Rite' of the 'Supreme Council 33°,' is that perhaps why?

Another example is that the 'English Illuminati' rituals deal in several places with some of the names that appear in some of their 33°, like the prodigy of Noah from the Bible's 'Table of Nations' and the resultant Aryan race of man that issued from one of his three sons, Japheth. A reference is made in the 'Revived English Illuminati' series to 'Mizpah' or the 'watchtower' or 'the heap of stones' and the covenant with God between Jacob and Laban. This is a covenant with God that followed that of Abram and Isaac. The initial letters 'J. and G.' that can be found either side of the revived Illuminati symbol or underneath the Illuminati Logo, may be deciphered by reference to the English Illuminati text in the ceremonies. 'J. and G.' may stand for 'Japheth' and his son 'Gomer'. Another ceremony no longer worked by 'Supreme Council 33°,' 'is their 21° of 'Noachite, or Prussian Knight.' It also refers to the prodigy of Noah. These Noachites are the Aryan peoples supposedly descended from Japheth, who legend describes travelling to north Europe and leaving a history of the Noachites in a Prussian salt mine found in 553 AD.[60]

DATING OF THE PRUSSIAN ILLUMINATI RITUALS 1896?

The four front covers of the revived Illuminati Rituals are not dated. There is no mention of rituals for either of Reuss' *'Ludwig Lodge'* in Munich in 1880 or the revived *'Ludwig Lodge'* in Berlin in 1895. The first printed material produced by Reuss was his *Mysteries of the Illuminati* pamphlet,

printed in 1894 in Berlin. The layout and printing style, as well as the one Illuminati logo that is used in 1894, is different from all the other images and printed material used by the Prussian and Dresden Illuminati.

The undated document *Bestimmungen für die Minerval-Logen des Ordens der Illuminaten* or *Provisions for Minerval lodges of the Order of the Illuminati* (see figs 51 & 52), is similarly devoid of Illuminati images. They just have some printer's scrolls and artwork that may also indicate that it was an early production. However it seems very unlikely that the rituals would have been produced at this time.

The *History of the Order of the Illuminati* printed in 1896, has the Pentagram on a blazing Sun with a bottony cross in the centre, printed on several pages, but none of them with the initial letters 'J.G.' could this mean they were not printed in Dresden by Leopold Engel? These initial letters appear for the first time on the *Innere Ordens-Ordnung* document printed in Dresden, which also has no date.

However, Leopold Engel joined Reuss' 'Prussian Illuminati' in 1896 and then re-located the Illuminati headquarters to his home town of Dresden in 1897. I imagine that Engel achieved this coup by probably promising to bank roll the printing and publishing of the Illuminati rituals and ordinances. For this reason, I believe that the first printed revived Illuminati documents were produced after 1897.

The last possible date that the rituals could have been printed, I believe, was after Reuss and Engel fell out in March 1902, this was when Engel and Reuss agreed to warrant the new 'Mother Ludwig Lodge' of Illuminati working out of Reuss' new 'Grand Lodge of Germany.' By which time you would imagine that the rituals would have to have been finished and available. I, therefore, believe that the German 'Revived Illuminati' rituals were produced sometime between 1896 and 1901.

DATING OF ENGLISH RITUALS 1902?

We now know for definite that the original German Rituals for the Illuminati 'Minerval, Scottish, Knight Rose Croix and Synods' rituals, were all sent to Westcott by Reuss via book post on 3 February 1902.

> *Today I sent you as Registered Book post-parcel the rituals of the Illuminati: Minerval, Synods, Scottish Knight, and Rose-Croix.*

In the supporting letter, Reuss mentions that the 'Sacred Word' of the last or priest degree:

> *I have given you orally while in London.*

---

60 Blanchard J., 1920, *Scotch Rite Masonry Illustrated 19-33 Degrees.*

This was in January 1902, when Reuss was passed through all eight grades of the Rosicrucian Society, the S.R.I.A., at a special ceremony held over two days.

The rituals must have been translated by Westcott sometime after February 1902. The ACTA has no record of Westcott ever receiving the translated rituals and he kept this out of his official diary for some reason. However, the eight or nine months until Westcott comments on the 'Rose-Croix Grade' to Reuss in the October 1902 letter, was more than ample time to have all the rituals translated, especially if he was using someone else to translate them and pay.

GERMAN RITUAL & TRANSLATIONS

There was a time when I thought the rituals might have been four of those five documents sent to Westcott on 17 October 1901, until I found the 3 February letter. One of the five pamphlets however, was the *Innere Ordens-Ordnung* from Dresden, (see fig 81). We know that two of the others were the *Geschichte des Illuminatens Orden,* 1896 and the *Die Mysterien der Illuminaten,* 1894, also with the handwritten dedication dated 17 October 1901, they were both anonymous pamphlets but written by Theodore Reuss, making three in total.

However it was to transpire that the fourth enclosure was probably the *Bestimmungen fur Die Minerval-Logen* or Provisions for Minerval Lodges. It has a similar dedication from Reuss on the inside front page, but it is not exactly the same as the other three documents. If that is the case then Westcott's Diploma as an Illuminate issued on 29 July 1901, could easily be the fifth.

We must assume that Westcott had these 3 February, 1902, Illuminati rituals, translated from German into English by some unknown translator at some unknown date. We do know that Albert Essinger from the Sanitary Wood Wool Company, had help translate the German letters of Fräulein Sprengel for Westcott in 1888, was he therefore also the one who translated these German documents? I am not a handwriting expert but, on closer inspection, I am reasonably sure that Westcott transcribed the 'rituals,' *History* and *Mysteries,* when compared to a number of other documents in the archives (see figs 80 a, b, c.)

It would seem that the rituals took eight months to translate into English, as Westcott would have needed to know what was in the rituals, before he could write to Reuss on 12 October to say that the Illuminati Rose-Croix grade is too similar to the Ancient & Accepted Rite 18° degree ceremony, for use in England.

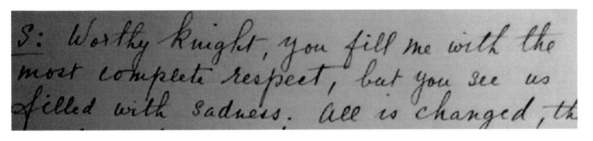

Fig 80 a - Sample of the handwriting from the Rose-Croix Ritual 1902

Fig 80 b - Sample of the handwriting from the History of the Order of the Illuminati 1902

Fig 80 c - Sample of the handwriting from the Zelator Ritual 1905

Here is a timeline for both the German printed material and the undated English translations of them. I have indicated when the German material may have been sent. All this material can be found in the Library and Museum of Freemasonry and online by using the references below.

However, it seems, after the 8 July 1902 consecration of the Berlin S.R.I.A. college designated the 'Societas Rosicruciana in Germania' or S.R.I.G. in an unsubstantiated note Reuss states:

I will send you the German Rituals which it's best you translate into English and will confer on you a warrant to found other Illuminati Lodges in England and more much more.

There is no evidence that these other rituals were sent by Reuss or received by Westcott in July or August 1902. One suggestion I would like to make is that they might refer to the longer sections of the missing 'Minerval' and 'Synod Grades.'

They consist of the lectures and questions for a 'Minerval' that were offered in German to Westcott in July 1902 to complete all the rituals he had already received earlier in February 1902, which I have not found.

The Hamburg Illuminati Warrant designating Westcott an Illuminati Regent was issued by Reuss on the 17 September 1902, after the 8 July consecration in Berlin.

Its receipt was not recorded in the ACTA, so it is quite conceivable that these other so called German rituals could have been sent with this warrant, but that leaves only three months to translate them, which does not seem a reasonable amount of time to complete this task.

The 'Revived English Illuminati' rituals prove something else, that Reuss had something real and deliverable in 1902. This is contrary to what Engel wrote in 1906, about Reuss' Order "being only on paper." It was real and it was based along practical masonic style of Illuminati rituals.

GERMAN PRINTED MATERIAL TIMELINE

29th July 1901
Westcott's Diploma as an Illuminate
German - *Bestimmungen fur Die Minerval-Logen* - Provision for Minerval Lodges (undated)

17th October 1901
1. German - *Innere Ordens-Ordnung* or *Inside the Order*, 26 pages.
2. German - *Die Mysterien der Illuminaten* 1894 sent 17 October 1901.
3. German - *Geschichte des Illuminatens Orden* 1896 sent 17 October 1901.
4. German - Unknown document or *Bestimmungen fur Die Minerval-Logen?* (Above)
5. German - Unknown document.

3rd February 1902.
1. German - *Minerval Grad.* Item ID: L32073, 3 leaves; 29 x 22.5 cm.
2. German - *Andreas - Ritter* Item ID: L32074, 4 leaves; 29 x 22.5 cm.
3. German - *Rosenkreuzer.* Item ID: L32075, 6 leaves; 29 x 22.5 cm.
4. German - *Ritual der Synoden.* Item ID: L32071, 2 leaves; 29 x 22.5 cm.

ENGLISH TRANSLATIONS

Westcott had rituals translated into English by some unknown translator at some unknown date.

They were:

1. The English Translation: *Minerval grade.*
2. The English Translation: *Andreas Knight grade.*
3. The English Translation: *Rose Cross grade.*
4. The English Translation: *Ritual of the Synods.*

INNERE ORDENS-ORDNUNG
Inside the Illuminati Order

INTRODUCTION

I have already introduced the twenty-six page printed document called the *Innere Ordens-Ordnung* or *Inside the Order,* in Chapter I.

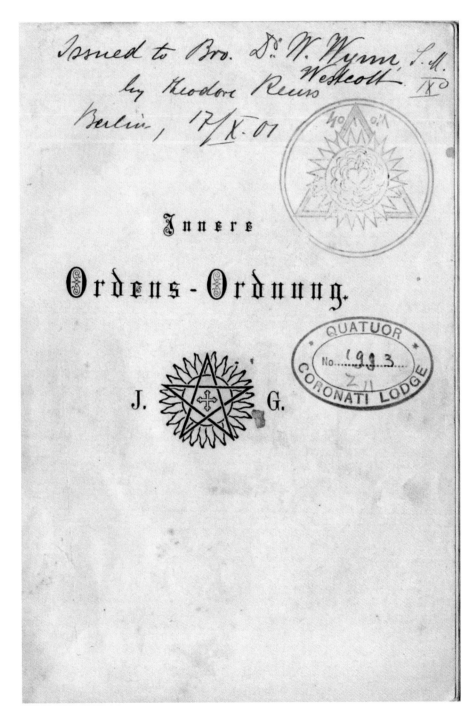

Figure 81 - Front page of 'Innere Ordens-Ordnung' or 'Inside the Order.'

INNERE ORDENS-ORDNUNG
(continued)

The *Innere Ordens-Ordnung* or *Inside the Order,* were written in German and were the Constitutions and Regulations of the Illuminati Order and had been printed in Dresden, Germany.

The *Innere Ordens-Ordnung* booklet, (see figs 7a, b, c, and fig 81). Has a dedication on the front page of the document, which means it must have been sent to Westcott by Theodore Reuss.

> *Issued to Brother Dr W. Wynn Westcott*
> *S.M. IX° by Theodore Reuss, Berlin, 17/X/01.*

The handwritten initial letters after, Westcott's name that look like 'Ill.' are in fact the letters 'S.M.' which stands for Supreme Magus and have been erroneously interpreted by previous archivists.

The date is not in cipher, Reuss has simply used the letter 'X' for the tenth month of October, followed by a full stop and the abbreviated version of the year, '01' making the date 17/10/1901.

The image in the top right hand corner of the cover of the *Innere Ordens-Ordnung* document (see fig 81) has a distinctive rubber stamp mark in blue ink from the 'Prussian Illuminati.' It was not part of this document but added afterwards. It consists of a double circle around the outside, with a double equilateral triangle or sacred delta touching the inside, on which is overlaid the rune letters spelling ᚺ ◊ ᚱ ◊ ᛗ or Z.O.ʃ.O.M. [61]

The blazing Sun is superimposed over the triangle. Inside the glory is a circle with several rows of what looks like petals and in the very centre is the image of the flaming (sacred) heart.

The second image however on the front page is printed in black ink and therefore belonging to the Dresden Order of the Illuminati booklet.

It consisted of a 'flaming star' with a five pointed star or pentagram superimposed on top. Inside the pentagram is a bottony cross in the very centre.

The bottony cross exhibits four trinities at the points of the cross and is the cross symbol used in both the 'Epopt Grade' rituals used in the 'Bavarian Illuminati' rituals and the 'Synod Grade' of the 'English Illuminati' rituals.[62] According to the Illuminati ritual this is the pentagram symbol of the Illuminated man, the son crucified.

It has the initials J. and G. either side and is one of four different positions of the these two letters, on three different rubber stamps (see figs 11, 81, 83, 84b). Only one part of the printed document, the other three rubber stamp marks.

I speculate in the introduction of chapter I, that these letters stand for Japheth and Gomer, son and grandson of Noah from Biblical times.

The last page of the *Innere Ordens-Ordnung*, (see fig 7c) is signed by Leopold Engel. Printed above his signature is 'Der Geheime Areopag.'

This translates as 'The Secret Areopagus' and is equivalent to the 'Grand Lodge of the Illuminati' in their terms.

Engel was directed by the Custos-Office or 'Grand Lodge'. This consists of three people and a council, which are called the Custos, the Vice-Custos and the Archivist. They are assisted by a supervisory board of five members of the Order elected by the ordinary voting members.

The Office of the Custodian and the Supervisory Board are the 'Secret Areopag.' They organised all the current Illuminati (religious) Orders and manage the Order and supervised the entire organisation.

The other blue stamp mark on the front cover is the Quatuor Coronati Lodge, No. 2076, London, No. 1993 blue stamp library mark and is mentioned as from the Donor. This document is currently the property of Quatuor Coronati Lodge, No. 2076.

---

61 See page 26 & 27 for more detailed description.
62 See fig 90 page 169.

Chapter IV - Revived Illuminati Regulations and Rituals

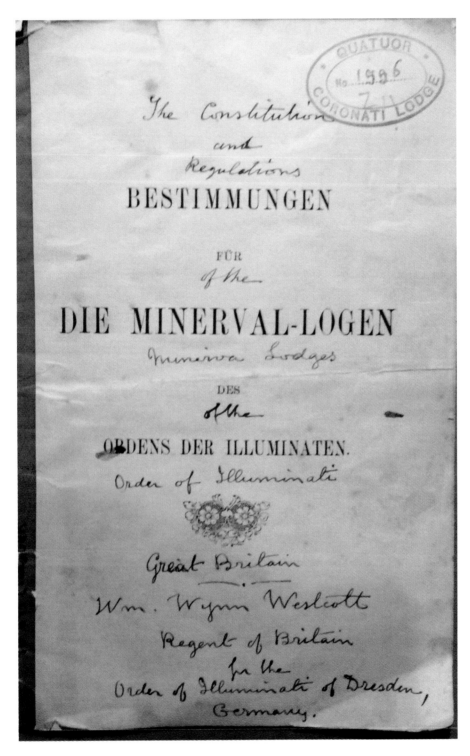

Figure 82 - Cover page for The Minerval Lodges

CONSTITUTIONS AND REGULATIONS

INTRODUCTION

It is an undated document and was probably sent with Westcott's Certificate as 'legitimately Minerval in the Order of the Illuminati,' and letter that the Order of Illuminati is lawful, on 29 July 1901.

The German word 'Bestimmungen' translates as 'Regulations' but it is translated on the cover page by Westcott or his translator as, 'Constitutions and Regulations.'

This document also has a Quatuor Coronati Lodge No. 2076, oval blue ink stamp mark on the top right hand side of the front cover, No.1995.

The *Bestimmungen für die Minerval-Logen des Ordens der Illuminaten* or in Westcott's handwriting next to the German text it says:

> *The Constitution and Regulations of the Minerval Lodges of the Order of the Illuminati.*

It is a fifteen page A5 pamphlet, published by Bitterfield, Germany: Druck von E. Baumann.

The original (see fig 82), has the following inscription on the inside cover, (see fig 84a) and with the initial letters replaced states:

> *Theodore Reuss, Regens J.G.*
>
> *To the Most Wise Brother,*
>
> *Dr William Wynn Westcott.*
>
> *Secretary General, (Swedenborg Rite)*
>
> *Illustrious & Senior Warden.*[63]

The front cover, in Westcott's handwriting is already talking about the 'Order of Illuminati, Great Britain' with 'Wm. Wynn Westcott as the Regent of Britain.'

Westcott did not accept the position as 'Regent of the Illuminati' until 21 August 1902, a year later. So the inscription on the inside 'Theodore Reuss Regens J.G.' refers to Reuss being the Regent J.G. in Germany, not Westcott.

The other significant thing here is that Westcott has written that the document is from the 'Order of Illuminati of Dresden,' not from Berlin at this stage; refer to the bottom of fig 82.

The Constitutions and Regulations of the Minerval Lodge give us a good understanding of how a 'Revived Illuminati Lodge' worked and they are very different from the original 'Bavarian Illuminati' statutes.

They insist on such a close level of supervision of its 'Minerval' members and their studying and reading of a set number of books on art and science, with proof of their diligence.

Figure 83 - Last page for The Minerval Lodges

What is significant about the last page above, which is probably the first document that Westcott received. Is that it features the red ink stamps marks from both, Reuss' Prussian Illuminati with the ᚺ ◊ ᚱ ◊ ᛗ or Z.O.ſ.O.M. and the Dresden Illuminati of Engle, (see fig 83). They were not part of the printed document but added.

63 The Library and Museum of Freemasonry 'Call number YG 699 (ILL) GER.'

Chapter IV - Revived Illuminati Regulations and Rituals

WOMEN MEMBERS

Later you will find under 'Membership and Admission' item 1, that Ladies are mentioned and then later 'women visitors' are mentioned in item 9 'Work.'

I do not think the Revived Illuminati were integrated or a mixed-sex organisation, as this is the only mention of women that I can find. They are not mentioned at all in any of the rituals.

It gives the impression that they are not actively involved with the 'Resurrected Illuminati Order' at all.

I have also highlighted the following entry in the text for your information;

Ladies belonging to the Order may only visit the lodge on special days set apart for this purpose.

Westcott's translation and adaptation of the constitutions of the German Illuminaten-Ordens are undated.

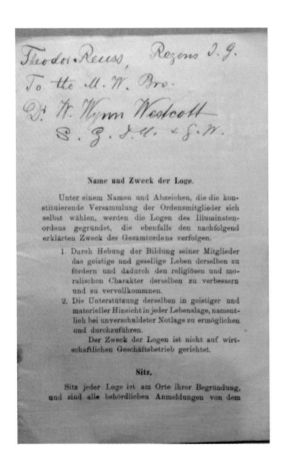

Figure 84a - Inside dedication Reuss J.G.

Figure 84b – Dresden blue stamp mark

NAME AND PURPOSE OF THE MINERVAL LODGES

The lodges of the Illuminati are founded under a name and sign, which the representative assemblages of the members of the Order choose themselves, here set forth as follows:

1. To advance the spiritual and social life of the members of the Order by the improvement of their culture and thus to elevate and perfect their religious and moral character.

2. To enable members to benefit by each other's help and support both spiritually and materially, particularly in cases of undeserved adversity.

3. The purpose of the lodges does not extend to the furtherance of business affairs.

SITUATION

Every lodge is to be held at the place of its founding and all the notifications to the authorities are to be made as required by law by the chosen board of directors of the lodge.

FOUNDATION OF LODGES

1. The Minerva lodges are founded by the trustees of the Illuminati Order in Dresden and are subject to the authority of that Order or of their designated representatives. All decisions of the trustees are, therefore, to be obeyed. All members of the Order are at liberty, when supported by two others, to present their proposal for the foundation of a lodge.

2. Every Minerva lodge forms a district of its own inside that of the whole Order, without, however, possessing the right of free administration of the monies of the lodge, its properties, or the exercise of any peculiar rights. In the same way, no lodge has the power to curtail the rights of any member of the Order which have been obtained by their connection with the general Illuminati Order. Every lodge possesses unrestrained freedom within its own limits which are explained by the following regulations, and undertakes the whole responsibility to the government of the country, as also to the officials of the superior Order (the trustees at Dresden).

3. The first sittings of the lodge are presided over by a representative of the trustees; as soon as possible, at latest after the third sitting of the lodge, must follow the election of officials from among the members, and directly afterwards the notification to the authorities of the existence of a lodge of the Illuminati Order (the central office of the administration of the Order being Dresden) must be drawn up at the place of its founding.

MEMBERSHIP AND ADMISSION

1. Every member of the Illuminati Order, without distinction, may apply for admission to any other lodge, his admission depending upon the decision of the members. Ladies belonging to the Order may only visit the lodge on special days set apart for this purpose.

2. Membership to a lodge is inadmissible without a previous general admission to the Order. The president has to see that he is dealing with a real member of the Order.

3. Respectable persons, who announce themselves to the president or a member of the lodge for admission, must therefore first be introduced in a well-known manner into the general association of the Order and later on into the sphere of activity of the lodge.

4. The 'Introductor' or (Magus) takes all responsibility and also retains the office of leader (Magus) in the lodge.

5. When a suitable member of the Order has been found for a Minerva member, the president must obtain from the trustees the probation papers of the same, and must decide within the official college, whether, after perusing these papers, the admission is to be countenanced or not. If the proposition is supported, then the name of the member is loudly announced by the president at the next sitting, and is immediately put to the vote.

Should a black voting ball fall, the president, in order to assure the same, must have the voting repeated; if a black ball again occurs, the members of the lodge in order to control it, must hand the remaining balls to the president, each separately, thus giving him an opportunity of recognising, without it being noticed by the others, who it was who threw a black ball. The president must have an interview with this member, in order to hear his reasons. When this has occurred, the president calls together the chief officials of the Order, and imparts to them the reasons which caused the member of the Order to throw black, without mentioning his name. Then it must be decided whether these reasons shall be considered justifiable or not. The result is made known at the next lodge, again without mentioning the name. If the reasons given are considered sufficient by the official college, the announcement of his membership is delayed for one year.

If the reasons are considered inadequate, the second ballot immediately takes place. If three black balls fall, the ballot must be delayed, without enquiry, for a whole year. If, however, five black balls fall, the candidate must be definitely refused.

6. No member of a Minerva Lodge may be at the same time a member of another Minerva Lodge, unless it be as an honorary member.

7.The introduction of a member into a lodge occurs by ritual.

8. Every member possesses an inalienable voice at every ballot.

OFFICIALS

1. The official college of a lodge consists of one or two presidents, one or two secretaries, and one or two treasurers.

2. The officials are elected yearly at the general meeting of the lodge. In order to obtain an authentic election, it is necessary to have three quarters of the voting members present. If this is not obtained, the decision is left to the trustees. The result of every election must be immediately transmitted to the trustees.

3. The first president takes over the direction of the lodge meetings, as well as the representation on every occasion when desired by the interests of the lodge or of the Order. As the president, he belongs to the Areopagus, and is a delegate of his lodge as soon as this is necessary. In cases of inability, his office is conducted by the second president.

The secretary is the registrar and recorder for all writings and documents. A copy of the protocol of every lodge meeting, as well as a copy of all notifications within the lodge must be sent by him to the trustees immediately, without being demanded. The treasurer has to look after the affairs of the treasury, and must supervise the inventory of the lodge and take every care of it.

4. The authorisation for practising the official duties is certified by the trustees after every election. Until such certificate is received, no sitting of the lodge may take place.

FEES

1. Every member of the Order, who enters a lodge, no longer pays his Order fee to the trustees, but to the treasurer of the lodge, and obtains a receipt from him.

2. The fees are arranged as follows:

   a. The lodge fee for every member of the lodge is at least 12m (Marks) per annum.

   b. If a member of the Order at his voluntary estimation engages to pay an amount less than 12m (Marks), then his amount must be increased.

   c. This increase, upon demand to the lodge administration and upon the decision of the lodge officials, may be dispensed with.

   d. The voluntary estimation of a member of an amount more than 12 Marks per annum remains of value after his admission into the lodge.

   e. The half of all this amount must be transmitted quarterly to the general treasury of the Order, together with a detailed statement.

   f. All results from collections , any kind of arrangement, donations etc. which are obtained by order of the decisions of the lodge, as well as the remaining half of all amounts are used up by the lodge itself, which has free use of this income according as the lodge may require it.

WORK

1. In order to fulfil the purpose of the Minerva lodges, the work of the same includes the teachings of every Order, mutual instructs, animation of free talk, the culture of friendship and sociable intercourse.

2. Members are to be taken up or visitors to be greeted, according to the existing ritual.

3. Within the Minerva lodges, only the first part of our doctrines is used for general argument. Propositions with the resulting discussions on any favourite subject, but which must as much as possible suit themselves to the scope of the Order, are desired, the only exceptions being all propositions and discussions regarding politics or matters which may bring suspicion upon the Order or lodge as to any particular political leaning or any attitude towards existing parties.

To learn to understand everything down to its very roots, by practicing the greatest tolerance. A good understanding and not opposition is the working purpose of the Minerva lodges.

Expounders, who fail in this, may be deprived of their speech by the president.

4. Lecture of the sciences is supported in all its branches. The president must pay attention to the wishes of the leaders of the Order in this respect.

5. The president has the right to appoint members of the lodge, who after a certain period of time must give a lecture on a subject adapted to the scope of the Order.

6. Every member is bound to make accessible, by means of short or long lectures, his knowledge within the lodge so far as this can be done without harming him.

7. Every member, upon his admission, must address all those present, stating what it is he expects of the Order or lodge.

8. The lodges naturally determine special evenings, on which, without ritual, social intercourse is permitted, or on which special lectures are held, at which the friends or relations of the members of the Order are permitted to attend, as well as guests, these latter having to be introduced by some member. Guests must always pay a voluntary or a fixed fee to the treasury of the lodge.

9. Further, the lodges set apart evenings as desired, on which female friends or relations may be admitted under the rights of a member of the lodge.

10. Great public arrangements of the lodge are permissible, but every apparent show is avoided. At any rate the permission of the trustees must first be obtained.

11. The nature of the timely publication of a lodge date is naturally determined by the superiors.

12. It is the duty of every member to inspect the work of the lodge to which he is invited. If prevented, he must apprise the secretary of this in writing or verbally through another member, sending his dispensation fee.

13. The extent of this dispensation fee, as well as fines, for repeated non-attendance of members of the lodge, may be determined by the lodge.

14. Christmas or Easter, or both, shall be devoted by the members of the lodge, if possible, to some deed of charity. The nature of the same as well as

the method for obtaining the means for this purpose are determined at the general meetings of the lodges.

15. Regarding the dates of the lodge, the secretary must keep an exact protocol, a copy of which must always be sent immediately to the trustees in Dresden.

16. All end resolutions once passed by a lodge, which bear fruit within a working year and thereafter, can only be taken up again at a general meeting. These separate resolutions should be collected and made accessible to every member. Every new member, before admission, must be well versed in the existing resolutions of the lodge. Printing is permissible.

17. Daily arrangements of the lodge.

    a)   Opening of the lodge.
    b)   Reading of the protocol.
    c)   The greeting and introduction of visiting brethren.
    d)   Admission of new members.
    e)   Lecture.
    f)   Discussion regarding the same.
    g)   Public questions and answers.
    h)   Matters concerning the lodge.
    i)   Closing the lodge.

GENERAL MEETING

1. Eight days after the foundation day of the lodge, a general meeting of all members is called, on which occasion new officials are chosen and resolutions are passed, as far as is required according to the decision of the Mineral lodges.

2. The trustees in Dresden can of their own accord or upon demand of the lodge, or at any time, call a special general meeting under their direction or that of the superiors of the lodge, which call must be obeyed.

INSPECTION

All Minerva lodges, by order of the trustees and through their authorised representatives, are inspected and these representatives must be permitted a clear insight into all conditions of the lodge.

FREE ENTRY AND DEPARTURE

1. Every member of the Order has the right, to visit existing lodges three times from the day after he has proved himself to the superiors as a member of the Order or some other lodge. After the third visit, he must decide upon joining the lodge. More frequent visits of a non-member of the lodge can be granted according to the decision on the lodge.

2. If a brother when moving from one lodge place to another desires to become a member of the latter lodge, after paying three visits he must submit himself to admission by ballot.

3. Every visiting brother and also every joining brother, is bound to pay three previous visits to the lodge before his admission, is also bound, upon the command of the president, to express himself freely with regard to his travelling observations, the purpose of his journey and the reasons for his moving, and he must also hold forth on any subject which appears of interest to the members of the Order.

4. The retirement from a lodge can occur at any time after notification to the superiors, without retirement from the Order being necessary. Members changing their place of residence can be dismissed after corresponding formalities.

5. Every member leaving a lodge receives a certificate bearing the seal of the lodge, and signed by the officials, which certifies as to his membership of the lodge. In the same manner, certificates of this nature can be provided for travelling members if desired.

These latter must be returned upon the completion of the journey.

6. A member of a lodge, who does not adhere to the demands made on him, in accordance with his membership to the lodge or Order, with regard to the resolutions or general order resolutions, can be turned away if so decided.

DISSOLUTION OF A LODGE

1. If the number of members in a lodge is only three, and if after a period of three months this number is not increased, the lodge must be dissolved. Any ready money and inventory falls to the Order of Illuminati.

2. If within a lodge party disputes should arise, or quarrelling and misunderstandings regarding the rules and teachings of the Order, opposition to the existing arrangements of the trustees, the lodge is dissolved, drawing confiscated in its capital and inventory, both of which fall due to the Illuminati Order to be disposed of as they think fit.

Alterations in these decisions of the Order are only made by the trustees of the Order, and require to be certified by the stamp of the trustees

In authenticity of these decisions for the Minerva lodges of the Order of Illuminati is confirmed by the addition of their seal.

END OF MINERVAL CONSTITUTIONS

J. G.

Minerval = Grad

Figure 85 - Front page of the Revived Illuminati 'Minerval Grade' (reproduction)

RITUAL MINERVAL GRAD
Minerval Grade

THE PROPOSED RITUALS OF THE ORDER OF

ENGLISH ILLUMINATI 1901

ILLUMINATEN ORDEN, GERMANY. MINERVAL GRAD

The original front cover of the German Minerval Grad ritual is blue paper with the Illuminati logo in the middle of the page with the bottony cross in the centre, (see fig 85). The translation of the Minerval Grade is in William Wynn Westcott's handwriting on seven pieces of A4 exercise paper, with faint green/blue ruled lines and a pencil ruled margin down the left hand side. It is written using a quill in black ink. The original cover page now has a Quatuor Coronati Lodge No. 2076 oval stamp mark and has the following inscription inside, 'Sent by Theodore Reuss to William Wynn Westcott.' The Library and Museum of Freemasonry online entry for the manuscript says: 'Reuss, Theodor, 1855-1923, the former owner Westcott, W. Wynn (William Wynn), 1848-1925. The current owner is Quatuor Coronati Lodge, No. 2076, London, as the Donor.

INTRODUCTION

Reuss supplied Westcott only with the 'opening' and 'closing' of the Minerval Grade and a very short admission ceremony. I was originally quite surprised and disappointed that was all that there was, as this is the root and marrow of the Illuminati Order and the Minerval Grade contains most of its teachings.

The 'Revived English Illuminati Minerval Grade' 'opening' and 'closing' seems to be quite unique. It is not to be found in the exposes books written by John Robson or Abbe Barrel or in C.W. Heckethorn's Illuminati rituals. Neither is there one in the original 'Bavarian Illuminati' rituals of Adam Weishaupt, that have been reproduced in *The Secret School of Wisdom*.[64]

I believe that this is deliberate and is the only part of ritual that there was in the 'Revived English Illuminati Minerval Grade' and that it was created for those Freemasons who were used to an 'opening' of the lodge and a 'closing' of the lodge.

In many ways this 'opening' was something that created the sacred space for the operation of the 'Revived English Illuminati Minerval Grade' and when the work was completed the 'closing' ceremony also sealed the sacred space.

In the 'opening' ceremony, the members use the 'blinding sign' before the candidate comes into the Lodge. The sign also helps explain the Minerval word used, that can also be found on the Illuminati jewel of the Minerval Owl. The initial letters are P.M.C.V. (see fig 86).

The image is used on the front of many of Weishaupt's books, but with this difference.

When he uses it the pages of the book that the owl sits on are blank and there is no P.M.C.V. exhibited.

They stand for the Latin words, *Per Me Coeci Vident,* which translates into English as 'Through me let the blind see.' There may have been a second higher meaning to the same 'blinding sign.' That could also mean 'blinded by the light' in sense of an enlightened 'man,' who has followed the path of knowledge, or of Gnosis or light.

In this ceremony, the head of the Lodge is called the 'Magnate Magus,' Westcott would have

Figure 86 - Minerval Owl with P.M.C.V.

64 Wages, Markner & Singh-Anand, 2015.

been particularly interested in the *History of the Order of the Illuminati*'s use of 'Magus' as the same word is used for the head of his S.R.I.A. Rosicrucian Society in England, 'Supreme Magus.'

According to the John Robinson 1787 expose, the Illuminati 'Magus' and the 'Illuminati Rex' 'Roi' or 'King,' were the highest ranks in the 'Bavarian Illuminati' and these titles were only communicated upon the qualifying brethren by Adam Weishaupt himself. The 'Magnate Magus' would rule the Lodge as he was perceived as a wealthy and influential businessman, while the 'Illuminati Rex' would rule the country or province. But Westcott at this early stage was offered the lower rank or title of 'Regent in Great Britain and Ireland.'

Generally in all Bavarian Illuminati correspondence and rituals, the name of the society is replaced by the symbol of the 'Sun' i.e. '☉.' The candidate is also usually referred to by the initial letters as 'O.N.,' neither is the case in the 'Revived Illuminati' Minerval ritual for example. The letters 'O.N.' are an abbreviation for the Illuminati name of the candidate, they represent '☉ Name' or 'Order Name.'

During the admission ceremony of the Minerval, the candidate is told that the process:

Is either shortened or lengthened according to the worthiness of the man.

We can assume that no two ceremonies were therefore exactly the same. The candidate is presented with an apron and the symbols on it are explained in the ceremony.

Where did this ritual come from? On recently reading Weishaupt's 'Bavarian Illuminati Minerval Grade' system,[65] it seems to me, more like a school curriculum than a masonic ritual and one you would expect from a University professor.

Essentially in his system, a candidate fills in his application form and writes down a great deal of their personal details, so that other members can really get to know the man or woman.

Which, in my opinion is a very good system and it would work very well today in Freemasonry, where all too often the candidates are left alone to work out what is going on for themselves.

Illuminate members were given an empty journal to write down what they have read that week. This enabled their mentor to ask them questions on what they have learned from the material contained in the book supplied from the societies' reading list. Why? Is it because everyone is different and they will learn at a different pace.

This, I believe, may be the "personal pupillage" and "question and answer system," that was something asked of every candidate before being admitted in to 'Bavarian Illuminati Minerval Grade.' This is also something that Westcott asked Reuss for in paragraph two of his 12 October 1902 letter, (see fig 48). I can find no record of the personal pupillage documentation ever being sent by Reuss or received by Westcott. However, the questioning of a candidate can be found in the Addendum in the book *The Secret School of Wisdom.*[66]

This would tend to suggest, as I have speculated, that the Minerval Grade may have been produced much later in the short life of the Illuminati Order, by Freemasons who prefer a ritual system, rather than the very long lectures, that Adam Weishaupt wrote as the foundation stone of his Illuminati system.

What follows next are the English translations as transcribed by Westcott of the 'Revived English Illuminati' sections of the 'Minerval Ritual.'

I have reproduced the translation errors and the translator's English, which may have been improved at some later stage by Westcott before these rituals were actually used. The text in black is that spoken during the ceremony. The text in red is the original rubric of the ceremony, which I have highlighted to avoid any confusion and to help the reading of the ceremonies.

My notes have been highlighted in blue to distinguish them from the original ceremony. The originals can be found in the Library and Museum of Freemasonry.

---

65 Wages, Markner & Singh-Anand 2015.

66 Ibid.

OPENING OF THE LODGE OF THE MINERVAL

Magnate Magus: Dear brethren, the hour of our work calls us. Let us begin. Do you acknowledge me?

(He makes the blinding sign)

Witnesses: We acknowledge you as the lawful Magus.

(They make the blinding sign).[67]

Magnate: I also recognise you thanks to the Divine light which aides me in finding you, and which illumines us all and may further enlighten us in our work. Let us therefore ask the support of Him who must be obeyed.

(All cross their arms over their breasts).

Prayer: Thou eternal power which was, is and will be, which enlightens us that we may find the right paths and walk with confidence therein, grant us in our undertakings today thy indispensable blessing, that the work done in thy science may flourish, grow, blossom and bear rich fruit. Amen.

ADMISSION IN THE LODGE OF THE MINERVAL

Magnate: brethren a fellowman who is still groping in the dark desires to be enlightened by the light from the East, who is worthy and has sealed his vow of scary silence by his signature. Lead him in. (Candidate is fetched)

My friend! You expressed the wish to be admitted into the society of Illuminati brethren. But before initiating any man be his admission ever so desirable into the grade of the I.O.,[68] he must go through the Minerva grade, which is either shortened or lengthened according to the worthiness of the man. In this time you will not learn to know any of the members, and the more secret intimate authorisation [arrangements] of the Order with respect to the grades will also be kept back from you for the present, and you are not permitted to enquire about same. Upon your admission as a Minerva you undertake to work actively on behalf of the Society.

---

67 P.M.C.V. Per me Coeci Vident-translates as "Through me
   let the blind see." (see fig 86).
68 I.O. Illuminati Order.

You promise us with your signature, strictest secret and unquestionable obedience, the document which you sign reads as follows:

(He reads) Is the signature here shown yours?

Reply: Yes!

And you acknowledge by a loud "Yes!" that you desire to become a member of the Order?

Reply: Yes!

Then we would explain to you that only he is admissible who does not close his ears to the cries of woe of the miserable, nor his heart to generate pity, who is the friend and brother of the unhappy, who has a heart full of love and friendship, who is steadfast in adversity, writing in the accomplishment of any duty commenced, undaunted in his efforts to overcome difficulties, who does not despise [much] the weak, whose soul is sensible of great deeds, anxious to rise above petty things and to prove himself by good deeds, fleeing from indolence, who does not regard any knowledge whatsoever as useless. Who, when it is a question of truth and virtue has the courage to do as his heart dictates in material of the approval of the majority. Only he is admissible, who asks his conscience, please place your hand on this book which contains our precepts according to which we act, and reply to my question:

"Will you, be measured with this measure and prove yourself to be worthy?"

Reply: Yes!

Then I will turn to your obligations. You have already satisfactorily replied in writing to a number of questions which were submitted to you. The chief questions I will ask you once more and you must reply to them with a loud "Yes" (see copy)

Give me your hand in place of an oath.

(The witnesses rise, hand-pressure, then to the witnesses)

"Is this brother worthy to be admitted?"

Witnesses: Yes! (The Magus places his hand on the head of the probationer)

Magus: I now initiate you by this touch as a lawful Minerva in the name of the honourable Society of Enlightened Brethren and assure you of their protection and support, but they will not aid you should you have iniquities through your own faults, or should you sin against the power and support of the Order.

But should you become a traitor, you see here in this sword all the members of the grade rising up in arms against you. Do not hope for safety then, whosesoever you may flee to, from the shame and reproach of your heart and conscience, the revenge of your betrayed brothers would follow you and eat into your very vitals. As an outer sign of your membership I hand you these documents, from which you will see that you will be recognised as a member of the Order under the name of ………….

For reasons which will be clear to you without further explanation, and which prove to you that we wish to be men amongst men, we lay aside more worldly names.

(Reads the document)

There is added one sentence: (Reads) let this be your staff to guide you to the temple of truth in the land of spirits.

(Hands him the apron)

As a sign that you wish to be in our midst as a man amongst men, take this apron and gird yourself therewith.

(Explains the symbol)

The three cornered piece turned down, represents the person awakened to spiritual life; that you should gird yourself with it indicates your earnest wish to attain this spiritual life. The white colour is the purity of this desire, the light blue bordering, means that only by being impressed with the earnest belief can the higher and highest stages be attained.

The (Jewel) symbol which you herewith suspend shows the Seal of Solomon, a triangle with one point reaching upwards and another downwards. The meaning of the downwardly directed point has just been explained to you, the second is a representation of the spiritually awakened man: the goal which we all strive after. Examine this symbol frequently and remind yourself of the higher sublime purpose and goal which we are striving after!

(Free speech)

CLOSING OF THE LODGE OF THE MINERVAL.

Brethren the work is completed and the light of the East has been given to a man who has hitherto groped in the dark.

May it enlighten him and warn him, for love and friendship, and help him to wise deeds and actions.

(To the Inner guard/guides)

"Brother, lead the newly initiated into the hall."

(This is done)

Therewith close all the work and thank the eternal light because our eyes see clearer, our spirits are more clear, our spirits are more cheerful and we have made another step towards the light.

My brethren, in the name of Him who must be obeyed, I hereby close this meeting of enlightened brethren according to old custom, (raps and makes the blinding sign).[69]

END OF MINERVAL GRAD RITUAL

---

69 P.M.C.V. Per me Coeci Vident-translates as "Through me let the blind see," (see fig 86).

Chapter IV - Revived Illuminati Regulations and Rituals

J. G.

Schotten = Grad

Figure 87 - Front page of Ritual Schotten Grad or Andreas Knight (reproduction)

RITUAL SCHOTTEN GRAD
Andreas Knight Grade

THE PROPOSED RITUALS OF THE ORDER OF ENGLISH ILLUMINATI 1901

ILLUMINATEN ORDENS - SCHOTTEN GRAD (ANDREAS KNIGHT GRADE)

The original front cover of the German 'Schotten Grad' ritual is on green paper with the Illuminati logo in the middle of the page with the bottony cross in the centre, (see fig 87).

The translation of the Andreas Knight Grade is in William Wynn Westcott's handwriting on eleven pieces of A4 exercise paper. With faint green/blue ruled lines and a pencil ruled margin down the left hand side. It is written using a quill in black ink. The original cover page now has a Quatuor Coronati Lodge No. 2076 oval stamp mark and has the following inscription inside, 'Sent by Theodore Reuss to William Wynn Westcott.' The Library and Museum of Freemasonry online entry for the manuscript says: 'Reuss, Theodor, 1855-1923, the former owner Westcott, W. Wynn (William Wynn), 1848-1925. The current owner is Quatuor Coronati Lodge, No. 2076, London, as the Donor.

INTRODUCTION

The 'Andreas Knight Grade' is the Illuminati name for the 'St. Andrews Knight Grade.' This ceremony would be the equivalent of the 'Scottish Novice Knight' of the 'Bavarian Illuminati' system, grade number four. They were called 'Illuminatus Dirigens' or 'Directing Illuminati.' The 'Minervals' were 'Lesser Illuminati' and the 'Scottish Knights,' 'Greater Illuminatus.'

In this 'English Illuminati Schotten (Scottish) Grad,' just like in the 'Bavarian Illuminati' system, they confer knighthood on the candidate, with a sword, head, heart and shoulder and a brotherly kiss.

The candidates are referred to as brother 'N.N.' or 'Novice Notuma.' The word 'Notuma' appears in many different 'Templar' workings in Freemasonry, it is an anagram of 'Aumont,' who was in fact Pierre d' Aumont 1313 who was the Grand Regional Master of the Temple in Auvergne during the persecution of the Knights Templar Order by King Philip IV of France. Aumont allegedly fled to Scotland and became the first Grand Master of the Templars in Scotland, and the restorer of the Order there after the death of the 23rd and last Grand Master of the Templars, Jacque De Molay in March 1314.

Unlike the Bavarian Illuminati ceremony, which does not feature this part at all, after the oath in the English Illuminati Schotten Grad, the candidate says:

As a sign hereof I grasp this dagger and pierce therewith this skull. May the like overtake me should I ever become a traitor! Amen!

This is typical of the vengeance degrees of the 'Masonic Knights Templar,' where the Notuma is avenging the death of their Grand Master Jacques De Molay. Stabbing the skull is also used in the Elu Cohen and in the Grand Elect Knight Kadosh 30° of 'Ancient & Accepted Rite Supreme Council 33°,' but there the similarity ends. However the jewel of 'St. Andrew Knight' in the 'English Illuminati Schotten Grad' is very similar to that of the '29° Grand Scotch Chevalier of St. Andrew,' 'Supreme Council 33°.'

The Magus admits the N.N. as a Schotten (Scottish) or Andreas Knight, of the High Illuminati Order, by the power of his office and embraces him with a brotherly kiss, so that he may always remain the friend of your friends. In this grade, part of the Illuminati logo is explained;

Whoever does not reply 'J' is no real and true Schotten of the Illuminati! Outside the Lodges one makes himself known by saying: **"I know J and G and the flaming star."** *"Gomer"* is an outside word.

Before this, the letters 'J' and 'A' are exchanged, the ritual indicates the 'J' is for Jehovah and 'A' is for Adonai. The letter 'A,' however, could also stand for 'Aumont.'

What follows next are the English translations that were transcribed by Westcott, of the 'Revived Illuminati' sections of the Schotten (Scottish) Ritual' of the St. Andrews Knight. I have reproduced the translation errors and the translator's English, which may have been improved at some later stage by Westcott before these rituals were actually used. The text in black is that spoken during the ceremony.

RITUAL SCHOTTEN GRAD
ANDREAS KNIGHT GRADE

Officers of the Lodge:

Magus: H.B.G.M. and G.M. Honourable Brother Grand Master and Grand Magus.
Chanc: M.H.B.H.C. Most Honourable Brother High Chancellor.
Cerem: M.H.B.M.C. Most Honourable Brother Master of Ceremonies.
N.N. The Novice Notuma or Andreas aspirant.

Magus: (knocks) Most Honourable Brother Master of Ceremonies, cover the Lodge!

Cerem: (Closes the doors and announces). H.B.G.M. and G.M. the lodge is covered.

Magus: O, Most Honourable brother High Chancellor take to the honourable brothers the password 'Gabaon'[70] and bear it into the innermost circle, there to take your place.

Chanc: H.B.G.M. and G.M. The brethren have given me the password 'Gabaon.'

Magus: Therefore, it is fully time to commence our duties. (Lights 2 large and 2 small lights and M.G. 1 small light) Therefore, O honourable brethren and A.R.[71] I open this high Schotten Andreas Lodge of the great and mighty Order of the Illuminati in the name of the Great Creator of all words, with theory of this degree: Rabboni, Rabboni, Rabboni our salvation is Nemesis! 4 * 4 (knocks).

(Prayer)

Father of truth and eternal source of all light, permeated with the feeling of our own unworthiness we stand accompanied by your spirit and desire to enter thy service. May our recognition of the eternal law surmount every other feeling of our humanity? May the thought of thy presence and holiness abound within us, so that we may at all times hearken unto thy voice which speaketh

within us, with great humility and obedience, in order that we may firmly grasp the truth and virtue with true love and energy for majesty of moral dispositions, and thereby accomplish the holiness in which only sense, love and law shall dwell as the image of the Godhead.
Amen!

All: (Complete the sign and clap 4*4, the call comes before prayers).

Magus: What is our work in this Midnight stillness?

Chanc: A worthy and tried one, brother ...., one who seeks after truth begs to be admitted as a member in this degree of our high Order.

Magus: Most Honourable Brother Grand Chancellor prove him once more, and if he is willing to take the great vow of obedience and silence, and to sign in the vestibule, and will promise to fight for friendship and truth, until death, then prepare him beforehand in the signs of humility and of blind obedience, and after he has repeated his affairs to the M.H.B.H.C., leads him before the door of the innermost circle.

Cerem: (Makes the arm sign) H.B.G.M. and G.M. Your commands shall be obeyed. (C. goes out, brings the signature of the candidate, all his valuables and the admission - Order, all of which he hands to the Magus with the words): "H.B.G.M. and G.M. the applicant has signed."

Magus: Then let him start on the great journey. (Music)

Cerem: (Goes out) Are you ready seeking brother N.N. to start the journey in blind obedience,[72] under guidance, if so, confide yourself to me, and clothe yourself with this symbol of humility.
(Both walk around the pale fire in the vestibule. To the first time the Chanc. Who has softly come out, presents himself before him with the questions which he reads out to the seeker, receiving his answers).

Chanc: (One rap as a Schotten).[73] What seekest thou brother, in this holy circle at this midnight hour?

Cerem: (For the candidate). He wishes to fight for truth and friendship in a circle of comrades with the same desire.

---

70 Gabaon is a Greek form of the name Gibeon, 8 miles NW of Jerusalem on the route to Joppa. "In the 14° of the Ancient & Accepted Rite, Gabaon is a significant word in the high degrees." Oliver says. (Landm., i. 335.) "in philosophical Masonry, heaven, or, more correctly speaking, the third heaven, is denominated Mount Gabaon, which is feigned to be accessible only by the seven degrees that compass the winding staircase." These are the degrees terminating in the 'Royal Arch.' Gabaon is defined to signify 'a high place.' ['Scotch Rite Masonry Illustrated.' 14° GRAND ELECT, PERFECT AND SUBLIME MASON Volume I, page 351].
71 A.R. for Andreas Ritter St. Andrews Knight.

72 Blind Obedience - Sign of a 'Minerval,' cover the eyes with the hand.
73 Scottish Knight

Chanc: Then answer the following questions, seeking brother.

Seekers: (Replies shortly) Yes! Yes! Yes!

Magus: Then let the seeking brother and comrade in arms start the journey in the innermost circle, and give him the password so that he may gain admission! (Chanc: goes away softly).

Cerem: (Whispers to the applicant, to repeat aloud with him three times, both of them seeking their way to the circle. "Rabboni, Rabboni, Rabboni, and Lodge No. XX" At the third time they all three stand in the middle, 4 long steps from the Altar).

Magus: (4 # 4 on the sword) who calls on our great Master in the name of the N.N.

Chanc: The seeking brother is called N.N. who here holds his signed oath stating that he is prepared to lay the same on the altar.

Magus: Then give him light on his way. Let him reach his goal under the arch of friendship through the 4 great steps. At the same time listen to the words which I hear read to you: (Exodus III - 13)

"And Moses said unto God, Behold, when I come unto the children of Israel, and shall say unto them, the God of your Fathers hath sent me unto you; and they shall say to me, What is his name? what shall I say unto them? And God said unto Moses, I am that I am: and he said. Thus shalt thou say unto the children of Israel, I am hath sent me unto you."
(At the 4 step the seeker repeats, I am that I am)

(C. had previously taken off the bandages, covering his eyes. All three formed a royal arch or arch of friendship, after the 4th Ch. & C. Step back. During these steps, soft music)

Magus: Brother N.N. by means of close friendship, accompanied by tried brethren and in the name of the Great I am that I am, draw nearer to the inner most circle in your search after truth.

Are you prepared, brother N.N. to repeat here, strengthened by your former vow, that you desire to be initiated, if so reply in a loud voice "Yes!" - Yes - Yes!

Magus: (Covers himself).[74] Then kneel down. Place your right hand on this sword and upon this book, which contains our laws, and repeat what I shall say to you:

"I .... N.N. .... Herewith do solemnly promise to faithfully fulfil the Reverses,[75] I also promise the most faithful obedience to the illustrious heads of the Order of Illuminati and the true mandates of the same Br. ......A.R...... (N.N.) who stands before me. To love my brothers in arms and brethren of the Order as myself and to strive diligently for the sacred work of the Order. I also promise that I will rather suffer death than betray the secrets of my friend or his wife's honour. In sign hereof I grasp this dagger and pierce therewith this skull. May a like overtake me should I ever become a traitor! Amen!"[76]

Magus: Therewith admit thee N.N. as a Schotten or Andreas Knight of the High Illuminati Order. By the power of my office lent to me by the M.M. Be a striver after truths, and brotherly love. May thy friend and his wife's honour be dear to thee. (With a sword, head, heart and right shoulder). I take from thee the symbol of humility and clothe thee with the robe of honour of a Scottish Knight, the colour of which shall be to thee as a symbol of hope, purity based on hope, so that it may help thee in finding the truth. (This is done)

Magus: I embrace you with a brotherly kiss, so that you may always remain the friend of your friends. (This is done).

Magus: Stand up 'Notuma' N.N. and receive the old master word (in the ear Adonai giving back to the other Jehovah. It is only given in the Lodges, the speaker says "A" the replier replies in his ear "J").[77]

Magus: Whoever does not reply 'J' is no real and true Schotten of the Illuminati! Outside the Lodges one makes himself known by saying: **'I know J and G and the flaming star.' 'Gomer'** is an outside word. Let yourself be known to the H.B.B.G.Ch. & G. Cer. (This is done).[78] Now you must receive a pair of white gloves, wear the same as a symbol of the purity of your hands from all falseness.

END OF RITUAL SCHOTTEN GRAD

75 Probably a translation or transcription error?

76 A Skull is mentioned in several places in many of the old unworked grades of the Ancient & Accepted Rite, first in 9°, then in 17° and finally in the 32°. There used to be a rite of vengeance for the dissolution of the Knights Templar and the death of the Grand Master, even to the point of stabbing a skull. These grades are no longer worked in full.

77 The word 'Notuma' is simply an anagram on Aumont. Pierre d' Aumont 1313 who it is said to have become the first Grand Master of the Templars in Scotland, and the restorer of the Order after the death of De Molay. The letter 'A' stands for Adonai or could refer to Aumont again.

78 'J' is also used here as the initial letter of Jehovah.

74 Covers his head.

Illuminaten Orden

J. G.

Rosenkreuzer = Grad

Figure 88 - Front page of Rosenkreuzer or Rose-Croix Grade (reproduction)

RITUAL ROSENKREUZER GRAD
Rose-Croix Grade

THE PROPOSED RITUALS OF THE ORDER OF

ENGLISH ILLUMINATI 1901

ILLUMINATEN ORDEN, GERMANY, ROSENKREUZER GRAD ROSE-CROIX GRADE

The original German Rosenkreuzer Grad ritual, is in a red A4 cover, with typed text and with the bottony cross in the centre, (see fig 88). The translation of the Rose-Cross Grade is in William Wynn Westcott's handwriting on six pieces of A4 exercise paper. With faint green/blue ruled lines and a pencil ruled margin down the left hand side. It is written using a quill in black ink. The original cover page now has a Quatuor Coronati Lodge No. 2076 oval stamp mark and has the following inscription inside, 'Sent by Theodore Reuss to William Wynn Westcott.' The Library and Museum of Freemasonry online entry for the manuscript says: 'Reuss, Theodor, 1855-1923, the former owner Westcott, W. Wynn (William Wynn), 1848-1925. The current owner is Quatuor Coronati Lodge, No. 2076, London, as the Donor.

INTRODUCTION

I now present below the actual ritual for the English Illuminati Rose-Croix. But before I do, I would like to make a comment on the similarity of this ritual to that which was already in use in England during the period we are discussing, because, it shows why Westcott was uncomfortable and could not 'work' it as part of an Illuminati system.

The ceremonies of the English Illuminati Rose-Croix or more properly, the revived 'Prussian Illuminati' and the 'Ancient & Accepted Rite 18°' are not the same! But they are very similar. The biggest similarities between the two rituals are in the 'opening' and 'closing.' The biggest difference between the two is that in the 'Supreme Council 33°' of the 'Ancient & Accepted Rite 18°' the ceremony confers masonic knighthood on the aspirant. In the English Illuminati Rose-Croix ceremony it does not confer Knighthood. On the last page of the Illuminati Rose-Croix ritual it confirms this, by saying you are admitted as a companion:

In my official capacity I now admit you as a lawful perfected companion in the illustrious Knighthood of the Rose-Cross of the honourable and mighty Order of the Illuminate.

One paragraph further on, the ritual itself gives Westcott all the ammunition he ever needed not to go ahead with the Illuminati system in England, when towards the end of the Illuminati Rose-Croix ceremony the ritual includes the lines:

In the chapters of the well-known English 'Ancient & Accepted Masons,' the degree is called Knights of the Pelican and Eagle, Prince of the Rose-Cross.

So, we know that the members of the Revived Illuminati at least knew where their Rose-Croix degree ceremony had come from and that is the English 'Supreme Council 33°,'18th degree. This would have made it much easier for Westcott to come to the correct conclusions, if they had only told him.

To repeat myself, the English Illuminati confers its masonic knighthood in the previous grades of 'Novice Notuma' and the 'Andreas Knight Grade' or the 'Scottish Grade' of 'Novice and Knight.'

What then is the purpose of the 'English Illuminati Rose-Croix Grade?' The 'Revived Illuminati' ceremony then goes on to confer many Rosicrucian secrets. I believe that it is in explaining the alchemical and cabalistic explanation of the Logos or Grand Word. The 'Ancient & Accepted Rite 18°' ceremony does not really use the name Logos in the same sense in its ceremony, but the 'Revived Illuminati' ceremony does give more Rosicrucian explanation of the 'Word' I.N.R.I.! The word was already used in the 'Andreas Knight Grade.' Having completed a side by side comparison of the two rituals here is the detail:

THE NUMBER OF WORDS IN EACH

	A. & A. R. 18°	English Illuminati	
OPENING	514 words	460 words	Same
INTERMEDIATE	904 words	0	N/A
1ST POINT	2,469 words	661 words	Similar
2ND POINT	2,119 words	177 words	Similar
3RD POINT & Agape	642 words	0	N/A
CLOSING	220 words	157 words	Same
	5,568 total	1,455 total	

A SIDE-BY-SIDE COMPARISON

OPENING: The ceremonies are almost the same and there are fifty words difference. I do not know if it is because of the translation between English and German, but the 'Ancient & Accepted Rite 18°' uses the title 'Most Worthy Sovereign' for the head of the Rose Croix chapter and the translator has used 'Most Mighty Sovereign' for the 'English Illuminati Rose-Croix' rituals. There is nothing much in common until the section that starts; "what is the hour?" The reply from the 1st General is the same when describing the veil, Temple, rent in twain, darkness, blazing star, cubic stone, blood, water and the Word is lost.

INTERMEDIATE DEGREES: There is no conferring of the Intermediate Degrees in the English Illuminati Rose-Croix ceremony. There is a single mention in the English Illuminati Rose-Croix ceremony of Babylon, which is also mentioned in the 'Ancient & Accepted Rite 18°' Intermediate Degrees, but not in the same context and nothing else at all, as the aspirant is already considered a Knight, an 'Andreas Knight.'

1st POINT: The questioning of the knight is very similar before the journey around the seven circles, where the candidate is in search of the three virtues Faith, Hope and Charity or F. H. C. In the English Illuminati rituals, the virtue 'Charity' is instead called 'Love.' I believe this is because in the German language 'Charity' is called 'love' or 'Liebe,' the words in German have virtually the same meaning. The English Illuminati Rose-Croix oath is completely different at the altar. Both ceremonies quote Isaiah LIII, 4-5 but the 'Ancient & Accepted Rite 18°' quotes a little bit more besides. As you can see from the table of words used the 'Ancient & Accepted Rite 18°' has 2,469 words and the English Illuminati only 661 words.

2nd POINT: there is no detailed explanation or 'rubric' in the 'English Illuminati Rose-Croix' ceremony. The 'rubric' is the words used, to explain to people conducting a ritual 'how to' do

it.' For example, there is no rubric to explain the carpet used with a sphinx or how the ladder is introduced to the ceremony in the 'English Illuminati ceremony'. In both ceremonies Raphael guides the aspirant in a similar way and the same words are used in both ceremonies. As previously mentioned, in the 'Ancient & Accepted Rite 18°' ceremony, there is no mention of the 'Logos' or 'Shibboleth' that is used in 'English Illuminati Rose-Croix' ritual. But both ceremonies refer to the Alpha and Omega. There is no conferral of knighthood in the 'English Illuminati Rose-Croix' ceremony; you only become a 'lawful perfected companion.' The three signs that are exchanged are very similar but not exactly the same. There is no similarity at all between the 'English Illuminati Rose-Croix' ceremony after the Grand Word, I.N.R.I. is communicated and the end of the 'Ancient & Accepted Rite 18°' 2nd Point. The 'English Illuminati' ceremony has 177 words and the 'Ancient & Accepted Rite 18°' the 2nd Point has 2,119 words.

3rd POINT: One of the biggest differences is that The English Illuminati Rose-Croix ritual has no 3rd Point or sharing of the Agape.

CLOSING: There is some similarity in closing in both ceremonies. The English Illuminati ritual without the prayer has 157 words and the Ancient & Accepted Rite 18° has 220 words.

What follows next are the English translations as transcribed by Westcott of the Revived Illuminati sections of the Rose-Croix Ritual. I have reproduced the translation errors and the translator's English, which may have been improved at some later stage by Westcott before these rituals were actually used. The text in black is that spoken during the ceremony. The text in red is the original rubric of the ceremony, which I have highlighted to avoid any confusion and help the reading of the ceremonies. My notes have been highlighted in blue to distinguish them from the original ceremony.

OPENING OF THE ROSE-CROIX GRADE

Officers of the Lodge:

M.M.S∴ Most Mighty Sovereign, S∴ (Sovereign)

I.G.M∴ Illustrious Great Marshall, M∴ (Marshall)

R∴ Raphael

"Most mighty sovereign of the R.C. degree and most Illustrious Great Marshall, invite the members of our knighthood to a solemn chapter of the Rose-Cross!"

I.G.M∴ M.W.S∴ the members of our knighthood of the R.C. are gathered and await your commands.

M.W.S∴ I.G.M∴ assure yourself of the fact that the chapter is secure against the profane. (This is done)

I.G.M∴ The Chapter is secure in the East and West, in the North and South.

M.M.S∴ Are all the knights in order? (All make the sign and give the word)

I.G.M∴ All the knights are in order and I give the great password.

M.M.S∴ I.G.M∴ What hour is it?

I.G.M∴ It is the ninth hour of the day!

S∴ Then it is about the hour when the veil curtain of the Temple was rent in twain and when darkness overspread covered the earth, when the pillars were split, true Light departed from us, the altar was thrown down, the Blazing Star was eclipsed, the Cubic Stone pours forth blood and water, the 'Word' was lost to us! and despair and tribulation sat heavily upon us.
Consumatum est![79] We swayed with grief. My companions and knights, prepare to humble yourselves, and to prostate yourselves before Him who is, and was, and evermore will be!

Companions: M.W.S∴ we are prepared! (All kneel to the East, bowing three times)

S∴ (Prayer) Eternal, unfathomable Spirit, who hast created everything that is, and who keeps and governs it, truth is thy inextinguishable light, and justice thy law, whereby thou alone announces thy presence, let the first shine forth, and the latter govern us in all our undertakings and dealings, so that in due time we may stand before thy judgement seat as worthy servants of thy power and glory! Amen! (Takes the Bible, 3# swings it over his head and the altar, and speaks). Rex regnantium et Dominus dominantium,[80]

All: (Repeat beat their breast, bows to the Earth three times and stands up)

S∴ (Reads). Mathew III 13-17.
"Then cometh ...., in who I am well pleased."
Our great Emanuel, give us hope, faith and love! Amen! (Raps 7 times, then all make the finger sign and shout 3 times).[81]

All: Hosanna! Hosanna! Hosanna!

S∴ (Makes the finger sign) Honoured companions, knights and brethren, with strengthened faith, renewed hopes and greater love we will commence our task today, and I herewith declare this chapter of the Rose Cross opened, in the name of the great Emmanuel. The power of my positon!
(Raps 7 times, all knights repeat with their hands)

Benedictus Dominus Deus Noster qui dedit nobis Sigum! (Makes a big cross) take your places great knights!

---

79 It is finished. John 19:30.

80 King of Kings and Lord of lords. Timothy 6:15.
81 Raise the right hand to the brow with the fingers, only the index finger being straight.

CEREMONY OF INITIATION INTO ROSE CROIX

S∴ What is the subject to-day I.G.M.?

M. A worthy Andreas Knight, whose life is well known, desires and requests the permission to become a companion and Knight of the Red Cross.

S∴ Is he thoroughly prepared to receive this high honour?

M∴ Yes

S∴ Then lead the wise and chosen Raphael to the applicant before the altar. (Raphael fetches the applicant), he raps 4#4, Illustrious replies 7 times, then outside also 7 times and Raphael calls) "Hosanna! Hosanna! Hosanna!"

M∴ (Announces to S) A Knight of the Rose Croix knocks! (Make all dark)

S∴ Let the companions lament! (Music, Death March of Brethren)

R∴ H.S.V.H.K. R.*C.* Here you see a worthy Andreas-Knight, who presents himself to the High Chapter desiring to be made a Knight of the Rose Cross.

S∴ Worthy knight, who are you?

Candidate:
I am of noble birth, from the tribe of Judea!   J.

S∴ Which is your fatherland?

Candidate: Babylon!   B.

S∴ What do you know?

Candidate: Masonry   M.

S∴ What is your grade?

Candidate: Andreas Knight of East and West of the high Order of the Illuminati!

S∴ Give me the sign! (This occurs)

S∴ How old are you?

Candidate: 33 years.

S∴ Worthy Knight, you fill me with the most complete respect, but you see us filled with sadness. All is changed, the veil in the Temple is rent, the pillars are spilt, and the 'Word' is lost!

We only have hope, that you will help us to find it again. Now will you promise to help us?

Candidate: Yes, Almighty and Wise Sovereign!

S∴ Then approach the altar; place your right hand on the book of truth, the sword and compass, and repeat the following after me:

> *"In the presence of all the Very Worthy and Illustrious Knights, I Andreas Knight, promise, as an honest man and Illuminate, to help search for the lost word, and to keep the word, when found, in spite of everything, as a secret, under the threat of being turned out of all the lodges and chapters. So help me God!" (Take hands).*
>
> *"Now follow your leader Raphael on your first journey of 33, eleven to North [Wisdom] eleven to South [Beauty] and eleven to West [Strength]!"*

(Raphael leads him slowly through a dark. room to the pillars F. H. L. and draws his attention to these letters; soft music is heard, and S: leads: Isaiah LIII, 4-5).[82]

Surely he hath borne our griefs, and carried our sorrows: yet we did esteem him stricken, smitten of God, and afflicted. But he was wounded for our transgressions, he was bruised for our iniquities: the chastisement of our peace was upon him; and with his stripes we are healed.

R∴ (For the candidate) H: G: S: I again present to you the worthy A.R∴[83]

R∴ N.N. who has completed the 33 year journey![84]

S∴ What did you discover, worthy Knight?

R∴ (For the candidate) we have searched, but only found on the pillars the 3 letters F. H. L.[85]

S∴ I congratulate you on your success, for these three letters represent the three virtues by means of which you will find that which is lost. You also travelled round 7 circles and of these 7 circles the first represents the 6 periods of the creation of the world, ...which will now come to an end with the second coming of Emmanuel. For the time will go into Eternity, which is represented by the 7th circle. Of these virtues 'Faith' is the substance of all things which we hope, the proof al all things

---

82 F. H. L. Faith, Hope and Liebe (Charity is the same as Love in German).
83 Andreas Knight.
84 N.N. is the name of the Novice in Illuminati ceremonies.
85 F.H.L. translated from the German as 'Liebe' or 'Love' or 'Charity,' hence forward.

which we do not see; 'Hope' puts no man to shame. 'Love' is the true self denied.[86]

R∴ (Soft music during the wandering) I lead you through the valley of deepest night, of death, and of greatest pain; but clothed with Faith, Hope and Love we overcome all despair and attain the clearer heights where our heavenly Master has reigned for all eternity. Almighty Sovereign, the worthy Knight has passed with me through the valley of death; strengthened by the virtues of F. H. L. he did not stumble, but reached his goal, and he now demands his reward! (All illuminated as brightly as possible)

S∴ My Worthy Knight, whence do you come?

R∴ (For candidate) Through night and darkness.

S∴ What was your support?

R∴ (As above) The example of our Saviour!

S∴ What was your object?

R∴ The lost word!

S∴ As so far you have found and followed the right path, you are doubtless prepared to ascend the ladder of secrecy which leads to the temple of perfection.

Step = what is the name of the virtue which leads from Earth to heaven?   F.*

Step = which virtue comforts you in sorrow and in shame?   H.*

Step = which is the greatest human virtue?
                                                        L.*

Step = whence come you? (Reply)   Judea.

Step = through which town did you come?

                                        Nazareth.

Step = who led you?   Raphael

Step = from what branch did you descend?

                                        Judea

Cand:
             I. N. R. I.!

S: All hail worthy Knight. You have certainly with holy zeal, found again the Lost 'Word'! Three times all hail to you, all hail to us and thrice thanks to the agony of Him who helped you and us! These four letters designate Him of whom Saint John says. In the beginning was the Word, and the Word was with God, and the Word was God. It is the 'Logos' and this true Shibboleth, the password 'Logos' will lead you to the altar. Draw near to the altar, and listen.

"I am Alpha and Omega, I am the beginning and the end, says the Lord our God!" Now kneel down."

In my official capacity I now admit you as a **lawful perfected companion** in the illustrious Knighthood of the Rose-Cross of the honourable and mighty Order of the Illuminate. It is the highest dignity which the Order can bestow, may you always show yourself worthy of it. I clothe you with the sign of this new and high honour of our Order, (Gives him the Jewel and Apron) wear it at all the Chapters of the Rose-Cross.

In the chapters of the well-known English 'Ancient & Accepted Masons,' the degree is called 'Knights of the Pelican and Eagle, Prince of the Rose-Cross.' I will now communicate to you the signs and words of this highest dignity degree of the Illuminate Order.

The first sign is generally called the sign of Adoration or of veneration!

1) Raise your eyes to heaven, clasp your hands outwards, raise them to your brow, then let them fall on your hip or sword.

2) Raise the right hand to the brow with the fingers, only the index finger being straight, as a sign that there is only ONE God![87]

3) The sign of the good shepherd: Cross the arms under the left breast; place your ear to the mouth of the other, and say: I. and N; the other replies: R. and I: to which you retort: Immanuel: the other says: Pax vobiscum. At the same time you make the second sign towards heaven, the other points downward.

The last and greatest secret of all philosophical masonry and cabalistic Rose-Cross Orders is contained in this key-word of the great Order of Illuminati. This word now discovered I.N.R.I. has a threefold meaning:

---

86 'L' is Love.

87 The finger sign is also mentioned in the opening.

1) Jesus Nazarenus Rex Judaeorum

2) Igne Natura Renovatur Integra (All Nature Will Be Renewed by Fire; an alchemists' aphorism)[88]

3) The climax of all occult sciences according to the poem of Hermes.

I. **Ioithi.** The active creative principle, the manifestation of the fructifying and generating principle.
N. **Nain**. The passive principle, the form for all generated and created matters.
R. **Rasith**. A combination of the above two principles, and the constant eternal transformation of all created things.
I. **Ioithi.** Again the creative, godly principle as a symbol of the eternal circle of the world and all things created.[89]

The sphinx on the carpet is the emblem of I.N.R.I.

I. = Human head; N. = Bull; R. = Lion; I. = Eagle

The odours which we have to use for set purposes in the Order are:

Sulphur - Aloe - Storax - Laurel - Musk - Juniper

*   *   *   *   *   *

Saturn - Jupiter - Mars - Sun - Venus - Mercury

And Magnetic stone = Moon!

When entering and leaving the chapter R.C. meeting and when the nights stand in order, they make the sign of the Good Shepherd and give the entrance password, 'Golgotha'. The great legal password is 'Logos'; the holy word is 'I.N.R.I.'!

Take your place in the West amongst the crusaders of the high and illustrious knights.

CLOSING OF THE ROSE-CROIX GRADE

S∴ I.G.M., what is the hour?

M∴ M.M.S., it is the hour when the holy word was found; when the cubic stone was changed to the mystic rose; when the night of egotism was overcome by the new commandment; "Love one another, and Love thy neighbour as thyself."

R∴ (Reads: St. Mark XIV, 15 - 20)
(This is generally left out)

> *"And he said to them, Go into all the world and proclaim the gospel to the whole creation. Whoever believes and is baptized will be saved, but whoever does not believe will be condemned. And these signs will accompany those who believe: in my name they will cast out demons; they will speak in new tongues; they will pick up serpents with their hands; and if they drink any deadly poison, it will not hurt them; they will lay their hands on the sick, and they will recover. So then the Lord Jesus, after he had spoken to them, was taken up into heaven and sat down at the right hand of God. And they went out and preached everywhere, while the Lord worked with them and confirmed the message by accompanying signs."*

S∴ Brethren and comrades of the high and illustrious knighthood of the Red-Cross let us carry this new commandment in our hearts, so that it may live in our deeds for the good of mankind. Amen!

All: So mote it be: (Clap seven times, all make the sign of the good shepherd and shout)
"Hosanna! Hosanna! Hosanna!"

S∴ Pax vobiscum! - 0 - 00 0000![90]

M∴ (Repeats) - 0 - 00 0000! (knocks)

S∴ I close this High Chapter of the Rose Croix in the name of the Great Emanuel!

Peace be with you!

END OF ROSENKREUZER GRAD RITUAL

---

88 Pike Albert, 1857, Magnum Opus, features these words in his 18° Rose Croix lecture.

89 Another Hermetic traditional name of I.N.R.I. One suggestion is: The whole purpose of the alchemical and Cabalistic symbols is to awaken the inter-physical cosmological Christ. The process is designed to achieve this by awakening the aspect of the Godhead within the aspirant. Alexi Petrou 2015.

90 Peace with you.

Chapter IV - Revived Illuminati Regulations and Rituals

J.　G.

Ritual der Synoden

Figure 89 - Front page of Synods Ritual (reproduction)

RITUAL DE SYNODEN
Ritual of the Synods

THE PROPOSED RITUALS OF THE ORDER OF ENGLISH ILLUMINATI 1901

ILLUMINATEN ORDEN, GERMANY, RITUAL DE SYNODEN (SYNODS)

The front cover of the original German Minerval Grad ritual is opaque beige paper with the Dresden Illuminati logo in the middle of the page with the bottony cross in the centre, (see fig 89).

The translation of the Synods Grade is in William Wynn Westcott's handwriting on five pieces of A4 exercise paper. With faint green/blue ruled lines and a pencil ruled margin down the left hand side. It is written using a quill in black ink. The original cover page now has a Quatuor Coronati Lodge No. 2076 oval stamp mark and has the following inscription inside, "Sent by Theodore Reuss to William Wynn Westcott." The Library and Museum of Freemasonry online entry for the manuscript says: 'Reuss, Theodor, 1855-1923, the former owner Westcott, W. Wynn (William Wynn), 1848-1925. The current owner is Quatuor Coronati Lodge, No. 2076, London, as the Donor.

INTRODUCTION

The Synod Grade is not listed or called by this name in the Bavarian Illuminati series of grades, where it is listed as grade nine and called the Presbyter, Priest, or Epopt grade.[91]

Reuss, it would seem, only supplied Westcott with the 'Opening' and 'Closing' of the Synod Grade in 1901. Why was that? Was it perhaps only to give him a flavour of what the ceremony was like? Reading through them both, I am not so sure now! It might be that this 'opening' and 'closing' ceremony topped and tailed the several lectures that this grade already consisted of in the Bavarian Illuminati degrees. It might have been these longer parts, consisting of the lectures that were offered in German to Westcott in July 1902 to complete all the rituals he had already received in February 1902.

In fact there are no 'opening' or 'closing' ceremonies to be found in any of the Bavarian Presbyter, Priest, or Epopt grades in the books written by Barruel, 1799, Heckethorn, 1875 and Wages, Markner & Singh-Anand, 2015, so this is another completely new part of an Illuminati ceremony.

The word 'Synod' is mentioned in the Bavarian Illuminati rituals, as the name of the assemblies of the Epopt or Priest grade, which would indicate that they are based on the same construct. Especially as they both have the same kinds of qualification for membership. This was to have received both the Minerval and Andreas Knight Grades.

Why are they named differently? The Epopt ceremony was not liked very much by Weishaupt when it was finished, so he asked Baron Knigge to re-write it again in 1783. This directly resulted in Knigge leaving the Order for good. Is this Synod grade perhaps one of Knigge's versions of this grade used by others much later, deliberately renamed Synod, because it was a masonic version of Weishaupt's much more 'priestly' lectures, that perhaps Knigge did not like much?

The Synod grade name does, however, appear much later in the Illuminati rituals of the O.T.O. in 1925, in their collection of grades and degrees, so this is not the only appearance of this degree.

In the Bavarian Illuminati series of grades, the Synod grade was the sixth grade and would have been in their 'Third Order' called the 'Lesser Mystery Class' of the Presbyters, Epopt or Priest grade. The English Illuminati rituals did not have this 'Order' distinction.

The Regent or grade seven in the Bavarian Illuminati 'Greater Mysteries Class,' was not supplied by Reuss, even though Westcott was named a 'Regent,' as such. However Westcott only officially accepted the position of Regent for England and Ireland in October 1902 at the end of the process.

I believe that Reuss would have thought that Westcott did not really need this particular ritual, because he was already the Provincial head of the Illuminati Order. Unless of course Westcott really did want it, so he could eventually appoint Regents in other countries outside of Europe, in the British Empire for example? This may have been a small issue or a big issue in the scheme of things. In the S.R.I.A., Westcott was already negotiating for

---

91 See Chapter V section 353: Organisation list of Bavarian Illuminati Grade Structure and the merged grades on the next page.

several colleges in India, one in Durban, South Africa, another in Buena Aires, South America, to go alongside his existing Australian College and the proposed college in New Zealand. In fact, in a letter to Reuss in 1902, Westcott calls himself the 'Magus Mundo', or Magus of the World!

Another reason for only giving Westcott the 'opening' and 'closing' ceremonies may have been that the Bavarian Illuminati Presbyter, Epopt or Priest grade is very long indeed and the second part of it is all read in Latin. For example, Abbe Barruel said in his book (Barruel, 1799) that "the discourse of the Hierophant" takes two hours to read and during his preamble in the book he suggests that meetings start in the afternoon, because the ceremonies are so long.

What is certain is that they are both different ceremonies. The Bavarian Epopt grade expresses 'Universal Love' and that 'fathers shall become the Priests and the absolute Sovereigns of their family' and that one of their 'great mysteries' is that 'Reason shall become the only book of the law.'

The English Illuminati 'Synod Grade' 'opening' and 'closing' ceremonies have a completely different theme running through them, nothing like Weishaupt's and are a very masonic type of ritual, using several different officers to conduct the ceremony instead of just one person (the Hierophant) in the 'Bavarian Illuminati' who reads all the large passages. The Revived English Illuminati continues the Knights Templar theme of 'Novice Notuma' and the J.G. letters standing for 'Jehovah' and 'Gomer' the son of 'Japheth' from the 'St. Andrew Knight Grade' and develops the Teutonic Knights story of Noah's prodigy from a Teutonic Knight point of view.

The main word communicated in the Bavarian 'Epopt ceremony' is *I.N.R.I.* meaning Iesus Nazarenus Rex Iudaeorum. This is the Grand word already used in both the English Illuminati 'Andreas Knight Grade' and the 'Rose-Croix Grade' ceremony. The English Illuminati Synod Grade,' however, also introduces a new password 'Mizpah,' a word from the Bible meaning a 'watchtower' and is also the name of a certain pile of stone or stone pillar set up in Gilead, marking a 'covenant' between Jacob and Laban his father in law, to honour his daughter and all women, Genesis 31.49. It is then linked to a second 'covenant' made by the Gileaditish general Jephthah to help him defeat the Amorites. Jephthah was not a Semite but a Noachite from the prodigy of Noah's line of Japheth and Gomer. The town of Gilead is where Jephthah lived and where the moral lesson of ominously keeping your oath or covenants and that of others, should enable you to keep your oath even at their own peril.[92]

The most senior member of the Synod in this grade was called the Hierophant and this title is used in both rituals, which refers back to the chief priests in the 'Eleusinian Mysteries'. The Eleusian ceremonies were held every year in honour of Demeter and Persephone. This seems to be the only link back to Ancient Greece in the Illuminate rituals.

We must assume from the four 'English Illuminati' grade ceremonies found in the Library and Museum of Freemasonry, that the Revised Illuminati, reorganised the original thirteen grades, into four grades with only one grade in each Order. Probably combining the four Minerval grades into one and completely dropping the three masonic grades or 'craft degrees' from the Illuminate system. The two Scottish Knight Grades merge into one grade. The Lesser and greater priest grades become one, no longer called Epopt but now Synod. The Regent grade seems to be incorporating the Magus or Philosopher and the Rex or King grade of the ruling Areopagite and one Supreme Magus are selected from these grades. See below for how the grades were merged:

I. The Nursery-Minerval (Brethren of Minerva).
II. Masonry-Illuminatus Dirigens. (Director or Scotch or Andreas Knight).
III. Mysteries-Synod-Presbyter, Epopt or Priest.
IV. Areopagite. (Grand Lodge)-Regent-Provincial Superior.

What I cannot explain is, why if you add the English Illuminati Synod/Epopt 'opening' and 'closing' ceremony to the Heckethorn revelations and the Bavarian Illuminati lectures, from *The Secret School of Wisdom;* do you only now get the whole of the Synod/Epopt ceremony?

Westcott was not supplied with the whole rituals by Reuss in 1902, only the 'opening' and 'closing' of a Synod. However, the names of the officers involved here seem different to the others. Heckethorn supplies us with a description of the regalia and arrangement of the apartments as well as the ritual, but not the 'opening' and 'closing' of a Synod. While in the book *Secret School of Wisdom,*[93] they do not have the 'opening' and 'closing' for the Lesser Priest (Presbyter) Grade, but do have the lectures.[94]

From Heckethorn's Epopt (or priest), we can see that the grade consisted of two lectures and an admonishment, with the repeating of the word I.N.R.I. as the only secret and no oath! As we do not have the ceremony, only the 'opening' and 'closing,' we do not know if the Revived Illuminati had an oath in this grade.

---

92 See Judges 11:29-40.

93 Wages, Markner & Singh-Anand, 2015.
94 *The Secret Societies of All Ages,* Heckethorn C.W., 1875.

OPENING OF THE RITUAL DE SYNODEN

Officers of the Synod Grade:

H. - Hierophant, who is the leader of the Synods
T. - Treasurer:
S. - Secretary:

Inside archive folder Presented by the Hierophant (Sometimes called Altmeister) takes his stand at a white covered table on which stand two unlighted lights. To the right (side) the Treasurer, to the left (side) Secretary.

Secretary: What is the duty of the Illuminati before opening the Synod?

S. To assure oneself that everyone who is present is a lawful member of the Order.

H. Fulfil this duty.

S. I beg of those present to prove to me by means of the sign, that they are lawful Minerva members.

All. (Make the blinding sign).[95]

H. Ask for the password (The treasurer passes it to his right-hand neighbour, and (so) on until it comes to the turn of the Secretary, who gives it to H)

S. All the members present are lawful Minerva members, and I give you the password of 'MIZPAH.'[96]

H. Peace be with you! Dear brethren of the honourable Order of the Illuminati, do you recognise me as the lawful Great-Magus of the Illuminati Order, and as such justified in conducting this Synod?

All. Yes!

H. Then I will clothe myself in the raiment of a Hierophant, who is the leader of the Synods, and I command you to clothe yourselves with symbols of your grades, in order to start the proceedings worthily. **Bro. S.** Where will the H. step?

S. Towards morning!

H. Why?

S. In order that he may be near the very source of light to show the Minervals the way in which they can come out of the dark into the clearness and from clearness to light.

H. How can this occur?

S. By means of directions and examination of the Minerva's, and by opening the Synods.

H. For this purpose I require your agreement, for without innate harmony I cannot conduct the work, nor can I promise and open the Synods.

All. We feel our selves quite in harmony with you.

H. Bros. Treas. & Sec., then help me to open the Synod.

(Secretary lights the candle to the left, treasurer that to the right of H. raps and all rise & speaks)

H. No commencement and no end limit's the deeds of the Almighty! No short duration of the times measures the eternal workings of nature. Where ever we look God's laws are practised. Whoever acknowledges them, acknowledges Him! Eternal source of light, enlighten our understanding and strengthen our Will in the fulfilment of your laws, so that we may work untiringly and steadfastly in the building of your temple, to which you have called us! Amen!

All. Amen (Everyone presses hands simultaneously right and left)

H. (after a short pause) our work today is; etc. etc.

---

95 Sign of a Minerval, cover the eyes with the hand. The Illuminati motto :P.M.C.V. Per me Coeci Vident, "Through me let the blind see."

96 Mizpah is called a watchtower a stone or pillar raised to mark the covenant between Jacob and Laban (Father in law) at Gilead. Genesis 31:49 Therefore was the name of it called Galeed and Mizpah; for he said, The LORD watch between me and thee, when we are absent one from another. Gilead/Galeed. This is also the town where Jephthah resided, and where he assumed the command of the Israelites in a time of national danger. Here he made his rash vow; and here his daughter submitted to her mysterious fate (Judges 10:17 ; Judges 11:11 Judges 11:34).

CLOSING RITUAL DE SYNODEN

(After the work and after all business has been transacted)

H. Can anyone suggest anything which might further our today's work?

(If all are silent or after considering suggestions)

Then help me to close the Synod. For what purpose are we gathered together?

S. To find the most holy in the temple of the Eternal, and to comprehend same.

H. When shall we succeed in our purpose?

S. The powers of mankind and his final purpose are reckoned out and measured far beyond the short span of this earthly life.

H. In the same way our works and our researches are measured out beyond the short span of a Synod meeting and we must interrupt our work at the correct time in order that at a later hour we may continue our work with renewed vigour. Let us extinguish the lights, for the night refreshes mankind for fresh deeds, orderly, dear Minerva's!

S. (Extinguishes his light, H. raps once and speaks)

H. The millions of worlds which we shall see rolling above our heads at night announce to us the presence of the Eternal!

Treasurer. (Extinguishes his light and H. speaking and again rapping once)

H. Rest, love and bliss be the price of our work accomplished this day. Amen

All. (Shake hands simultaneously right and left so that at the time of shaking hands a strong chain is formed from H. around the entire Synod and back again to H)

H. MIZPAH! Peace be with you.

END OF RITUAL DE SYNODEN

Chapter V

Heckethorn's Bavarian Illuminati Rituals

HECKETHORN'S BAVARIAN ILLUMINATI

THE SECRET SOCIETIES OF ALL AGES AND COUNTRIES.
Written by Charles W. Heckethorn.
Published in 1897
Book 1, starting on page 395

Commentary

I have retained Heckethorn's numbering of the sections that appear in his book. Before the publishing of *The Secret Wisdom School*[97] in 2015, there were no reliable sources for authentic rituals of the original Bavarian Illuminati. Virtually all the other sources of the rituals came from the Illuminati's detractors and the vast majority of authors have used them, like from Robinson 1789 and by Barruel, 1799. In the absence of the full EPOPT GRADE ceremony and any mention of the REGENT GRADE as part of the revived English Illuminati rituals, I had always intended, therefore, to insert these rituals found in Heckethorn's book, to compare them with the English Illuminati rituals, as both rituals seem thin and there is no real detail. However, now we have three versions to compare to those of the Illuminati detractors.

The Masonic grades and Scottish grades came from Baron von Knigge's masonic order, that Weishaupt was admitted into known as 'The Rite of Strict Observance,' which much later became the C.B.C.S. in Switzerland.

I now present a transcription of Heckethorn's work, *The Secret Societies of all Ages and Countries* published in 1897.[98]

THE TERM ILLUMINATI

Section 351: The Term Illuminati. The name of 'Illuminati' has frequently been adopted by various sects. The end of the sixteenth century saw the Alombrados in Spain and in 1654 the Guerinets were founded in France, both societies of visionaries and ghost-seers. In the second half of the last century there was an association of mystics existing under that name in Belgium. Other fraternities, calling themselves Illuminati, and formed in more recent times, will be found mentioned in this work; but the society of which I am about to speak now is the best known of all Illuminati Orders.

FOUNDATION

Section 352: Foundation of the Order. Adam Weishaupt a student in the University of Ingolstadt, learned and ambitious, and attracted by that love of mystery which is a prominent characteristic of youth, meditated the formation of a philosophico-political sect. When twenty-two years of age he was elected Professor of Canon Law in the same University, a chair which had for twenty years been filled by the Jesuits; hence their rage against, and persecution of, Weishaupt, which he met boldly, returning hatred with hatred, and collecting partisans. The great aversion he then conceived for the Jesuits appears in many of the statutes of the Order he founded. Jesuits, he often declares, are to be avoided like the plague.

The sect of the Illuminati was founded in 1776 by Weishaupt, who adopted the pseudonym of Spartacus, but it was years before its ritual and constitution were finally settled. Weishaupt, in order the better to succeed, connected himself with the Freemasons, by entering the lodge 'Theodore of Good Counsel,' of Eclectic Masonry, [The Rite of Strict Observance] at Munich, and attempting to graft Illuminism on Freemasonry. Many members of the craft, misled by the construction of his first degrees, entered the Order; but when they found that Weishaupt meant real work and not mere play, they hung back. The society was instituted for the purpose of lessening the evils resulting from the want of information, from tyranny, political and ecclesiastical.

ORGANISATION

Section 353: Organisation. The society was by its founder divided into classes, each of which was again subdivided into grades, in the following manner:

---

97 Wages, Markner & Singh-Anand, 2015, *Secret School of Wisdom*, London: Ian Allan.

98 Heckethorn C.W., 1897, *The Secret Societies of All Ages and Countries*.

BAVARIAN ILLUMINATI GRADE STRUCTURE

THE NURSERY:

1. *Preparatory Literary Essay*
2. *Novitiate (Novice)*
3. *Minerval (Brethren of Minerva, Academy of Illuminism)*
4. *Illuminatus Minor*

MASONRY SYMBOLIC:

This grade was conferred only on such persons as by high intellectual attainments, social position, and tried fidelity, was considered capable of advancing the objects of the Order.

5. *Apprentice*
6. *Fellow-Craft*
7. *Master Mason*

SCOTTISH:

8. *Illuminatus Major or Scotch Novice*
9. *Illuminatus Dirigens or Scotch Knight*

MYSTERIES:

Lesser Mysteries:

10. *Presbyter, Epopt or Priest.*
11. *Prince or Regent.*

Greater Mysteries:

12. *Magus or Philosopher.*
13. *Rex or King, Homme Roi, or Areopagite*

In the Nursery and Masonry grades, the candidate was merely tried and prepared for the Mystery grades. If he was found unreliable, he was not allowed to go beyond; but if he proved an apt scholar, he was gradually initiated into the latter, where all that he had been taught before was overthrown, and radical and deistic theories and plans were unfolded, which were in 'nowise' immoral or subversive of public order, but only such as, at the present day, are held by many men of just and enlightened views.

INITIATION INTO THE GRADE OF EPOPT OR PRIEST

Section 354: Initiation into the Degree of priest. The candidate for the priesthood, the first grade in the Lesser Mysteries, was taken, with his eyes bandaged, in a carriage, following a roundabout way, to the house where the initiation was to take place.

On his arrival there his eyes were unbandage, and he was told to put on the apron of the Scotch Knight, the cross of St. Andrews, and the hat, take the sword into his hand, and wait before the first door till summoned to enter. After a while he heard a solemn voice calling:

Enter, orphan, the fathers call thee, and shut the door behind thee.

On entering he beheld a room, the walls of which were covered with rich red hangings, and splendidly illuminated.

In the background stood a throne under a canopy and in front of it a table, on which were placed a crown, sceptre, sword, valuables, and chains. The priestly vestments were displayed on a red cushion. There were no chairs in the room, but a stool without back stood at some distance from the throne, facing it.

The candidate, on being introduced, was told to choose between the things on the table or the vestments on the cushion. Should he, contrary to all expectation, declare for the crown and its concomitants, he would at once be expelled; but if he chose the priestly dress, he was addressed with:

All hail, thou noble one!

And invited to take a seat on the stool and listen to the explanation of his future duties, which, as intimated above, were simply to act as an instructor of the uninitiated.

The lecture being ended, a door at the back was opened, and the friend who had introduced the candidate entered in the priest's dress, which consisted of a white woollen toga, descending to the feet; the neck and sleeves were edged with scarlet silk ribbons, a silk girdle of the same colour encircled the waist.

The deacon alone had, moreover, a red cross, about a foot long, on his left breast, fig 90. The candidate was led into the inner room, the door of which had in the meantime been opened, and in which was seen an altar, covered with red cloth; above it hung a painted or carved crucifix.

On the altar itself were placed the book of the ritual, a Bible bound in red, a small glass dish with honey, and a glass jug with milk in it. A burning lamp hung over the head of the deacon, who faced the altar; the priests sat on both sides, on red-cushioned benches.

The candidate was admonished, and promised to renounce the enemies of mankind, evil desires, the spirit of oppression, and deception; having done this, he was divested of his Masonic clothing, and having promised in presence of the crucifix to be faithful to the Order, the assistants put on him the priestly dress, and then let him eat some of the honey and drink some of the milk, as a sealing of their covenant.

The priest's sign was laying both hands in the form of a cross flat on the head; the grip consisted in presenting a fist, with the thumb held straight up; the other would then make a fist, pressing it on that presented to him, but so as to enclose the vertically presented thumb. The word was I.N.R.I.

This was then followed by a long lecture of a moral and scientific character.

INITIATION GRADE OF REGENT

Section 355: Initiation into the Degree of Regent. This grade was conferred only on such persons as by high intellectual attainments, social position, and tried fidelity, was considered capable of advancing the objects of the Order. [Like Westcott]

The place of reception consisted of three rooms. In the last there stood a raised richly-decorated red throne under a canopy for the Provincial; to the right stood a white column, about seven feet high, on which was placed a crown, resting on a red cushion; suspended from the column were a shepherd's crook of white wood and an artificial palm branch. On the left hand stood a table with a red cover, on which were placed the garments of the Regent, which consisted of a kind of cuirass made of white leather, with a red cross on it.[99]

Over this was worn a white cloak, with another red cross embroidered on it. The collar and cuffs were red. The Regents wore tails, white hats with red feathers, and red laced half-boots on their feet. [Similar to C.B.C.S. regalia today] The cross on the cuirass of the Provincial was irradiated with golden rays.

The room was hung with red, and well lighted up. The Provincial alone occupied it, seated on the throne; the other Regents were in the middle room. The first room was set aside for preparation; it was hung with black, and in its centre, on a platform, stood a complete human skeleton, at whose feet lay a crown and a sword.

The candidate was led into this room; his hands were manacled, and he was left alone for a little while, during which time he could hear the conversation carried on in the middle room.

"Who has brought this slave hither?"
"He came and knocked."
"What does he seek?"
"Freedom; he beseeches you to free him from his bonds."

"Why does he not apply to those who have bound him?"
"They will not set him free; his servitude benefits them."
"Who has made him a slave?"
"Society, the State, false Religion."
"Does he respect persons?"
"Ask him who was the man whose skeleton he sees before him; was he a king, nobleman, or beggar?"
"He does not know; he only knows that he was a man like one of us. He wants only to be a man."
"Then let him be introduced."

The candidate was then brought into the middle, and finally into the last room, and after some more catechising, invested with the dress of the Regent. The sign was holding out both arms towards a brother; the grip taking hold of his elbows, as if to support or raise him up. The word is REDEMTIS.[100]

Figure 90 - Cross Bottony of the Bavarian Illuminati

THE GREATER MYSTERIES

Section 356: The Greater Mysteries. The Greater Mysteries, with their two grades of Magus and Rex, were never worked out by 'Philo,' as Baron de Knigge called himself.

MAGUS GRADE

But according to statements found in the writings of Weishaupt, the Magus grade was to be founded on the principles of Spinoza, showing all to be material, God and the world One, and all religions human inventions.

---

99 We can assume this would be a red bottony cross as used in the Epopt Grade. Fig 90,

100 The French word for Redemption.

A B C D E F G H I/J K L M
12 11 10 9 8 7 6 5 4 3 2 1

N O P Q R S T U V X Y Z
13 14 15 16 17 18 19 20 21 22 23 24

Figure 91 – Heckethorn, Cipher 1897

† The common cypher of the Illuminées confift in *numbers* correfponding to letters in the following order :

12.	11.	10.	9.	8.	7.	6.	5.	4.	3.	2.	1.
a.	b.	c.	d.	e.	f.	g.	h.	i.	k.	l.	m.
13.	14.	15.	16.	17.	18.	19.	20.	21.	22.	23.	24.
n.	o.	p.	q.	r.	s.	t.	u.	w.	x.	y.	z.

Figure 92 - Abbe Barruel, Cipher 1799

HOMO REX

The second, or grade of Homo Rex, taught that every peasant, citizen, or father of a family is a sovereign, as in patriarchal life, to which all mankind must be brought back, and that consequently all state authority must be abolished. Weishaupt never intended these grades to become known to any but the most trustworthy of his followers; but the discovery of his correspondence and secret papers revealed also this part of his scheme.

NOMENCLATURE

Section 357: Nomenclature and Secret Writing of the Order. The most important person of the Order after Weishaupt was Baron de Knigge, who assumed the pseudonym of 'Philo.' All the leading members equally adopted such pseudonyms.

Thus we have seen that Weishaupt took the name of Spartacus, who in Pompey's time headed the insurrection of slaves; Zwack, a lawyer, was known among the initiated as 'Cato.'' 'Nicolai' the bookseller, was known as 'Lucian.' Professor Westenrieder was known as 'Pythagoras.' The Canon Hertel, as 'Marius' and so on.

The places whence the members wrote to one another were also designated by fictitious names: thus Bavaria was called Achaia; Munich was called Athens; Frankfurt-on-the-Main became Thebes; Heidelberg, Utica; and so on.

The brethren dated their letters according to the Persian era, called after the king who began to rule in Persia in 632 before Christ, Jezdegerd, and the year began with them on the 21st March.[101]

CIPHER

They corresponded in the Illuminati, until initiated into the higher grades, in Cipher, which consisted in numbers corresponding to letters in the following order:

The Heckethorn 1897 cipher as we can see (fig 91); it is exactly the same cipher as that found in the Abbe Barruel account in 1799, (fig 92).

101 See Chapter I, Westcott's Diploma as Illuminate 1901.

HIGHER MYSTERIES CIPHER

When admitted to the higher grades, they used either the one or the other hieroglyphic ciphers, (see fig 93).

The word 'Order' [for Illuminati Order] was never written in full, but always indicated by a circle with a dot in the centre, thus. ⊙

The Order made considerable progress, including among its members priests, prelates, ministers, physicians, princes, and sovereign dukes. No doubt, few of them were initiated into the higher degrees. The [new] Elector of Bavaria became alarmed at the political tenets betrayed by some recreant brothers of the Order, and at once suppressed it in all his territories.

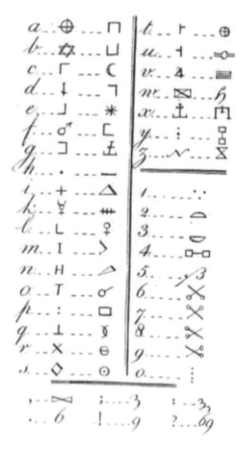

Figure 93 – Heckethorn, Scottish Knight Cipher

SECRET PAPERS AND CORRESPONDENCE

Section 358: Secret Papers and Correspondence. It was only after the suppression of the Order that the mode of initiation into the higher grades, and the true doctrines taught therein, became known. A collection of original papers and correspondence was found, by illegally searching the house of Zwack, in 1786. In the following year a much larger collection was found at the house of Baron Bassus, another member.

From these we learn that one of the chief means recommended by the leaders for the success of the Order was that of gaining over the women — not a bad plan, and not objectionable when the aim is a good one.

There is no way of influencing men so powerfully as by means of the women, says the instructor.

These should, therefore, be our chief study. We should insinuate ourselves into their good opinion, give them hints of emancipation from the tyranny of public opinion, and of standing up for themselves; it will be an immense relief to their enslaved minds to be freed from any one bond of restraint, and it will fire them the more, and cause them to work for us with zeal. &. Similar views are enunciated in a letter found among the correspondence:

The proposal of Hercules (a member not identified) to establish a Minerval school for girls is excellent, but requires circumspection..... We cannot improve the world without improving the women.....But how shall we get hold of them? How will their mothers, immersed in prejudices, consent that others shall influence their education? We must begin with grown girls. Hercules proposes the wife of Ptolemy Magus. I have no objection; and I have four stepdaughters, fine girls. The eldest in particular is excellent. She is twenty-four, has read much, and is above all prejudices. They have many acquaintances..... It may immediately be a very pretty society..... No man must be admitted. This will make them become more keen, and they will go much farther than if we were present..... Leave them to the scope of their own fancies, and they will soon invent mysteries which will put us to the blush..... They will be our great apostles. . . . Ptolemy's wife must direct them, and she will be instructed by Ptolemy, and my stepdaughters will consult with me..... But I am doubtful whether the association will be durable women are fickle and impatient. Nothing will please them but hurrying from

degree to degree; ..... which will soon lose their novelty and influence. To rest seriously in one rank, and to be silent when they have found out that the whole is a cheat (!), is a work of which they are incapable..... Nay, there is a risk that they may take it into their heads to give things an opposite turn, and then, by the arts in which they are adepts by nature, they may turn our Order upside down.

And a circumstance, affecting the personal character of the founder, which was brought to light by the discovery of the secret correspondence, but was totally unconnected with the principles advocated by the Order, contributed as much as anything else to give the Order of the Illuminati a bad name. Another circumstance was taken advantage of by the enemies of the Order to crush it.

In the handwriting of Zwack was found a description of a strong box, which, if forced open, should blow up and destroy its contents; a recipe for sympathetic ink and how to take off impressions of seals, so as to use them afterwards as seals. A collection of a hundred such impressions with a list of their different owners; a set of portraits of eighty-five ladies in Munich, with recommendations of some of them as members of a lodge of sisters illuminates; injunctions to all superiors to learn to write with both hands, and to use more than one cipher; and other matters.

REFUTATION OF CHARGES

Section 359: Refutation of Charges. So says Robison in his book the *Proofs of a Conspiracy*.[102] But he does not say that this. "Zwack, a counsellor, holding some law office," was a judge and electoral councillor, in a published letter disproved all the scandalous charges brought against the Iluminati, showing that the idea of utilising the influence of women was taken from an essay on the 'Mopses,' and that the list of recipes given above was copied by him for his own private amusement and instruction, he being a criminal lawyer and judge, from the works of the Jesuit, Kircher and other orthodox authorities, and had not the slightest connection with the Illuminati. The 'set of portraits of eighty five ladies in Munich' was actually stolen by the police from the wardrobe of von Zwack's wife!

SUPPRESSION

Section 360: Suppression. The society having been established in the small state of Bavaria, and so quickly suppressed, never made any lasting

---

102 Robison A.M. John, 1798, *Proofs of a Conspiracy.*

impression on the affairs of its own time, nor on those of the future. All the terrible effects attributed to its doctrines by Robison and other opponents of the Order existed more in the imagination of the writers than in reality.

If, as Robison says in his *Proofs,* the founders only wanted liberty to indulge their ambition and passions, they might, and, according to the secret correspondence quoted, seem to, have done so without the cumbrous machinery of a society whose members appeared so unmanageable. Weishaupt was deprived of his professor's chair, and banished from Bavaria, but with a pension of eight hundred florins, which he refused. He first went to Regensburg,[103] and afterwards entered the service of the Duke of Saxe-Gotha. Zwack also was banished, and went into the service of the Prince of Salms, who soon after had so great a hand in the disturbances in Holland. Of the German society of the Illuminati, it may truly be said that it was before its time; all enlightened nations now adopt and advocate its aims. But it was not without its influence on the French Revolution, and it may have inspired Bahrdt with the idea of the German Union.

ILLUMINATI IN FRANCE

Section 361: Illuminati in France. As early as the year 1782, Philo and Spartacus had formed the plan of introducing Illuminism into France, especially as some adepts already existed in that country. Dietrich, the Mayor of Strasbourg, was one of them; Mirabeau was another, who had been initiated at Berlin, to which city he had been sent by Louis XVI, on a secret mission. On his return to France he initiated the Abbe Talleyrand de Perigord, and Bode, privy councillor, at Weimar, known in the sect as Amelius, and William, Baron de Busch, whose sectarian name was Bayard, who shortly after came to Paris, continued the work of initiation, choosing their adepts chiefly in the masonic lodges. The most zealous and trusted members were formed into a 'Secret Committee of United Friends.' According to a book published about 1790, and entitled *Essai sur la Secte des Illumines,*[104] their manner of initiation, their oaths and doctrines, were of the most frightful kind. Let us go a little into details.

LA SECTE DES ILLUMINES
CEREMONIES OF INITIATION

362: Ceremonies of Initiation. The large mansion of Ermenonville, about thirty miles from Paris, and

belonging to the Marquis de Gerardin, who gave J. J. Rousseau during the last days of his life an asylum, and afterwards a tomb on his estate, was said to be the chief lodge of Illuminism.

The famous impostor Saint Germain presided in it. On the day of initiation the candidate was led through a long dark passage into a large hall hung with black. By the feeble light of sepulchral lamps he perceived corpses wrapped up in shrouds. In the centre of the hall stood an altar built up of human skeletons; spectres wandered through the hall and disappeared, leaving an evil odour behind.

At last two men disguised as spectres appeared, tied a pink ribbon, smeared with blood, and having the image of the Lady of Loretto [which refers to the Holy House of Loreto, the house in which Mary was born] on it, round his forehead. Into his hand they placed a crucifix, and hung an amulet round his neck.

His clothes were laid on a funeral pyre; on his body they painted crosses with blood. His 'pudenda' [Genitals] were tied up with string. Five terrific figures, armed with daggers, and clothed in bloodstained garments, approached him, fell down before him, and prayed.

At the end of an hour or so the candidate heard mourning sounds, the pyre was lit up, and his clothes burnt, A gigantic semi-transparent form arose from the flames; the five figures on the ground fell into fearful convulsions; and the voice of an invisible hierophant burst from the vault, and uttered the following oaths, which the neophyte had to repeat.

OATH OF LA SECTE DES ILLUMINES

Before the Oath is administered it is said a sword is pointed at the breast:

> *Shouldst thou become a traitor or perjurer, let this sword remind thee of each and all the members in arms against thee. Do not hope to find safety; whithersoever thou mayest fly, shame and remorse as well as the vengeance of thine unknown brothers will torture and pursue thee.*
>
> *In the name of the Crucified, I swear to sever all bonds uniting me with father, mother, brothers, sisters, wife, relations, friends, mistress, king, superiors, benefactors, or any other man to whom I have promised faith, obedience, gratitude, or service.*
>
> *Name and curse the place where you were born, so that you may dwell in another sphere, to which you will attain only after having renounced this pestilential globe, vile refuse of the heavens!*
>
> *From this moment thou shalt reveal to thy new chief all thou shalt have heard, learned,*

---

103 Regensburg was where the Rose-Croix charter was signed.
104 de Luchet, Jean-Pierre-Louis, 1789, *Essai sur la Secte des Illuminés.*

and discovered, and also to seek after and spy into things that might otherwise escape thy notice.

Honour and respect the Aqua Tofana[105] as a sure, prompt, and necessary means of purging the globe by death of those who seek to vilify the truth and seize it from our hands.

Avoid Spain, Naples, and every other accursed country; also avoid all temptation to betray what thou hast now heard. Lightning does not strike so quickly as the dagger which will reach thee wherever thou mayest be.

The candidate having repeated these words, a candlestick with seven, black wax tapers was placed before him, together with a vessel full of human blood. He had to wash himself with the blood, and drink half a glassful. Then the string round the 'pudenda'[106] was untied, he was placed in a bath, and on leaving it regaled with a dish of roots.

CREDIBILITY OF ABOVE ACCOUNT

363. Credibility of above Account. - 'No doubt all this sounds very horrible, and is very incredible. But as to the horrors, they were simply theatrical; and as to credibility, writers near the time when these horrors were said to have been practised seriously believed in them!

The Abbe Barruel, who gives some of the above details in his work,[107] does "not hesitate to consider them as historical truth." [Barruel and Robinson are the two main protractors of the Illuminati.]

The Marquis de Jouffroi, in his 'Dictionary of Social Errors,' positively asserts that the meetings at Ermenonville were scenes of the grossest debauchery. Why should we doubt that they also were occasions for all sorts of ridiculous absurdities?

Note: In the *(London) Monthly Magazine* for January 1798 there appeared a letter from Augustus Bottiger, Provost of the College of Weimar, in reply to Robison's work, charging that writer with making false statements, and declaring that since 1790 "every concern of the Illuminati has ceased." Bottiger also offered to supply any person in Great Britain, alarmed at the erroneous statements contained in the book above mentioned, with correct information.

HECKETHORN OATH OF AN ILLUMINATI

Commentary

It was C.W. Heckethorn that suggested that, "The Oath administered to the Illuminati is based upon the Oath of the Jesuits." For this reason I have included what C.W. Heckethorn wrote about the *Essai sur la Secte des Illumines* in France and their Illuminati Oath on the previous page. Below is his version of the Jesuit Oath.

I believe that both the Heckethorn oaths may have been exaggerated for a frightening effect on audiences in the 1890s. I also believe that Heckethorn used the information contained in Robison's and Burrell's accounts and not the actual rituals of the Bavarian Illuminati as his source.

THE JESUITS OATH

Heckethorn. Volume. I, Pages 285[108]

This is what Heckethorn said about the Jesuit oath in his book:

335. Initiations:

In the name of Christ crucified, I swear to burst the bonds that yet unite me to father, mother, brothers, sisters, relations, friends; to the king, magistrates, and any other authority to which I may ever have sworn fealty, obedience, gratitude, or service.

I renounce . . . the place of my birth, henceforth to exist in another sphere. I swear to reveal to my new superior, whom I desire to know, what I have done, thought, read, learnt, or discovered, and to observe and watch all that comes under my notice.

I swear to yield myself up to my superior, as if I were a corpse, deprived of life and will. I finally swear to flee temptation, and to reveal all I succeed in discovering, well aware that lightning is not more rapid and ready than the dagger to reach me wherever I may be.[109]

---

105 An imperceptibly slow poison.
106 Pudendum a person's external genitals, especially a women.
107 Barruel, Abbé Augustin, 1797-98, *Memoirs Illustrating the History of Jacobinism.*

108 Heckethorn C.W., 1897, *The Secret Societies of All Ages and Countries.*
109 Only those words above in red appear in both the French Illuminati and Jesuit oaths.

THE PROPOSED ENGLISH ILLUMINATI RITUAL OATHS

No part of the above French Illuminati oath or Jesuit oath is used in the revived Illuminati English rituals. In comparison, here is a summary of what oaths there are as documented in Chapter IV:

ENGLISH ILLUMINATI-MINERVAL OATH:

The proposed English Illuminati did not have an Oath in the Minerval Grade. "Give me your hand in place of an oath."

ENGLISH ILLUMINATI - ANDREAS KNIGHT GRADE OATH:

I .... N.N. .... Herewith do solemnly promise to faithfully fulfil the Reverse I also promise the most faithful obedience to the illustrious heads of the Order of Illuminati and the true mandates of the same Br. ......T.R....... (N.N.) who stands before me. To love my brothers in arms and brethren of the Order as myself and to strive diligently for the sacred work of the Order. I also promise that I will rather suffer death than betray the secrets of my friend or his wife's honour. In sign hereof I grasp this dagger and pierce therewith this skull. May a like overtake me should I ever become a traitor! Amen!

The mention of his wife's honour, underlined, links nicely to the covenant between Jacob and Laban who was the father in law, to honour his daughter.

The mention of stabbing the skull is in allusion to the Knights Templar revenge on Phillip IV of France (1268-1314) called the 'Fair.' For his part in causing the Templar's downfall and although a dagger is used it seems to be in a different way. This reference has been removed from the modern 'Ancient & Accepted Rite' rituals.

The candidate was called N.N. for Notuma and the 'Word' used was Gabaon.

ENGLISH ILLUMINATI-ROSE-CROIX GRADE OATH:

In the presence of all the Very Worthy and Illustrious Knights, I Andreas Knight, promise, as an honest man and Illuminate, to help search for the lost word, and to keep the word, when found, in spite of everything, as a secret, under the threat of being turned out of all the lodges and chapters. So help me God!

The 'Word' used here was 'I am that I am' or 'Jehovah.' They also use 'Faith,' 'Hope' and 'Love.' They also used three versions of I.N.R.I., the alchemical (Igne Natura Renovatur Integra), the old Rosicrucian or hermetic (Ioithi Nain Rasith Ioithi) and the Christian (Iesus Nazarenus Rex Iudaeorum).

ENGLISH ILLUMINATI-OPENING AND CLOSING THE SYNODS

I do not have the whole ritual of the Synod, but after consulting the original Illuminati rituals in *The Secret School of Wisdom*,[110] it mostly consists of lectures. The English Illuminati version only has the opening and closing of the Synod, so there is no oath to compare with C.W. Heckethorn's oath of the Illuminati.

The word in the Bavarian Illuminati 'Epopt Grade' was I.N.R.I. and in the revived Illuminati I.N.R.I. and MIZPAH.

ENGLISH ILLUMINATI-WORD OF THE REGENTS GRADE

I do not have any of this ritual and therefore no oaths, just a few words from Heckethorn's account in Section 355, which includes the 'Word' of the grade, which was REDEMTIS, from the French word for 'Redemption.'

We also know that Westcott was given the Regent's 'Word' when Reuss visited his house in London in January 1902, to be advanced into the S.R.I.A. Clearly he was prepared by Reuss to become the Regent for Great Britain at that time.

END OF HECKETHORN'S ACCOUNT

---

110 Wages, Markner & Singh-Anand, 2015, *The Secret School of Wisdom*, London: Ian Allan. The first paragraph above is similar but not the same as the second paragraph of the Minerval Oath that can be found on page 70 of The Secret School of Wisdom, but I could find nothing else the same. [A.M.L. 2015]

Chapter VI

Characters in the revived Illuminati story

Dr WILLIAM WYNN WESTCOTT

Driving force behind the S.R.I.A.

The pivotal character behind the introduction of the Illuminati into England and the British Empire in 1902 was William Wynn Westcott (1848-1925).

In his professional capacity, he had risen to become the North East London Coroner, having qualified as a doctor in medicine. In his personal life, he had risen through the ranks of Freemasonry and several esoteric Orders over the same period of thirty years, to become the head of the Rosicrucian Freemasons.

Westcott had an air of superiority and was a natural leader, who thought big and seemed a bit blustery. He was cheerful, but also direct and serious, with the passion and force to move mountains and the opportunism needed to establish his own court of influence, with the capability for good governance.

This is perhaps what astrologers would say about him if they used his Chinese year of birth 1848 and his Sun sign of 17 December to characterise him.[111] Someone with charisma, charm, wit and showmanship, he was the centre of attention, a highly sought after friend and companion.

In a very different role as the North London Coroner, in 1900, he used his skills to manage and organise proceedings with great acumen. The standard role of a Coroner is to confirm and then certify the death of an individual. Westcott was very concerned at the time that more should be done to work out 'the cause of death,' particularly of murder victims and especially suicides. He had a huge influence into the investigation of the

Figure 95 - Westcott's personal bookplate

circumstances of death on behalf of the coroner's office. A coroner's court is the highest court in the land, so he held huge responsibility in his mundane life as well as in his private life.

By 1902 he had been the head of the now flourishing order of Rosicrucian Freemasons for ten years. They were called the 'Societas Rosicruciana in Anglia' (S.R.I.A.). He had been a member for twenty two years.

At the time of the resurrected Illuminati he was the leader and Supreme Magus of the S.R.I.A. with several colleges in England and one in Australia. With potential colleges in (Penang) Malaya, (Natal) South Africa, (Christchurch) New Zealand, (Buenos Ayres) Argentina and four in India (Peshawar, Rawal Pindi, Madras and Bangalore). I believe this means that Westcott was in the mood to setup other orders too like the Illuminati. The S.R.I.A. also had a daughter constitution in Scotland called the S.R.I.S. which had warranted colleges in America, Canada and Greece. So a college in Berlin, of the Prussia Empire in the very homeland of the ancient Rosicrucians was a great prize, in his grandiose plans for the future of the society.

I believe that his powerful, positive influence began when he was admitted into the society in 1880 and he clearly worked hard from the very start. This started when he was the secretary of the Metropolitan College in London, where he helped Dr William George Robert Woodman (1828-1891) while he resided in Devon. Woodman was the ageing head of the S.R.I.A. and had been the

Figure 94 - Portrait of Westcott, 1906

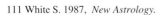

111 White S. 1987, *New Astrology.*

founding secretary of the society in 1867. Woodman then qualified by right as the Senior Substitute Magus in 1877 to become the second Supreme Magus in 1878. However, he could not find a reliable replacement as secretary of the London College and for the Society. Not until Westcott volunteered seventeen years later, first as the secretary of the premier college in 1884. Then, after only three years as college secretary Westcott became the Secretary General of the whole society in 1887. His qualification for such a role, I believe, probably came from his high positions in another order, that of Supreme Grand Senior Deacon in the 'Swedenborg Rite' since 1876 and their Grand Secretary from 1886.

Westcott had added to Woodman's library with his own personal collection of books and purchased many more, creating the very valuable Rosicrucian High Council Library, with other significant and valuable donations from other members. He was instrumental in producing the Metropolitan College Transactions, which contained the best papers delivered in that college, a publication that started in 1885 and continues today, something almost as valuable as the Library itself. He had lectured in colleges up and down the country and encouraged their members to write papers in York, Newcastle and Manchester and their college transactions are also to be found in the High Council Library.

Described by some as a hooting owl, he certainly looked like one and strangely had an owl as the crest on his personal bookplate, which can be still found in some of his books in the High Council Library, (see fig 95). I do not know when Westcott started using the image of Minerva as a book plate. The Roman Goddess Minerva was the Etruscan counterpart to Greek Athena. His bookplate

Figure 97 - Annie Kenney and Christabel Pankhurst

probably pre-dates the introduction of the resurrected Illuminati, as it can be found in his books printed after 1890.

Westcott can be blamed for making several whopping big mistakes while writing a History of the S.R.I.A. for the new millennium in 1900. His diary shows that he approached enough of the senior members to get a good understanding of the founding and history by return letter. The people he selected let him down and these senior Freemasons replies missed the publishing deadline and when he did finally receive them, they were woefully empty of any detail, as the correspondence left in the archives now show.

There were no formal archives or collection of material, that he could cross check or that he could refer to in his time and his crime was that he mistook and mis-interpreted badly the letter written by the Reverend Thomas Fitz Arthur Torin Ravenshaw (1829-1882) Grand Chaplain (1868). Thinking it was about the founding and history of the Rosicrucian Freemasons, which centred on Robert Wentworth Little. On closer inspection, in fact it was about Robert Wentworth Little and the founding of the Red Cross of Rome and Constantine. Both societies were being formed at the same time and by R.W. Little, all the characters mentioned in the letter were also members of both originations, having found the original, it was an easy mistake to make. (Ravenshaw, 1870). Besides all this Westcott was a freethinker, he had blazed a trail and shot for the stars and the successful future of the society was his reward and high office, all from his own efforts.

Figure 96 - William Wynn Westcott 1894

CAPABLE OF SETTING UP THE ILLUMINATI

Clearly from this we can see that Westcott was very capable of setting up the English Illuminati. The real point is that you can imagine he was also very cautious about the Illuminati after the whole 'Golden Dawn' debacle, where co-founders turned on each other and yet others plotted their down fall. In fact, that is exactly what was going on behind the scenes in the Illuminati in Berlin and Dresden with Reuss and Engel.

But it may have been the new breed of Edwardian women shaking off the Victorian age in 1900, as part of the 'suffragette movement' that was gathering momentum at the time, for example Pankhurst, (see fig 97), who founded the Women's Franchise League in 1889 and the hope of equal rights for woman, which might have also helped inspire the founding of English Illuminati!

An order that I had always assumed must include women, just like the Theosophical Society that started in New York, America in 1875 and then spread around the world in 1878. Westcott and all the protagonists of this story were all keen Theosophical Society members with contact with esoteric minded women and only Westcott stayed the course as the Theosophical Society changed its emphasis from its founding interest in the Western Mystic tradition in New York, to the Eastern traditions once they set up when it moved to India.

But where in our story do you hear a single mention of a woman being involved with the resurrected Illuminati in Germany or England come to that! Only if you look again at the Illuminati ordinances will you find that there is a place for women, but only as visitors. The 'Golden Dawn' and the *Ordre Martinist* however did admit women. The 1797 exposes written about the Illuminati did accuse them of educating women and children, an order well ahead of its time.

Westcott was a relatively young man when he started the 'Golden Dawn' at forty years old. Macgregor Mathers was even younger when he became Imperator in 1891 at the age of thirty seven. It was at this date that Mathers received the 5=6 grade, while in Paris in July 1891 and created an active inner order for the 'Golden Dawn' and he started a new Temple in Paris 1893, where Papus was admitted in 1895 at the relatively young age of thirty. Papus for example was only twenty three when he became the President of the 'Ordre Martinist,' while Theodor Reuss was a mature forty at this time.

The 'English Illuminati' would be based on the revived 'Bavarian Illuminati' and founded on the purest principles of improving MAN, teaching him/her about the immortality of the soul after death and raising men and women above their

Figure 98 - Supreme Magus S.R.I.A. 1903

natural animal state to become better human beings.[112]

The new esoteric order was likely to have been started and run from Westcott's house in 396 Camden Road, North, London, (see fig 99).

It would have been spread though his existing contacts in the now failed 'Golden Dawn,' which had imploded in 1900-1901 and changed its name. This was after the Horos Legal Case and the successful convictions in London of two bogus former members of the Paris 'Golden Dawn.'

Westcott would have attempted to spread the order nationally through the heads of several other esoteric and fringe masonic organisations he knew in Great Britain. One was the Secretary General of the 'Societas Rosicruciana in Scotia' or S.R.I.S., a sister independent society, Robert Smith Brown VIII° in Scotland, who was approached by Westcott in 1902 to take on the 'English Illuminati' order and many other senior spiritual and interested members of both the S.R.I.A. and S.R.I.S. as well.

Who was Westcott the man? The so called 'Magical Mason' and how did he rise and what caused his fall and what were his twilight years composed of as the head of the English Rosicrucian Society of Freemasons.

His story is told here through his diary entries and people who knew him. What were the other many orders he belonged to and in who he played a major part?

---

112 See Chapter IV - Illuminati Order rituals.

WESTCOTT AND THE SRIA

From the society's *Golden Book* a record of members, William Wynn Westcott, XI° (1848-1925) who officially styled himself 'Dr Wynn Westcott,' was admitted a Zelator on 15 April 1880, this was nine years after being admitted a Freemason. After only four years he reached grade VIII° and Secretary of Metropolitan College in 1884, having progressed rapidly through the college office's and ranks of the society. I say that because it would usually take seven to eight years in most colleges in the S.R.I.A. to get that far normally and something like sixteen years to advance that quickly in London to this high rank. Even today this was rapid advancement as London has so many more members in its college, three to four times the size of an average size S.R.I.A. college around the world.

It was exceptional for Westcott to receive his Grade 9° in 1886 only six years after being admitted to the S.R.I.A., as it is usually one year between each grade at least. But his contribution to the society was also exceptional; as it is clear from the minutes that Westcott increased the number of colleges, attendance and admissions to the society.

The administration of the society stepped up a gear or two with Westcott as secretary. I believe it was Westcott who first 'Latinised' the name of the society, changing it from the 'Rosicrucian Society of England' in 1867 to the 'Societas Rosicruciana in Anglia' in 1885. For some reason, this innovation started first while he was secretary of Metropolitan College and it appeared on their convocation notices first and then he changed the name for the whole society on High Council's convocations, Latinising it from 1889 onwards, this was while he was the Secretary General of the S.R.I.A. (1887-1891).

All credit to the existing members of Metropolitan College, because they made Westcott work his way through all the offices in college until he became Celebrant in 1889, after nine years. It was on the death of Dr W.R. Woodman, that Westcott became the third, and longest serving, Supreme Magus (1892-1925, see fig 98).

Finally, his contribution to the society can be gauged by the large number of articles and papers he delivered, which was greater than any other member. In 2010 I found a wooden trunk filled with his original drafts and some published papers, in all some 200 works in the S.R.I.A. archives, some are re-worked for different organisations he lectured. He also took the library of 72 books donated by Woodman and in several years turned that into a collection of 365 books from purchases and donations made by many different members and adding his own Hermetic collection started for 'Golden Dawn' members.

To his credit Dr Westcott did not join or rule over every order he was offered. A good example was in 1899 when Frater John Yarker offered the Chiefship of 'Red branch of Eri' (Irish Chivalric Order) to Westcott, which he declined. Westcott had been admitted a knight of ERI in 1880 with others. In the archives we have (1886) F.G. Irwin's[113] own bound ritual book which is a copy of the *Ritual of the Knight of the Red Branch*, 1697 (Order of ERI) belonging to an American ship's captain called Brother P. Wilson. It also has a letter bound in with it from Captain P. Wilson to Bro Yarker dated 29 December 1886, asking him to start a *Red Branch of Eri Province*. There other examples of him declining orders, like the 'Swedenborg Rite' and the 'Ancient and Primitive Rite,' the 'Fratres Lucis' and the 'English Martinist Order.'

THE FAMILY MAN

From the biography that can be found in the Library and Museum of Freemasonry, we know that William Wynn Westcott was born in Leamington, Warwickshire, England on 17 December 1848. His family was probably descended from the 'Westcotes of Leicester.' There is still a district of this name in South West Leicester; they were formally known as the Ruding's family of Leicester & Worcestershire.[114] He was the son of Dr Peter Westcott, a doctor and surgeon of Oundle, Northamptonshire, which is South East of Leicester.[115]

Figure 99 - Home & Head Quarters, 396 Camden Road

113 Captain Francais George Irwin (1828-1893).
114 Fairbairn, 1905, *Crests of the families of Great Britain and Ireland.*
115 *Who's Who*, 1914.

His mother was Elizabeth Mary Ellis, however she died when he was only three in 1852 and his father died in 1858, when he was 10 years old. He was adopted by his uncle Richard Westcott Martyn, who lived at Bridge House, Water Street, Martock, Somerset, who was also a medical practitioner and born in Plymouth, Devon, where there is also a strong historical family connection with the Westcott's. William attended a school in South Petherton, Devon. He then studied at Kingston Grammar School in Kingston-upon-Thames, Surrey from 1858 to 1865. He then went to University College, London. He became a Member of the Royal College of Surgeons in 1870.

He became a Licentiate of the Society of Apothecaries and graduated with a Bachelor in Medicine degree in 1871. He joined his uncle as a general practitioner in Martock, Somerset, where he worked for ten years. It was probably during this time that he got to know the West Country Freemasons, Captain Francais George Irwin, (1828-1893) and Benjamin Cox (1828-1895), they were both involved with many of the orders that Westcott joined much later.

F.G. Irwin lived at 1, Brislington Crescent, Bristol, until 1890, when he moved to 2 Russell Villars, Runell, Gloucester, where he died. He was the Intendant General (Provincial Grand Master) of the 'Red Cross of Constantine,' 'Rose and Lily Conclave No. 10,' which met at Western-super Mare.

It was at this masonic centre, where seven different Lodges meet that he would have come across, B. Cox who was a member of the 'St Kew Lodge No. 1222,' which also met at the Western-super-mare masonic centre, it was at least 40 miles North West of Westcott's home in Martock. While his own mother Lodge called the 'Parret and Axe Lodge, No. 814' met at the George Hotel, Crewkerne at the time, (see fig 102). It still meets today in South Street, Crewkerne, in Somerset and is very local, only eight miles south of his home in Martock. It was while living in Martock that Westcott wrote to Irwin, who introduced him to John Yarker in 1876, when Westcott became a 'Grand Officer' in the 'Swedenborg Rite.'

After this, he moved to Langley Villa, Sunny Gardens, Hendon, Middlesex, in 1881. It was while living in Hendon that he studied the Qabalah and other metaphysical subjects, during a voluntary period of retirement at the age of thirty three.

Westcott also worked with W. H. Martindale on *The extra Pharmacopoeia of Unofficial Drugs and poisons*, (see fig 100), which is annotated by Westcott. His career took off when he was appointed Deputy Coroner for Central Middlesex and Central London, based at Hoxton, London in 1881.

Before the suicides of his wife, daughter and son, Westcott wrote a very important study on suicide and how it was not a crime in itself. In it he says that there were only two other books on the subject, the first in English in 1840 and another in Italian. It was called *A Social Science Treatise: Suicide, Its History, Literature, Jurisprudence, Causation, and Prevention,* published in 1885. It was dedicated to his employer at the time Dr George D. Thomas, who was the Central Middlesex Coroner.

Westcott, with this work on suicides and his joint work on unofficial drugs, may have been partly responsible for the change in British Law. The Coroners Act of 1887 made significant changes, repealing much of the earlier legislation. Coroners then became more concerned with determining the circumstances and the actual medical causes of sudden, violent and unnatural deaths for the benefit of the community as a whole. Westcott took his diploma in Public Health in 1892 and was appointed the Medical Officer of Health for Islington, but only retained the post for a short

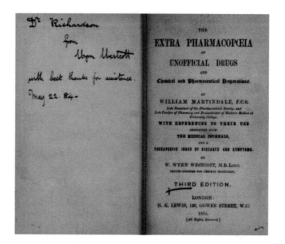

Figure 100 - Extra Pharmacopoeia 1884

time. He was appointed H.M.'s Coroner for North East London in 1894-1918[116] and served as President of the Coroners' Society from 1909 to 1910.

It may only be of slight interest to mention that according to the *Who's who* of 1920, it was Dr Wynne Edwin Baxter who was the Middlesex Coroner, who conducted the inquests into the deaths during the 'Jack the Ripper' or 'Whitechapel Murders' of 1888 to 1891, which did not involve Westcott at all. The inquest of one of 'Jack the Ripper' suspect's was held at Chiswick, by the coroner Dr Thomas Bramah Diplock and the suspect was named Montague John Druitt. He was named as such by Assistant Chief Constable Sir Melville Macnaghten in a private handwritten memorandum of 23 February 1894, only released to the public in 1966. However, the coroner's jury concluded that Druitt had committed suicide, by

---

116 *Who's Who*, 1914.

drowning while in an unsound state of mind. Some modern novelists have suggested that Druitt may have contacted Westcott over his proposed suicide, especially as several of Druitt's family were also suicidal. Although Westcott was a Freemason and a Doctor and had started the 'Golden Dawn,' he never actually lived at 34 Blythe Road, Hammersmith, London W14 0HA, near Olympia which was the address of the 'Golden Dawn's' Temple at the time, which was erroneously linked to the Ripper suspect because Druitt was found drowned at Chiswick, with a return rail ticket to Hammersmith, on 31 December 1888, which is very tenuous, but worth mentioning here, only out of interest.

Westcott (age 44) 'bachelor of medicine .... former son of Peter Westcott of Oundle, Northamptonshire, surgeon,' became a member of the Middle Temple on 16 March 1894.[117] He served as Justice of the Peace for Stoke Newington; Past President of the Society for the Study of Inebriety; Vice-President of the Medico-Legal Society and National Sunday League and Divisional Director for Islington of the Red Cross Society.

Figure 101 - Last known picture in South Africa 1924

These are some of his home addresses, in the English census; he is recorded as a student living in the home of Robert Billings, South Petherton, Somerset in 1861. He was then living as a general practitioner, with his uncle, at Bridge House, Martock, in 1871. Then living at Langley Villas, Sunny Gardens, Hendon, Middlesex. Then living at the same address with his wife, with one son, three daughters and two servants in 1881. As a surgeon and deputy coroner, living at 396 Camden Road,

Islington, London. With his wife, two daughters, one son and one servant in 1891 and as coroner, living at 396 Camden Road, with his wife, two daughters and one son in 1901 (see fig 99).

FAMILY

Here is a short biography of his family members. Westcott married **Eliza Burnett** Westcott (1851-1921) the daughter of Edmund Crawford Burnett, the ceremony was held at St. Matthew's Church, St. Pancras, London, on 18 February 1873 and the couple raised two sons and three daughters. She may have committed suicide in Tunbridge Wells in 1921.

Edmund William Martyn Westcott (1874-1907) the eldest son was born in Somerset and at the age of 33 died after six years of illness, following the amputation of a leg in 1901.[118] The initials E.W.M.W. can be found on a number of *'Golden Dawn'* drawings in the S.R.I.A. archives. Was Edmund the artist of this material? His father shared his artistic eye and produced some fair drawings in ink that can also be found in his several scrapbooks in the archives.

Ida Grace Westcott was born in Somerset in 1875 and was the only child to outlive their father. All I can find out about her was that music was her profession.

Elsie Bridget Wynn Westcott (1877-1918) was born in Somerset and married Fergus Edward Hamel on the 18th October 1895. He was admitted into to the Metropolitan College SRIA on 8 January 1903. He resigned on 1 July 1935, having reached the chair on 9 April 1914 and received his grade 8°, according to the S.R.I.A. Golden Book. It is Fergus Hamel that, allegedly, was given some of Westcott's 'Golden Dawn' material before he left for South Africa, along with Dr William Elliot Carnegie Dickson (1878-1954).

Lilian Margret Westcott (1880-1924) was born in Hendon and married Albert Frederick Gee (1863-1934) on 25 September 1902 in Lewisham and three weeks later, before leaving for Natal, he was admitted into the Metropolitan College S.R.I.A. as a Zelator and remained that rank until he resigned on 1 January 1923, his Golden Book membership No. 0588. Gee was a native South African and worked on the Natal Railway. Westcott and his wife lived with them and their Grandchildren in Durban. Lilian, who had been a chronic invalid, died on 13 February 1924 aged 44 years old.

---

117 Register of admissions to the Middle Temple archive.

118 Gilbert R , 2012, *A Magus Among the Adepts.*

George Wynn Westcott (1883-1906) born in London, began a promising medical career but died suddenly in 1906 aged 23 years old, probably of suicide.

There are no mentions of either death of his children or wife in Westcott's ACTA for 1906 or 1925. After Edmund's death, Westcott left for the first time for Africa on 13 April 1907,[119] to be with his daughter Lilian. While in Africa, he attended a meeting of the brand new S.R.I.A. Ladysmith College. (Clegg was the Celebrant, Goodman as secretary and Williams) on 1 June. He and his wife left Durban to return to England on 13 June 1907.

Elsie (Westcott) Hamel aged 41, committed suicide in 1918. Westcott retired as a Coroner after her death and he also decided to retire from public office completely, but carried on as Supreme Magus and attended Metropolitan College meetings until he finally immigrated to Natal in 1920. Westcott announced very little in his ACTA[120] December 1919:

> *I gave general notice about this time that I found it necessary to go to Natal, for health and family reasons.*

He offered his resignation, which was rejected by High Council and continued in office as Supreme Magus of the S.R.I.A. in absentia for five years. They left for Natal in South Africa on 12 March 1920 to stay with Lilian Gee. They arrived on 6 April, with severe damage to their furniture. He gave notice to the S.R.I.A. in December 1920, that he would return to England for a visit and arrived on 11 February 1921.

However, during this fateful visit the most awful tragedy struck and in early August, his wife **Eliza Burnett** fell to her death from a window in a house where they had been staying in Tunbridge Wells. See *The Times,* London; 'Fatal Fall into Courtyard' 10 August 1921. All it said in his ACTA[121] was simply:

> *After consultation with the Fraters....I left for Durban, Natal.*

Two weeks later on 26 August Westcott left London for Durban, he arrived alone on 17 September 1921. Westcott died at 39, Rapson Road, Durban, South Africa on 30 July 1925.

I hope this book in some small manner will help repair some of Westcott's tarnished reputation, in some people's eyes. It may have been caused in some small way because he did not defend himself at the time. I believe that he should have followed through and produced some of the proof that he had amassed of his innocence, against some of the false claims of *'Golden Dawn'* forgery. He could have easily made a good case in his own defence and perhaps admitted some of his errors, but Sagittarius/Capricorn's do like to keep their little secrets.

FREEMASONRY
Brief summary of his memberships[122]

Craft Freemason, Westcott was initiated as freemason in the Parrett and Axe Lodge, No. 814, Crewkerne, Somerset on 24 October 1871, he was passed on 19 December that year and raised on 16 April 1872, he served as Worshipful Master in 1877. The Lodge was a warranted in 1860 and met at the George Hotel in Crewkerne and then moved to the Town Hall before settling at its current home in South Street, Crewkerne, and (see fig 102). He became a joining member of Lodge of Brotherly Love, No. 329, Yeovil, Somerset in 1873 and

Figure 102 - Banner of the Parrett & Axe Lodge

joined the research lodge called Quatuor Coronati Lodge, No. 2076, London in 1886, where he served as Worshipful Master in 1893. He served as Provincial Assistant Grand Director of Ceremonies for Somerset in 1877. He was appointed Past Junior

---

119 (HCL1242C, 1905) ACTA.
120 (H.C.L. No. 1242D, 1907) ACTA.
121 Ibid.

122 Most of the biography was obtained from the online information attached to the Westcott photograph in the Library and Museum of Freemasonry. GBR 1991 P 10/16/85.

Grand Deacon by the United Grand Lodge of England on Wednesday the 4 June 1902.[123]

In the **Holy Royal Arch**; he was exalted in the Chapter of Brotherly Love, No. 329, Yeovil on 30 April 1873, where he served as First Principal in 1889. He was appointed Past Grand Standard Bearer by the Supreme Grand Chapter of Royal Arch Masons of England on 4 June 1902.

In **Mark Masonry** he was advanced in William de Irwin Lodge, No. 162, Yeovil in 1873, where he served as Worshipful Master in 1878. This Lodge became dormant, but on its revival in 1887 Westcott was elected Worshipful Master. He served as Provincial Grand Senior Warden for Somerset in 1887.

In the **Ancient and Accepted Rite** he was perfected in Alfred Chapter, No. 13, Taunton, Somerset on 15 February 1875. He became a joining member of Bayard Chapter, No. 71, London in 1879; Invicta Chapter, No. 10, London in 1898 and Durban Chapter, No. 127, Durban, Natal, South Africa in 1922. He was awarded 30° in 1878 having gone through the chair as M.W.S.

In the **Red Cross of Constantine** he became a member of Rose and Lily Conclave, No. 10, Weston-super-Mare, Somerset, but seems to have been only a casual member. Probably introduced by F.G. Irwin who was the Inspector General based there.

In **The Royal Order of Eri** (Red Branch Knights of Ulster and its Appendant Orders) Westcott was admitted by F. G. Irwin in 1880. In 1886 he was sent a Charter by John Yarker to admit Knights and Commanders. He revived and reorganised the Order in 1917 before he left for South Africa, serving as Grand Master and Senior Knight Grand Cross.

I believe that the **Swedenborg Rite** became an important order to Westcott while living in Somerset. He must have seen the article written by John Yarker in *The Freemason* on 4 November 1876 and he wrote to his friend and mentor F.G. Irwin at number 1 Brislington Crescent, Bristol, on 12 November 1876 asking to become a member. Irwin was, in fact, only the behind the scenes organiser for John Yarker. According to several letters in the S.R.I.A. archives Irwin had a Canadian 'pen pal', called George Canning Longley and it was he that was working behind the scenes with Lt. Colonel W.J.B. Moore in Canada, to introduce that order into Great Britain and Ireland. Longley also introduced into Canada many

side orders too, obtained for him by Irwin. The Canadian 'Swedenborg Rite' Warrant was dated 1 July 1876. At the time there were only four members, J. Yarker, F.G. Irwin, S.P. Leather and K. Mackenzie. Irwin in his reply to Westcott's letter, suggested:

If you care to go in for working it then ....I would appoint you Master and as such your name will appear in the Grand Warrant, and as a Grand Officer.

The net result was that Westcott, after being a Freemason for only five years, received his first Grand Rank, that of Supreme Grand Senior Deacon in 1876 and his name appeared on the Supreme Grand Lodge and Temple for Great Britain and Ireland, Warrant for the 'Swedenborg Rite,' issued to John Yarker.

Westcott was admitted to Emanuel Lodge, No. 1, held at Manchester in 1876. It moved effectively to Bristol in 1877 but meetings were allegedly held in Weston-super-Mare. Thus from the letters of the Lodge secretary Benjamin Cox to Irwin, it would seem that it was a hollow affair, with few meetings and equally few members, no printed rituals and few manuscript versions to copy. Westcott served as Worshipful Master in 1886. He was a joining member of Hermes Lodge, No. 8, London in 1886. He became the Worshipful Master of Pythagorean Lodge of Instruction in 1887; it was formed in London on 1 November 1879. He served there as Worshipful Master in 1888. He served as District Senior Grand Warden of the Western District in 1887.

He was promoted to Supreme Grand Junior Warden in 1879-1891. He served as Supreme Grand Secretary from 1886-1902, Westcott tried to resign in March 1902 over the Swedenborg affair, but Yarker asked him to stay for at least one more year and promoted him. I believe he was informed of his promotion by Yarker in a letter received on 30 July 1902, two months after his Past Grand Rank promotion in the craft. He became the Supreme Grand Senior Warden 1902-1903, second only in rank to Yarker.

But, Westcott resigned as Grand Senior Warden and Grand Secretary of the Swedenborg Rite, in a letter to Yarker on 8 March 1903,[124] I think he became completely disillusioned with the 'Swedenborg Rite' due to Papus going behind his back in 1899 to get a dispensation for his Paris, INRI Lodge and Temple No. 14. Then for not paying for members' certificate and then in 1902 discovering the problems caused by Papus mistaking the 6 degrees of the 'Swedenborg Rite' for the 96 degrees of the 'Ancient & Primitive Rite,' and publishing these mistakes in France,

---

123 (HCL1242B, 1897) ACTA.

124 (HCL1242B, 1897) S.R.I.A. archives.

back in 1900. This then led to Reuss very quickly swapping the 'Swedenborg Rite' for the 'Ancient & Primitive Rite of Memphis and Mizraim,' in his German collection of rites, effectively dropping the 'Swedenborg Rite' and Westcott's potential role in Germany and France. The problem here, was that he had wasted all that time and effort in helping Reuss set up a Provincial Grand Lodge and the warrants for six German Swedenborg Lodges and it had all come to nothing because of Papus. Not to mention the time spent overcoming the reputational damage that was nearly caused to him, by the so called irregularity or making masons clandestinely by the 'Swedenborg Rite,' in Germany, that might have put him under the spotlight of United Grand Lodge of England, in January 1901.[125]

The **Society of Eight** only ever had eight members at any one time, according to its constitutions.[126] It was founded by Francis George Irwin and Fredrick Holland (1854-1917) a friend, neighbour and local masonic brother of Mathers in 1883. The other members were William James Hughan, Kenneth Mackenzie, John Yarker, Frederick Hockley, Benjamin Cox and Rev. William Alexander Ayton. Then later W.W. Westcott and S.L. Mathers joined. It is very interesting that Fred Hockley told Fred G. Irwin that he did not want W.W. Westcott to become a member in August 1883 and threatened to resign, but he died in 1885, it was only then that Westcott became a member, but by the end of that year, Mackenzie had argued with the founder Holland and told F.G. Irwin that the 'Society of Eight' was quite dormant, there is no mention in Westcott's ACTA of the 'Society of Eight.'[127] It is very interesting that Yarker planned to use the 'Society of Eight's' members as the Provincial heads of the English 'Ordre Martinist' in 1895.

Westcott was probably not an early member but was very aware of the **Fratres Lucis** Order. In 1901 we find that he mistook the rituals sent to him by R.S. Brown for Lawrence Archer's 'Apex' or 'Sat B'hai.' The 'Fratres Lucis' is a European system of enlightenment from the 14th century Florence, that takes its teachings from the Hermetic teachings in Egypt which came from Persia. It was inclusive of Jews, when so many European esoteric orders excluded them and it was defiantly not an 'Indian Order of Light.' It claims Robert Fludd, Count St. Germain, Count Cagliostro, Mesmer, Swedenborg and Martinez de Pasqualez as alleged members of the Order. In more recent times J. Ragon and Eliphas Levi were alleged members.

You can read more, in A.E. Waite's book.[128] But, it would seem there were only nine members that we can account for in the archives of the 'Fratres Lucis,' they are M.V. Portman, F.G. Irwin; H.F. Irwin; B. Cox; K.R.H. Mackenzie, J. Yarker, G.C. Longley, A.W. Adair and F. Hockley.

In the (original) **of August Order Light,** Westcott was introduced to the order by F.G. Irwin and admitted by the founder Maurice Vidal Portman, Grand Hierophant, on 1 June 1871, while Westcott's home address was still Martock, Somerset; this is according to his first 'August Order of Light.'[129] It is based on Indian lore and his certificate was signed by the founder Portman alone. Dr Maurice Vidal Portman (1861-1935), was a learned student of oriental lore, a Freemason, Occultist and Politician who worked for the Civil Service in both India and the Andaman Islands, the order did not really progress in England before 1900.[130]

This order is not to be confused with another Order of Light from India, but it is from a different source. In 1872, an Indian officer, Captain James Henry Lawrence Archer (1823-1889), introduced the **Royal Oriental Order of Sikha (Apex) and the Sat B'hai**. It consisted of a series of titles with Hindu names and passwords, caste marks and symbolic devices and the Order began to falter in England after its introduction. Kenneth Mackenzie worked with Lawrence Archer to translate the rituals into English, but was frustrated by Archer's absences away in Scotland and then by his illness. With little or no progress a letter from John Yarker' dated 13 April 1882, which includes the following paragraph and quote:

> *The gentleman introduced by me was Maurice Vidal Portman .... who is a grandson of Viscount Portman. He is Political Superintendent under the Viceroy of India, & a Judge of the Civil Courts; though a very young man. He has gone over to the native faith & is a Priest of Mahadeva & Buddha, an Initiate in almost all of the Occult Societies of India.*

John Yarker claims to have given Portman the 'Sat B'hai' in return for the 'August Order of Light' and been involved with Kenneth Mackenzie's amalgamation of the two Indian Orders of light, they wrote a new amalgamated code in 1886.

However, after his retirement Bro. Portman approached his friends Bro. Thomas Henry Pattinson (1851-1940) and Bro. Dr Bogdan E. J. Edwards, MBE (1860-1923) to take over the 'August Order of Light' and make whatever alterations they thought necessary to attract

---

125 See Chapter I, Irregular Freemasonry and Greiner role.
126 Constitutions that were found in S.R.I.A. archives in 2015.
127 See Chapter VI-People-John Yarker.
128 Waite A.E., 1924, *Brotherhood of the Rosy Cross.*

129 The certificate is found in the S.R.I.A. archives in 2015.
130 Ibid.

Yorkshire Freemasons and the rituals were very extensively revised after that by Pattinson and Edwards, who as founders became the two Arch-Presidents.

Before its re-launch, Westcott was chosen by Portman in 1901 to revise the rituals.[131] Westcott wrote to Yarker and R.S. Brown a friend of Portman for their rituals, which he borrowed and there was much contact with Pattison and others in Westcott's ACTA in 1901, leading up to the re-founding of the Garuda Temple, No. 1 in 1902. Where the Order first met is not known, but during Bogdan Edward Jastrzebski Edwards (1860-1923) lifetime meetings were held at 81 King's Arcade, Market Street Bradford.[132]

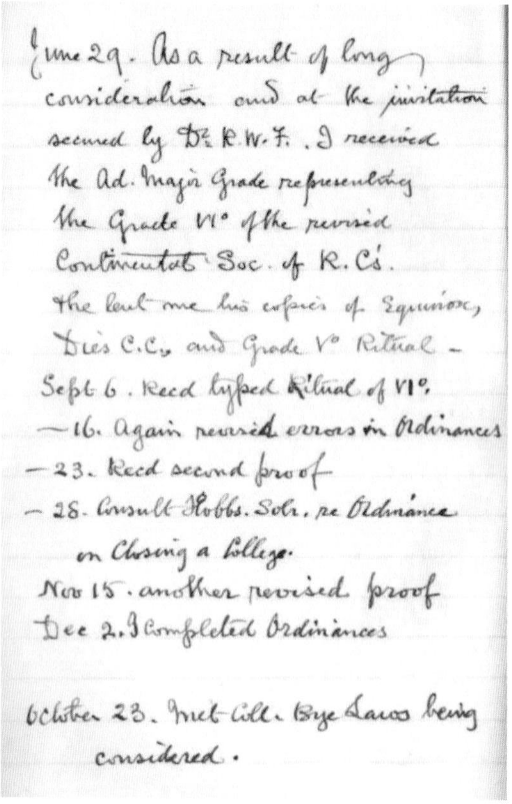

Figure 103a - Westcott admitted into Stella Matutina

They opened the Bradford Temple on 9 January 1902, a meeting Westcott could not make as Supreme Magus as he was in the chair of the Metropolitan College advancing a number of candidates.

The second Westcott certificate of initiation from the revised 'August Order of Light' looks like the modern certificates of today and Westcott 'Passed the dark mystery and was one in the circle of light,' in the 1st and 2nd degrees, it is dated 6 of September 1903 and signed by Bro. T. H. Pattinson and Bro. Dr Bogdan E. J. Edwards. Later, Westcott held the role of 'Chief of the Council of

Instruction' and he delivered 21 lectures in Bradford between 1903 and 1917, he retired from the 'August Order of Light' in 1920.[133]

According to Andrew B. Stephenson's detailed history of the order, within a short time they had set up home in the disused basement of a pub in King Street, Bradford. In 1939 the headquarters of the Order leased the two top floors of a warehouse in the re-named Godwin Street Bradford and the Temple was later relocated to York and then Halifax, Yorkshire. During the end of the Bradford phase, a second Temple, Garuda Temple, No. 2 was opened in A. B. Stephenson's' home. The location was the attic to be precise at number 38, Westcombe Park Road, Blackheath, London SE3 7RB in 1970. This house grew to become the centre of many other small Orders, until Stephenson emigrated and moved to New Zealand in 2006.

NON MASONIC
Brief summary of memberships

The non-masonic **Golden Dawn** was founded on 1 March 1888 by three members of the S.R.I.A. They were W.G.R. Woodman who would have been called the Imperator; S.L. Mathers the second in command or Praemonstrator, and Westcott who was the real powerhouse behind the forming of the order as the Cancellarius or secretary.

None of them had been admitted to the order by anyone or by ceremony and all assumed the grade of 5=6 of the 'second order.' Westcott and Mathers effectively ran the 'first and only order' together for the first three years, with Woodman as the figure head.

Then, after W.G.R. Woodman's death at the end of 1891, Westcott became the Supreme Magus of the S.R.I.A. and handed over the running of the 'first order' to Mathers. But, in January 1892 Mathers had to relocate with his wife to Paris because of financial difficulties, having been sacked from his job and falling on hard times. In Paris, while flat hunting in June 1892, he met a Belgium member of the 'Continental Order' and acquired the first of the Adept Grades of the 'second order' and only one ritual the 5=6. With Westcott's financial help they set up the Adept's Temple in Hammersmith and started admitting members to the 'second order' at the end of 1892. Westcott however left the new 'second order' to Mathers to run from Paris whilst he concentrated on running what had now become the 'first order' from London.

Then, according to Mathers own testimony, in a public court case held in 1911, he admitted forcing Westcott out of the 'Golden Dawn' completely in

---

131 Howe E, 1972, *Fringe Masonry in England 1870-1885*.
132 Wright R., *August Order of Light history*.

133 Stephenson A. B. (Supreme Magus Emeritus*) August Order of Light history*.

1897 by deliberately leaving incriminating 'Golden Dawn' papers in a hansom cab with Westcott name on them to be found by the Police.

Westcott quit and contented himself with running the S.R.I.A. and only kept in touch with his baby, the 'Golden Dawn,' through other members. He watched their original 'Golden Dawn' implode three years later, when Mathers accused Westcott of forgery in February 1900. This backfired and Mathers was expelled from the London Temple after investigation by some of the members. Westcott kept a watchful though distant eye on the order and let sleeping dogs lie, as the London members of the 'Golden Dawn' renamed it in German, *Goldene Morgenröthe* meaning 'Golden Dawn' and changed the order beyond comparison, from its original ideal of a practical Rosicrucian Order. This was something which Westcott had nothing to do with. Mather's reputation suffered again in 1901, after the dreadful Horos court case which was printed in the press, the proceedings also implicated Mathers.

What many people do not know, as the details only came to light in Westcott's ACTA in 2014, is that Westcott progressed from Grade V° in 1915 to Grade VIII° of the **Stella Matutina** in 1916. He did this in four full ceremonies, conducted by Dr R. Felkin and 'others.' As a direct result the 'Secret Stella Matutina College' of the S.R.I.A., (see fig 103b) was formed by Arthur Cadbury Jones, the Secretary General of the S.R.I.A. at the time. Dr Felkin was made a grade 9° in the S.R.I.A. as a result and then travelled to Australia and then New Zealand, as the Chief Adept of Australia for the S.R.I.A. and to bring the 'Stella Matutina' to the inhabitants. What is significant about Westcott's advancement is that none of the founders of the original 'Golden Dawn', Woodman, Mathers or Westcott had ever been through a ceremony of that order before. They had found a cipher manuscript of an 'organisation' and Mathers had been tasked with turning these notes, into the 'first order' ceremonies of his own making and all three founders had assumed their high ranks.

In my opinion what is called by some the 'Stella Matutina' is in fact a completely different order, to that of the 1888 'Golden Dawn.' Although I believe that they are both probably both from the same shared source. My next book will cover this subject in more detail.

The evidence has been hidden away all this time in a number of very interesting entries in a couple of Westcott's ACTA. To repeat myself what many people will not have realised is that Westcott progressed through the 'second order grades,' by full ceremony, from VI° to the VIII°, of the 'Stella Matutina' between 1915-1916. Later these grades will be designated 6=5, 7=4, 8=3.

The first entry can be seen in Fig 103a, on 29 June 1915.[134]

ACTA: 1915

June 29. - *As a result of long consideration and at the invitation, seconded by Dr R.W. Felkin. I received the Adept Major Grade representing the Grade VI° of the revised Continental Society of Rosicrucian's. He lent me his copies of the Equinox, Dies C.C., and Grade V° Ritual.*
September 6. - *Received typed Ritual of VI°.*

Those of you, who are students of 'Golden Dawn' history, I hope will keep an open mind and ask yourself, why did Westcott go through these ceremonies in 1915? It is so many years after the fall of the 1888 'Golden Dawn' in 1900 and 27 years since it was launched. It was Dr Felkin who brought the 'Stella Matutina' to Westcott's attention, after his personal investigations in Germany of a number of years. Many people continue to think that the 'Stella Matutina' was just another version of the 'Golden Dawn,' but I believe that it was something else, much more on that at another time.

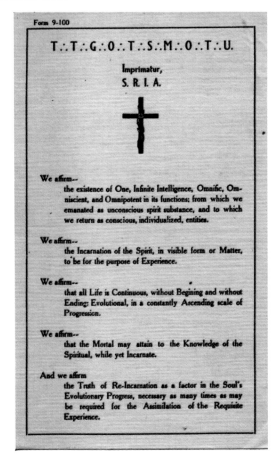

Figure 103b - Secret Stella Matutina College

---

134 Westcott's Acta 1905-1917.

Figure 104 - Westcott's Martinist Certificate 1899

In the **Martinist Order**, John Yarker makes Westcott an Initiator without ceremony on 10 February 1895, an equivalent to Provincial Grand Master, of a Lodge De L'Ordre Martinist No.45, (see fig 120), Westcott's Martinist Initiator Warrant 1895.

Yarker suggests to R.S. Brown in 1895 that they use the surviving 'Society of Eight' as the foundation of the 'Martinist Order' in England. Yarker produced an 1899 list of members and officers with their rank in the order in brackets; J. Yarker (UP), R.S. Brown (U.B.), G.S. Hunter (B.I.), G.A. Turner (B.A.), Dr W.W. Westcott (B.O.), Fred Holland (B.Rec.) was issued a Certificate of 'D 'Initiator' for Birmingham. F.F. Schnitger (B.Tr.), Dr G. Dickson (B.G.). It may only be a coincidence that the list has eight members! Yarker, Holland and Westcott were original 'Society of Eight' members.

Papus visited Westcott in London on 7 June 1899 and said the Soc. Ros. in France, the 'Kabbalistic de la Rose-Croix' was a small body of 7 - 12 men and promised Westcott a diploma in the Rituals.

Westcott received his Papus 'Certificate D'Initiation,' (see fig 104) and the date, when deciphered,[135] turns out to be 8 July 1899. This is only days before Westcott received in the post the 'Proposal of alliance from the Ordre Kabbalistique De La Rose-Croix of Paris,' this was sent on 13 July, (see fig 119). Westcott's Warrant of

'Inspector Principal & Doctor en Hermetisim' or as it says on the 'CHARGE' 'Representative of the Order in London' is dated 7 December 1899, (see fig 123). On 2 February 1900, Westcott received two Martinist Grand Officer Jewels from Papus, one for Westcott and the other for Yarker, (see fig 124). In June 1901, Theodor Reuss was made 'Special Inspector for the Martinist Order' in Germany and Papus was made a 'Prussian Illuminati,' Berlin. All communication with Papus and the Martinist Order stopped and all the letters cease in the archives and there are not even any notes about Papus in Westcott's ACTA after 1902.

In the **Prussian Illuminati**, Westcott was made a Minerval without ceremony on 29 July 1901, (see fig 23) and probably received the certificate in the post on 30 August 1901, sent by Reuss. Westcott was considered to be the Regent of Britain of the Minerva Lodges of the Order of Illuminati in Great Britain sometime in October 1901. During his January 1901 visit, Reuss conveyed the 'Sacred Word' of the 'Priest Degree' or 'Synods Grade,' which according to Heckethorn was the same as the Regent's Word. There is no proof, but an unsubstantiated note that said he was admitted by full ceremony on 8 July 1902. However, Westcott only accepted officially "the position as Regent" on 26 August 1902, but in the same letter rejects the Illuminati grades because their Rose Croix ceremony is too similar to the 'Ancient & Accepted Rite' 18th Degree.

---

135 The Martinist Cipher code was supplied in a letter to Westcott from Papus in the S.R.I.A. archives.

In the **Theosophical Society,** I am not sure when Westcott became a member. He may have been a member of the original 'London Lodge' founded in 1878 by C.C. Massey. There is no evidence of such, but when Anna Kingsford and Edward Maitland broke away from the 'Theosophical Society' 'London Lodge' in 1884 and formed the 'Hermetic Society,' Westcott became an Honorary member and he and Mathers contributed and read papers to their meetings until Kingsford's death in 1888.

Allegedly, Westcott joined the 'Theosophical Society' (Eastern Philosophy) proper in June 1887, a month after Helena Petrovna Blavatsky arrived to live in London and where she founded the 'Blavatsky Lodge' in the May of 1887. His contribution of over forty different papers to Blavatsky's magazine *LUCIFER* starts in October 1887, with two reviews of his work. Blavatsky banned all membership of Rosicrucian organisations on 9 October 1888, as a measure to thwart the 'Golden Dawn,' but afterwards was persuaded to correct her mistake. Westcott was personally invited on 19 August 1890 to join the 'Esoteric Section' of the 'Theosophical Society,' which he did with twenty others.

The fences must have been mended as Westcott founded the Theosophical Lodge Adelphi, in 1891 with Percy Bullock and John Watkins. We know that W.B. Yeats was also a member of this 'Theosophical Society Lodge.' When Westcott retired in 1920, to Natal in South Africa, he began to work on behalf of the 'Theosophical Society' until his death.

PUBLISHING

Westcott published many works in a variety of publications and, in addition to writing his own work, some that have never been published, see the picture in (fig 105). He also wrote an introduction to many other authors' books. His medical treatises on unofficial drugs were published 1883-1921, assisting William Martindale (1840-1902) in that undertaking and on other subjects such as alcoholism and suicide in 1885. In 1907, he wrote about his *Twelve years experiences of a London Coroner.*[136]

The first ever esoteric book that he wrote and published was on *The Isiac Tablets of Cardinal Bembo,* on the hieroglyphics of a Ptolemaic Egyptian Solar and Luna calendar.[137] His second publication was a translation of the *Sepher Yetzirah*

of the Hebrew Rabbis.[138] Yet another translation of *The magical ritual of the sanctum regnum: interpreted by the tarot trumps.*[139] Then the *Numbers: their occult power and mystic virtues,*[140] both of these volumes were drawing from Eliphas Levi works.

He wrote many articles for the Societas Rosicruciana in Anglia; over sixty-one papers appear in the Metropolitan College Transactions, which was started by Westcott in 1885, the last was read posthumously in 1937. If you look at the list of the High Council Library books, you can actually see the names of the books Westcott used, as the basis of research in his papers; many annotated by him in the margin and on the front cover signed or rubber stamped by him with his signature.

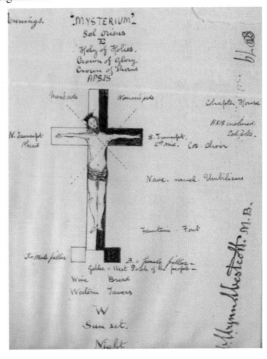

Figure 105 - Westcott drawing from a scrap book

In the back of one of his several ACTA or official diaries, is a complete list of the forty dated lectures read to Metropolitan College, twenty two lectures to the 'August Order of Light' and some thirty lectures delivered to the other S.R.I.A. colleges.

One of my most exciting finds, in 2010, was a large wooden chest, which contained eighty-seven specially bound numbered papers that were either handwritten or typed by Westcott, with one omission and one duplicate number. These were presumably a master set of papers see the list of 'Westcott's box of numbered papers' over the page.

---

136 Wynn Westcott W. M.B., D.P.H., J.P. 1906, *Twelve years experiences of a London Coroner.*
137 Westcott W., 1887, The Isiac Tablets of Cardinal Bembo. The S.R.I.A. has a 4 x 5 foot replica in the library.

138 Westcott W. W. 1893. *The Book of Formation, and the 32 Paths of Wisdom.*
139 Westcott W. W., 1896, *The magical ritual of the sanctum regnum: interpreted by the tarot trumps.*
140 Westcott W. W., 1911, *Numbers: their occult power.*

He could pick up and take along any of these papers to read at the twelve colleges in the society at the time.

The box contained much more than this and there were over one hundred and thirty seven different titles; as several numbered papers had different versions and variations of the title, some are heavily annotated. It also contained a sample of each of his printed and published works, by some unknown compiler of this collection; we assume the contents had been unread for at least sixty years, based on the date of the last item.

Westcott also researched and compiled a series of nine monographs that he also edited and published entitled the *Collectanea Hermetica*, which started in 1893 and ended in 1902. There were also, in the Westcott Box, his eight contributions to *Ars Quatuorum Coronatorum*, the transactions of Quatuor Coronati Lodge, No. 2076, London, a list can be found in their *Concise Index 1917* and includes:

QUATUOR CORONATI RESEARCH LODGE PAPERS;

Religion of Freemasonry and the Kabbalah.
(1886-88) Volume 1: pages 55-9
Mason's marks and the secret alphabet of Cornelius Agrippa.
(1890) Volume 3: pages 77-8
Symbolism of the Tabernacle.
(1893) Volume 6: pages 12-16
Rosicrucians and their connection with Freemasonry.
(1894) Volume 7: pages 36-47, 83
The Magic Roll.
(1903) Volume 16: pages 254-6
Notes on a curious Certificate and seal.
(1906) Volume 19: pages 241-2
Freemasonry in its relation to Essenes.
(1915) Volume 28: pages 67-79
Resemblance of Freemasonry to cult of Mithra.
(1916) Volume 29: pages 336-47

WESTCOTT BOX OF NUMBERED PAPERS

No. 01, Thoughts on the Zodiac, 1885
No. 02, Rosicrucian Thoughts on the Ever-Burning Lamps, 1885
No. 03, Alchemy and Chemistry, 1886
No. 05, The Ten Sephiroth, 1887
No. 06, Kabbalah, 1888
No. 07, The Shaman, 1888
No. 08, The Basilisk or Cockatrice, 1889
No. 08, Man, 1889
No. 09, The Mandrake, 1889
No. 10, Blavatsky's Early Race, 1892
No. 11, Death, Essay on [The], 1893
No. 12, Hiram, Chiram, and Hermes, 1893
No. 13, Tabernacle of Moses, 1893
No. 14, The Modern Mystics 1894/1900/1912
No. 15, Royal Arch, on an older ritual, 1894
No. 16, Clairvoyance and Dreaming, 1895
No. 17, Angels, 1890, 1912, 1915, 1917
No. 18, The Devil, Hebrew and others , 1900
No. 19, The History of Astrology, 1901
No. 20, My Occult Life- Symbolism Sphinx, 1903
No. 21, Talismans and Charms, 1904
No. 22, Serpent Myth, 1905
No. 23, Dreams, 1906
No. 24, The Supernatural, 1906
No. 25, The Ruins of Zimbabwe, 1907
No. 26, Robert Fludd and his works, 1907
No. 27, Time and Space, 1907
No. 28, Necromancy, Sorcery and Magic,
No. 29, Glastonbury Abbey, 1909
No. 30, Divining Rod, 1909
No. 31, Man as Spirit and Soul, 1910
No. 32, Paracelsus, Life and Writings, 1910
No. 33, Divination and its History, 1910
No. 34, Ancient Mysteries, 1910
No. 35, Star Lore of the Bible, 1911
No. 36, Religion, Philosophy and Occult Science of China, 1911
No. 37, Curious Birth Custom, 1912
No. 38, Easter Island, 1913
No. 39, The Golden Age & Others, 1913
No. 40, Mysteries of Egypt, 1913
No. 41, Rosicrucians: Past and Present:, 1913
No. 42, Man's Blood and Generation, 1913
No. 43, Symbolism of Stones, 1914

No. 44, Head, Heart and Hand, 1914
No. 45, The Essenes and Freemasonry 1914
No. 46, The Mistletoe Bough, 1914
No. 47, The Sense of smell & Incense, 1915
No. 48, The Symbolism of Knots, 1915
No. 49, Bells and Sounds, 1915
No. 50, Angels at Mons notes on the, "Light" 1915
No. 50, Angels, "The Occult Review" Oct, 1917
No. 50, Life and Death, 1915
No. 51, Circumambulation, On The Rite of , 1915
No. 52, Fairies and Elementals, 1915
No. 53, Resemblance of Freemasonry to Cult Mithra, 1916
No. 54, Symbolism of Keys, 1916
No. 55, A New Spiritual Development, 1916
No. 56, Spiritualism and Occult Arts & Supplements, 1917
No. 57, Stonehenge and the Druids, 1917
No. 58, The Number Four and Man, 1917
No. 59, Trial of Ordeal, 1917
No. 60, Limitations of Science, 1917
No. 61, Fate, Fortune, Luck, 1917
No. 62, The Golden Fleece, 1918
No. 63, Reincarnation and Birth Emblems, 1918
No. 64, Progress in Spiral Cycles (of Human Progress) 1918
No. 65, The Zodiac and its Symbolism, 1918
No. 66, Candlemas, candles and wax, 1918
No. 68, Spiritualism of Magic, 1919
No. 69, Life and Death, 1919
No. 70, Anomalies in masonry, 1919
No. 71, Society of Rosicrucians, 1919
No. 72, Rosicrucian Society during fifty years, 1915
No. 73, Data of the History of the Rosicrucians, 1916
No. 74, Intellectual moderation, 1908
No. 76, Hebrew Rabbis,
No. 77, Jubilee Convocation, 1919
No. 78, The Kabalah Hebrew Letters,
No. 79, The Mystical Number 666 Revised, 1922
No. 80, Mystical Reverie upon the Sphinx, 1890
No. 81, The Carnival,
No. 83, The Four Pillars Zelator Grade, 1912
No. 84, Judaism, 1913
No. 85 , Sound, Voice Poetry and Music, 1924
No. 86, Clairvoyance & Pre-vision, 1752, 1912
No. 87, Playing Cards and the Tarot in Divination, 1922

THEODOR ALBERT KARL REUSS

So called irregular mason!

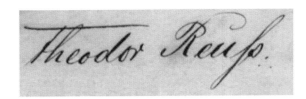

Theodor Reuss (1855-1923), was a Bavarian by birth and it must have been here that he nurtured his affinity with the 'Bavarian Illuminati,' which was founded in Munich in 1777. He was an ambitious and a very capable journalist and singer, who was the son of an innkeeper of Augsburg, a city approximately the same distance North West of Munich as Ingolstadt, the home of the 'Bavarian Illuminati,' is North of Munich.

Reuss was the first Freemason we know, to have resurrected the Illuminati in Munich in 1880. His resurrected Illuminati rituals are not like the original Weishaupt ceremonies, but something much more masonic like in character. Much easier to use as they do not contain any of the very long lecture material, found in the original Weishaupt ceremonies. Unfortunately they do not contain any description of the furniture or setup of the lodges and very little rubric or the movement of the officers and the candidate during the ceremonies, something you do find in more modern day ritual books, which in my opinion may show just how old these resurrected Iluminati rituals may be.

Why did he resurrect the Illuminati, first in Munich and then Berlin? In the words of his main rival Leopold Engel:

Diese Person behauptete, doss in ihr sich noch die alten Überreste des Ordens konzentrierten, dass eine bedeutende Anzahl von wurdigen Mannern sic hunter ihrer Obhut noch befande, die nur warteten, den geeigneten Führer zu erhalten und dass dieser Fuhrer der Schreiber dieser Zeilen sein Könner, wenn er nur wolle.

Translating it in my words, Leopold Engel thought that Reuss believed that there were considerable numbers of Illuminati left over from the original 'Bavarian Order.' That these people or scribes (Schreiber) were very worthy men, only waiting for the right leader or master (Führer) to come along and guide them in the older system, if they wanted to do so.

FREEMASONRY

Reuss first became a regular Freemason in London in 1867. It was in a German speaking lodge that used the 'Schroder Ritual' working under a warrant from the United Grand Lodge of England, while he was living in the City.

He was probably proposed into the lodge by a friend who was their 'Director of Ceremonies' at the time, Henry Klein a shop proprietor who sold sheet music, an interest they both shared.

Reuss was initiated into the 'Pilgrim Lodge No. 238' on Wednesday 8 November 1876. He was passed to the Degree of 'Fellowcraft' on Tuesday 8th May, 1877 and raised to the degree of 'Master Mason' on Wednesday 9 January 1878. I also believe that while living in London, Reuss joined many other masonic orders too.

Figure 106 - Theodor Reuss as young man

He was allegedly exalted into the 'Holy Royal Arch' on 7 May 1877; the date does not however fit, one of the dates is wrong as he was still only a Fellowcraft at the time, the 'Holy Royal Arch' qualification being a 'Master Mason.' One masonic photograph of him reproduced in the *Oriflamme* Magazine shows Reuss in a 'Master Mason's' apron (see fig 107),[141] but also wearing the 'Thrice Illustrious Master's Collarette' and the 'Breast Jewel' of the 'Royal and Select Masters.'

There is another photograph of him in a Worshipful Masters apron and a top hat, (see fig 108).[142] The top hat is still worn by the Worshipful Masters and members of the Pilgrim Lodge today.

---

141 *Oriflamme* magazine 1912 and E. Howe, page 88.
142 *Oriflamme* magazine 1912.

Figure 107 - Reuss wearing Royal & Select Masters

But I believe that this picture may only imply that he became a Worshipful Master of a 'Schroder Lodge,' at some time, it may have been in Hamburg in 1902, but he was certainly not the Worshipful Master in the 'Pilgrim Lodge' having searched through a list of their Worshipful Masters, which survives.

The 'Pilgrim Lodge' was consecrated in England in 1779 under the name of *Der Pilger* and met at the Mitre Tavern, Fleet Street, London. It was formed under the 'Moderns Grand Lodge' and then later became part of the 'United Grand Lodge of England' in 1813. It has the privilege to work in the German language, in the beginning they used the 'Zinnendorf Ritual' a distinct Swedish System that had been introduced in to Germany, they now use as mentioned the 'Schroder ritual.' The 'Pilgrim Lodge' is also one of the nineteen lodges that have the privilege of nominating, each year, a member of their lodge for appointment as a 'Grand Steward,' a prestigious lodge indeed and is therefore known as a 'Red Apron Lodge.'

Ellic Howe[143] tells us that in the *Oriflamme* magazine, according to Reuss' own 'Grand Lodge' under the 'Sovereign Sanctuary Constitution,' published by the 'Ancient & Primitive Rite' Germany, that its craft lodges were to use the 'Pilgrim Lodge's' by-laws and the 'Hamburg Lodge' (Schroeder) ritual, as adopted by the 'Pilgrim Lodge' in 1852. This means that Reuss was using the ritual from its source in Hamburg,

the home of Schroder and he used the by-laws of his Mother Lodge in London.

The Schroeder ritual was the very first German Masonic Ritual that we know of that was created in 1801, by Friedrich Ludwig Schroeder (1744-1816) and first adopted in Hamburg in 1811. It was specifically for Germans, who had, up until then, only practised their masonry in either, the French or English language depending on the 'Grand Lodge' it belonged to. The Schroeder ritual was fashioned on a purer form of 'English (Ancient) Freemasonry' and was currently available to 'German (Moderns) Freemasons' and this may have been part of the problem, because it was probably considered by some Germans as not German enough, even though it was written and performed in the German language.

For example, one part the present 'Schroeder Installation Ceremony' is a direct translation from the 'English Emulation Ritual.' Top hats are worn at the meetings by all the members of the 'Pilgrim Lodge,' visitors wearing either the hats provided or if they wish their own.[144] During these four years spent in London, I do not believe Reuss would have had enough time to gain enough useful masonic contacts for his next project in Germany.

Figure 108 - Reuss wearing W.M. apron and a top hat

---

143 December 1902 issue.

144 See website of the Pilgrim Lodge, 2015.

MUNICH

In January 1878, Reuss was not only made a Master Mason, but he also wrote for the *Times* as a war correspondent from the Balkans. This prompted him to move to back to Bavaria and Munich in 1878, with his new wife Delphina Garbois, who was from Dublin. It was here that he conceived and executed his childhood scheme to resurrect the 'Illuminati Order.' What was his project?

There is a clue or two in a letter he wrote to Wilhelm Hübbe-Schleiden, in 1893 see translation over the page. In the letter he says "I became a member of the Freemasons, the Scots-brethren, the Rosenkreutzer, the Illuminati and the Theosophists, among others."

It was while in Munich in this year that he got behind with his lodge dues and was promptly excluded from the 'Pilgrims Lodge' in London, which is understandable in the circumstances. The 1880 Munich Illuminati project also seems to have failed. This may have been caused by the nature of his job, travelling as a journalist and performing as an accomplished bass, opera singer.

He was also a close friend of Richard Wagner (1813-1883), as a young man he knew Wagner the famous German composer, whom he met in 1873 at the age of 18 years old. He may also have sung on occasions privately for one of Wagner's greatest fans at the time, Ludovicus Rex Bavariae, Ludwig II, the reclusive 'Swan King' or 'mad king of Bavaria' (1863-1886). Ludwig II prided himself as a model for the Grail King, one of Wagner's famous operas and also the French 'Sun King' Louis XIV. Ludwig II was certainly also interested in the occult, which may have inspired Reuss. In 1882 he went to Bosnia and Herzegovina as a war correspondent and all this travelling would have made it too difficult to be able to administer a new revived Illuminati order.

LONDON

We know he left Munich for London in 1885 alone and re-married a financially well-endowed wife who bore him a son. Albert Franz Theodor Reuss (1879-1958), a self-educated zoologist lived in Berlin. It was an interest in Lepidoptera that led him to collect various reptiles, including many poisonous snakes. Albert was also a talented painter of snakes that were the subjects of most of his works. Reuss was artistic himself and in 1885, for example he appeared at a concert given by the Literary and Artistic Society at which he sang arias from the Magic Flute, Reuss would have liked the strong connection to Egyptian Freemasonry in this opera. He also sang at a Ballad and Operatic

concert at the St James's Hall and the Musical Review, a critic predicted that he would have 'a good career in this country'.[145]

There was plenty of time to re-join the 'Pilgrim Lodge' over the next ten years, but he did not. Reuss was a modern socialist and revolutionary, he was probably also distracted by his involvement with the 'Socialist League and International Workers Association' in England and this got him into hot water. There were also accusations of spying for the Prussian Government as a journalist. Reuss was even expelled by Karl Marx's daughter Eleanor, who was suspicious of Reuss's activities as a spy whilst being a journalist. On 5 October 1887 the *London Evening News* published an article by him on the machinations of London anarchist circles which can only have confirmed current suspicions of such political activities. On 7 January 1888, William Morris printed an extensive list of alleged Prussian police spies in 'The Commonweal.' Reuss was described as now Bismarck's political agent on the Central News of London. He was a contributor to the *Suddeutsche Presse* at Munich and the *Berliner Zeitung* at Berlin. All of which is probably true, but for example the author who conducted so much research on Reus that I have used, Ellic Howe, was himself a very successful English spy, cycling around Germany as a student collecting examples of German typefaces and printed material, while a student leading up to the Second World War. Perhaps a case of "the pot calling the kettle black."

BERLIN

Reuss was in Berlin in 1889 in his capacity as the *Central News* agency's representative there, which lasted until 1891. Reuss also represented the *London Daily Chronicle* at Berlin and must have travelled repeatedly between London and Berlin.

It was during this period in Berlin that Reuss significantly wrote on the LUDWIG Lodge Illuminati letterhead, to the head of the original 'German Theosophical Society,' Wilhelm Hübbe-Schleiden on 30 October 1893, see below.[146]

The letterhead on which he wrote had the title, *The study lodge of the Illuminati Chapter, called Ludwig.* However Reuss had put a line through the second row of the printed letterhead, which read *des alten und angenommenen Freimaurer.* This translates as 'the old and accepted Freemasons. The original printed letterhead would therefore have read, "The study lodge of the old and accepted Freemasons (Illuminati Chapter) called LUDWIG in the Orient of Munich." The word 'Illuminati

---

145 Howe E. 1972, *Fringe Masonry in England 1870-1885,*
146 Cod MS W. Hübbe-Schleiden 239, *Spezialsammlungen und Bestandserhaltung, Staats-und Universitatsbibliothek Gottingen.*

Chapter' only added in brackets by hand afterwards.

So the Munich 'Ludwig Lodge' in 1880 would seem to have been originally, a teaching Lodge of the 'Ancient and Accepted Freemasons,' which is unusual in itself for that particular order. It was called 'LUDWIG,' only later did it become a 'Lodge of Instruction' for the 'Illuminati Chapter' called LUDWIG, but based in Berlin in 1893.[147]

The language of the letter I was told uses old style German words. But with a little help from a modern day German member of the S.R.I.A. and his Mother, who wish to remain anonymous, they came up with this translation for us (see fig 109):

This letter seems to infer to me that after becoming a Freemason in London, Reuss joined a separate 'Scottish Rite' organisation where he received the 'Rose-Croix' degree. This was all before his involvement with, the 'Resurrected Iluminati.' I have found no other reference to this except in this letter

In this letter he also a little contentiously mentions at the end of the first paragraph, his different understanding and opinion of the down to earth Illuminati 'teachings of karma.' Perhaps a little controversial when Wilhelm Hübbe-Schleiden was the head and founder of the original (Eastern orientated) 'Theosophical Society' based in Hamburg.

Die Unterrichtsloge
des alten und angenommenen freimaurer
Illuminaten Capitels
genannt
LUDWIG
Im Orient Munchen

Berlin, den 30.10.1893

Geehrter Herr!

Im Verlaufe meines Suchens nach Möglichkeit wurde ich Mitglied der Freimaurer, der Schottenbrüder, der Rosenkreutzer, der Illuminaten, der Theosophen, u. a. und ich fand die Lehre vom Karma unvollkommen ausgebildet im Fundamentalsatz des inneren Zirkels des großen Illuminaten legitals: Alles rächt sich hier auf Erden!
Ich lege Ihnen eine Beitrittserklärung bei, falls Sie die selbige unterzeichnen wollen, bin ich zu weiteren Auskünften bereit. Kosten entstehen Ihnen gar keine.

Hochachtungsvoll
Theodor Reuß

The Study Lodge
Ancient and Accepted Freemasons
Illuminati Chapters
called
LUDWIG
In the Orient Munich

Berlin, the 30.10.1893

Honoured gentleman!

In the course of my search, I became a member of the Freemasons, the Scots-brethren, the Rosenkreutzer, the Illuminati, the Theosophists, among others, and I found the teachings of karma imperfect in the fundamental theorem of the inner circle of the great Illuminati law: Everything is avenged here on Earth!
I will give you a declaration of accession if you want to sign the same, I am ready to give you further information. Costs are not incurred at all.

Respectfully
Theodor Reuss

Figure 109 - Letter to Wilhelm Hübbe-Schleiden 1893

What is so interesting is that this letter was sent long before Reuss ever met Westcott in 1901 or ever discussed setting up an S.R.I.A. College in Germany 1902. So the reference to *der Rosenkreutzer* in the letter may only refer to one of the other uses of the word in the German language.

I suggest it is used as 'Rose-Croix' not 'Christian Rosenkreutze,' or 'Rosicrucian Society.' Why, because this use of the word Rosenkreutzer is also the heading used by Reuss on the title page of the 'Illuminati Rose-Croix ritual,' (see fig 88).

Wilhelm was also the editor of the *Sphinx Magazine* in 1893.

I was to find out much later, that Hübbe-Schleiden was to correspond with Dr Robert Felkin about meeting up with Dr Rudolf Steiner in 1910, with regard to the 'Continental Rosicrucians' and the 'Stella Matutina,' which is another part of that story.

---

147 Also briefly mentioned in Chapter I, 'First Illuminati letter.'

REVIVED LUDWIG LODGE 1895

Reuss was still thinking about the Illuminati as he wrote his first anonymous Illuminati book, *Die Mysterien der Illuminaten* under the pseudonym Caratheodoro, but he had it published by Druck von Trowitsch & Sohn in Berlin in 1894, the year before he moved back permanently to Berlin with his family.

One of the first things Reuss did when he returned to Berlin from London in 1895, was turn his research into reality and revived the Illuminati Order, and re-opened the Munich 'Study Lodge of the Illuminati Chapter called Ludwig in the Orient of Munich,' of his comparative youth and built so much more upon it. I do not know when Reuss added the additional grade, of the 'Rose-Croix,' to his revived Illuminati. He had already joined a number of other different orders.

It was this, I believe, that Reuss and Karl Kellner (1851-1905), began to discuss at length during 1895, the founding of what they called the 'Academia Masonica.' The grandiose idea was to make it possible for questing brethren to become acquainted *with all* the existing Masonic degrees and systems. Karl Kellner had discovered 'The Hermetic Brotherhood of Light' teachings that suited his pure in-spirit and almost priest like ways. Kellner did not like the unscrupulous but talented Leopold Engel or his pans for the Illuminati. So, when Engel turned up on the scene the following year, Kellner was not sympathetic to his involvement and would have nothing more to do with the 'Academia Masonica' and Reuss and left him on his own. That is until Reuss finally broke off all contact with Engel for the second time in June 1902, only then did his friendship with Kellner resume, it was only then that Kellner asked Reuss to obtain the 'Ancient and Primitive Rite' from Yarker with its 90° and 95° of the combined 'Rites of Memphis and Mizraim.' So that they could build their 'Templars of the East' with all the degrees, grades and rites Reuss had already obtained from France and England in 1902 with the help of Papus, Westcott and Yarker, three men that Reuss could get along with. The 'Oriental Templars' was Reuss' new name for the 'Academia Masonica,' however Kellner's death ended their original plan.

I speculated in Chapter I, how and where Reuss and Engel met? It was most probably in the new Western orientated German section of the 'Theosophical Society' on 29 Aug 1896 in Berlin.'

Reuss was elected vice president and Engel was elected the treasurer at the same meeting, under the leadership of Franz Hartmann. They were both writers, Reuss a journalist and Engel the editor of a spiritual magazine called *Wahrheit-Sucher* (1896-1897) which mentioned Reuss by name in the September 1896 edition. After only one year, the magazine changed its name to *Das Wort* (1897-1923).

Most of the people in this Illuminati story had been members of the 'Theosophical Society' at one time or other and most of them, for some reason or other left the organisation. Up until now, the first mention of the 'Theosophical Society' associated with Reuss was in one of Ellic Howe's otherwise excellent books on Reuss, which are at times in direct conflict with this new body of evidence, where he alleges that:

Reuss went to London in December 1901 and saw Westcott, whom he had already met in Theosophical Society circles a decade earlier.

There is no evidence of either of the above being actually true, as Westcott absolutely did not meet Reuss in 1901. They only corresponded after the Papus introduction in June and there is no mention of a previous meeting. Their first meeting was in January 1902 as the S.R.I.A. archives show. Westcott may have been very involved with the London 'Theosophical Society,' but nowhere does it mention that Reuss attended Theosophical meetings at this time or while living in London.

However, ten years before this Reuss while in London, is thought to have attended the funeral of Madame Helena A. Blavatsky at the crematorium in Woking where her ashes were put in a casket and returned to her home address at 19 Avenue Road, Regents Park. She died of a kidney infection after a bout of influenza on Friday 7 May 1891 and which was reported in the evening press on Saturday 8 May. There is no indication in Westcott's ACTA that he attended the funeral.

On 9 November 1896, Reuss admitted to the 'Illuminati Ludwig Lodge' the enthusiastic and pushy potential Illuminati called Leopold Engel and added strength to his new cause, but ultimately with dire consequences. Reuss suggested in 1912, in his historical edition of the *Oriflamme*, that he was first to admit Leopold Engel as a Freemason and that his father Carl Engel became the Dresden Illuminati 'Archivist and Seal keeper.' The father was from St. Petersburg, Russia, was he a Russian Freemason? Leopold Engel was born in St. Petersburg and quotes himself as a Freemason from the Orient of Petersburg, was this after meeting Reuss?

From Engel birthdates and star signs,[148] we know he was affronted by setbacks and he wanted instant satisfaction and positive encouragement, he was also a sore loser that would kick back and pout if he did not get his own way, as we will find. Did Theodor Reuss take his eye off the ball, as he

---

148 White S. 1987, *New, Astrology.*

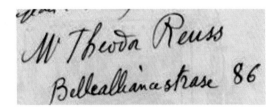

Figure 110 - Reuss' Home address and Illuminati Ludwig Lodge address

travelled the world with his job as a war correspondent in peace time in, London, New York, Munich and Berlin? He reported on the Imperial Manoeuvres for a number of years after 1896 and, in the spring of 1897, travelled to Greece and Turkey on behalf of the Berlin *Das Kleine Journal* to report on the current hostilities between those countries.

It was probably during this last wandering phase that Engel set up his own 'Revived Illuminati Order' in Dresden in 1897, using Reuss' material, probably out of pure frustration with Reuss. But Engel and Reuss had made up by 1899, when the two Illuminati orders were amalgamated into one. Engel had probably persuaded Reuss dexterously to relocate the headquarters from Berlin to Dresden, where Engel lived and already ran his own esoteric newspaper *Die Wort* or 'The Word.' This resulted in Engel offering to help Reuss and the 'Revived Illuminati Order' by printing all the Illuminati material in Dresden.

GRAND LODGE OF GERMANY

Forming a new 'Grand Lodge of Germany,' would account for why Reuss held a meeting at his home on 12 March 1901 to re-open the Illuminati's 'Ludwig Lodge,' in Berlin. Reuss was its 'Worshipful Master,' and August Weinholtz was the Senior Warden, and Max Rahn as the Junior Warden. Engel however was relegated to the more junior role of Conductor.

But I think what Reuss did was gain agreement from those present for a Berlin based 'Grand Lodge of Germany' as an umbrella organisation for all the new degrees rites and orders he was hoping to obtain, from France and England, including the 'Revived Iluminati Order.' This Grand Lodge of his own making was declared totally independent of all others.

However, it would seem that Reuss was very much a man who would rather stay at home and let the world come to him after all his travels, whenever he could. He based the new Order of the 'Resurrected Illuminati' just down the road from his Berlin home. It was, after all, then the capital city of the new Emperor of Prussia.

His home address was 86 Belle Alliance Straße, Berlin and he seems a very much a home loving man. He ran several of his Orders just six doors down the road at Number 74 Belle Alliance Straße, Berlin. This information did not come to light until you compare the home addresses on the Papus letters and those of the 'Ludwig' and 'Swedenborgian Lodges,' (see fig 110).

The idea of a new Grand Lodge was not as strange as it sounds because, in greater Germania, at that time there was a complete mixture of Freemason Lodges, working in German, French and English languages, reporting to three different German Grand Lodges in Berlin alone and there were different 'Grand Lodges' belonging to other countries like England and France, each with their own competing 'Grand Lodges.' All these 'Lodges' and 'Grand Lodges' were competing sometimes for the same German members and their membership money. They did this by offering them completely different higher grade orders associated with each.

Reuss, like many other German Freemasons, but perhaps only the revolutionary kind, felt at the time, that what was really needed for the sake of sanity and order was one governing body for all masonry. Where you paid just one subscription fee to join and only worked in your native tongue. Even today, many Freemasons will be members of many different Grand bodies at one time and pay an annual subscription to each, to remain a member. Membership also implied a distinct path of progression, through their approved grades.

Some 'Grand Lodges' nowadays actively encourage their members not to join 'this order' or 'that order,' making it a very complicated path of progression to follow and this only makes it more difficult to understand the point of some of these degrees, grades and rites. This becomes even more complicated in the higher orders or 'haute grades' where you not only duplicate the fees you pay, but you may be in, for example, three different types of 'Rose Croix degrees' belonging to three different 'Grand Lodges.'

There needed to be a logical, systematic progression from one degree to the next and from them into the higher degrees and other orders for those who wished to, both then and now!

NON MASONIC MEMBERSHIPS

Papus went to Berlin on 24 June 1901 and exchanged a number of orders with Reuss, these included the 'Ordre Martinist,' but not with Engel.

Tactful Reuss and stubborn Papus shared the same Sun sign and were so alike, insightful and imaginative,[149] that they got on with each other and Reuss had issued an 'Illuminati Warrant' to Papus to become the French representative of the Illuminati in Paris.

Papus made Reuss the 'Sovereign Delegate' of the 'Ordre Martinist' in Berlin. During this visit, Papus must have told Reuss the story of how he had obtained the 'Swedenborg Rite' from Yarker, directly through their Martinist relationship and probably explained that Reuss would have to go the long way around and use Westcott as the 'Grand Secretary' to get his warrant for Germany. Reuss probably explained that he did not want just the one 'Swedenborg Lodge,' he wanted five across Germany.

However, forming the 'English Illuminati' in Great Britain in 1901 was only one part of this grandiose plan. Theodor Reuss had already set up a relationship with a 'Schroder Lodge' in Hamburg, called the „Phonig" Order, of which he may even have been a member. England and the English Freemasons, it would seem, had much very much more to offer Reuss in terms of potential candidates for the 'English Illuminati.' While some of the senior English Freemasons also had orders and degrees that they could bestow in return on Reuss and he wanted to take them!

ORIFLAMME MAGAZINE
Reuss' Grand Lodge newspaper

You can build a picture of how Reuss started to lay the foundations of his several orders in the six editions of the 1902 *Oriflamme* magazine in the S.R.I.A. archives, starting in May 1902, (see fig 111), they are issues 5, 6, 7, 8, 9, all written in German.

The *Oriflamme* magazine charts the first year of the Grand Lodge's life and the early development of Reuss' orders.

They contain a few articles, which should have been interesting to its audience, but even the translator I used remarked how boring they were.

Confirmed by Ellic Howe "The majority of the articles are of little interest," and he could speak German!

It was clearly designed to be the mouthpiece of the Berlin based 'Prussian Illuminati' under the 'Ludwig Lodge' in 1902, and to showcase the other German High-grade Freemasonry. Especially the

newly acquired, but short-lived, 'Swedenborg Rite Provincial Grand Lodge' with its potential five attached Lodges that had been newly acquired from John Yarker through W.W. Westcott as its 'Grand Secretary.'

The arrival of the 'Swedenborg Lodge and Temple of the Holy Grail No. 15' was first announced in January 1902 edition. But it was also on the front cover of the May 1902 issue No. 5 (see fig 111). On page 2, it announces that:

> *On 26th April, the founding celebration of the Lodge Ludwig was celebrated by the brethren in Berlin in the most appropriate way.*

The *Oriflamme* also contained the first announcement and first meeting of the S.R.I.A.'s English Rosicrucian daughter constitution of the 'Societas Rosicruciana In Germania' or 'S.R.I.G.' to be held on 8 July 1902 and I speculate that Westcott attended.

The magazine was also in direct competition with Leopold Engel's *Das Wort* magazine, which had started in 1900.

Reuss' *Oriflamme* magazine commenced publication, initially as a monthly, with the issue dated January 1902, although it cannot have been published until a month later.

However, it also proves that the 'German Rosicrucian College' only formally met once in July 1902. There was another proposed on 28 September, but it seems to have been cancelled.

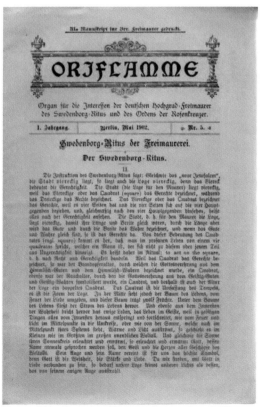

Figure 111 - Prussian Illuminati magazine Oriflamme

---

149 Ibid.

ORIFLAMME LODGE CALENDAR

Meeting dates from the Oriflamme Magazine

The fonts and puntation used here are those found in the *Oriflamme* written in German.

„Rosenkreuzer Orden" Am 8. Juli Kapitelsikung.

„Zum heiligen Gral." Am 10.Juni VI. Loge, dann Tempel Arbeit.

„Ludwig" Or. Berlin.

Am 27. Mai	I Besorderung.
Am 3. Juni	II. Inftruftion, ev. Rez oder Zeichnung.
Am 17 Juni	III. Beforderung.
Am 28. Juni	Johannis und Rofenfeft.

Camtliche Arbeiten beginnen um 8 Uhr abends.

Die Beamten werden gebeten, ftets eine halbe Ctunde vor Beginn der Arbeit im Rlubzimmer zur Befprechung der Tagesordnung fich einzufinden.

„Phonix" zur Wahrheit Or(der) Hamburg

„Phonig" Or. Hamburg.

Am 27Mai	I. Reception unb Inftruktion.
Am 10. Juui	I. zeichnung
Am 24. Juni	Johannisfest. Beamte um 6 ½ Ahr.

Beginn der Festloge 7 Uhr. Safelloge 9 Uhr. Um 8. Juli I zeichnung.

TRANSLATION

"**Rosenkreuzer Order** [S.R.I.G.] On July 8th Chapter (of improvement) confirmation. On September 28th next (proposed meeting).

"To **The Holy Grail**." [Swedenborg Lodge No.15] -On 10th/19th June, June 10th. Lodge work, then temple work grade VI.

"**Ludwig Lodge**" Order. Berlin. [Illuminati]

On May 27th	I.) Transport
On June 3rd	II.) instruction or subscription
On June 17th	III.) Transport.
On June 28th	St. John's and Christian

Rosenkreuzer work will start at 8 clock in the evening.

The officials are asked to (arrive) always an hour before starting the work in the Club Room to discuss the agenda.

"**Phonix**" zur Wahrheit Hamburg [Johannisloge] (Sprengel of Hamburg) three degrees.
On 2nd September Phonix zur Wahrheit (Phoenix Under Fire Hamburg has the oldest Lodges in Germany from the English Constitution Lodge, and they still meet today).

"**Phonix Order Hamburg**. [Schroder Lodge]

On May 27th	I.) Reception without instruction
On June 10th	I.) Drawings
On June 24th	St. John's Festival. Officials at 6½

o'clock. Start of Festive lodge 7 o'clock. Safe (home) lodge 9 o'clock . To July 8th I.) Drawing

THE MEETING DATES

1902 - Oriflamme Issue No. 5	6	7	8	9	10	11
	MAY JUN	JUL	AUG	SEP	OCT	NOV
S.R.I.G.(Rosicrucian)		8th		28th		
Swedenborgian Holy Grail Lodge	10th/29th		11th	10th		
Illuminati Ludwig Order	27th 3rd/28th		8th	16th/27th/30th	14th/21st/28th	
Phonix zur Wahrheit, Order				2nd		6th
Phonix (Schroder) Order	27th 24th	8th/22nd/29th	5th/12th/26th 29th		14th//28th	13th/27th

Figure 112 - Meeting dates in Oriflamme magazine.

From the different *Oriflamme* magazine issues in the archives, we can piece together and see that the 'S.R.I.G.' only met once that year, although a second meeting in September was planned. The 'Phoenix Lodge' that used the Schroder Ritual met the most often. There were some months when several rehearsal meetings were held. The Ludwig Lodge met three times a month in September and October.

I have no explanation for the sudden appearance in September of the 'Phoenix zur Wahrheit Order,' in Hamburg, but the founding of this new lodge was mentioned in the January 1902 edition. There is a Schroder lodge of this name today[150] and this Province of Hamburg has the oldest English Constitution lodges in Germany.

They call their masonic parishes or chapelry in German, 'Sprengel'. This translates to a Diocese or parish, a region which is supervised by a priest or bishop.

Germany also had a masonic Sprengel Law concerning none encroachment of provincial lodges. Does this mean that 'Fräulein Sprengel' mentioned in connection with the Golden Dawn means, woman of the Diocese?

There was no issue of the *Oriflamme* for August as can be seen above, what it says in September:

To our subscribers and colleagues, the August edition of 'Oriflamme' was unfortunately suspended due to the summer holidays. To make up for that there will be a double-issue at the end of the year. The works handed in by brothers will be taken to print as soon as possible and we thank you sincerely for the interest that our magazine gets, not just from members but from people who are not part of the lodge. The editor September Issue No.8

A LIST OF REUSS' WRITINGS:

The Matrimonial Question from an Anarchistic Point of View (1887); by Reuss, Charles Theodore
Die Mysterien der Illuminaten (1894); The Mysteries of the Illuminati by Caratheodoro.
Geschichte des Illuminaten-Ordens (1896); History of the Illuminati Order by anonymous.
Was muss man von der Freimauerei wissen? (1901); what do you need to know about Freemasonry? By Peregrinus.
Was ist Okkultismus und wie erlangt man occulte Kräfte? (1903); what is occultism and how do you get occult powers? By Peregrinus.
Was muss man von Richard Wagner und seinen Ton-dramen wissen? (1903); what do you need to know about Richard Wagner and his sound dramas? By Peregrinus.
Lingam-Yoni; oder die Mysterien des Geschlechts-Kultus (1906); Linga-Yoni Mysteries of Gender Cult.
Allgemeine Satzungen des Ordens der Orientali schem Templer O.T.O. (1906); General Statutes of the Order of the Oriental Templar OTO.
Parsifal und das Enthüllte Grals-Geheimnis (1914); Parsifal, the Revealed Grail Secret of Ur-Uter.
Constitution of the Ancient Order of Oriental Templars (1917).
Die Gnostische Messe' (1920); The Gnostic Mass.
Das Aufbau-Programm und die Leitsätze der Gnostischen Neo-Christen (1920); The Construction Program and the Guiding Principles of the Gnostic Neo-Christians.
Die Arte Magica Ararita (Die Magie des Hochaltars); The Magic of the High Altar.
De Nuptis Secretis Deorum cum Hominibus; The secret weddings of the gods with the people.
De Homunculus (Von der Bereitung des Humunkulus); From the Provision of the Humunculus.
Die Eucharistie, das Geheimnis des Abendmahls; The Eucharist, the mystery of the Lord's Supper.
Das Erotische in Goethes Faust und die Tantriks; The Erotic in Goethe's Faust and the Tantriks.
Das Kreuz und die Sexual-Religion; The Cross and the Sexual Religion.
Die neuen Illuminaten und ihre Einrichtungen und Händel; The new Illuminati and their institutions and Handel.
Pranatherapie. von Theodor Regens; Pranotherapy an article on sympathetic cures. By Theodor Regens.
Oriflamme (1902-1914) numerous articles published in his periodical.

OTHER PSEUDONYMS USED BY REUSS:

Caratheodoro, Peregrinus, Merlin Peregrinus, Charles Theodore, Hans Merlin, Theodor Regens.

---

[150] Phoenix under Fire, website 2015.

DR GÉRARD ANACLET VINCENT ENCAUSSE

A French Rosicrucians or the Martinist known as Papus.

What many people do not know about Dr Gerard Encausse (1865-1916), or Papus as he was known, was that he was admitted a member of the 'Resurrected Illuminati' in 1900 and was their representative in France in1901. Also that he went on to play a key role in what happened next.

It was Papus that introduced Westcott to Reuss and not as many have thought over the years, that Reuss sought out and contacted Westcott directly.

It was also Papus' alleged relationship with Mathers in the Paris Temple of the 'Golden Dawn' that was one of the reasons why Westcott did not promulgate the 'Ordre Martinist' in England also why Westcott would later ignore the opportunity to form a concordat between the 'S.R.I.A.' and the 'Ordre Kabbalistique De La Rose Croix' Paris in 1899.

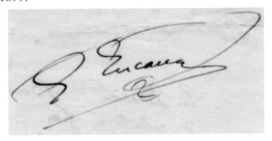

Figure 113 - Gerard Encausse signature

This was an Order founded by Stanislas de Guaita (1861-1897), as we will find out. It was an Order in which Papus was only the General Manager not the Grand Master as many people have thought, as a letter signed by François Charles Barlet (1838-1921) in the S.R.I.A. archives. He was the 2nd Grand Master of Ordre Kabbalistique De La Rose + Cross, Barlet had become the head of the order on Stanislas de Guaita's death.

Some of the above decisions concerning Papus may have also significantly influenced Westcott's decision with regard to the 'Prussian Illuminati.'

The finding of the two key Papus letters (June and July 1901) in the S.R.I.A. archives, which mentioned the Illuminati, was only a co-incidence. It happened while scanning approximately twenty five letters from Papus to Westcott for an S.R.I.A. member who is also a modern day Martinist.

This correspondence was found in an ordinary large A4 brown envelope that had been stored with a number of other nondescript packages over the last 100 years in the S.R.I.A. archives. They were probably left undisturbed as they looked so unimportant and were not immediately accessible to most people as they were all written in French.

These essentially Martinist letters, rituals, constitutions and personal correspondence between Papus and Westcott tell half the story of Papus' failed second attempt to spread his 'Ordre Martinist' in England through Westcott in 1900. The first attempt was through Fredrick Holland (1854-1917) and John Yarker in 1895. Yarker's Manchester home address was registered as the forty fifth and last 'Ordre Martinist' Lodge in the World at that time.

A good example of Westcott's lack of understanding of the French is best highlighted, when he had to ask other members of the S.R.I.A., the difference between the 'Ordre Martinist' and the 'Ordre Kabbalistique De La Rose + Cross,' the description that Westcott used in the ACTA for the 'Ordre Kabbalistique De La Rose + Cross,' in his ACTA was simply 'French Rosicrucian Order.'

I also believe that like Yarker, Westcott did not really appreciate the subtlety and depth of the ceremonies of the 'Ordre Martinist,' an organisation which he had been a member for four years before he ever met Papus. I believe that Westcott may not have even read through the French rituals. Many have thought that the first English rituals were produced by the head of the 'American Martinist Order,' Edouard Blitz in 1900. It transpires on further investigation that John Yarker paid for the rituals to be translated in 1895. Yarker's and Blitz's rituals can be found today in the Library and Museum of Freemasonry, London.

Figure 114 - Dr Gerard Encausse or Papus

Figure 115 - The Papus signature

Although Westcott had an 'Initiator's' certificate, dated 1895, he probably did not go through any of their three degrees and experience them. I believe that having not been through the wonderful ceremonies, he also did not benefit from practicing the several unique Martinist lessons to be learned, Westcott therefore did not promulgate the order, which was his loss.

PERSONAL LIFE

Born at Coruña in North West Spain on 13 July 1865, Gerard Encausse's mother was Spanish and he had a French father, Louis, a chemist. The family moved to Paris when he was four years old, where he later received his education at the College Rollin. Papus was also one of the youngest Grand Masters of all the people in this story. He set up his own 'Ordre Martinist' and became the President and wrote the rituals when he was only twenty five years old in 1890.

He became a physician, a General Practioner and was, allegedly, a great success with his patients. He received his Doctor of Medicine degree in 1894 upon submitting a dissertation on Philosophical Anatomy. He opened a clinic in the rue Rodin which was quite successful.

He was winner of the Faculty of Paris Hospitals. (Laureat des hopitaux des Paris). He was ex-Head of Laboratory at the Charity Hospital of Paris, (Ex-Chef de Laboratoier a l'Hospital de la Charite.) also called the Hospital Brothers of Saint-Jean-de-Dieu, a former Paris hospital founded in the early XVIIth century. It was closed and destroyed around 1935 to make way for the new Faculty of Medicine. He was a Medical Consultant at the hospital St. Jacques or Saint-Jean-de-Dieu (Medecin de Consultations de l'Hospital St. Jacques). He was also the Public Education Officer. This information comes from researching the several different letterheads he used in his correspondence with Westcott. Much of this information is contained in his letterhead for The Villa Montmorency, 10 Avenue des Peupliers, 10 Auteuil, Paris, on which he used to write his first letter to Westcott.

The Villa Montmorency is his last known home address. It is still a very exclusive, expensive private area in Paris, the equivalent of a "gated community" situated on a hillock of the 16th arrondissement of Paris where many famous people have lived. As a young man, he studied the Kabbalah, occult tarot, the sciences of magic and alchemy, especially the writings of Eliphas Lévi (1810-1875), who died long before Papus could meet him, spending it is said a great deal of time at the Bibliothèque Nationale in Paris studying his works.

It might help readers who do not know very much about some of the people already mentioned in the story of the Revived Illuminati in connection with Papus. That I explain who some of them are and a little bit about the new primary source material. I have broken it down into the different Orders that Papus was a member of and their name appears written in bold letters.

FREEMASONRY
Brief summary of memberships

In **Freemasonry**, it is generally thought that Dr Encausse or Papus was not a Freemason. However he was a Swedenborg Freemason from 1899 onwards and formed a Temple and Lodge in Paris.

Not being a Freemason usually means that he was not a member of a Lodge that was recognised by the United Grand Lodge of England.

One of the reasons for this maybe that Papus was received as a 'Ordre Martinist' in 1882, when he was only seventeen years old, too young to be admitted a Freemason as a Lewis or son of a Freemason at the age of 18, or as a non-Lewis at the age of 21.

Figure 116 - Martinez de Pasqually

This may also be historically understandable, after the significant changes made to Freemasonry in France, after the French Revolution by Napoleon Bonaparte's brothers and again a little later during the Franco-Prussian War in 1872. Very few Lodges in France would have been recognised by the English, or by any other European country.

However Papus must have been a Freemason to take on the 'Swedenborg Rite' from John Yarker, as the Rite did not make Freemasons.

Papus may have been a member of a really interesting Paris 'Ancient & Accepted Scottish Rite Lodge' that was called Le Libre Examen Loge. But it would be unrecognised outside of France, as its Grand Body the 'Grand Loge de France,' was a Grand Lodge working underneath an 'Ancient & Accepted Scottish Rite Supreme Council.' Papus was very strongly associated with it, on four levels, his family links, where it met, when and why it changed and became an Adoption Lodge in 1902 and the new Adoption rituals that Papus obtained for that lodge.

Both his sister and his brother in law were both members of Le Libre Examen Loge. Louise Deullin (sister) was its first Grand Senior Warden in 1902/3 and is considered as one of the original founders of 'French Adoption Freemasonry.' Pierre Deullin (brother in-law) was a member of the old male only Le Libre Examen Loge. He was one of those old members of the Le Libre Examen Loge that petitioned the 'Grand Loge de France,' to allow the attachment of a women's' only 'Adoption Lodge' to the original. This failed and it became the first or founding Lodge in the world of the 'American Adoption Rite.' Deullin was also the Senior Warden and Secretary' of Papus's 'Swedenborg Loge I.N.R.I.'

Papus was probably instrumental in obtaining the 'American Adoption Rite' ritual from Yarker on behalf of his sister. The ritual that was used for the first time in 1902 by its members is still used today. These rituals are very different from the old 'French Adoption' rituals, which were either modified men's rituals for women or 'White Table Lodges' (table blanche) meetings, called off after the men's Lodge meeting was closed.

The Ritual is different because the 'American Adoption Rite' was a series of ceremonies specifically written for women, inculcating moral lesson learnt by women from female characters in the Bible.

The old French lodge was called Le Libre Examen Loge and probably met in the buildings where Papus once lived and where his office was based at '5 Rue de Savoie.' It was also the place where all his other orders met. It was where the famous 'Merveilleux' bookstore was held, I say this because we find out that the women members of the Le Libre Examen Loge wanted to use its books

after their lodge meetings in 1903. More research is needed here.

So Papus certainly did become a 'Swedenborg Freemason.' Then several years later he became an 'Ancient & Primitive Rite' Freemason in 1902.

NON MASONIC MEMBERSHIPS

The origins of **Martinisim** come from the writings of Martinez de Pasqually (1727-1774) and his 1758 'L'Ordre des Chevaliers Maçon Elus Cohens de l'Univers,' a theurgical way of reintegration for Freemasons, (see fig 116). His thoughts were written down for his two students, Louis Claude de Saint-Martin and Jean-Baptiste Willermoz, in the 'Lessons of Lyon,' in France 1774.[151] The lessons were left for them to debate and discuss, just before Pasqually left on military service.

Figure 117 - Henri Viscount Delaage

Fatefully for him, to the Caribbean never to return and he died in Saint-Domingue later in 1774. Pasqually's father was a French member of the 'Scottish Rite Freemasonry' who believed in the hereditary succession and passed his 'Scottish Rite' warrant on to his son, but Martinez had no son and therefore no successor.

The two Pasqually students went their own separate ways and from Willermoz we inherit the 'Scottish Rectified Rite' a reformed variant of the 'Rite of Strict Observance,' a purely masonic rite, later called the 'Chevaliers Bienfaisants de la Cité-Sainte' or 'C.B.C.S.' From Saint-Martin we received 'Martinism,' a silent 'way of the heart,' a way to attain 'reintegration.' Martinism is a form of Christian mysticism and esoteric Christianity.

151 Osborne M. (MSG 2017) *Lessons of Lyon.*

Concerned chiefly with the fall of the first man, his state of material privation from his divine source, and the process of his return, called 'Reintegration' or illumination. The Martinist and Illuminati have much in common and that was masonic education!

Modern Martinisim, as you may know it, started when Gerard Encausse made the acquaintance of Henri Viscount Delaage (1825-1882) (see fig 117), his 'Martinist' initiator, who just before he died in 1882, consecrated the young seventeen year old Encausse with the name 'Papus S∴ I∴'

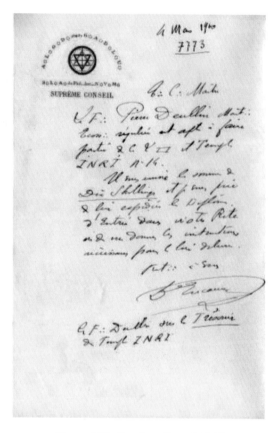

Figure 118 - Suprême Conseil 1900

His nom de plume: 'Papus' means 'physician,' and comes from his reading of Eliphas Lévi, whose translation of the *Nuctemeron of Apollonius of Tyana* was printed as a supplement to *Dogme et Rituel de la Haute Magie.*[152]

Eliphas Lévi was, for a short time, a Freemason before he died and was visited by Kenneth Mackenzie in Paris, who wrote an interesting study of his visit, which was published in the S.R.I.A. Rosicrucian Magazine transactions. Levi came to London, probably the year of Lord Edward Bulwer-Lytton's death to meet with the surviving members of a mysterious 'English Rosicrucian order' in

January 1872, of which Levi was an alleged member. This is relevant because Papus was deeply affected by the intellectual doctrines of both Eliphas Lévi and Stanislas de Guaita.

Six years later he was to meet Pierre-Augustin Chaboseau (1868-1946) who had been initiated into the 'Traditional Martinist Order' in 1886, at the age of twenty, by his aunt Amelie de Boise-Montmart. Papus, who was a member of a different 'Martinist' stream, realised there was something missing from his branch of 'Martinisim.' In 1887 the 'L'Ordre des Supérieurs Inconnus' (S∴ I∴) was founded as, it was a fusion of the 'Ordre des Elus Cohen' and the 'Rectified Rite of Saint-Martin.' The two esotericists swapped initiations in 1888 and merged them to form 'L'Ordre Martiniste.'

That same year, 1888, Papus and his friend Lucien Marcel (Chamuel) a famous French 'éditeur' of many occult books, founded the 'Librarie du Merveilleux,' (or wonderful library) first in the Rue de Trévise and then from 1894 to 1898, at number '5 Rue de Savoie.'[153]

This was Papus' work address for a time and also for all his orders. Chamuel and Papus launched the monthly review of esoteric subjects called *L'Initiation* and the magazine's motto was 'The Supernatural does not exist.' This became Papus' mouth piece to the esoteric world and articles in 'L'Initiation' would feature many of those people mentioned above. Yet another esotericists, who wrote articles was Paul Sédir (1871-1926). He was featured in the *L'Initiation*, a copy of which is in the S.R.I.A. archives. What is so important about Paul Sédir is that he would later be Papus' successor in the 'Ordre Martinist' in 1916. The magazine remained in publication until 1914, back copies of which can also be found online.[154]

In 1888-9, the editorial address of *L'Initiation* was the 14 rue de Strasbourg, this is where Papus lived that year in a modest dorm like room, and the administration address was at 54 rue Saint-André des Arts in Paris. The edition of *L'Initiation* on 15 October 1896 features the 'Director's address' for Papus, as the Villa Montmorency and the Administration address has moved to 5, Rue de Savoie, which as we will see is a very significant address. Later in November 1896, we see that the 'Prière d'adresser tous les échanges:' "Please address all exchanges to the Villa Montmorency, number 87, Boulevard Montmorency" and the administration address has changed to 3, Rue de Savoie, next door, another address in the same road and its telephone number at the time was: 282-67

Papus joined the **Kabbalistic Order of the Rose-Croix,** in the year that it was founded in1888, by the Marquis Stanislas de Guaita (1861-1897) and by Oswald Wirth (1860-1943).

152 Lévi E., 1861, *Dogme et Rituel de la Haute Magie.*

153 Pierrot J.1984, *L'imaginaire decadent, 1880-1900.*
154 http://www.iapsop.com/archive/materials/l_initiation.

Wirth is well known today for his famous tarot decks. Stanislas de Guaita became a famous French Rosicrucian poet after he published two collections of poetry *The Dark Muse* (1883) and *The Mystic Rose* (1885), which became popular at the time. The 'Kabbalistic Order of the Rose-Croix,' consisted of a society with a number of other significant esotericists, like Alexandre Saint-Yves d'Alveydre (1842-1909), Saint-Yves was greatly influenced by Papus and, publically, was the first person to rightly suggest a much earlier date for the Great Sphinx of Giza than was generally assumed at the time and he wrote against anti-communism in favour of an elite ruling class, extreme views that Papus may well have shared.

Papus joined this French Rosicrucian Order with a number of other people who would later become 'Martinist,' including Joséphin Péladan (1858-1918), who was also greatly influenced Stanislas de Guaita. But by 1899, Papus had argued with Péladan and he went off to form his own new infamous 'French Rosicrucian Order' called the 'Salon de la Rose-Croix' for painters, writers and musicians who were more esoterically minded and wished to express their spirituality in artistic forms, while Papus remained a member of the 'Kabbalistic Order of the Rose-Croix,' and became their General Manager, who worked under the Grand Master for the rest of his life.

By 1891, Papus claimed to have come into the possession of the original Martinist papers of Jacques de Livron Joachim de la Tour de la Casa and Martinez de Pasqually (1727-1774) and to have been given authority in the 'Rite of Saint-Martin' by his friend Henri Viscount Delaage before he died. He formed a Martinist 'Suprême Conseil' of twelve men in 1891, see the letterhead in (see fig 118), who all came from the 'Kabbalistic Order of the Rose-Croix.' Stanislas de Guaïta and Joseph Péladan were also Council members.

Papus re-wrote the three 'Martinist' rituals and became the President or Grand Master of the 'Ordre Martinist' at the very young age of twenty six. The three degrees were called in French, 'Associe, Initie and Adepte.' These became the modern 'Martinist' degrees of 'Associate, Initiate and S∴ I∴' which we now associate with Gerard Encausse and Augustin Chaboseau. There is a fourth 'Martinist Degree,' that of being an S∴ I∴ 'in the chair of the Lodge' or the 'Master's Degree' or sometimes it is just called an S∴ I∴ administrative degree.

It was Papus under Charles Barlet the Grand Master who attempted to introduce the 'Ordre Kabbalistique De La Rose' into England with the help of the S.R.I.A. in 1899, as the proposed concordat documentation in the archives show, (see fig 119).

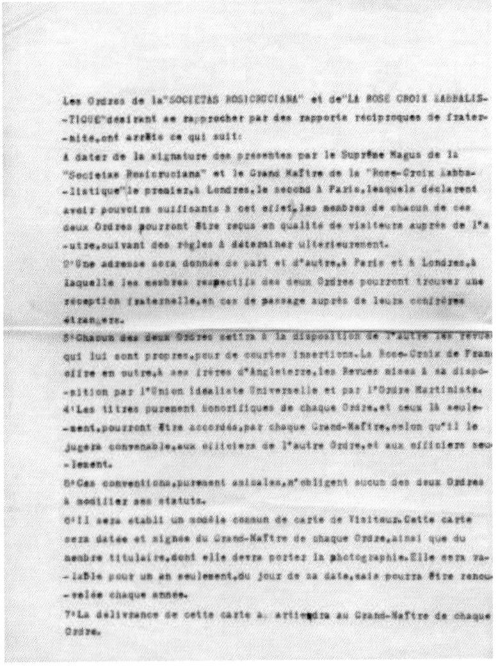

Les Ordres de la "SOCIETAS ROSICRUCIANA" et de "LA ROSE CROIX KABBALIS-TIQUE" desirant se rapprocher par des rapports réciproques de fraternite, ont arrête ce qui suit:
A dater de la signature des presentes par le Suprême Magus de la "Societas Rosicruciana" et le Grand Maître de la "Rose-Croix Kabbalistique" le premier, à Londres, le second à Paris, lesquels déclarent avoir pouvoirs suffisants à cet effet, les membres de chacun de ces deux Ordres pourront être reçus en qualite de visiteurs auprès de l'autre, suivant des règles à déterminer ulterieurement.
2° Une adresse sera donnée de part et d'autre, à Paris et à Londres, à laquelle les membres respectifs des deux Ordres pourront trouver une reception fraternelle, en cas de passage auprès de leurs confrères étrangers.
3° Chacun des deux Ordres mettra à la disposition de l'autre les revues qui lui sont propres, pour de courtes insertions. La Rose-Croix de France offre en outre, à ses frères d'Angleterre, les Revues mises à sa disposition par l'Union Idealiste Universelle et par l'Ordre Martiniste.
4° Les titres purement honorifiques de chaque Ordre, et ceux là seulement, pourront être accordés, par chaque Grand-Maître, selon qu'il le jugera convenable, aux officiers de l'autre Ordre, et aux officiers seulement.
5° Ces conventions, purement amicales, n'obligent aucun des deux Ordres à modifier ses statuts.
6° Il sera etabli un modèle commun de carte de Visiteur. Cette carte sera datée et signee du Grand-Maître de chaque Ordre, ainsi que du membre titulaire, dont elle devra porter la photographie. Elle sera valable pour un an seulement, du jour de sa date, mais pourra être renouvelée chaque année.
7° La delivrance de cette carte appartiendra au Grand-Maître de chaque Ordre.

Figure 119 - Ordre Kabbalistique De La Rose Concordat

We first hear of **Martinism in England**, or as I shall refer to it the 'Martinist Order' when John Yarker was made a Docteur en Science Hermetique of the 'Ordre Martinist' by the Free University of Paris in 1891, which seems far too early a date for his admission, based on how little Yarker did with the order in England. From another source, he was allegedly made an 'Ordre Martinist' on 10 October 1899, one date that is very early the other date that is too late.

But, according to Barry Loft who should know, because of his considerable collection of Yarker material, Yarker did not become a Martinist until 24 July 1893:

> *....and it was through him that members were registered by Papus (with a number) in Paris. It was all very informal. There were no fees and no obligation to do anything but maintain secrecy. Rituals had to be returned to him 'on honour' within three days.*

This 1893 date fits with the early foundation correspondence between J. Yarker and R.S. Brown (Secretary General of the Scottish S.R.I.S.) found in the S.R.I.A. archives, letters that are written in January/February 1895.

Today it is possible to access the contents of the 'Ordre Martinist' archive.[155]

155 'Ordre Martinist' archive: https://www.facebook.com/permalink.php?story_fbid=10154404032888623&id=112119848622.

NON MASONIC MEMBERSHIPS (continued)

In 1895 there were forty five numbered 'Ordre Martinist' Lodges listed in the world and John Yarker's, is the last one named on that 'Ordre Martinist' list and it is very interesting in the context of this story that the warrant was issued in the name of 'one' of Yarker's many orders:

Lodge No. 45: Ancient & Primitive Rite of Masonry (Withington, England)

The 'Ordre Martinist' archive also contains the following:

- *Fact Sheet for John Yarker, 1 slip.*
- *2 letters of John Yarker: 02/22/1894 (1f), 09/01/1895 (1f)*
- *Lack f. 45-1 (ranked in mss 5486-13?).*

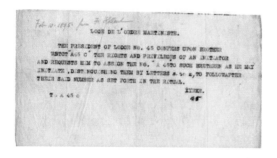

Figure 120 - Westcott's Martinist Initiator Warrant

The earliest English letter on file in the 'Ordre Martinist' archives in France is dated 22 February 1894 and the last 1 September 1895. This proves conclusively that John Yarker was the head of the English 'Martinist Order' in Great Britain. This also proves to me that it was not Fredrick Holland as some authors have said. In fact as recently in 2015 a member of the S.R.I.S. in Scotland purchased the Fredrick F. Holland's 'Deluge Special a Birmingham' certificate No.133. It is similar in every way to Westcott's but undated. This shows that Holland was considered a Provincial Grand Master in Birmingham only if you like, of the 'Martinist Order' like Westcott was in London, but with Yarker as it head. It's worth mentioning in passing here that the first Papus attempt to launch the 'Ordre Martinist' in England can be traced through Westcott's ACTA. It was made in 1895, through the ageing John Yarker who was then already sixty two years old and Frederick Holland was its first 'Secretary' in England as we will see. The beginning of the real organisation of UK Martinisim may only have begun on the 25 January 1895, with a letter from John Yarker to Robert Smith Brown who was the Secretary General of the 'S.R.I.S.' in Edinburgh:

R.S. Brown I have not received your form yet but he (Holland) is secretary. Discuss the rituals and adopting a uniform translation. I have suggested to Holland we might revive his 'Hermetic Society of Eight' with this as Ritual, a corresponding society in which members might take up some particular study.

The 'Hermetic Society of Eight' was not revived. In another letter from Yarker to R.S. Brown on 8 February 1895 he informed him he had received back rituals and laws and that he, had appointed Holland secretary and he had named the first members.

Two days later, in parallel, Westcott received a letter from the secretary Holland, he has signed the note in the top right hand corner and it is the very basic, simple 'Martinist Initiator Warrant' from Yarker, (see fig 120) it says:

On the 10th February 1895.
From the Lodge De L'Ordre Martinist,

'The President of Lodge [Yarker] No.45 confers upon brother WSTCT [Westcott] "A45 C" the rights and privileges of an INITIATOR [Provincial Grand Master] and requests him to assign the No. "A 45 to such brethren as he may initiate, distinguishing them by the letters a to z to follow after their said number as set forth in the ritual.

XYRKR. TO A 45 C.

From this you can see that the number of John Yarker's 'Martinist Lodge' was number 45 in the 'Ordre Martinist Roll.' At the time Westcott held the position of 'Grand Brother Orator', which is also one of the offices held in a 'Martinist Lodge.' Yarker's *The Regulations of the Martinist Order in England* is also dated 1895.[156]

Papus, like so many participants in this story, joined the **Theosophical Society** but in Paris, France. He joined the 'Theosophical Loge Isis' in Paris on 25 October 1887 for a short time, but within a year he had become involved in a dispute with a senior French Theosophist. This led to the intervention of Colonel Olcott one of the original founders and this resulted in the dissolution of the 'Isis Loge.' They formed a new Theosophical 'Loge Hermes' and Papus was the 'Correspondence Secretary.' Later hostilities broke out again this time between Blavatsky and Papus and he resigned at the same time as Joséphin Péladan and the remaining French Theosophist dissolved the 'Loge Hermes,' preferring a more Western form of mysticism instead.

---

156 Library and Museum of Freemasonry, London.

Papus was also alleged to be a member of the **Hermetic Brotherhood of Luxor** (or of Light), which supposedly taught a form of Eastern sex-magic. Kenneth Mackenzie in his Cyclopaedia,[157] under *Light, Brothers of,* says it was established in 1498 in Florence and among its members was - Pasqualez, Cagliostro, Swedenborg, St. Martin, Eliphas Levi and many eminent mystics. The 'Hermetic Brotherhood of Light' was also the order that Reuss' close friend Carl Kellner came across on his travels and later became central to the high degrees of the O.T.O. much later. It would seem that Papus received this order from Reuss or from Kellner.

This is not to be confused with the '**Fratres Lucis**' order, that George Longley asked Fred Irwin if he could be admitted into the order in his letter of 17 January 1877. R.A. Gilbert confirmed this in his book,[158] when he said that Fred G. Irwin, "was an advanced member of the society of students of Magic called 'Fratres Lucis'." Westcott went on to confirm that F.G. Irwin was a senor Adept in Westcott's history of the S.R.I.A.[159] he said that John Yarker, Fred Irwin, George Longley and Kenneth Mackenzie, were involved with the Fratres Lucis, from the American school of Rosicrucianism of Paschal Beverly Randolph (1825-1875). Certainly Westcott, in the ACTA, declined all the advances to be recognised, by the American Rosicrucians who were Randolph's successors, very early on in the 1900s and the S.R.I.A. had nothing to do with that organisation or the other two competing Rosicrucian orders in America. Those of Ruben Swinburne Clymer's (1878-1966) 'Fraternitatis Rosea Cruis' and Harvey Spencer Lewis' (1883-1939) very slick organisation called, the 'Ancient and Mystical Order Rosae Crucis,' A.M.O.R.C.

In the **Golden Dawn**, Papus allegedly is given an honorary initiation into Macgregor Mathers' version of the 'Hermetic Order of the Golden Dawn' in its 'Ahathoor Temple' in Paris, on 23 March 1895. These were meetings that were held not far from where Papus lived. This is one of the reasons I have discussed the 'Golden Dawn' here. This honorary initiation into the 'Golden Dawn' was probably Papus' reward for putting Mathers in touch with a mysterious Dr Thiessen four years earlier, not previously mentioned. We are told he was a senior member of the 'Ordre Martinist' and also allegedly in touch with the hidden superiors of the 'Continental Rosicrucian' order, allegedly the

order behind the 'Golden Dawn.' It was them that I allege gave Mathers a new ritual for the 'second order' 5=6 ritual. The 1887/8 'Golden Dawn' cipher manuscript only contains information on the 'first order' it did not have a 'second order' element in 1888.

Dr Thiessen is often referred to as Frater *Lux Ex Tenebris.* Was that his motto or was it the organisation's name? As Lux et Tenebris is also the motto of the old French 'Rite of Perfection,' or 'Scottish Rite.' We are also told that Dr Thiessen was a Belgian living in Liege and that he was a high grade 'Freemason' and a member of the 'Ordre Martinist.' These are probably some of the reasons why Papus might have known the Belgian.

Figure 121 - Dr Gérard Encausse portrait

I do not think Papus was ever very happy with Mathers at the time and was clearly offended by him, according to what Westcott wrote in the ACTA during Papus' visit on 7 June 1899, concerning one of their few face to face conversations. Papus later resigned from the 'Golden Dawn' to concentrate on expanding the 'Ordre Martinist' he was trying to promulgate.

Papus was not a member of the **Hermetic Society of Eight**; the English members of the 'Martinist Order' were simply going to use the eight members of the 'Hermetic Society of Eight' as their Provincial Grand Masters as most of them were already Martinist.

---

157 Mackenzie K.R.H. 1987, *The Royal Masonic Cyclopaedia,*
158 Gilbert R.A. 1983, *The Magical Mason.*
159 Westcott W.W. 1916, *The Data of the History of the Rosicrucians.*

AFTER PAPUS

Jumping to the end of Papus life, after the First World War had broken out, Dr Encausse/Papus joined the French army medical corps. He returned to work in his old hospital, which had been turned into a military hospital. He then contracted tuberculosis, probably from one of his patients and died on 25 October 1916, at the young age of 51.

When he died, Papus had not appointed a successor. It even seems that what he really wanted was the dissolution of the 'Ordre Martinist' as he had known it, after he was gone and he entrusted Georges Loiselle to carry this out his wishes, in the event of his death.[160]

Figure 122 - Papus writes letter of introduction

Heri-Charles (Teder) Détré (1855-1918) became the next Grand Master of the 'Original Ordre Martinist' and he wanted to restrict membership to male Master-Masons, just as Blitz had wanted to do in America, but with this difference, Détré wanted, preferably, masons who belonged only to Yarker's 'Antient & Primitive Rite of Memphis & Mizraim.' It was no longer ruled by John Yarker, now deceased, who had been at one-time Détré's friend. In the end, Détré wanted all the women who had previously been received into the rank of 'Associate,' to be eventually excluded, over time.

However, after only two years he was succeeded, on his death, by Jean Bricaud (1881-1934) who made the 'Ordre Martinist' even more masonic and moved its headquarters from Paris to his home city of Lyon. Perhaps significantly it was the former home of both Pasqually and Willermoz. He made women feel even more excluded.

At the death of Jean Bricaud in 1934, he was succeeded by Constant Chevillon (1880-1944) who considered that women were an integral part of humanity and should have full access to initiation. Chevillon cut the relationship between the 'Antient & Primitive Rite of Memphis & Mizraim' and the 'Elus Cohen.' He was, unfortunately, shot by mistake by the Vichy regime in 1945 at the end of the war.

There are today many 'Martinist Orders' that have mixed sex Lodges and Orders that have a strict masonic membership and some with no masonic qualifications at all, with both male only and mixed membership. The present day members of the Hermetic Order of Martinist or 'H.O.M.' which consists entirely of S.R.I.A. members, does not claim a direct descendancy from this original Papus organisation or from Frederick Holland or Yarker, nor were any of the Papus warrants used by the S.R.I.A. The direct lineage of H.O.M. comes after several changes of direction, made by the successors of Papus after his death. We are told that H.O.M. came via Victor Blanchard in 1921 and then through a Frenchman living in England called Louis Bentin alias Sâr Gulion in 1958. Then it passed to Desmond Bourke (Sâr Olibius) in 1978. The H.O.M. are different from many other 'Martinist Orders' in that they only admit men who are Freemasons, very much like Edouard Blitz had wanted to do in 1900!

PAPUS MEETS WESTCOTT FOR THE FIRST TIME

We know that Papus introduced Westcott to Reuss in 1901 for certain, but when did Westcott first meet Papus? It was after Westcott received a letter of introduction from Papus on the 7 June 1899, which is simply recorded in his diary, "Papus had asked for an interview with him in London". It was many years later that I found the letter in the archives and it is addressed very formally in French, indicating this was their very first ever contact. In it Dr Encausse states that he is in London for only three days and that he wishes for an interview, to discuss several subjects, unspecified, and to give Westcott a copy of his latest book on Martinisim, (see fig 122).

In the right hand corner of the letter is blue stamp mark, probably from where he was staying in 11 Upper Bedford Place, Russell Square. Since

---

160 http://omrunis.canalblog.com/archives/2011/11/14/.

Figure 123 - Westcott certificate No. 192, 'Inspector Principal & Doctor en Hermetisim'

the damage inflicted to this area of London during the Second World War, it no longer exists.

Meanwhile, the next day on the 8th June 1899, Papus called in on Westcott at his home at No.396 Camden Road, Islington, London, "With regard to making an alliance in France and the Rosicrucian Freemasons in England." It is all very vague. I do not think Westcott actually knew what Papus wanted to talk specifically about as we will see from his diary entries. It is only with hindsight, that I now realise it must have been a meeting mainly to do with an alliance between the S.R.I.A. and the 'Order of Kabbalistic Rose-Croix,' which only had twelve members in charge at the time. It was not about the 'Order Martinist,' and very little to do with the proposed changes to the 'Martinist Order' in England that Yarker had discussed with Westcott, in letters written earlier in 1899, when Yarker proposed that Westcott takeover the 'Martinist Order' in England, replacing himself.

In a removed note that I had found, used as a page marker in an unrelated book in the library, that seems to have been torn from one of the ACTA, Westcott after this meeting is left thinking.

That the Soc. Ros. in the France area was a small body of 7-12 men, who had all passed exams in occult knowledge and Hebrew from the 3rd Grade in Sanskrit and desired a fraternal esoteric alliance with the Soc. Ros. in Anglia. Not for exchange of pledges or ritual, but for empathy.

What is left in the ACTA about the meeting is only to do with Mathers and adds to my contention that Westcott did not really trust Papus' relationship with Mathers. This is something that I believe may have clouded the whole 'Revived Illuminati' introduction via Papus. In the ACTA Westcott wrote the following about the meeting:

That he knows Mathers, and is friendly with him - but had no communications with him for several years. Mathers is not admitted to the French Rosicrucian Society." Also that Mathers has said to him. *"I am an officer of high grade in a Rosic Society, in which Moses had been a member of an inferior grade."* Papus adds, *"I answered to him that is good for you but did not argue the contention."* He (Papus) says, *"Mathers gave him a fanciful degree which erred in teaching the Duality and not the Trinity. The French Society of Rosicrucians is male only but not necessary masonic, but has bona fides Hebrew, Sanskrit and other exams. He (Papus) also spoke of Martinisim and gave me (Westcott) his book and promised him a diploma and the (Martinist) Rituals.*

The 'rituals' mentioned above are mentioned in the ACTA with a hint of annoyance aimed at Papus. They are Martinist rituals that Westcott stated that he had already seen before in 1895 and that they had been translated from the French years ago.

As mentioned elsewhere, John Yarker had paid for these 'Ordre Martinist' Rituals to be translated and transcribed in 1895, a short time after he was admitted and these rituals are now in Library and Museum of Freemasonry and are kept with the slightly later Blitz English translations. Two days later, Westcott received in the post from Papus a certificate of membership of the 'Ordre Martinist,' called a certificate of D'Initiation officer and a copy of two books *Science Occult* and *Magic et Hypnotism* as gifts. On 12 June, Westcott wrote and thanked Papus and sent him 'our ordinances,' from the S.R.I.A.

A month later, and I think completely out of the blue, on 13 July 1899 Westcott received in the post a "Proposal of alliance from the 'Society Kabbalistique De La Rose Croix of Paris'", from Papus and someone called Barlet. I do not think that either Westcott or anyone else in England knew who the 'Ordre Kabbalistique De La Rose Croix' was and the English Rosicrucians had similarly never heard of Barlet the Grand Master.

For that reason there was a formal investigation into 'Ordre Kabbalistique De La Rose Croix,' which ended badly for Papus and Barlet. A mistake was made by the 'Assistant Secretary General,' Frederick Leigh Gardner VII° (1857-1930) of the S.R.I.A., who contacted on behalf of the society, the Junior Substitute Magus, who had been living in Paris since 1891, which made sense, but it was MacGregor Mathers.

It was probably Mathers' response to Gardner's approach that put the S.R.I.A. off the alliance and the fact that it would give Mathers more power than he deserved in France, as their representative, as he had not been involved in the S.R.I.A. society at all over the last nine year period. This reply is reproduced in the ACTA using original spellings.

I am well known among the Haut Monde Parisian as Count Mac Gregor of Glenstrae my hereditary Stuart title, which the Hanoverian Government annulled; but which I claim in spite of them; therefore your authority to me from the Metropolitan College had better be addressed to me as G.S.L. M. Mathers Mac Gregor, Comte de Glenstrae, by which I am known in the Parisian World.

G. Mathers

I think, quite legitimately, Mathers wanted the High Council to give him a letter of authority, so he could formally contact the *'Ordre Kabbalistique De La Rose Croix'* and represent the S.R.I.A. in Paris. But Mathers wanted the High Council to write to him under a very exaggerated 'title' that was politically and rationally ridiculous. I also believe that Mathers knew the high quality of the twelve members under its banner and desperately wanted to entice them into his Paris Temple of the

Golden Dawn, something that Westcott dreaded and wanted to thwart. The warrant to form a new 'Ordre Kabbalistique De La Rose Croix' in England was never used by Westcott who said:

I do not think we English Loyalists in London can be represented in France by a Frater who lays so much stress on Roman Catholic Jacobite titles   W.W. Westcott.

How did Mathers react to this rebuttal and to not being made the society's representative in Paris? On 8 December, Gardner brought around to Westcott's house, the reply he had received from Mathers, in which he had decided to suspended Gardner from the 'Hermetic Society of the Golden Dawn,' in the 'second order.'

I do not know if Westcott or his High Council had ever become aware of some of what was going on behind the scenes in the 'Ordre Kabbalistique De La Rose Croix,' all was not well! In 1890, Joséphin Péladan one of the co-founders and great friend of Stanislas de Guaita had a disagreement with Papus and left both the 'Ordre Martinist' and the 'Ordre Kabbalistique De La Rose Croix' to create a quasi-Catholic Mystic Order for artists and musicians called the 'Salon De La Rose + Cross,' with him as the leader of the new order and he allegedly took the titles of 'Imperator' and 'Super Magician.' So, it would seem that Papus in 1899 was indeed offering Westcott the 'Ordre Kabbalistique De La Rose Croix' with Papus as only in his role as the General Manager not as the head or Grand Master. On 7 December 1899, the ACTA states*:*

Received from the Martinist Order and the French College of Hermetic Science, the certificates of Inspector Principal & Doctor en Hermetisim.

One of these two documents was the 'CHARGE' of 'All the necessary powers for the purpose of representing the Martinist Order in London, (see fig 123), Westcott called this 'Inspector Principal.' The word 'Charge' on the certificate may come from "the Unknown Agent charged with the work of initiation," an expression of Willermoz.

The other was his Certificate of D'Initiation as an S:. I:., backdated and signed by 'Docteure G. Encausse and Papus,' using both names, on 8 July 1899, in Martinist cipher. This is what Westcott must have called his 'Doctor en Hermetisim' certificate. They were both returned to S.R.I.A. ownership in 2015. The certificates have no discernible date on them, unless you use the Martinist cipher.

As a result, on 8 December 1899, Westcott made Dr Gerard Encausse, an 'Honorary Associate of the High Council of the Society Rosicruciana in

Anglia (S.R.I.A.)' and Westcott posted the certificate on 11 January 1900.

This seems a personal exchange of titles and certificates between the heads of two orders. It was entirely appropriate for Westcott to make him an honorary member, even if Papus was technically a non-mason at the time or only a Swedenborg Freemason or was he?[161]

His rank was recorded and acknowledged in the S.R.I.A. High Council minutes.

Papus then sent Westcott two 'Ordre Martinist' collar jewels. Which I was later to find out was in fact their equivalent to 'Ordre Martinist' or 'Grand Rank' to wear suspended from a white collarette for both himself and John Yarker on 2 February 1900, (see fig 124).

The breast Jewel design is new to me, however as I have not attended a 'Supreme Council' meeting of the 'Ordre Martinist,' perhaps they all wear this insignia today? It is very unusual in Martinist

wedding of Pierre Deullin (1873-1912) and Louise Encausse (1878-1960) (see fig 127), to which Westcott was invited but did not attend and was held on 31 May 1900, at Eglise Notre-Dame d'Auteuil.[162]

LE LIBRE EXAMEN

The next day on 7 March 1900 Westcott heard separately from Deullin as the Senior Warden of a French Lodge with regard to the 'Swedenborg Rite.' This letter to Westcott was on written on behalf of Papus, (see fig 125). The letter is dated 5 March. Deullin was also a 'Martinist,' as can be seen by the Martinist titles and abbreviations used in the letter. He introduced himself to Westcott as a member of the 'Swedenborg INRI Lodge No.14' and was offering his adherence to that Lodge and the 'Swedenborg Rite.' This is with regard to the

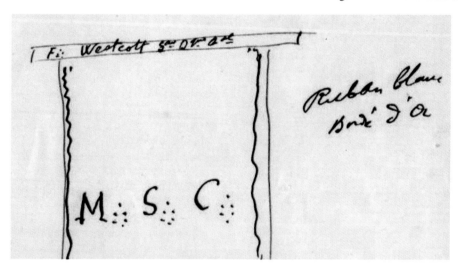

Figure 124 - Detail of Westcott's Breast Jewel

circles I mix in, I can only conclude that M.∴ S.∴ C.∴ are the initial letters of 'Martinist Supreme Council' The Martinist collar and jewels, warrants and certificates were never used by Westcott or the S.R.I.A. in England as part of any 'Martinist Order.'

Westcott thanked Papus and forwarded the Martinist Jewel to Yarker the very next day. At the end of February, Westcott sent out in the post to several friends a copy of his latest printed S.R.I.A. college paper. This particular one was on 'Angels.' He states in his ACTA, "My Angels lecture to Papus, a present." was sent to Papus on 20 February in Paris as a gift.

The point is that on 6 March Papus wrote and thanked Westcott for the 'Angels' lecture. Westcott must also have been sent an invitation to the

suggestion made by Papus to Yarker in 1899, that he obtains his (esoteric) members for the proposed 'Swedenborg Lodge and Temple No.14' from among the members of the Le Libre Examen Loge No.217.

This was a very interesting period in time for this highly regarded Paris Lodge, which has an incredible history, as between 1900 and 1903 its male members were trying to attach a woman's only American type 'Adoptive Lodge' to itself and re-introduce woman's Freemasonry back into French Masonry through this Lodge. What was Papus' involvement, more research is needed here.

It succeeded in 1903, but became a women only lodge with its own 'Grand Lodge Body'[163] in a long drawn out battle with its own 'Grand Lodge' the 'Grand Lodge de France,' which was then I believe

---

161 See next section on Le Libre Examen Lodge No.217.

162 Invitation in the S.R.I.A. archives.
163 Snoek J. 2011, *Initiating Women in Freemasonry: The Adoption Rite.*

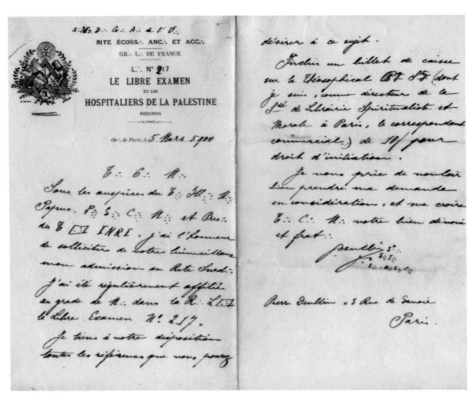

Figure 125 - Le Libre Examen No. 217

still subservient to the 'Supreme Council of the French Ancient & Accepted Rite' who did not recognise women's Freemasonry at the time, an affair that caused much of a stir in Paris.[164] It dropped the 'Adoptive Rite' and now is 'The Grand Lodge of France ' that works the first three degrees of the 'Ancient and Accepted Scottish Rite.'

That makes the letterhead used by Deullin more interesting, especially when he wrote to Westcott. It starts with the identity of the 'Supreme Council 33°' of the French 'Accepted Scottish Rite,' 'Rite Ecoss∴ Anc∴ Et Acc∴' Next comes the name of its 'Grand Lodge' the 'Grand Lodge de France'; 'GR∴ L∴ De Franc.'

Its history is even more interesting because of the possible connection with the letterhead that Reuss used in 1893, which was of the 'Accepted Scottish Rite' revived 'Illuminati Chapter of Improvement, Ludwig Lodge' in the Orient of Munich 1880.[165] The 'Grand Lodge de France' foundation date is 1773 and it changed names to 'Grand Orient de France' in 1799 at the time of the French Revolution. Benjamin Franklin who was mentioned earlier in *The History of the Illuminati Order;* was a member of the Paris Lodge Les Neuf Sœurs attached to the 'Grand Orient de France.' In 1894 many lodges broke away from the 'Grand Orient de France' and reformed the 'Grand Lodge de France' and brought back the 'Scottish Rectified

Rite' (Willermoz) from Switzerland. In 1904 the 'Grand Lodge de France' broke the last administrative links between the Grand Lodge of France and the Supreme Council. The 'Grand Lodge de France' and now enjoys full independence and total sovereignty, is constituted in association according to the law of 1901. In 1913 the old 'Grand Lodge de France' became the 'Grande Loge Nationale Française.'

The number of Deullin's Lodge is number 217 on the list of old 'Grand Lodge de France roll of Lodges.' The Lodge name is Le Libre Examen. This Lodge was amalgamated or re-united with the older Lodges of 'les Hospitaliers de la Palestine' and 'La Persévérance Ecossaise' in 1899 as implied by the letterhead, (see fig 125). Deullin was a Past Master of the Lodge and we assume a member of the 'Ordre Martinist' as he uses the Martinist greeting, 'Très Cher Maitre' in the letter and his rank of '3rd S∴ I∴,' of the 'Martinist Order,' after his signature.

For some reason, he also sends a receipt of his membership of the 'Theosophical Society' to add additional credibility. Deullin mentions the Society of 'Librairie Spiritualiste et Morale in Paris,' or the 'Moral and Spiritual Bookstore' which he and his friend Auguste Jacqute, ran in direct competition to Lucien Chamuel's 'Librairie du Merveilleux' (wonderful library), a library already mentioned that was based at the same address, that he gives at the end of the letter, 5 Rue de Savoie.

It is a strange co-incidence that Le Libre Examen Loge had amalgamated in 1899? This is

---

164 A row previously mentioned in, Gilbert, R.A. 1986, *The Masonic Career of A.E. Waite.*

165 See this Chapter – Reuss, Berlin, LUDWIG in the Orient of Munich.

the period when Papus approached Westcott and the S.R.I.A. about the 'Order of Kabbalistic Rose-Croix' and restarting the 'Ordre Martinist' in England. It was also the year that Papus first asked Yarker for a 'Swedenborg Rite' warrant for his 'I.N.R.I. Lodge and Temple No. 14 in Paris, something which is mentioned in this letter, as this was going to be the source from which 'Swedenborg Rite' members will be recruited.

This is also the address of all Papus Orders in France, is this where the 'Grand Lodge de France' Le Libra Examen Lodge' held its meetings or is it just Deullin's correspondence address? The 'Adoption Rite' row in 1901-1903 Paris could be one reason why Papus possible membership of his brother in-law and sisters Lodge may have been overlooked or hidden or he did not admit. Translation and transcription of the letter from Deullin, dated 5 March 1900:

Figure 126 – Brochure INRI Paris T & L

Next, chronologically, Papus received from John Yarker the 'Grand Hierophant' of the 'M.M.' between March and May 1900, a dispensation to open the 'Swedenborgian Lodge I.N.R.I. No14' to receive masons until such time as it had enough members to be properly warranted or chartered.

Then, on 29 May, Papus wrote to Westcott on yet another letterhead, this time on his new French 'Swedenborg Rite' headed note paper, (see fig 126) with a 'Rite Swedenborg' rubber stamp seal on the second sheet after his signature, with purely administrative questions, but again mentioning his brother in-law:

> *Très Cher Maitre. By this letter I send you the* <u>*brochure of constitution of the Lodge and INRI Temple in Paris.*</u> *I would be grateful if you could answer the following questions: Do I have to have diplomas given to the members of my Lodge or have to wait for the ones you send to each member of the Lodge? In the latter case, how should I announce the English diplomas and the affiliation to our Lodge? It just happens for our Frater Deullin and I have several others waiting, fraternally Papus.*

I had missed this in the correspondence before, but this letter implies that Papus may have sent Westcott a copy of the 'Brochure' with this letter

---

RITE ECOSS.: ANC.: ET ACC.:
GR.: L.: DE FRANC;
L.: NO.217;
LE LIBRE EXAMEN
BY LES
HOSPITALLERS OF PALESTINE
RÉUNIS

Ord.: De Paris le ...... 5th Mars 5900

T :. C :. M :. (Très Cher Maitre)

Under the auspices of the Most Illustrious Brother Papus:. Papus, P. .::. S ::. C :. N ::. and President:. of the Lodge INRI. I have the honour to solicit my adherence to the Swedenborgian Rite.

I have been regularly affiliated with the rank of Master in the (Respectable Lodge) in the Le Libre Examen Lodge No. 217.
I would like to provide you with all the references you may wish for on this subject.

Includes a receipt on the Theosophical Society (of which I am the director of the Society of Librairie Spiritualiste et Morale in Paris, the commercial correspondent) of 10 francs for the initiation fee.

I beg you to take my request into consideration, and believe me. T :. C :. M :. Very Dear master your devoted and fraternally.

P. Deullin, 3rd
S .::. I .::.
I.::. M.::. S .::. C.::.

Pierre Deullin = 5 Rue de Savoie, Paris

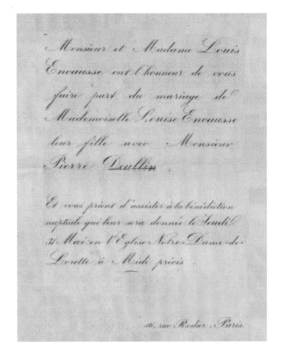

Figure 127 – Papus sister marriage to Deullin

in, that caused all the problems when Reuss went on to copy the details in 1902.[166]

This would mean that Westcott had every opportunity of translating the document and correcting the mistakes made by Papus in 1900, with the Swedenborg grade mistakes and the wrong history of the 'Swedenborg Rite' issued to his French candidates, two years earlier. The Papus brochure however is not in the S.R.I.A. archives.

It is interesting to note that the address on this 'Swedenborg Rite letterhead' is number 4, Rue de Savoie in Paris. When you look on Google Maps, you see that numbers 5 and 4 Rue de Savoie are directly across the street from each other, so they perhaps used different rooms in the same street at different times, (see fig 131).

The letterhead motif of Papus' 'Swedenborgian Rite' contains many symbols it seems from many different orders, (see figs 19 and 126), but it does not seem to include the 'Illuminati Symbols' or those of the 'Martinist Order.' In the bottom left corner is the equal arm cross with roses in each quarter that is that of Papus's 'Order Kabbalistique De La Rose Croix,' which Papus offered to Westcott in 1899. In the bottom right corner is the 'Sphynx,' could this represent some form of 'Egyptian Freemasonry' or 'Hermetisim?'

They probably also represent some of the symbols of Yarker's 'Ancient Primitive Rite,' which Papus thought he had mistakenly obtained. On the curtain or the arch-work are the signs of the horoscope and the signs for the planets. Inside that are the B and J columns of 'craft masonry,' inside

these on the right is the ladder and the pelican in its piety, symbols of the '18° of the Rose Croix' of the 'Ancient and Accepted Rite' and opposite those the 'Masters words' M & B, the acacia and the working tools of the 3° in the 'craft.' The Ouroboros, the triangles of the elements and interlaced triangles with three spheres are all depicted, to name just a few of the many symbols; there are so many more.

RUSSIA

There was a strong mystical presence in Russia, especially after the Napoleonic Wars, when many Masonic Lodges in Europe were closed. There were at least three 'Ordre Martinist Lodges' in Russia, one in run by Le Comte Valérien Mouravieff from Saint-Petersbourg. Another in Butatar near Gdansk run by Grégoire von Mébès and the last in Warsaw.

There is also on file a message from the French spiritualists to His Holiness Nicholas II. Emperor of Russia (1868-1918). *Message des spiritualistes français à S.M. Nicolas II Empereur de Russie.* Finally there is a paper without text, signed by Nicolas Emperor of Russia, Empress Alexandra and the President of France Felix Faure 1895-1899. *Papier sans texte signé par Nicolas, empereur de Russie, l'impératrice Alexandra et le président Félix Faure.*

Figure 128 - Encausse in Russia

---

166 See Chapter I, Figure 19 - General Information about the Lodge and Temple of Perfection 1900.

206

Chapter VI

Papus first visited Russia in January 1900, following an impressive spiritual séance at the Romanoff court he was invited back again to give a series of conferences in February 1901. Papus was there for three weeks explaining the 'Archemeter' which was a Stanislas de Guaita cube, for keeping track of all manifestations of the immaterial. The Empress Alexandra granted him an audience just before he returned to Paris.

Papus returned to Russia again in 1905, and 1906, serving Tsar Nicholas II and Tsarina Alexandra, both as a physician and as an occult consultant.

PROTOCOLS OF THE ELDERS OF ZION

Papus actually became one of several occult advisers to Russian Czar Nicholas II.

While in Paris he continued to write anti-Zionist articles in support of the Czar. I was really surprised to learn that Papus was accused, much later in 1920 after his death, of having helped forge some of the Protocols of the Elders of Zion documents with his friend Nizier Anthelme Philippe, one of Papus' Martinist protégées. I have not found any proof of this terrible accusation.

If he was involved in some way with these forgeries it was unforgivable, because they were used in both the Russian Revolution and by the Nazis in the Second World War to persecute Jews and many other groups of people.

Having read them one of the masonic letters it is fairly incriminating, signed by a 'Ancient & Accepted Rite' type 33° mason, who definitely did not seem to know the masonic jargon he used very well. Of course, it may be partly just a very bad translation into English. If so, this sheds more doubt on their authenticity. They were used to smear Freemasons in the Protocols, as well as journalist and Jews.

The protocols document, are alleged, to be secret minutes from an 'Ancient & Accepted Rite' type meeting. They are called Protocols, from the First Zionist Congress held at Basel, Switzerland in August 1897. Many authors now believe that some of the Protocols were plagiarised from nothing more than a much earlier satire, written by Maurice Joly.

In his book *Mein Kampf* written later in 1925, Adolf Hitler corrected some of the ridiculous anomalies in the masonic documents that were written in the Protocols, as if they had a more reliable source for the language that was used in them.

Some of *Mein Kompf's*, anti-Jewish and anti-Freemasonry rhetoric is, however, based on some of the sentiments contained in the Protocols and was even allegedly given to school children to read at one point during the Second World War. None of which however can be blamed on Papus.

WAS PAPUS LOSING CONTROL
Or just fighting for survival?

The following letter from Papus to Westcott that was written on 9 March 1902, (see fig 129), gives an incredible insight into some of the problems that Papus was facing at the time with Deullin. The letter gives Westcott details of some of these troubles that he was having at the time.

He writes to Westcott that he has prepared a magazine for the 'Swedenborg Rite' and that it will soon be published. It would seem that he is suffering with the deaf Hostility of the 'Grand Orient of France,' who he calls the 'Atheists French Freemasons,' as their organisation did not believe in the 'Supreme Being' something which is a prerequisite of being a regular Freemason, the letter speaks for itself, (see fig 129) and the transcript, (see fig 130).

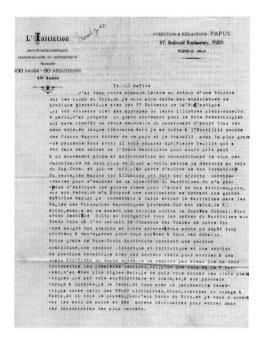

Figure 129 - Scan of letter dated 9 March 1902

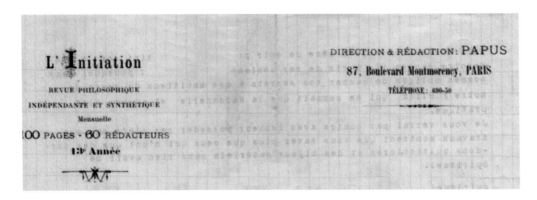

L'**I**nitiation

REVUE PHILOSOPHIQUE
INDÉPENDANTE ET SYNTHÉTIQUE
Mensuelle
100 PAGES · 60 RÉDACTEURS
13ᵉ Année

DIRECTION & RÉDACTION: PAPUS
87, Boulevard Montmorency, PARIS
TÉLÉPHONE: 690-50

9 March 1902

Tr. Ill Maître

I received your kind letter (10ᵗʰ February) after returning from a tour on the Rhine, where I went to experiment with practical hermetic Eminent F.F.1. all "R.C." that have preserved many ancient mysteries of their illustrious predecessors.

In Paris, I have prepared a great movement for the Swedenborgian Rite, which will soon have its monthly review appearing first or every two months, in French. But, I exposed myself to the deaf Hostility of Atheists French Freemasons of this country and I work with great caution.

We had to separate from the F∴ Pierre Deullin, who was dismissed from the Martinist Order for taking part in an atheist and anti-Christian movement in restoring the club Jacobins. I do not see it Frater, which way to read the disorder within the 'Suprême Conseil' and which is no longer part of our training.

Moreover, non-illuminated Masons have made considerable efforts to take over the leadership of Martinism. In America, a large sum was offered for the purchase of our Archives, (by E. Blitz) then, on my refusal, I was offered a combination giving me Grand Master MAC S.∴. I was offered, if I agreed to bring Martinism into the rules of the profane Masonic Powers (C.B.C.S.). On my refusal, the F∴ Blitz, is trying at the moment, a revolt against the 'Suprême Conseil.' We have removed Blitz and reorganized all Lodges of Martinism in the US, where it traded in Grades of the Order despite our statutes and our defence. They are too precious a deposit to save, and must stop these details.

Our grade of Martiniste Rosicrucians contains section s both symbolic, historical and of initiation sections and a practical section with tight real secrets to arrive at real keys of the Greater work. I ask nothing better than to transmit the first section, to you and the F∴ Yarker, you are not more worthy. But, I cannot give you the keys in practice only by experiment and orally, and in my next trip to London, I will, if you have an airtight laboratory as that of the old Rosicrucian alchemists. Alternatively, combine a trip to Paris, and if you can, could drink juice 'on the banks of the Rhine, and give you the passwords and your means to get into the most secret laboratories.

You will thus be able to see why Martinism has sacred duties vis-a-vis its former founders and why we are obliged to hide our secrets from the ambitious of the kind of our F. Blitz who knows only Masonry and has no practical key

I'll see you happily through these keys as your own work shows, that you know more than those who have only have a multi-coloured Cordon (of Grand Martinist Rank) and a Jewel (of office) without having anything Spiritually.

By this letter, I am sending you, Tres. Illustrious Master, papers prepared for the Lodge INRI. Soon I will publish the newspaper.

Fraternally to You: Papus

Figure 130 - Transcription of Deullin and Blitz letter 1902

PIERRE DEULLIN

Papus' brother in-law, Pierre Deullin (1873-1912), has now been dismissed from the 'Martinist Order' for taking part in an atheist and anti-Christian movement and an attempt to restore the 'Club Jacobins.' The 'Jacobins Club' had an incredible influence on the French revolution. 'The Society of the Friends of the Constitution' after 1792 was renamed the 'Society of the Jacobins, Friends of Freedom and Equality.'

In May 1793, they were led by Maximilien de Robespierre, the leaders of one of the factions succeeded in side-lining the other faction and controlled the government until July 1794. In 1794, the 'Thermidorian Reaction' pushed this faction out of power, the 'Jacobin Club' was closed and many of its leaders, including Robespierre, were executed. At its peak, there were at least 7,000 chapters throughout France, with a membership estimated at a half-million or more. It was this widespread yet highly centralised organization that gave the 'Jacobin Club' its formidable power. The cultural influence of the Jacobin movement during the French Revolution revolved around the creation of the Citizen and the rights of man.

What a terrible organisation to be accused of trying to restore to power.

The political character and history of some of the old Le Libre Examen Loge No.217 members lends itself to the continued heavy influence of left wing members being in the lodge and Deullin was a Past Master among them.

Additionally in the letter, Papus says that there is disorder within the 'Suprême Conseil' and the 'Grande Loge de France.' Yes and as already mentioned the 'Grande Loge de France' broke away completely from the 'Suprême Conseil' in 1904 and became the Grand Lodge for Women.

I believe that this was caused by the failure of the male members to get proper approval of their proposed 'Adoptive Rite Lodge,' of woman only, attached to the Le Libre Examen Loge, mentioned earlier. Papus' reputation would have been tarnished by his brother-in-law and sister's involvement with both issues, all fermented in the Le Libre Examen Loge.

EDOUARD BLITZ

Who was this Edouard Emmanuel Blitz (1860-1915) from America? Papus had a meeting at the *Librarie du Merveilleux* bookstore at 5 Rue de Savoie, on 20 June, 1894, with Edouard Blitz who was then initiated a 'Martinist.' Only a few days later, Papus gave Blitz a charter for the 'Osiris Lodge No. 37' in America. That would give Blitz full authority as a Sovereign National Delegate of

the 'Ordre Martiniste' to install and develop 'Martinism' in the United States. Then, on the evening of 20 July 1894, in his apartment at 12 rue des Filles Dieux, Blitz received from Paul Sédir, whose real name Yvon Le Loup, further documents probably from the 'Ordre Kabbalistic Rose-Croix' to assist him in establishing American Martinist lodges.

In America, Blitz was accused by Papus of trying to change the whole running of the 'Ordre Martinist.' In fact at one point he wanted to close down the French Order and preferred to turn it into an offshoot of the 'Swedenborg Rite' in America and later more significantly to become part of the Swiss, 'Scottish Rectified Rite' (C.B.C.S.) thereby putting the 'Ordre Martinist,' on a more masonic footing. To put this into perspective, it shows that Papus was fighting his own 'Grand Lodge Wars' on two fronts, over his 'Ordre' Martinist,' in America and in England during the time of the introduction of the 'English Illuminati.'

Figure 131 - Number 5 Rue de Savoie

Was it so different in France and is this why Papus allegedly wanted to close down the Martinist Order on his death?

I have seen documents online written by Blitz as the 'Grand Prior C.B.C.S.' of America, suggesting that Zurich would make Papus the 'Grand Prior' of the 'Scottish Rectified Rite' or 'C.B.C.S.' in France, on condition that he should give up the 'Ordre' Martinist' altogether. The reason Blitz gave was that they, the 'C.B.C.S.' in Switzerland, were the true and rightful inheritors of the ethos of Martinez de Pasqually, Jean-Baptiste Willermoz and Louis-Claude de Saint-Martin.

Papus was having none of it and did not join them, which is credit to him! But he might have thought at the time that he had failed with his version of 'Martinisim?'

It is true that Blitz saw the potential of the 'Martinist Order,' but thought that the 'Free Initiation' policy of the 'Ordre Martinist' did not work in America, where members just did not pay at all for anything. It was meant to be a 'Martinist philosophy,' not free membership.

So he felt that only Freemasons should be admitted, he wanted to therefore get rid of all the women members that had joined him from the 'Theosophical Society,' who Blitz said turned their 'Martinist' meetings into frivolous chats.

Blitz did offer a large sum of money to buy the papers of Jean-Baptiste Willermoz and the 'Cohen Temple of Lyons' archive material that had come into Papus' possession in 1893, only because he wanted to translate them into English. Papus was accused by Blitz, of dragging his feet over the task. What the American really wanted was just to be able access all the fabulous material that was available, but in English.

Figure 132 - Papus in his office at 5 Rue de Savoie

The rest of the letter is about Papus wishing to share the keys of philosophy with Yarker and Westcott in person, rather than by putting his sentiments in a letter.

From this tale of Edouard Blitz and Papus, you can see that some of the problems that a foreign order can cause, especially when establishing it in different country and the immense problems that there are in using different languages.

Yarker had already experienced this in 1895 and had translated the 'French Martinist' ritual into English, before Blitz did exactly the same thing the next year in parallel.[167] When you are admitted in to 'Martinisim,' to this very day, you are told about the fabulous writings of Martinez de Pasqually, Jean-Baptiste Willermoz and Louis-Claude de Saint-Martin and this makes you want to read them for yourself and see what they said and thought, it

is information that is available to you but it is very difficult to find it in English!

This is exactly the problem that Westcott faced with the 'Resurrected Illuminati,' for example, Adam Weishaupt wrote many books about the Illuminati, but they were all in German and few were ever translated, I can only find three

These are some of the many problems that Westcott may also have been experiencing in 1902.

The problems of translating Illuminati rituals, ordinances and support material like the *History* and *Mysteries*. If Westcott had gone ahead he would have to pay for them all to be translated out of his own pocket. Although Reuss wrote perfectly good English as a journalist, could he be relied on to tackle the huge amount paperwork and background material that needed completing?

Using the 'Ordre Martinist' as an example, even 100 years later, I have seen comments online, by many modern 'American Martinists' complaining at the lack of English translated material available!

What I think Papus means in the letter, is that Blitz was too interested in acquiring degrees, promotion, regalia, titles and control, and did not spend enough time on the esoteric study and self-development side. To a certain extent this is also what happened after Papus died in 1916.

Papus' successors fought over the succession, control, titles, regalia, promotion, how many degrees there should be and even whether women should be allowed to be new members.

On 13 February 1902:

The Supreme Council in France discontinued the post of Sovereign Delegate General for the United States. Edouard Blitz was no longer the director of the Martinist Order in America.[168]

The Décret du Suprême Conseil was signed by Sédir, Sénéra, Sabrin, Jacques Burg, G. Phaneg and Papus et A. C.

From Google Earth we have a glimpse of the front door of number 5 Rue de Savoie (see fig 131).

In (fig 132) we actually see Papus at work inside his office at number 5 Rue de Savoie.

---

167 Library and Museum of Freemasonry, London.

168 Garver P.A. 2003, Edouard Blitz (1860-1915) and *American Martinism.*

A LIST OF PAPUS' WRITINGS:

Anarchie, indolence et synarchie : les lois physiologiques d'organisation sociale et l'ésotérisme 1894
Library and Museum of Freemasonry: 1660 PAP fol.

L'Occultisme Contemporain. 1887. PDF scans from Gallica.

Clef absolue de la science occulte: Le Tarot des bohémiens 1889.
.https://archive.org/details/clefabsoluedelas00papuuoft.

Absolute Key to occult science. The Tarot of the Bohemians. 1892.
https://archive.org/details/cu31924028930571.

La Science Des Nombres 1934.
http://www.labirintoermetico.com/06Numerologia_Cabala/Papus_La_Science_des_Nombres.pdf.

L'Occultisme. 1890.

Le Livre des Splendeurs; Etude sur les Origines de la Kabbala; 1894. High Council Library.

*La magie et l'hypnose : recueil de faits et d'expériences justifiant et prouvant les enseignements de
l'occultisme; avec dessins de: Ange Bossard* 1897. Library and Museum of Freemasonry: SRIA .

Traite Elementaire de Science Occulte, 1898. High Council Library/ Library and Museum of
Freemasonry: SRIA 843. https://archive.org/details/cu31924028930571.

Martinésisme Willermosisme : Martinisme et Franc-Maçonnerie 1899. Library and Museum of
Freemasonry: A 699 (MAR) ENC.

The Tarot of the Bohemians, 1910. High Council Library/ Library and Museum of Freemasonry: SRIA.
839 https://archive.org/details/tarotofbohemians00papu.

Martinez de Pasqually, 1895. High Council Library/ Library and Museum of Freemasonry: SRIA 842.

Martinisme et Franc Maconnerie, 1899. High Council Library.

*Louis Claude de Saint-Martin*s. Library and Museum of Freemasonry: A699 (ILL) ENC.

La Russie Aujourd'hui, 1902. High Council Library.

Grimorium Saturni (Volume II):*Traite Elementaire de Science Occulte*, 1973.

https://archive.org/details/GrimoriumSaturnivolumeIiTratadoDeCinciasOcultasVol.I.

JOHN YARKER

A man of many decorations and Orders

In deference to Barry Loft, who is in the process of producing a comprehensive history of John Yarker (1833-1913) and because he has supplied the S.R.I.A. with transcriptions and much useful material., I will content myself with quoting the information that is on file in the S.R.I.A. 'Golden Book' and reproducing the online biography that the Library and Museum of Freemasonry have produced to accompany the photographs they have of John Yarker. However, I could not resist inserting a few purely speculative personal traits, based on his date of birth.[169]

Born at Swindale, Shap, in Cumbria on 17 April 1833, the son of John Yarker, a scripture reader and his wife, Ann, née Fell and was baptised there on 21 April that same year. In the English census, he is recorded aged 18 years old, living with his parents as a commercial clerk, at Reather Street, Manchester, which used to run from Rochdale Road towards Oldham Road in Collyhurst and it is all-but-lost to redevelopment except for the short Reather Walk today. He lived with his father, mother and five brothers in 1851 He married Elizabeth Jane Lund at Chorlton, Manchester on 4 January 1857. He became involved in several commercial ventures and travelled extensively in America, the West Indies and Cuba on business around 1864. The couple moved to 'The Poplars' 90 Burton Road Withington in 1876 and raised three sons and three daughters.

On first impressions, I believe that John Yarker would appear, as a can do type of person, someone who you would imagine wanted to 'rush out' and both 'do' and 'experience' everything. However, what would have surprised you is that there were times when he wanted only to sit back and ponder, understand and judge. His reflective side was the 'wiser half' of Yarker and, in fact, he did not much like rushing in where angels fear to tread. He was the type who would weigh everything forty times and then sleep on it again to be absolutely sure.

He was involved in several commercial ventures and always seemed to have enough money until the end of his life when business was not so good. He was not rich, but he was generous to a fault and eager to please. Someone who enjoyed travelling extensively for business and his masonic membership would have helped make contacts in these countries, which is where many of his side orders originated from.

Yarker had that dark haired eager Boy Scout, boyish look about him in his youth, which was exaggerated by his small stature, but he was always elegantly turned out, a dapper sort of chap, with a sporty air of coquetry.

Someone who had been drawn away from the hardy sensible shoes of Cumbria and backpacking, to embrace Manchester city life and international commercial travel, someone who looked the typical British man abroad.

Later, in 1881, he was living as a doting caring parent and the manager of a mercantile business, a merchant, involved in trade with Turkey. He was living at West Didsbury, with his wife Elizabeth Jane, three sons called John Lewis, Thomas Edward, William Francais and with three daughters, Eliza Edith, Amy Beatrice and Anne Elizabeth.

Then, as a director and shipping merchant in 1900, when he was the Director of the General Merchants and Shippers, 'Smith & Pass Ltd,' Atlantic Chambers, Number 7 Brazennose Street, Manchester. Several of the letters written to Westcott in the S.R.I.A. archives are written on this business letterhead, (see fig 133).

If Turkey was a country that was still part of their business, this ally of Germany in the First

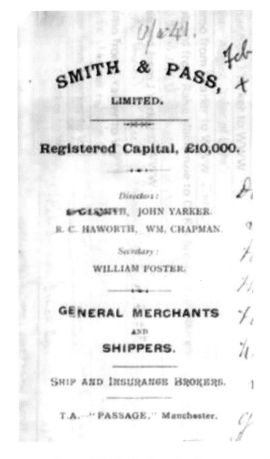

Figure 133 - Yarker's work address

---

169 White S. 1987, *New Astrology.*

World War may have gone cold in the years leading up to the conflict, which may have financially affected his business. He was still living at 'The Poplars,' with his wife, one son and three daughters in 1901 and finally as a retired clerk, shipper and author, living at the same address with his wife, three daughters and one visitor in 1911, where he eventually died.

NON MASONIC MEMBERSHIPS

He received many civil decorations, including 'the Star of Merit' of the Rajah of Calcutta in 1886, (see fig 139), the Order of Melusine, Knight from the Princedom of Lusignians (Jerusalem, of Cyprus and of Armenia) in 1886 and Nischal al Ifrikhar or Order of Glory from the Sultan Abdul Hamid of Ottoman, Turkey in 1905.

Figure 134 - Imperial Constantine Order of St George

He also received the Imperial Constantinian Order of St. George (see fig 134), granted by Prince Demetrius Rhodocanakis in 1871. This may have been because both Charles F. Matier (who was living in Manchester at the time) and John Yarker defended Prince Rhodocanakis against Robert Wentworth Little and the resurrection of the Red Cross of Rome and Constantine in the Masonic press. This was an ancient Civic Order of which Prince Rhodocanakis believed that he and his family were the rightful heredity heirs and that R.W. Little should not have used the insignia and regalia of this order for the masonic Order. The upshot of their campaign was that Thomas Taylour, commonly called Earl of Bective, declared the English branch of the Red Cross Order and changed its title from 'Imperial Ecclesiastical Order of the Red Cross of Rome and Constantine' to the 'Military and Masonic Order of the Red Cross of Constantine,' on 29 March 1871. There was a year

recess and the next meeting of the Grand Conclave was held on 7 March 1872, but they still carried on using the emblems of the Constantine Order of St. George.

It was nice to read one commentator's anonymous words on the British Columbia and Yukon website:

> *Yarker was neither a degree-monger, nor a charlatan, for he believed what he wrote, that the many degrees he had discovered all predated regular Freemasonry. He never invented evidence but accepted, uncritically, the invented evidence of others.* [170]

In the **Theosophical Society**, Yarker was elected an Honorary Fellow in 1879 and then into the **Society of Science, Letters and Arts** in 1882, he was the awarded a Gold Medal in 1887, and for whom he served as a council member for five years.

In the **L'Ordre Martinist** in Paris of France, it is alleged that Yarker was installed as a Docteur en Science Hermetique by the Free University of Paris in 1881. This, however, was seven years before Papus formed the L'Ordre Martinist in Paris. There are two other dates often quoted, the first 1891 and from another source 10 October 1899. But, as mentioned before, according to Barry Loft, Yarker did not become a Martinist until 24 July 1893, Loft goes on to say that it was through him that members were registered by Papus (with a number Lodge No.45) in Paris. It was all very informal, there were no fees and no obligation to do anything but maintain secrecy. Rituals had to be returned to him "on honour" within three days.

It is very interesting to note that John Yarker claimed to A.E. Waite that he had been initiated by a non-mason.[171] In that book, the author gives us one version of his name as 'Baron Surdi of Prague.' However, the name of his 'Martinist Initiator,' I believe has been lost for years and is the Baron Adolphe de Leonhardi.[172] This was because it has been misspelt many different ways over the last hundred years, mainly due to the shocking handwriting writing style that Yarker used. However, the name 'Leonhardi' associated with Austria, South Bohemia and Czech, turned up in the 'Ordre Martinist Archives, Paris.'

The 'Ordre Martinist' archives show that, a Martinist circle came into being in 1893 at České Budějovice, (Budweiz, South Bohemia/Austria 1900/Czech). It was led by Baron Adolf Franz Leonhardi (1856-1908). In 1895, the circle was turned into a lodge which was called *U modré*

---

170 Freemasonry.bcy.ca.
171 Gilbert, R.A. 1986, *The Masonic Career of A.E. Waite*, AQC Vol 99 1986.
172 Member of Lodge No. 12 Martinist Order Archives, Paris.

hvězdy (The Blue Star) Lodge Number 12. With a vague address, Platz, Austria, this was apparently later moved to Prague, which finally concurs with R.A. Gilbert's quote mentioned above.

The same archive also contains an 1893 letter 'Password for the 2nd semester' meaning a password was supplied to the Baron Leonhardi by Paris, in the same year that he is alleged to have admitted Yarker a Martinist! Could this mean they both became 'Martinist' the same year?

There are three different attempts to spell the name Leonhardi,[173] by someone employed to transcribe Yarker's version of the Martinist Rituals in 1895, (see fig 135). These names appear with question marks, next to the signature, one of the *Baron de Tulvidi? Sulvidi? or Inardi?* This appears to be a note made by the copyist, who you would have thought had become an expert at Yarker's writing by then.

These papers are collected together with those of the 'Order of Marquis de St. Martin' to be found in the Library and Museum of Freemasonry. 'The Order of St. Martin' is a paper containing a short explanation of its ritual written by Frederick Holland and the paper has an 1894 watermark. This is the time of the communications between Yarker and Paris and before the 'Martinist rituals' are translated. The collection also contains a transcribed copy of Yarker's translation of the French documents, which are not dated, but probably sent in 1894, with the 'Regulations of the Martinist Order in England' of 1895.[174]

The heading on the top of the page is 'Supreme Conseil d'l'Ordre Martinist,' Charter No. 45, signed by the secretary Paul Sedir and the President: Papus. What gives more credence to all this activity in 1893, 1894 and 1895, is a letter in the S.R.I.A. archives from Yarker to Westcott on the 18/11/1893:

> *The address to write to about 'Martinisim' is Monsieur Jacque Bony, 38 Rue des Abondances, Boulogne, France, who is the secretary.*

This suggests that Yarker knew the secretary better than he knew the President, who was Papus at this time and that Westcott first became involved with 'Martinisim' in November 1893, several months after Yarker was admitted in the July. The 1893 date for being admitted a 'Martinist' seems also to fit with the 'Ordre Martinist' Archives in Paris today. They have a letter from Yarker dated 22 February 1894, which I have not seen. But, if I were to guess, it is a letter from a 'Martinist' asking if he could represent 'Martinisim' in Great Britain.

The result of this contact was that a forty fifth ''Ordre Martinist' Lodge was formed and it is listed in the 'Ordre Martinist' archives in Paris Lodge as:

> *'No. 45: Ancient & Primitive Rite of Masonry (Withington, England)'*

This 'Ordre Martinist' Lodge is named after one of Yarker's many orders and the lodge meetings were held at his home address in Withington.

This early foundation of the 'English Martinist' fits with the early correspondence in the S.R.I.A. archives, between J. Yarker and R.S. Brown, written in January and February 1895. This was probably the beginning of the attempted organisation of 'Martinisim' in Great Britain and may only have begun in earnest on 25 January 1895, with a letter from John Yarker to Robert Smith Brown, who I have already mentioned, who was the Secretary General of the S.R.I.S. in Edinburgh:

> *R.S. Brown I have not received your form yet but he (Holland) is secretary. Discuss the (Martinist) rituals and adopting a uniform translation. I have suggested to Holland we might revive his 'Hermetic Society of Eight' with this as Ritual, a corresponding society in which members might take up some particular study.*

The significance of this January letter is that it mentions the Rituals of Frederick Holland and the Society of Eight and that of Martinisim.

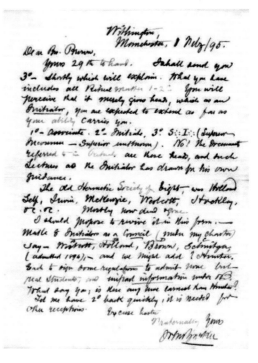

Figure 135 - Three Martinist Degrees 1 May 1895

173 Library and Museum of Freemasonry, [BE 699 (MAR) HOL fol.]
174 Ibid.

Figure 136 - John Yarker, Ancient & Primitive Rite

Having looked at the collection of early Martinist documents in the Library and Museum of Freemasonry, there are notes concerning Holland and the 'Society of Eight' and the transcriptions of Yarker's translations of the Martinist Rituals can be found signed by the Baron Leonhardi. In amongst these different documents at the bottom of the page ins the following note:

As to the old Hermetic Society of Eight, it is a past dream, though if you could get eight firm students, say, one through the Kabbalah & the others of other religions proving the assertion of the ritual, through Astrology, Theosophy, Hermeticism, then this ritual really hands the key down, but all should aim at the centre. The idea of eight was like the R. r. O. but really the eight angels of the Cubic or perfect stone. Eliphas Levi grand idea is the same ritual.

These notes and documents that are in the Library and Museum of Freemasonry, I believe tie up nicely with the 'Martinist' letters found in the S.R.I.A. archives and help corroborate the dates of documents and put them in a new context and in several different orders. In another 'Martinist' letter from Yarker to R.S. Brown on 8 February 1895, he informed him he had received back rituals and laws and that he, had appointed Holland 'Secretary' and he had named the first members. Two days later, in parallel, Westcott received a letter and certificate from Papus on 10 February 1895:

From the Lodge De L'Ordre Martinist, The President of Lodge No.45 confers upon brother

WSTCT (Westcott) "A45 C" the rights and privileges of an INITIATOR (Provincial Grand Master) and requests him to assign the No. "A 45 to such brethren as he may initiate, distinguishing them by letters a to z to follow after their said number as set forth in the ritual. XYRKR. (Yarker) TO A 45 C.

At the time Westcott held the position of Grand Brother Orator. Yarker's *Regulations of the Martinist Order in England* is also dated 1895. On 1 May 1895 letter, Yarker tells Brown about the first three Martinist Degrees and then mentions:

The Old Hermetic Society Eight," third paragraph, "was Holland, Yarker, Irwin, Mackenzie, Westcott, and Hockley etc. He then suggests "the following become Initiators (Provincial Grand Masters) Westcott-London; Holland-Bournemouth; Brown-Edinburgh; Schnitger-Newcastle and add W.S. Hunter-Glasgow.

In those days, the 'Initiator' had a special relationship with the initiated. The idea was to mentor them on a one to one basis in the 'Martinist' ways and the 'Ordre Martinist' was not designed to become a big order or necessarily a 'masonic order.' Another reason Yarker may not have pursued the Papus 'Ordre Martinist,' is that some of the original grades of Martinez Pasqually and Marquis de St. Martin and the 'Rites of Perfection and Knights of the Orient,' were already in the 'Ancient & Primitive Rite,' one of the reasons that I believe that Theodor Reuss also wanted the Rite in Prussia.

Again, in the Library and Museum of Freemasonry is a Ritual of 'Martinist' grade, in manuscript form, which was prepared by Edouard Blitz and another by John Yarker. They are typescript copies of 'first grade' ceremony, and related allocutions by John Yarker and Edouard Blitz, plus a carbon copy of the Blitz version.[175]

Yarker is elected an Honorary Member of the 'Osiris Lodge No. 37' (Nevada) of the 'Ordre Martinist' in the USA under Edouard Blitz. In September 1899, Yarker is made 'Sovereign & Grand Delegate 'of the 'Sovereign Grand Council of the Ordre Martinist' at Paris. Next month, on 10 October 1899, he is made 'Docteur en Hermetisme, ad honorem, de l'Universite Libre des Hautes, Etudes,' Paris.

The next year, Westcott received the designs drawn by Papus and then two Martinist jewels from Papus, one for himself and the other for John Yarker on 2 February 1900 to progress the order in the UK, but it did not happen, (see fig 125).

---

175 Library and Museum of Freemasonry [A 699 (MAR) RIT fol].

FREEMASONRY

In **Craft Masonry**, John Yarker was initiated as a Freemason at twenty one years old in the Lodge of Integrity, No. 189 (now No. 163), Manchester on 25 October 1854, three years before he was married. He was passed to the Fellow Craft on 15 February and raised a Master Mason on 25 April the following year.

He became a joining member of Fidelity Lodge, No. 623 (now No. 430), Dukinfield, Lancashire, on 29 April 1855, where he served as Worshipful Master in 1856-57, before resigning in 1858. It is very surprising that it only took two years to reach the chair instead of typically eight and that he was only a Past Master for another two years, before he resigned from his 'Mother Lodge,' after eight years in total, he demitted (resigned) from 'Craft Freemasonry' altogether in 1862.

This is perhaps why some people may have called him an irregular Freemason during the period of this story, because he was not a subscribing member of the 'United Grand Lodge of England.' However, he was an honorary member of several lodges and 'Grand Lodges.' Honorary members do not usually have to pay subscriptions and some of these lodges may not have had a similar requirement that he was a subscribing member of the 'U.G.L.E.' This also did not, however, stop him in those days of continuing in other side orders.

He was a member of at least six **overseas constitutions** in Freemasonry and was elected an honorary member of Geraldine Lodge, No. 227, Dublin, Irish Constitution in 1872. He was an honorary Past Senior Grand Warden of the 'Grand Lodge of Greece' in 1874; an honorary member and medallist of the 'Grand Lodge of Romania' in 1881; an honorary member of Ciro Menoti Lodge, No. 22, Italy in 1882 and La Verita Lodge, Italy, working under the 'Supreme Council of Italy' in 1883; an honorary member of Thorne Lodge, No. 282, Ontario, working under the 'Grand Lodge of Canada' in 1883; an honorary Master of Lodge Giordano Bruno, Palmi, Calabria in 1889 and Honorary Grand Master of the 'Grand Lodge of Cuba' in 1907.

In the **Holy Royal Arch,** he was exalted in Industry Chapter, No. 465 (now No. 361), Hyde, Lancashire, on 6 April 1856, where he served as the First Principal in 1860 and 1861. He attended St. John's Chapter, No. 407 (now No. 325), Eccles, Lancashire, in 1856 to take a Past Master degree and to demonstrate the Veils ceremony. He became a Founder and inaugural First Principal of Fidelity Chapter, No. 623, Newton, Lancashire in 1860.

In **Mark Masonry,** he was advanced in an unknown Lodge on 15 July 1855. He became a Founder and inaugural Worshipful Master of Fidelity Lodge, No. 31, Birkenhead in 1858.

In the **Ancient and Accepted Rite,** he was perfected in Palatine Rose Croix Chapter, No. 7, Manchester on 15 October 1862. He was expelled by the 'Supreme Council 33°' on 30 November 1870, eight years later, when he challenged the decision of 'Supreme Council 33°' at the festive board, after the meeting was held, to blackball four Irishman that Yarker had proposed into the Palatine Chapter. What Yarker did not know at the time was that it was a policy laid down by Capt. N. G. Philips 'Lieut. Grand. Commander and Sovereign Grand Commander 1874-1905 of Supreme Council

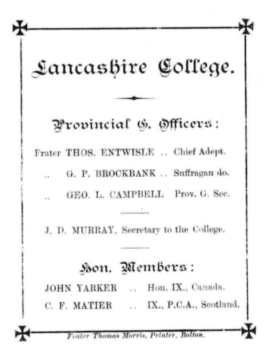

Figure 137 - S.R.I.A. Lancashire College 1882

33°,' that Irish candidates were not permitted to be 'Perfected' in England. But neither Yarker nor his candidates were informed about this prior to the meeting in October. Yarker never forgave the embarrassment caused to him by the senior member's actions.

In the **Cerneau Rite Supreme Council 33° New York,** Yarker was elected Honorary Member 33° on 24 August 1871 and received an 'Honorary 33°' of the New York 'Cerneau Scottish Rite,' a year after being excluded from the 'Ancient & Accepted Rite' in England. One year after that he was elected an 'Honorary Member' of the New York 'Cerneau Supreme Council' and their Representative in Great Britain on 15 November 1872. (Loft, 2015) The 'Cerneau Rite of 33°' was a direct competitor of the 'Ancient & Accepted Rite,' in the Northern Jurisdiction in the USA in 1801-06. While yet another New York Supreme Council was trying to earn that designation.

In the **Sovereign Grand Council of Ibérico,** on 5 October 1899, he was elected the Honorary Grand Master of the 'Sovereign Grand Council of Iberico 33-96°' and in 1910 the Honorary Grand Master and Vitam of the **United Supreme Council of Italy in Firenze**. Altogether he received over a dozen patents appointing him an honorary 33° of various Supreme Councils.

In the **Knights Templar,** he was installed in Jerusalem Conclave (now Jerusalem Preceptory, No. 5), in Manchester on 11 July 1856, where he served as Commander in 1862, before resigning in 1873. He was installed as a Knight of Malta in this Conclave. He became a joining member of Love and Friendship Encampment, Stockport, Lancashire (now erased) in 1860, where he served as Commander in 1861 and Antiquity Encampment, No. 1, Bath, Somerset in 1871. He served as Provincial Grand Vice-Chancellor of the Provincial Grand Conclave of Lancashire in 1861, for which he drew up by-laws in 1862. He was appointed Grand Constable by the Grand Conclave of England in 1864 after only ten years of masonic membership. He was elected an honorary member of St. Amand Encampment, No. 68, Worcester in 1869 and Royal Kent Preceptory, No. 20, Newcastle-upon-Tyne in 1895.

In the **Societas Rosicruciana In Anglia,** he was admitted into the Northern Counties, Lancashire College or Manchester College at their first meeting held on the 11 March 1871, by their new Chief Adept Charles Fitzgerald Matier VIII° (1840-1914), who I mentioned earlier with regard to Prince Demetrius Rhodocanakis, in fact all three lived in Manchester. Matier was received as a Zelator at a special ceremony in London consisting of three people, R.W. Little, W.J. Hughan and W.G.R Woodman on 28 February 1871. Matier's Golden book number was No.88 and authority was granted to Frater Matier as Chief Adept VIII° of Northern Anglia (1871-1877) to found a College of Rosicrucians at Manchester.

Yarker was admitted a Zelator and received as the Provincial Secretary on the same day by the new Chief Adept and his Golden Book number was the next recorded, No.89, being admitted with another local man, the Rev James Nixon Porter, G.B. No.90 and all three were entered in the S.R.I.A. Golden Book at the same time. Yarker's S.R.I.A. Latin Motto was 'Finis Coronat Opus.'

Yarker was made 'Grade 8°' on 1 January 1875 and resigned from the S.R.I.A. "to make room for others" on 20 November 1875. He did not stay long

enough to become the Chief when C.F. Matier stepped down in 1877. He was however made an Honorary IX° in 1896 by Westcott, (see fig 137).

In the **Red Branch of Eri**, according to W.W. Westcott's notes written in 1872, F.G. Irwin made the following knights of the Red Branch of Eri, which is an Irish Chivalric Order: Charles Scott (Supreme Magus Ireland/Hibernia), John Yarker, McLeod Moore, George C. Longley, J.K. Fletcher, Vincent Bird, Benjamin Cox, and H.F. Irwin (his son) into the first unit called the 'Brian Boru Faslairt' No.1' and then no one else until Westcott was admitted in 1880. F.G. Irwin was Chieftain 1858-1893, John Yarker Chieftain 1893-1913. John Yarker offered the Chief ship of Eri to C.F. Matier and then Lord Euston, both declined. On 10 November 1898, he once again offered the Chief ship of Eri to W.W. Westcott, it was declined. It was not until 1913 that Westcott became Chieftain until his death in 1925. John Yarker was a member in the second Eri unit called the Erminion Faslairt No.2 at Manchester. He admitted or knighted F. Schnitger, J. Armstrong and also Lord Euston and C.F. Matier into Eri in 1899. Yarker produced a number of drawings of the regalia in one of his ritual book, (see fig 138).

Figure 138 - Eri Knight's Star Jewel

In the **Ancient and Primitive Rite Sovereign Sanctuary (Memphis & Mizraim)** 33-96°, we know that, under a 23 February 1872 dispensation, John Yarker was made the Most Illustrious Grand Master General, establishing the 'Sovereign Sanctuary 33-96°' of the 'Ancient and Primitive Rite of Masonry' (Memphis & Mizraim) for England and Ireland under the authority of a Patent issued by the American Grand Master of that organization, General Giuseppe Garibaldi (1807-1882) 33-96°, Premiere Mason in Italy.

However, the first '**English Rite** of **Memphis**' meeting was held in London by Robert Wentworth Little (1838-1878), two years before Yarker formed his own 'Grand Lodge.' This was on Wednesday 28 December 1870. R.W. Little was the first 'Supreme Magus' of the S.R.I.A. This answers one of those odd queries about Yarker, why was he so anti R.W. Little and his London organisation, first in the Red Cross of Rome and Constantine and then over the 'Ancient & Primitive Rite of Misraim.' Robert Wentworth Little was the loser in this battle and it was probably this and other challenges to his leadership that made him very ill and he lived with tuberculosis for the last four years of his life with only one lung.

Yarker was never involved with the **Fratres Lucis,** which was an Order that belonged to F.G. Irwin, which he mentioned in a letter to Westcott on 29 June 1895. In the same letter, Yarker states that he has had nothing to do with founding any of Maurice Vidal Portman's Orders, they were 'Fratres Lucis' and the (Indian) 'August Order of Light,' which is not to be confused with another (Indian) Order of Light called (Apex) 'Royal Oriental Order of the Sikha Rote of Perfection Sat B'hai,' which Yarker was involved with and which was founded by J. H. Lawrence Archer. However, in another letter to Westcott, he goes on to say on 5 September 1908 that Portman gave Yarker and William Alexander Ayton the 'August Order of Light' and that Yarker gave Portman the 'Apex and Sat B'hai' and that Yarker then later amalgamated the two Indian Orders of Light.

In the **Sat B'hai,** he was involved at the very beginning with Captain J. H. Lawrence Archer and was appointed in 1872 to 'Censor' of the 'Royal Oriental Order of the Sat B'hai of Prag' in succession to Bro. R. S. Fitzgerald (killed at Delhi in 1857) and he was Co-Sponsor of the 'Royal Oriental Order of the Sikha (Apex).' On 23 September 1877, he was appointed to 'Perfection' in the 'Sat Bhai of Prag.' In 1886, there was a revised Code of 'Apex' and the 'Sat Bhai,' published. Much later, Westcott was 'chosen' by Maurice Vidal Portman in 1901, to revise the ritual

and to help establish the Order, as part of the 'August Order of Light' amalgamated with the Rites of the 'Royal Order and Sat B'hai' in Bradford, which was founded on 9 January 1902. (Loft, 2015)

In the **Society of Eight,** Yarker joined on the 11 December 1883, the same year it was founded by F.G. Irwin and Frederick Holland, who was a neighbour and friend of Mathers. The 'Society of Eight's' life was very short lived. See Chapter I for more information. The letter of 1 July 1895, in the archives, confirms that 'The Old hermetic Society of Eight' was of Holland's making and consisted of Holland, Yarker, Irwin, Hughan, Mackenzie, Westcott and Hockley at some time.

Figure 139 - Much older portrait of John Yarker

However, the correspondence between Robert S. Brown and John Yarker in 1895 concerning their new 'Martinist Order,' which he said was also co-founded by Frederick Holland, said that they might use the Martinist rituals in a revived 'Society of Eight' and to use the structure of eight for their 'INITIATORS' the equivalent of Provincial Grand Masters. Yarker, in the letter, suggested to Brown the following, a.) W.W. Westcott, b.) F. Holland, c.) F.F. Schnitger, d.) R.S. Brown, and add e.) G.S. Hunter, six with Yarker.

One month later he added two more names to the list of Martinist leaders, G.A. Turner and Dr G. Dickson, but this attempt to launch the 'Martinist Order' in Great Britain 1895 did not succeed, nor was the Society of Eight revived.

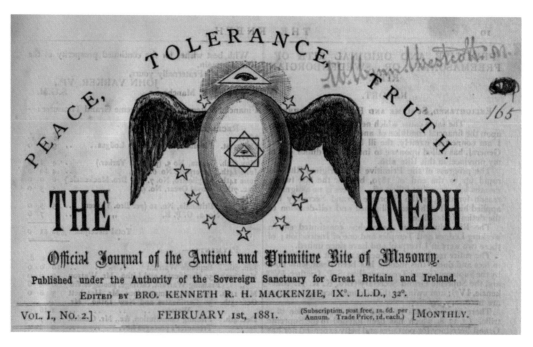

Figure 140 - The Kneph, publication 1881 sent in 1900

The **Swedenborg Rite** I wish to discuss here is the Beswick (1822-1903), version of the 'Swedenborg Rite,' as it was known in England. It was created by an Englishman living in America, who later moved to Canada, called Samuel Beswick. He resurrected the Rite based on his upbringing in the Swedenborgian Church as a minister and, allegedly, based on the writings of Emanuel Swedenborg (1688-1772) and his works.

The subject is referenced in his 1870 book, *The Swedenborg rite and the great masonic leaders of the eighteenth century* or *Swedenborg and Phremasonry*. From the correspondence in the S.R.I.A. archives between Francais George Irwin in Bristol and George Canning Longley in Canada, between 1876 and 1877, it is clear that F.G. Irwin had been put in direct contact with Samuel Beswick, through an introduction from George C. Longley as they both lived in Maitland, Canada at the time. I believe, from this correspondence, that Irwin did not want to run the order directly and so he passed it on to John Yarker. In 1876, a Canadian warrant was issued to John Yarker to form a Grand Lodge in Manchester, called the Emanuel No.1 Lodge and Temple. Yarker became the Grand Master, F. G. Irwin was the Grand Senior Warden and S. P. Leather was appointed the Grand Junior Warden on 13 January 1877 at their first meeting. Westcott was also placed on the founding warrant and became a 'Grand Officer' from the beginning. The Lodge was removed to Western-super-mare on 30 May 1877 under F.G. Irwin control. Later, Yarker offered Westcott to be Grand Master of the Swedenborg Rite on 10 February 1900, which he declined.

In the '**Order of Ishmael** 36°,' Yarker became the 'Sheikh of the Desert, Guardian of the Kaaba' in 1897 its full name was 'Ancient Oriental Order of Ishmael or of Esau and Reconciliation.'

The object of the order was to reconcile the two Semite descendants, of Abraham, a lofty goal. To reconcile Jacob who was the patriarch of the Jews and Ismael the patriarch of the Muslims. According to John Yarker's article on *Arab Masonry* in AQC 19, P. 243:

> In 1872 the late Bro. Mackenzie organised the "Order of Ishmael, the basis of which, he informed me, he had from an 'Arab in Paris.

Westcott became involved when he returned to Yarker an Order of Ishmael manuscript on 5 September 1908 and mentions the Arab from Paris. According to Mackenzie's Cyclopaedia (Mackenzie, 1987), the 'Order of Ishmael or of Esau and Reconciliation,' consisted of eighteen degrees and was divided into four classes, I have no idea where or when the additional degrees came from.

Yarker was also associated indirectly with several other secret orders like the **Ordo Templi Orientis** via Theodor Reuss and in a very small way with the **Hermetic Order of the Golden Dawn**, although he was never a member. Yarker joined the **Celestial Brotherhood,** or as it was known to the general public **The British and Foreign Society of Occultists** in a letter to Westcott dated 13 September 1890, it was a short-lived organisation. Similar, allegedly, in its workings to the 'Hermetic Order of the Golden Dawn,' it was founded by John Thomas (1826-1908), who was an astrologer and psychic. It involved a system of progressive grades, professed to receiving teachings from hidden Adepts on the inner planes and practiced magical and quasi-magical rituals. F.G. Irwin was also a member.

CONCLUSION
My own personal opinion

I think that both Papus and Reuss believed, like John Yarker, in the value of 'Ancient' Freemasonry and that is the real reason for their involvement in the higher grades or 'Hautes Grade.'

What I mean by that is the 'old speculative version of Freemasonry,' but not what is specifically called 'Operative Masonry.' They believed in what was speculative Freemasonry, with higher grades that existed before the forming of the first English Grand Lodge of Freemasons in 1717 by four existing London Lodges, which some would call 'Scottish Rite Masonry' and others the 'Holy Royal Arch.'

I believe, like some other authors before me, that Yarker was neither a degree-monger, nor a charlatan, for he believed what he wrote, that the many degrees he had discovered all predated 1717 the regular 'Modern's Freemasonry.' Here is what Yarker said for example in the first paragraph of his book:[176]

> *I here take the opportunity of recording my protest against the sceptical tendencies of the present generation of the Moderns' who are Masons, and against the efforts that are made, in season and out of season, to underrate the indubitable antiquity of the Masonic ceremonies.*

In this sense, what Yarker means by 'Modern's Freemasonry' was in fact two things. It was the introduction of a new organised 'Grand Lodge' structure in England that had been lost with the death of Sir Christopher Wren (1632-1723). It gave power and authority to masons who were members of that 'Grand Lodge' to hold an annual assembly of their private lodges. The four existing lodges that formed the first 'Grand Lodge of England' in 1717, in their first set of constitutions written by Anderson in 1723 stated: "and revived the drooping lodges of London."

The second new part of 'Moderns Freemasonry' was their new three grade ritual without any higher grades at all. Some of these 'Moderns' Freemasons thought that: *our system of degrees, words, grips, signs, etc., was not in existence until about 1717 A.D.*

Yet other, more enlightened, brethren thought that *they had only improved and enlarged, but not invented them.* I do not want to get any further into this historical minefield, only to say that there were existing French, German and Swedish Freemasons, that believed that there was an ancient system of Freemasonry long before 1717, just as the 'Ancients' Freemasons, believed, in both Scotland and Ireland and some of those in London, and later they formed their own 'Grand Lodges of Ancient Masonry' with higher grades, which have largely remained the same.

It was the 'Moderns Freemasonry' type of Freemasonry without any higher grades that was gradually introduced, across many countries in Europe after 1723, to the annoyance of many of the existing European 'Ancient Freemasons' who already had their existing 'Ancient Degrees.' The 'Ancients' began to call the missing higher grades that the English ignored 'Scottish Masonry' by which they probably meant the 'Holy Royal Arch Degree,' but also several other degrees taken before and after that exalted degree, which used to be worked separately in their old lodges and chapters, like the 'Ark, Mark, Link, Rose-Croix and Templar Degrees.' The reason for calling it 'Scottish Masonry' was that it was based on the Scottish system brought South with James I of Britain (1603-1625), as James VI of Scotland he was *an entered Freemason and Fellowcraft of the Lodge of (Perth and) Scoon (No.3)* on 15 April, 1601.

While reviewing the first (English) *The Constitutions Book of 1723,* written by Dr James Anderson a Scotsman, I noticed five pages concerning the masonic *King James VI of Scotland, the Royal Art, the King often being Grand Master, then the Grand Master and Grand Warden who had a Salary from the Crown, the annual Communication of the Masons of Scotland, and Scottish Architecture in general.* Starting on page 41 it goes on to page 46. *Upon his Demise, his Son King Charles I, being also a Mason, patroniz'd Mr. (Indigo) Jones too.* There was a reference to the higher grades; *If it were expedient, it could be made appear, that from this ancient Fraternity, the Societies or Orders of the Warlike Knights, and of the Religious too, in process of time, did borrow many solemn usages.*

One of the reasons the *Brethren and Fellows in and about the Cities of London and Westminster,* may have ignored 'Scottish Masonry' was its association with the Jacobite rebellion. They were the supporters of the descendancy of the Scottish Stuart Line from the Catholic King James II (1685-1689 of Britain). The third attempt to restore the Old Pretender was in the summer of 1715, the fourth Highland Rising in Glenshiel in 1719 and the final rebellion in 1745 by Charles Edward, later called the Young Pretender, culminating in the decisive defeat at Battle of Culloden in April 1746.

---

176 Yarker J. 1909, *Arcane School.*

The 'Scottish Rite' masonic system became popular in all the anti-English, anti-Georgian countries that supported the Jacobite Rebellion, specifically Sweden, France, Germany and America, all countries where Scottish Regiments fought against the English and their allies.

The big difference between those countries and England is that they never did have a union of the 'Ancients' Grand Lodge and the 'Moderns' Grand Lodge, which took place in England in 1813, that recognised one high grade system, that of the 'Holy Royal Arch' and tolerated other high grades attached to the older Ancients lodges. In Europe, the same battle must have raged but there was no compromise or Union of Grand Lodges in opposition. However, this compromise was not enough for many 'Ancients' like John Yarker.

Therefore, what I believe that Papus and Reuss wanted to do was add Yarker's many 'Ancient' Degrees and Rites collected over thirty years, to their own 'older collections of masonic systems.'

In France, Papus wanted to add them to his new creation the 'Order Martinist.' Which was a revival of the French based 'Elu Cohen' of Louis Claude Saint Martin and Martinez Pasqually. Papus had combined it in 1895 with a French 'Kabbalistic Rose-Croix' system and a French version of the C.B.C.S. of Jean Baptiste Willermoz. An earlier combination had developed over many years in Paris, first by Charles-Pierre-Paul, Marquis de Savalette de Langes (1745-1797) in the Paris Lodge Les Amis Réunis (1771). It was developed further by Savalette and the Marquis de Thomé in the collection of grades and rites called the 'Philalèthes system' in 1773, by adding the 'Elu Cohen' of Saint Martin and Martinez Pasqually. They then added the elements of the 'Rite of Strict Observance' or the 'C.B.C.S.' of Jean Baptiste Willermoz. The relatively new 'Illuminati system' was also added to the higher degrees but the 'twelve degree system' of the 'Rite of Philalèthes' in Paris, had started in 1773 long before the rise of the Illuminati in 1776.

The basic three ancient craft degrees of Europe were, I believe, found in Sweden or the several collections of the 'Swedish Systems,' just before the French Revolution finished them off in 1793.

In Germany, what Reuss wanted to do was add them to his revived 'Prussian Illuminati,' which was a new form of the 'Bavarian Illuminati' grades. There were also some Prussian Freemasons who wanted to get back to their old ancients system of Freemasonry, with its 'Hautes Grade,' that had been replaced by the introduction of the newish English 'Moderns' three degree masonic system. Frederick the Great for example was alleged to have had his own 'Ancient Swedish System' or 'Swedenborg Rite Lodge' shortly before he died in

1786. Some Prussian's too wanted the 'Elu Cohen,' 'Kabbalistic Rose-Croix,' 'C.B.C.S.' and the 'Order Martinist' systems from Papus.

It would seem that Papus and Reuss wanted to amalgamate all three people's collection of systems under their own Grand Lodges in their home countries!

Westcott, in one respect, was simply the facilitator as the 'Grand Secretary' of only one of Yarker's 'Ancient Rites' that of the 'Swedenborg Rite.' While Westcott, on the other hand, was the intended recipient of the new complete European systems, of both the 'French Empire' and 'Prussian Empire.' This was probably because he was assumed to have all the contacts necessary from the S.R.I.A. and the 'Golden Dawn' to promulgate them in the British Empire.

Yarker was sixty nine in 1902 and had them all in his several collections of degrees, grades and rites for many years and was getting drawn further into Reuss' sphere of influence just as he is trying to pass them all on to Westcott. Reuss' grandiose plans in Europe were enticing and when both Papus and Reuss requested Yarker's 'Ancient & Primitive Rite' it must have been too good to be true. They contained the 33° of the 'Cerneau Rite,' the 90° of the 'Rite of Memphis' and the 95° of the 'Misraim Rite.' They also included the 'Egyptian Freemasonry' of Cagliostro. This was all happening towards the end of 1902, when Westcott rejected the 'Revived Illuminati' and when Westcott was having none of the 'Ancient & Primitive Rite,' as it would further jeopardise his new 'Grand Rank,' in both the 'Grand Lodge of England' and the 'Grand Chapter of England' in June 1902.

I do not apologise for mentioning at this late stage the 'Cerneau Rite 33°,' it is a different form of 'Scottish Rite Masonry.' As it only goes to amplify that there were 'Grand Lodge Wars' all around the world, in America, England, Sweden, France, Switzerland and Germany, which impacted on the 'Grand Lodge Wars' in the rest of Europe in 1907-1916, when it all started again with the O.T.O. and Aleister Crowley.

The 'Cerneau Rite 33°,' rise and fall in America from 1807 to 1907, is a whole story in itself and too long to go into here. I believe that Yarker mistakenly used the 33° of the 'Cerneau Rite' in England as part of his 'Ancient & Primitive Rite.' Instead of the 33° of the 'Ancient & Accepted Scottish Rite' that was used in New York, by followers of Giuseppe Garibaldi's version of the Rite, with rituals dated 1881. However, the 'Cerneau Rite of 33°' was just as contentious and would have resulted in the same expulsion of Freemasons in England from lodges in amity with the 'United Grand Lodge of England' and the 'Sovereign Council 33°.' I mention it only to highlight that after the failed introduction of the Illuminati and Westcott's involvement, the 'Grand Lodge Wars' carried on, after Papus and Reuss had received from Yarker, his own created version of the 'Ancient & Primitive Rite 33°, 90°, 95°,' and you often see these designations after Yarker's, Reuss' and Papus' name in several different published communications.

These many 'Grand Lodge Wars' or battles for masonic supremacy, fortunately did not affect the rank and file members, who to their credit had little to do with them. They happened in the 1700s, the 1800s, the 1900s and echoes of these wars are still with us today.

What is the most interesting about all this is that the 'masonic world' was generally more interested in what Yarker said and wrote, rather than what he did. This is the real legacy of the man and his main contribution to the Freemasonry.

YARKER'S ARTICLES FOR QUATUOR CORONATI RESEARCH LODGE

John Yarker was a member of at least two research societies. He was elected an honorary member of the **Manchester Association for Masonic Research** in 1909. But before that he became a joining member of the prestigious Correspondence Circle of the Research Lodge, **Quatuor Coronati Lodge, No. 2076**, London in 1887. Westcott for example was a full member of Quatuor Coronati Lodge and their Worshipful Master and he only delivered six papers. Yet the transactions of the lodge contain no fewer than seventy three articles contributed by Yarker as only a correspondence member:

1888 - The Unrecognized Lodges & Degrees of
  Freemasonry before and after 1717, 1:107-11.
1889 - Geometry, Masonry, Symbols. 2:162
1890 - The 'Weise King', 3:61
1890 - William of Wykeham, and the Regius MS. 3:190
1890 - The Old Masonic Charges, Indenture, and
  Freedom. 3:192-3
1891 - The Old Masonic Charges, Indenture, and
  Freedom. 4:63
1891 - Nimrod as Buck and Mason, 4:69
1891 - Antiquity of Masonic Symbolism, 4:176-7
1891 - Armenian Architecture, 4:178
1891 - The Yezidis, 4:224-6
1891 - Sir Warburg's (Chester) Pulpit, 4:240;
1891 - Brahminical Initiation, 4:241;
1891 - The Regius MS. and Hali-Werk-Folk, 4:243-4
1891 - Sethos, 4:247
1891 - Lord Harnouester, 4:247
1892 - Brahminical Initiation, 5:21-3
1892 - Visvakarma, the God of Indian Masonry, 5:66
1892 - Introduction of Outside Rites into the Craft, 5:68-9
1892 - The Noose and Girdle, 5:145
1892 - Mach, 5:228
1892 - Yorkshire Masons and Freemasons, 5:228-9
1893 - The Nismesian Theory & French Legend, 6:34-5
1893 - Indian Masons' Marks, 6:62
1893 - The Masonic Society at Newcastle, 1581, 6:64
1893 - Regius and Cooke MSS. 6:147
1893 - Dermott and the Arms of the Ancient Masons, 6:65
1893 - Dumfries MS. No. 4, 6:147-8
1893 - Brahminical Caste Marks, 6:148
1893 - Who Was Naymus or Manus Grxcus? 6:148-9
1893 - The Chequered Floor & Masonic Tracing Board, 6:193
1894 - Purple Seal, 7:55
1894 - Freemason as a Surname, 7:55
1894 - Notes in Reference to H. A. B., 7:134
1894 - Catnach's Masonic Hymn, 7:191
1895 - The Alban and Edwin Legends, 8:34
1895 - Cagliostro's Rose-Croix Jewel, 8:161
1895 - Masons Marks, 8:233-5

1896 - Maçon, 9:23
1896 - Cowan, 9:26
1896 - Old Inscription, 9:115
1897 - Tomb of Randle Holmes, etc. 10:63
1897 - The Word Mason, 10:159;
1897 - The Orange Society, 10:194;
1897 - The Title Worshipful Master, 10:196;
1898 - Genuine Secrets, 11:87;
1898 - The Order of the Temple, 11:97-9;
1898 - Ancient Builders, 11:200
1901 - The Chivalric Orders, 14:56-7
1901 - The Alnwick Lodge, 14:136
1901 - Drummond—Earls of Perth, 14:138
1901 - Bro. Jesse Lee, of Manchester, 14:139-40
1901 - The Man with a Greek Name, 14:216-7
1902 - The Old Swalwell Lodge and the Harodim, 15:184-8
1902 - The Gateshead Charter of 1671, 15:194
1903 - The Gate side Charter, 16:89
1903 - Templar Burial Service, 16:89
1903 - The Kadosh Degree, 16:91
1903 - Royal Templar Certificate of 1779, 16:158-9
1903 - Patent of a Russian Grand Lodge, 1815, 16:160-1
1903 - The Haughfoot Lodge, 16:177-80
1904 - The Very Ancient Clermont Chapter, 17:84-7
1904 - The High Grades in Bristol and Bath, 17:88-90
1905 - The Kadosh Degree, 18:49
1905 - Obituary for Karl Kellner, 18:150
1905 - An Old York Templar Charter, 18:170-3
1906 - The Carolus of Our Ancient MSS, 19:31-5
1906 - Arab Masonry, 19:243
1907 - On Masonic History-Let Us Seek Truth, 20:15-25
1907 - Pasqually, 20:85-6
1908 - Two Ancient Legends Concerning the Is' Temple,
  Termed Solomon's Temple, 21:264-9
1910 - The Masons of Como, & the Masons' Marks, 23:97-8
1910 - Certificate, Issued at Bath by the Royal Grand Council
  of Ancient Rites, 23:322-3
1912 - The Charter of Larmenius 25:69-80

Figure 141 - John Yarker's AQC Articles for Quatuor Coronati Lodge, No. 2076

A LIST OF YARKER'S WRITINGS:

Abridged translation of Louis-Alphonse Cahagnet 's Magie Magnétique under the title Magnetic Magic 1898. (p. 560). Baillière. https://archive.org/details/magiemagntiqueo00cahagoog.

Freemasonry in Modern Times. Origin and Antiquity of Freemasonry; [Ref: BE 688/1 YAR] 1872.

Masonic Charges and Lectures. Scientific and Religious Mysteries and Antiquity [Ref: A 33 YAR] 1872; https://archive.org/details/notesonscientif00yarkgoog (p. 173). Quatuor Coronati Lodge No. 2076, London Volume III: J. Hogg.

Notes on the Scientific and Religious Mysteries of Antiquity: The Gnosis and Secret Schools of. https://archive.org/details/notesonscientif00yarkgoog (p. 173). J Hogg. (1872).

Officers, honorary members, privileges, principles and prerogatives. In S. S.-9. Masonry, 23rd February 1872 dispensation John Yarker, Most Illustrious Master General, (p. 4). Burnley: Burghope & Strange. (1873).

The Magians Mysteries; Masonry and the Crusades; Rite of Mizraim 1876. [Ref: BE 688/1 YAR].

Ancient and Primitive Rite, Lectures of a Chapter, Senate & Council: According to the Forms of the Ancient and Primitive Rite. (p. 117). J. Hogg. (1882). https://archive.org/details/lecturesachapte00yarkgoog.

Genealogy of the Surname Yarker: And Several Allied Families, (1882).

Lectures of a Chapter, Senate and Council: According to the Forms of the Antient and Primitive Rite Marconis. J. Hogg. (1882).

The Kneph: Crown Printing Company. (1886).

Masonic Charges and Lectures. Quatuor Coronati Lodge No. 2076, London Volume III. (1890).

The Very Ancient Clermont Chapter. (1904). QUATUOR Coronati Lodge No. 2076, London Volume XVII. https://archive.org/stream/arsquatuorcorona17free/arsquatuorcorona17free_djvu.txt.

An Old York Templar Charter. (1905). QUATUOR Coronati Lodge No. 2076, London Volume XVIII. https://archive.org/stream/arsquatuorcorona18free/arsquatuorcorona18free_djvu.txt.

The arcane schools. a review of their origin and antiquity with a general history of freemasonry and its relation to the theosophic, scientific and philosophic mysteries (p. 556). Belfast: William Tait. (1909). https://archive.org/details/The_Arcane_Schools_-_J_Yarker.

Secret High Degree Rituals Masonic Rite Memphis (ciphers appendix). (1911). https://archive.org/details/Secret_High_Degree_Rituals_Masonic_Rite_Memphis_-_J_Yarker (p. 82).

Masonry and the Crusades, (n.d.).

Modern Rosicrucianism 1872.

Bibliography

Agrippa von Nettesheim, H. C. (1533). *In Artem brevem Raymundi Lullii*. (p. 216). Latin: Soter J.

Andreae, J. V. (1681). *Allgemeine und General Reformation Beneben der Fama Fraternitatis*. Regensburg.

Apiryon, T. (1995). *Doctor (Albert Karl) Theodor Reuss, 33° 90° 96° X°*. Retrieved from hermetic.com:

Bain, D. (2014). *A New Dawn for Tarot*. In M. K. Goodwin, The original tarot of the Golden Dawn. Keswick: Forge Press.

Barruel, abbe. (1799). *Memoirs, illustrating the history of Jacobinism*. In a. (.-1. Barruel, https://archive.org/details/memoirsillustrat04barr.

BEEJAYWAY. (2015). *We Can Create Our Own World*. Retrieved from www.uk.pininterest :

Beswick, S. (1870). *Swedenborg rite and the great masonic leaders of the eighteenth century*.

Blanchard J., (1920), *Scotch Rite Masonry Illustrated 19-33 Degrees*.

Carr, H. (1992). *The Swedenborgian Rite*. Retrieved from Maine Lodge of Research: http://www.mainemason.org/mlr/swedenborg3.htm.

Cooper, W. (1675 and 1673). *The philosophical epitaph of W.C. Esquire, memento mori on his tomb*. London: T.R.

Cramer, D. (1624). *Emblemata sacra*. Francofurti : Sumptibus Lucae Jennisi.

De Quincey, T. (1865). *Confessions of an English opium-eater*. Boston: Ticknor and Fields.

Didier, C. (1843). *The extreme Oath of the Jesuits from the book Subterranean Rome*. Retrieved from www.reformation.org:

Didier, C. (1848). *Rome Souterraine*. In J. e. Oath, 2nd Edition (pp. 349-351). Paris: Paulin.

Ecker von Eckhoffen, (1779). *Freymäurerische Versammlungsreden der Gold- und Rosenkreutzer des alten Systems*.

Ecker von Eckhoffen, *Masonic Assembly speeches of gold and Rosicrucians of the old system* (p. 330). Amsterdam: Hof: Grau.

Engel, L. (1906). *History of the Illuminati Order - Geschichte des Illuminaten-Ordens 1906*.

Faulks, M. (2011). *In search of the grave of William Lilly*. www.youtube.com?v=62XLdOko-e8 abgerufen.

Gilbert, R. A. (2002). *William Wynn Westcott and the Esoteric School of Masonic Research*. Von www.freemasonry.bcy.ca:

Gilbert, R. A. (1987). *William Wynn Westcott and the Esoteric School of Masonic Research*. Ars Quatuor Coronatorum transactions, S.

Gilbert, R. A. (1995). *Chaos Out of Order: The Rise and Fall of the Swedenborgian Rite*. Retrieved from Freemasonry.bcy.ca:

Gilbert, R. A. (1983), *The Magical Mason: Forgotten Hermetic Writings: W. Wynn Westcott*. Aquarian.

Heckethorn, C. W. (1875). *The secret societies of all ages and countries*. London: R. Bentley and son.

Garver, P. A. (2003, Garver and T. Vincent). *Edouard Blitz (1860-1915) and American Martinism*. Retrieved from www.gnostique.net:
    http://www.gnostique.net/initiation/blitz.htm.

HCL1242A, (1881) *Acta (1881-1897) Rosicrucian Society January 1st 1881* - Precis of letters Written, S.R.I.A.

HCL1242B, (1897) *Acta (1897-1905) Agenda and Acta by the Supreme Magus or Sec. General,* S.R.I.A.

HCL1242C, (1905) *Acta (1905-1917) A record of the Acta of the M.W.S.M. of the S.R.I.A.*

HCL1242D, (1907) *Acta (1907-1925) A record of the Acta of the M.W.S.M. of the S.R.I.A.*

Hitchcock, E. A. (1858). *Swedenborg, a hermetic philosopher*.

Howe, E. (1972). *Fringe Masonry in England 1870-1885*. Ars Quatuor Coronatorum 85, 1972.

Howe, E. (1972). *Magicians of the Golden Dawn*. In A documentary history of a magical order. Red Wheel Weiser .

Howe, E. (1978). *Theodor Reuss: Irregular Freemasonry in Germany, 1900-1923*. Quatuor Coronati Lodge No. 2076 Vol. 91.

Howe, M. (1986). *Merlin Peregrinus*. In E. H. Möller, Vom Untergrund des Abendlandes (p. 339). Konigshause & Neumann.

Khunrath, H. (1609). *Amphitheatrvm sapientiae aeternae, promptings of eternal wisdom*.

Koenig, P.R. (2012). *Order of Illuminati*. Retrieved from www.parareligion.ch: http://www.parareligion.ch/illumin.htm.

Lévi, Eliphas (1861). *Dogme et Rituel de la Haute Magie*. https://archive.org/details/dogmeetrituelde00lvgoog. Paris: Germer Baillière.

Lilly, W. (1659). *Christian Astrology*. London: John Macock.

Llull, R. (1847). *The Book of the Order of Chivalry*. In R. L. 1315), https://archive.org/details/cu31924026512156 (p. 148). Edinburgh.

Loft, B. (2015). *John Yarker*. Yet to be published.

Lull, R. (1517). *Ars magna*. (p. 286). https://archive.org/details/illuminatisacrep00llul.

Mackenzie, K. R. (1987). *The Royal Masonic Cyclopaedia*. In I. J. Gilbert. Wellingborough: The Aquarian Press.

Mackey, A. G. (1887). *An Encyclopædia of Freemasonry and Its Kindred Sciences*.

Marrs, T. (2005, 2011). *Codex Magica*. (p. 598). Texas: River Crest Publishing.

Mirabeau, H. (1788). *De la Monarchie Prussienne*. (pp. T.V., p 96). London. https://archive.org/details/delamonarchiepr10miragoog.

Miller, E. S. (1933). *Occult Theocracy*. In L. Queenborough. Createspace.

Möller, H. (1986). *Merlin Peregrinus*. In E. H. Helmut Möller. Wuerzburg.

Papus, (1896). *The tarot of the Bohemians*. In The most ancient book in the world : for the exclusive use of initiates. London: G. Redway.

Peacher, W. G. (1992). *The Swedenborgian Rite*. Retrieved from The Maine Lodge of Research:

Phillip A. Garver, T. V. (2003). *Edouard Blitz (1860-1915) and American Martinism*. GNOSTIQUE.NET:

Pierrot, J. (1984). *L'imaginaire decadent, 1880-1900*. In The Decadent period.

Pike, Albert (1861) *The Inner Sanctuary* . [New York?] A:. M:. 5630 [1870.] 315 p. 8°.

Pike, Albert Part I. *The book of the Lodge of Perfection. Or[ient] of Charleston* [New York?] A:. M;. 5643 [1883.] 290 p. 8°.

Pike, Albert (1882) *Morals and Dogma of the A. & A. Scot. Rite of Freemasonry* 5632 IDEM.

Pike, Albert (1878) *The Book of the Words* 5638 (1878); IDEM.

Pike, Albert (1857) *The Magnum Opus*. N.D.

Pott, H. M. (1911). *Francis Bacon and his secret society*. San Francisco: J. Howell.

Publications, E. C. (1642). *England's Oaths*. A 1642 publication containing the oaths of Supremacy and Allegiance and the late Protestation.

Quincy, T. D. (1897). *Historico-Critical Inquiry Into the Origin of the Rosicrucians and The Free-Masons*. Soho Square London.: A. & C. Black.

Ragon, J. (1853). *Orthodoxie Maconnique*. Palace Royal, Paris.

Ravenshaw, R. T. (1870). *Ravenshaw letter: founding R.C. of R.& C. S.R.I.A.* - H.C.L.No.T43.

Reuss, T. (N.D.) *Bestimmungen für die Minerval-Logen des Ordens der Illuminate*, A5 pamphlet, published by Bitterfield, Germany: Druck
    von E. Baumann. Quatuor Coronati Lodge No. Z11 -1996.

Reuss, T. (1894). *Die Mysterien der Illuminaten*. In v. Caratheodoro, The Mysteries of the Illuminati .

Reuss, T. (1896). *Geschichte des Illuminatens Orden.* Anonymous, In History of the Illuminati Order. Bitterfeld.

Reuss, T. (1901, October 17th). *Innere Ordens-Ordnung. 'Inside the Order'* 26pp. Berlin: Quatuor Coronati Lodge No. Z11-1993.

Reuss, T. (1901, October 17th). *Minerval Grád.* [German typescript book, leaves 3] Berlin. Item ID: L32073, 3 leaves; 29 x 22.5 cm.

Reuss, T. (1901, October 17th). Rituale: der Synoden. [German MSS 2pp] Berlin. Item ID: L32071, 2 leaves; 29 x 22.5 cm.

Reuss, T. (1901, October 17th). *Rituale: Rosenkreuzer Grad.* [German MSS 6pp] Berlin: Item ID: L32075, 6 leaves; 29 x 22.5 cm.

Reuss, T. (1901, October 17th). *Rituale: Schotten = Grad Andreas.* [German MSS 4pp] Berlin: Item ID: L32074, 4 leaves; 29 x 22.5 cm.

Robison, J. (1789). *Proofs Of A Conspiracy, against all the religions and governments of Europe: carried on in the secret meetings of Free Masons, Illuminati, and reading societies.* Philadelphia: T. Dobson and W. Cobbet .

Schuchard, M. K. (2011). *Emanuel Swedenborg, Secret Agent on Earth and in Heaven:* Leiden, Brill.

Snoek J. 2011. *Initiating Women in Freemasonry: The Adoption Rite Stanislas, F. H. (1813).* Thuileur des trentetrois degrés de l'écossisme du rit ancien, dit accepté,. In F. H. 1830). Chez Delaunay, libraire, palais-Royal.

Wages, Markner & Singh-Anand. Wäges, Josef & Markner, Reinhard (editors), and Singh-Anand, Jeva (translator) 2015. *The Secret School of Wisdom.* London: Ian Allan.

Waite, A.E. (1924). *Brotherhood of the Rosy Cross.* William Rider.

Waite, A.E. (1911). *The secret tradition in freemasonry: and an analysis of the inter-relation between the craft and the high grades in respect to their term of research, expressed by the way of symbolism.* New York.

Weishaupt, A. (1787). *The improved system of the Illuminati* - Das verbesserte System der Illuminaten.

Westcott, W. (1895). *The Chaldean Oracles of Zoroaster.* London: privately printed.

Westcott, W. (1887). *The Isiac Tablets of Cardinal Bembo.* http://www.sacred-texts.com/eso/isi/index.htm . Bath: Robt. H. Fryar.

Westcott, W. (1893). *Sepher Yetzirah: The Book of Formation, and the Thirty Two Paths of Wisdom.* London: Theosophical Pub. Society.

Westcott, W. (1896). *The magical ritual of the sanctum regnum : interpreted by the tarot trumps.*

Westcott, W. (1902). *Andreas Knight degree.* [Westcott trans 11pp] UGLE L32079. London: Westcott trans.

Westcott, W. (1902). *Constitution Minerval.* Wm. Wynn Westcott, Regent of Britain translation . UGLE - IL09673. London.

Westcott, W. (1902). *History of the Order of Illuminati.* [Westcott trans] 1896 pages 1 – 35.

Westcott, W. (1902). *Minerval degree.* [Westcott trans.] UGLE L32077. London: Westcott trans.

Westcott, W. (1902). *Mysteries of the Illuminati,*1894 pages 39 – 47 (p. 47). London: English Illuminati.

Westcott, W. (1902). *Ritual of the Synods.* [Westcott trans 5pp] UGLE L32076. London: L32076.

Westcott, W. (1902). *Rose Cross degree.* [Westcott trans 14pp] UGLE L32078. London: Westcott trans .

Westcott, W. (1905). *Acta or official diary 1905 - 1917.* In W. W.-1. Westcott, Westcott papers list. London: H.C.L. No. 1242 C.

Westcott, W. (1911). *Numbers: their occult power and mystic virtues.* London: Theosophical Society Publishing.

Westcott, W. (1916), The Data of the History of the Rosicrucians. Printed privately, SRIA White, S. (1987). New Astrology. Pan Books.

Who's, Who. (1914). Adam & Charles Black. London: Macmillan.

Yarker, J. (1909). *The arcane schools.* (p. 556). Belfast: William Tait.

Yates, F. (1982). *Giordano Bruno and the Hermetic Tradition.* In V. 1.

Index

Abbot Vom Verdienst 93
Abode of the dead 87
Academia Masonica 43, 60, 67, 187
Admitting women 171
Adoption Rite women 34, 45, 73, 195
Ahathoor Temple, address at 1 Avenue Duquesne Paris 39, 199
Alchemy 91
Alfred Chapter No. 13, 176
Alombrados 93, 159
Altmeister/Hierophant 154, 155, 164
America 20, 41, 91, 96, 171, 209, 222
Ancient & Accepted Rite 20, 34, 39, 40, 50, 73, 76, 146, 176,
    206, 217
    Study group 50
    Scottish Rite Freemasonry 39
Ancient and Mystical Order Rosae Crucis 199
Ancient & Primitive Rite 40- 43, 73, 176, 198, 200, 215-219,
    227, 230-232
    Not the Swedenborg Rite, 96° not 6°, 41
Andreas knight grade 117, 120, 139, 140, 145, 153, 154, 166
Angels and Demons 25
Angels 71, 182, 203, 213, 216
Annual subscription 188
Anonymous, 61, 85, 97, 103, 119, 186, 214
    History of the Illuminati Order 29-30
Apron 52, 134, 136, 149, 160, 183, 184
Appears to and discloses himself to God 110
Archer, Capt. James Henry Lawrence (1823-1889) 177, 219
Archive project 24
Archivist 15, 17, 45, 67, 187
Aristotle 86
Asenath 87
Augsburg, Reuss parents' home 183
Augsburgerstrasse 82 in Dresden 39
August Order Light 177, 178, 181, 219
Aumont 139, 141

Barruel, Abbe Augustin de (1741-1820) 116, 154, 159, 162, 165
Bavaria 6-7, 92, 95
Bavarian Illuminati 15, 19-20, 27-29, 34, 36, 45-47, 57, 96, 115-
    117, 122, 124, 133-134, 139, 153-154, 157, 159-166, 183
    Magi ritual 29
    More Masonic type-Illuminati Rituals. 39
    No Rose-Croix Grade 73
    Rituals 27, 29, 73, 75
    The Secret School of Wisdom 37, 75
    Use the plain letters S.O.M.O. on tracing boards 51
Bayard Chapter No. 71, 176
Bective, Thomas Taylour, Earl (1844-1893) Lord Kenlis 215
Belgium 93
Beswick, Samuel (1822-1903) 41, 43, 220
Bible 33, 91
Bible and Women 195
Blazing Sun 27, 49-52, 64, 69, 122, 146-147
Blind Obedience 133, 135-136, 140, 155
Blitz, Edouard Emmanuel (1860-1915) 76, 78, 193, 200-202,
    208-210, 216
Bottony cross, 27, 28, 52, 64, 69, 85, 102, 118,122, 133, 139,
    145, 153, 161
Brahmins 91
Brian Boru Faslairt No.1, (Eri) 218
Brother P. Wilson 172
Brotherhood of the Illuminati Great Seal 49, 64, 69

Brown, Dan 24
Brown , Robert Smith 171, 177-178, 180, 197-198, 215, 219
Burke 96
Cabala 90, 91
Canon Danzer 95
Captain Anton von Fager 96
Caratheodoro 34, 101, 103
Carnegie Dickson, Dr William Elliot 24
Caspar Reuss 96
Castor 86
C.B.C.S. 73, 76, 78, 159, 161
Cerneau Rite
    Scottish Rite Freemasonry 41,72, 217, 222,
Chapter of Brotherly Love, No. 329, 176
Charity 20, 128, 146, 148, 194
Chemistry 91
Cherry, Martin 25, 26
Chevillon, Constant (1880-1944) 200, 227
Chiefship of Red branch of Eri 172, 176, 218, 219
Children 19
Chosen enlightened ones 110
Church schools 19
Cicero 86
Ciphers
    Abbe Barruel, Cipher 1799 162
    Heckethorn, Cipher 1897 162
    Heckethorn, Scottish Knight Cipher 162
    Hieroglyphic cipher 162
    Higher mysteries 162
    Martinist 180
    Minerval 162
Circe 87
College in Berlin, S.R.I.G. 30, 44, 54-55, 57, 62, 66, 67, 189-191
Conclusion 221
Conquer finiteness 110
Cossandey 95
Cox, Benjamin (1828-1895) 173, 176, 177, 218
Crowley, Aleister 27
    O.T.O. beginnings 30
Crusaders and Illuminati 88, 150
Custodian 27
Custos-Office 27, 57, 62-67, 122

Dapuis 88
Das Wort magazine 39, 187, 189
Dawson, Phillip 17, 23, 24
Dedication
    Bestimmungen für die Minerval-Logen des Ordens der
        Illuminaten 45, 102
    Die Mysterien der Illuminati 29, 119
    History of the Order of the Illuminati 24, 84, 85, 119
    Innere Ordens-Ordnung 29
    Library and Museum of Freemasonry 29
Deep down in the soul 87
Degrees 92
Degrees for women 34
Der Geheime Areopag, Secret Areopagus 27
Detractors 19, 20, 27
Détré, Henri-Charles (Teder) (1855-1918) 200
Deullin, Louise (Papus sister) 33, 195, 228-230
Deullin, Pierre 33, 195, 203-209, 228-230
    Pierre and Louise 33, 195, 203-205, 207, 209
    Louise Deullin founding Grand Junior Warden in 1901, 33

Dickson, Dr George (father) 180, 219
Dickson, Dr William Elliot Carnegie (1878-1954) son 83, 174
Die Grosse Freimaurerloge für Deutschland
    Address 74 Bellealliancestrasse 39
    Warrant 1900, 36
Die Mysterien der Illuminati 28, 29, 50, 103, 119
Die Unterrichtsloge des alten und angenommenen freimaurer
    genannt Ludwig im orient Munchen Ludwig Lodge 34
Diodorus 86
Discretion 111
Docetists degree, Weishaupt 29
Dr Bogdan E. J. Edwards, MBE (1860-1923) 177, 178
Dresden Illuminati 24, 25, 29, 33, 36, 40, 45, 49, 52, 57, 65, 120,
    125, 127,129
    Certificate 62
    June 1901, 35
    Statutes and Ordinances 65
Dresden 26, 27, 29, 30, 104, 118, 119, 122, 124, 126, 128
Duke Karl Augustus 93
Durable women 163
Duty of silence 90

Edmund William Martyn Westcott (1874-1907) 174
Educating women & children 171
Edwards, Dr Bogdan E. J. MBE (1860-1923) 177, 178
Egyptians 87, 88, 92, 96
Eleusinian 87, 91
Eliza Burnet Westcott (1851-1921) 174
Elsie Bridget Wynn Westcott (1877-1918) 174
Ellic Howe 28, 103, 117
Elus Cohen 139, 195, 196, 200, 222
Emanuel Lodge No. 1, 176, 220
Encausse, Gérard Anaclet Vincent Encausse (1865-1916)
(see also Papus) 20, 31, 35, 193, 194
    A list of writings 211
    After Papus 200
    Dr Gérard Anaclet Vincent Encausse 194
    Edouard blitz 209
    Freemasonry 194
    Le libre Examen Loge 203
    Losing control? 207
    Meets Westcott for the first time 200
    Non-masonic memberships 195
    Personal life 194
    Pierre Deullin 203-209
    Protocols of the elders of Zion 207
Edwardian Women 171
Engel, Leopold (1858-1938) 27, 34-37, 43, 45, 54, 56, 57, 62,
    66, 69, 75, 104, 117-122, 170, 183, 187-191
    Address 82 Augsburger Strasse in Dresden 39
    Dresden – Striesen, Augsburgerstrasse 77, 39
    Geschichte des Illuminaten-Ordens 1906, 29
    Member of a Russian Lodge 34
    No longer have any control 1902, 43
    No mention first letter 34
    Signature 28
English Illuminati 3, 9, 10, 12, 17, 19, 20, 21, 23, 27, 30, 36, 40,
    57, 62, 66, 73, 74, 75, 166, 189
Ephraim 87
Epopt Grade 27, 52, 159, 160, 161, 166
Eri (Red branch) 44, 72, 172, 176, 218, 219
Esoteric rituals 15, 19, 26, 110, 115, 169, 171, 181, 188, 195
Euston, Henry James Fitz Roy, (1848-1912) first Earl 218
Exchanging of degrees, orders and rites 30
Exodus 87

F.H.L., (Faith, Hope & Love) 149
Feasts 89
Female friends 129
Fireproof black steel trunk 24
Fischer 96

Five pointed star 27
Flaming (sacred) heart 27, 122
Foundation 159
Four German originals 25
France 95
Francis George Irwin (1828-1893) 170, 173, 176, 177, 199, 216,
    218, 219, 220, 221
Franck 95
Franklin, Benjamin (1705-1790) 96
Fraternitatis Rosea Cruis 199
Fratres Lucis 172, 177, 199, 219
Freemasons Hall 24
French Revolution 19, 194, 204, 208, 209, 222
Fuller, Tony 24

Gabaon 140
Garatheodoro 26, 29, 30, 103
    Caratheodoro 28
General Delegate 39
George Wynn Westcott (1883-1906) 175
German Grand Lodges 188
German High-grade Freemasonry 189
German Illuminati 31, 36
German S.R.I.A. (see S.R.I.G.) Warrant for a College in Berlin 43
Geschichte des Illuminaten-Ordens
    Engel 1906 29
    Reuss 1896 29
Gilbert, R.A. 33, 78, 174, 199, 204, 214, 215
God 20, 50, 86-88, 91, 110, 118, 140-141, 148-150, 155, 161,
    166, 170, 178, 191
Goethe 96
Golden Book 24, 172, 174, 213, 218,
Golden Dawn 171, 172, 174, 174, 178, 179, 181, 191, 193, 199,
    201, 220, 222
    Cipher MSS 40
    Women 171
Golgotha 92, 150
Gomer 120, 139, 140, 141, 154
Gordon, Robert 17, 23, 83, 101, 131, 137, 151
Grand Lodges
    France 39, 204
    Germania 39, 53, 118
    Grand Lodges of Europe 15
    United Grand Lodge of England 39
    Women's Freemasonry 209
Grand Lodges in Europe 19
Grand Masters 15, 20, 194, 199, 216, 219
Grand Orient, French Grand Lodge 37, 204, 207
Grandson of Noah 27 , 118, 122, 154
Greater Mysteries 161
Grunberger 95
Guerinets 93, 159

Hamburg. Religious-Regent of the Province 67
Hammel, Fergus Edward 174, 175
Hartmann, Franz (1838-1912) 34, 187
Harvey Spencer Lewis 199
Haute grades 188, 196
Heal sickness naturally 110
Held, Franz 54, 65, 67, 68, 75
Heliopolis 87
Hercules 86
Hermes, Otto (Custos) 67
Hermetic Society of Eight 34, 177, 180, 198, 199, 215, 216, 219
Frederick Holland 34
Hierophant 154, 155
High Council 15, 23, 24, 30, 45, 55, 59, 66, 67, 70, 73
    Library list 24, 42
    S.R.I.A. Alliance with Illuminati 30
High Masons/High Grade Masons 36, 37
Higher grade orders 188

History of the Order of the Illuminati 23, 25
Hockley, Frederick (1808-1885) 177, 216, 219
Holland, Fredrick (1854-1917) 34, 177, 180, 198, 200, 215- 219
Holy Grail Lodge No. 15 (Swedenborg T&L Berlin) 190
Royal Arch 37, 59, 60, 75, 78, 176, 183, 217, 221, 222
Holy truths 106
Homer 87
Homo Rex 115, 134, 147, 150, 154, 160, 161, 162, 166
Howe, Ellic Paul, (1910-1991), 28, 49, 57, 58, 177, 185, 189
Hübbe -Schleiden, Wilhelm (1846-1916) 34
Human passions 107
I.A.A.T. 92
I know J and G and the flaming star 139, 141
Ignis, Aqua, Aer, Terra 92
Initiator 44, 72, 180,
        Martinist Provincial Master 180, 194, 198, 216, 219
I.N.R.I.
        In Ancient & Accepted Rite and the Revived Illuminati 40
        Name new Swedenborg Lodge and Temple Paris 38
        Significant word S.R.I.A. 40
I.N.R.I. (alchemical) Igne Natura Renovatur Integra 150, 166
I.N.R.I., (Christian) Iesus Nazarenus Rex Iudaeorum 150, 166
I.N.R.I., (Hermetic) Ioithi Nain Rasith Ioithi 150, 166
I.N.R.I. 120, 144, 145, 146, 149, 150, 154, 155, 156, 166
Ida Grace Westcott 174
Illuminati 9, 11, 12, 15, 17, 19, 20, 25, 27, 28, 29, 30, 34, 35, 36,
        37, 39, 42, 43, 45, 47, 49, 50, 51, 52, 54, 56, 57, 59, 60, 62,
        64, 65, 66, 67, 69, 70, 73, 75, 76, 78, 79, 86, 88, 92
        Bavarian Illuminati, 9, 10, 13, 16, 21, 29, 30, 31, 38, 40, 51,
        53, 59, 60, 67, 88, 91
        Bavarian Illuminati Ludwig Lodge, 10, 13, 32, 37, 38, 48, 51,
        60, 66, 67, 83, 120, 185, 186, 187, 188, 189, 190, 191, 204
        Chance spotting, Illuminati 30
        Die Mysterien der Illuminati 29
        Dresden Illuminati 26, 27
        Dresden Illuminati 1899, 35, 126
        English Illuminati 30, 40
        French Illuminati 33, 164
        General Delegate 39
        German Illuminati 34, 36
        Grand Lodge of the Illuminati 27
        History of the Order of the Illuminati 23, 24, 29
        Illuminati images 26, 27
        Illuminati logos 20, 26, 28, 45, 50, 54, 56, 57, 85, 118, 133,
            139, 145, 146, 149, 150, 153
        Illuminati rituals 15, 25, 113
        Illuminati signatures 26
        Letters from Papus 32, 36,
        Ludwig Lodge 34, 120, 185-191, 204
        Masonic Illuminati rituals 34
        Minerval, Knight of St. Andrew, Rose-Croix and Synod
            Grades, 43, 113
        Mysteries of the Illuminati 29
        Prussian Illuminati 27, 34, 122
        Regent Warrant Hamburg 1902, 67
        Revived Illuminati 25, 29, 40
        The masonic type rituals 15, 115
        Women & the Illuminati 20, 58, 116, 154, 163, 171
Ingolstadt 34, 36, 92
Immortality of the soul 87
Impending First World War 97
Influence of women 163
Ingolstadt 36, 92
Initiation 86, 88
        Epopt or priest 160
        Homo Rex 162
        Magus 161
Initiation of women 203, 226
In quiet, without words, God 110
Inner one, secret 109
Innere Ordens-Ordnung 26-29, 118-122

Ioithi 150, 166
Irwin, Captain Francais George (1828-1893) 170, 173, 176, 177,
        199, 216, 218, 219, 220, 221
Isocrates 86
Israel 87

J & G and the flaming star 27, 139, 141
J. & G, Jehovah & Gomer 120, 139, 140, 141, 154
J. W. Hermes Lodge, No. 8, 176
Jao 91
Japheth and Gomer 27
Jason 86
Jean Bricaud (1881-1934) 200
Jefferson 96
Jehovah 91, 139, 141
Jephthah 20, 154, 155
Jesuits 20, 92, 93, 159, 165, 225
Jesus Nazarenus Rex Judaeorum 150
Joseph 87
Judea 149
Judged according to their works 108

Kingdom of Bavaria 11, 36, 93, 96, 116-117, 162, 185
Kneph Magazine 42, 72
Knigge, Adolph Franz Fredrich Ludwig (1752-1796) 94-95, 115-
        117, 153,159-162
Koenig, Peter-Robert 57
Krettmayr 95

L could stand for the German words Liebe, Licht or Leben or
        Living 28
        L in the very centre of the pentagram 28
L. is Lieber/Love 149
Ladies in Illuminati order 125-127
Le Libre Examine No. 217, 33, 136, 204-205
        Papus and Deullin 33
Legality of the Illuminati in Germania 45
Leichnitz, Max (Vice-custos) 67
Lenoir 88
Leonhardi von Platz, Baron Adolf Franz 34, 214-216, 227
Letter 'L' 65
Librarie du Merveilleux 196, 204, 206, 209
Library and Museum of Freemasonry 15, 17, 25-26, 28-29, 39,
        58, 60, 79, 84, 101-103, 120, 124, 133, 134, 139, 145, 153-
        154, 172, 175, 193, 198, 202, 210, 211, 213, 215, 216
Liebe, Licht, Leben 111
Logo 20, 26, 28, 45, 50, 54, 56, 57, 85, 118, 133, 139, 153
Logos 145, 146, 149, 150
Love, Light, Life 111
Lilian Margret Westcott (1880-1924) 174
Little, Robert Wentworth 25
Lodge of Brotherly Love, No. 329, 175
Loge Les Amis Réunis 117, 205, 222
London 96
Longley, George Canning (1827-1885) 176, 177, 199, 218, 220
Lord Engagiste Bazeilles 119
Love, light, life 111
Ludwig II of Bavaria 96
Ludwig Lodge 10, 13, 32, 34, 37, 38, 48, 51, 60, 66, 67, 83, 120,
        185, 186, 187, 188, 189, 190, 191, 204
        Die Unterrichtsloge des alten und angenommenen
        freimaurer genannt Ludwig im orient Munchen 34
        Lodge of Instruction of Ancient and Accepted Masons 33
Ludwig Mother Lodge
        Address 74 Bellealliancestrasse 39
Lupochewik, Mardim (Archivist) 67

Made women 58, 195
Magi ritual , Bavarian Illuminati 29
Magic 28, 33, 78, 90, 181, 182, 191, 194, 199, 202, 221-226
Magnetic stone = Moon 150

Magus Grade 161
Magus of the World 15
Magus 115, 122, 126, 127, 133-135, 139, 140, 141, 154, 155
Manassa 87
Mark Masonry 44, 72, 176, 217
Martinist 171, 180, 189, 193, 194, 196, 197, 198, 199, 200, 202,
    203, 204, 208, 209, 210, 214, 215, 216
    Baron Adolf Franz Leonhardi von Platz 34, 214-216, 227
    First English Martinists 1895, 30
    John Yarker Martinist warrant 30
    Initiator (Martinist Provincial Master) 180, 194, 196, 198,
    214, 216, 219,
    Martinist Lodge No. 12 in 1893, 33-34
    Reuss the Special Inspector 35
    Women and Martinisim 200
Masonry, Symbolic 149, 154, 160
Master builder 91
Matier, Charles Fitzgerald Lecade Wilson (1840-1914) S.M. of
    the S.R.I.S. 214, 218
Mathers, Samuel Liddell MacGregor (1854 – 1918) 39, 171, 177,
    178, 179, 181, 192, 193, 199, 201, 202, 219
    Address 87 Rue Mozart, Auteuil, in Paris 39
    Attacks on Westcott 1897 & 1900, 39
    Co-founder of the Golden Dawn in 1888, 39
    Count Mac Gregor of Glenstrae 202
McLeod Moore, Col. William James Bury (1810-1890) Canada
    41, 176, 218
Meat food 111
Memphis & Mizraim Rite, Yarker's Order, cover-up of mistake
    38, 40, 41, 72, 200, 219
Merlin Peregrinus 103
    Book 28
    Theodore Reuss 28
Merveilleux, Librarie du 196, 204, 206, 209
Metropolitan College S.R.I.A. 44, 58, 70, 72, 169, 170, 172, 174-
    175, 178, 181, 202
Minerval 126, 127, 128, 129, 130, 133-136, 154, 166, 170
Minerval Illuminati Certificate 47, 49
Minerva Lodge 127, 128, 129, 130
Mirabeau 95
Mizpah 118, 154, 155, 156
Möller, Helmut 28, 49, 225
Moral lessons for women 34
Moses 87
Mysteries 25, 118, 119, 120, 121, 153, 154, 160
Mythus 90

Nain 150
Name of the Order ⊙ 134
Nazareth 149
Nicolai 92
No beer 111
Noah 27, 118, 122, 154
Nomenclature 162
Not the only knowledge 89
Notuma 139, 140, 141, 145, 154
Nuremberg 92
Nursery 154, 160

O.N. 87, 134
O.T.O. 30, 57, 153, 191, 199, 222
    In the letters S.O.T.O.M, 97
    Letters of Ordo Templi Orientis 27, 220
Oaths, 115
    English Andreas knight grade 139, 141, 166
    English Minerval 135, 165, 166
    English Rose-Croix grade 146, 166
    English Synods 154, 166
    Heckethorn oath of an Illuminati 165
    Jesuit Oath 165
    Oath of la secte des illumines 164

Oath of the Jesuits 165
Occult Theocracy 64, 74
ONE God 149
Ordinances of the society 25
Ordre Martinist 30, 171, 180, 189, 193, 194, 196, 197, 198, 199,
    200, 202, 203, 204, 208, 209, 210, 214, 215, 216
    Organisation of Masonic High Grades 47
    Women and O.M. 171
Oriflamme Magazine 34, 40, 42, 72, 183-184, 187, 189- 191
    Mistake in January 1902 edition 40
Orpheus 86
Outer one, secret 109

P.M.C.V., Per Me Coeci Vident 133- 136, 156
Paid to translate and transcribe 25
Palace of Circe 87

Papus
    Address 4, Savoie Street 33
    A list of Papus' writings 211
    Adoption Lodge in Paris 33
    American Adoptive Rite 43
    Anti-Jewish and fascist beliefs 33
    Berlin 24th June 1901, 35
    Broke Berlin and Dresden Illuminati 36
    Cut out Engel 34
    Dispensation to recruit members 41
    Deullin, Pierre 33, 195, 203-205, 207, 209
    General Information about the Lodge and Temple of
    Gnostic Church or Eglise Gnostic 43
    Perfection in the East of Paris 1900, 41
    Gérard Anaclet Vincent Encausse 30
    German Illuminati 35
    Hospital where he worked 33
    Illuminati in 1901, 28
    Introduced Westcott to (Reuss) Illuminati 30
    Last letter from Westcott 42
    Le Libre Examine No. 217 Lodge 33, 136, 204-205
    Letter to Westcott 1901, 30
    Member of the Illuminati 30
    Mistake in 1900, 40
    Non-masonic memberships
    Ordre Martinist and Kabbalistic de la Rose-Croix 43
    Plagiarism in the L'Initiation 36
    Promotional pamphlet 1900, 40
    Russia to meet Martinists Tsar Nicholas II 33
    Sister, Louise Deullin 33
    Sovereign Delegate in Germania 34
    Travelling to Berlin 1901, 31
    Two letters to Westcott 30
    Villa Montmorency, 10 Avenue des Peupliers Auteuil Paris
    39, 194, 196
    Went unanswered 33
    Wrote again 33
Papus and Reuss
    How much they knew about these two rites 42
    Mistake 1902, 40
    Obtained from Yarker 'Ancient & Primitive Rite 43
Paracelsus 91
Paris 30-37, 39-44, 71-72, 75-76, 96, 117, 145-146, 164, 166,
    171, 176, 178-180, 189, 191, 193-200, 202-208, 214-216
Parishes or chapelry, Sprengel 191
Parrett and Axe Lodge, No. 814, 175
Paschal, Beverly Randolph 199
Paternoster, John 24
Pattinson, Thomas Henry (1851-1940) 177, 178
Pausanias 86
Pax vobiscum 149, 150
Pudendum women 165
Pentagram 27, 28, 52, 64, 67, 69, 85, 118, 122
Peregrinus, pseudonym 28, 49, 60, 101, 191

Peters, Mark 17, 25, 105
Phantasmagoria 91
Phi-Beta-Kappa Society 97
Phibetians 97
Phoenix zur Wahrheit Lodge (Hamburg) 190, 191
Pilgrim Lodge No. 238, 17, 28, 30, 43, 43, 58-60, 70, 183-185
Pigault-Lebrun 88
Political global events 19
Polluk 86
Pope 25
Potiphar 87
Primary source material 13, 15, 23, 26, 29, 57, 84, 101
Professor Westenrieder 95
Prolong life 110
Prussian Clubs and Societies Act 1892, 43, 59-60
      Create Grand Lodges and other societies 43
Prussian Illuminati 36, 57
Prussian Illuminati Ludwig Lodge, 34, 120, 185, 186, 187, 188,
      189, 190, 191, 204
Prussian Illuminati logo of Reuss 26, 28, 45
      Under the authority of Leopold Engel's 40
Prussian politics 19
Pseudonym 28, 34, 101, 159, 162, 187, 191
      Peregrinus 28, 49, 60, 101, 191
Pythagoras 93
Pythagorean Lodge of Instruction 176

Quatuor Coronati Lodge No. 2076, 58, 59, 124, 133, 139, 145,
      153, 223, 224

R.M. Ritter Meister 11, 27, 28, 57, 69
Rabboni 140, 141
Raphael 146, 147, 148, 149
Rasith 150
Recognised by whom 45
Regensburg 116, 117
Regent of Britain 45, 62-69, 75, 77, 85, 102, 120, 124, 153, 159,
      160-161, 166, 180, 187
Religious-Regent of the Province, 66
Reuss, Theodor Albert Karl (1855-1923) 17, 29, 69, 183
      A list of writings 191
      Address 86 Bellealliancestrasse 39
      Anonymous work 29
      Berlin 28-31, 33-45, 47, 53-60, 66-72, 75, 83, 85, 101-103,
            185-190
      Bestimmungen (Regulations) 45, 102, 118-120, 124
      Caratheodoro 28
      End English Illuminati 10th October 1902, 42
      Freemasonry 183
      General Delegate 36
      Geschichte des Illuminaten-Ordens 1896, 29, 34, 84, 116,
            119-120, 191
      Grand Freemasons Lodge for Germany 43, 44, 72
      Grand Lodge of Germany 53, 118, 188
      Introduced to Westcott, by Papus 30
      London 185
      Ludwig Lodge 10, 13, 32, 34, 37, 38, 48, 51, 60, 66, 67, 83,
            120, 185, 186, 187, 188, 189, 190, 191, 204
      Meets Engel 1895, 34
      Merlin Peregrinus 28, 49, 101, 191
      Mistake originated by Papus 40
      Munich 185
      New Grand Lodge 39
      Non-masonic memberships 189
      Oriflamme magazine & lodge calendar 189, 190
      Pilgrim Lodge 17, 28, 30, 43, 43, 58-60, 70, 183-185
      Prussian Clubs and Societies Law 43, 59
      Resurrected Bavarian Illuminati 27-29, 34, 75, 103, 125,
            169, 170 171, 183, 186, 188, 193
      Revived Ludwig Lodge 1895, 187
      Rosicrucian Society in Berlin, (Beswick/Yarker)

Swedenborg Rite and (Yarker) Ancient & Primitive Rite 43
Schroder Rite 43
Signature 28
Sovereign Delegate Ordre Martinist in Berlin 30
Traveling around Europe 1896, 34
Warrant 12th March 1901 backdated 1900, 35
Without checking any of the details with either
      Yarker or Westcott 40
Revived Illuminati
      A new head 30
      Four Revived Illuminati rituals 73
Reward and punishment after death 87
Rhodocanakis, Prince Demetrius (1840-1902) 214, 215
Richter 96
Ritter Meister, Master Knight 25, Rituals 23
Robert Fludd 91
Robinson, John (1739-1805) Proofs 133, 134, 159, 165
Rose and Lily Conclave No. 10, 176
Rose-Croix degree 12, 73-76, 115-117, 145-147, 150, 164, 186
      Side by side comparison 146
      Oath 166
Rosenkreuz 90
Rosenkreuzer Order (S.R.I.G.) Berlin 190
Rosenkreuzer Grade (Illuminati) 20, 55, 143, 145, 150, 190
      Christian Rosenkreuz picture (St. Jerome) 24
Rosicrucian Enlightenment 24, 89
Ruben Swinburne Clymer 199

Schroder Ritual 43, 44, 72, 184, 191
Schroder working 183
Sovereign Delegate Ordre Martinist in Berlin, 40
Sacred Word of Priest Degree 120
Samothrakies 86
Saxony 95
Schnitger, F.F. (Newcastle College) 180, 216, 219
School of wisdom 108, 110
Schroder Lodge in Hamburg 189
Scottish Rosicrucians 25
Seal of Solomon 136
Secret 15, 76, 90-92,109, 110-111, 116, 135, 141, 149, 166, 197,
      208, 214
Secret Areopagus 27, 47, 62, 65-67
Secret society 90, 93, 95, 96, 159-166
Secret 13, 19, 20, 27, 29, 60, 64, 67, 78, 90, 93, 109, 220
Secretary General of the S.R.I.A. (1887-1891) 170, 171, 172,
      179, 197, 198, 202, 215
Sensual one, secret 109
Seven planets 91
Seymour, Harry 11, 40, 41
Shepherd, Lucy 17, 24, 83
Sisyphus 87
Societas Rosicruciana In Anglia (S.R.I.A.) 15, 17, 19, 23-25, 30,
      33, 34, 36, 40, 42-45, 49, 54, 55, 57-62, 66, 70, 72, 73, 76,
      78, 79, 83, 84, 101, 119, 120, 134, 153, 166, 169,-181, 186,
      187, 189, 193, 196, 197, 199-206, 213-220
      Alliance with the Illuminati 1901, 30
      College in Berlin, S.R.I.G. 30
      John Yarker Martinist Warrant 30
      Letters from Papus 33
      Minutes of Alliance with Illuminati 30
Societas Rosicruciana In Germania (S.R.I.G.) 30, 44, 54-55, 57,
      62, 66, 67, 70, 189-191
Societas Rosicruciana In Scotia (S.R.I.S.) 169, 171, 198, 215
Society of Eight, (Hermetic) 34, 177, 180, 198-199, 215, 219
Solar mystery 87
Solar service 87
Son crucified 27, 122
Soul of the neophytes 87
Spartacus 159
Sphinx 34, 40, 111, 146, 150, 186, 197
Spiritual knowledge 86

Sprengel 190, 191
St. Jerome 24
St. Petersburg 26
Stephenson, Andrew B. 178
Strict moderation 111
Strobl 95
Students 92
Supervisory Board 27, 122
Suppression 163
Supreme Magus Emeritus 178
Supreme Magus 15, 17, 24, 169, 170, 171, 172, 173,175, 178
Swabian 96
Swedenborg Rite 43, 170, 172, 173, 176, 177, 188, 189, 190,
    194, 195, 198, 203, 205, 206, 207, 209, 220, 222
    No Scottish Rite Masonry 41
    Only 6° not 96°, 40
    Papus obtained dispensation not warrant 35
    Paris letterhead 40
    Swedenborg Rite Lodge in Paris 33
    The saga ended 1902, 33
    Warrant for Reuss 1901, 35
    Westcott resigned on 8 March 1903, 42
    Wrong history of founding 40-42, 206
Synods 17, 20, 27, 43, 60, 118, 120, 151, 153, 155, 166, 180

Tantalus 87
Term Illuminati 159
Theodore of Good Counsel 159
Theosophical Society 171, 181, 185-187, 198, 204, 205, 214
    29 Aug 1896 in Berlin 34
Theosophical Society and women 171
Theosophists 90
Theurgy 110
Three out of four finished 26
Thüringen 95, 96
True wisdom 107
Truth 13, 86, 88, 106-108, 111, 135, 136, 140-141,148

Unopened for approximately 80 years 24
Uzschneider 95

Vice-Custos 27, 67
Views expressed 19
Visitor's women 125, 195

W.E.C.D.
    Dr William Elliot Carnegie Dickson 24, 83
Wahrheit-Sucher, Magazine 1896-97, 34, 67, 187
Weishaupt, Adam 6, 9, 15, 29, 69, 75, 86, 92-96, 115-117, 118,
    119, 120, 133, 134, 154, 159, 162, 164
    Docetists degree 29
    Pictures by Engel 29
Twelve German Illuminati books 116
Westcott, Dr William Wynn 169, 189
    A list of Westcott's writings 182
    A member of the Illuminati 26
    Cancellarius or registrar 178
    Co-founder of the Golden Dawn in 1888, 39
    Edmund William Martyn Westcott (1874-1907) 174
    Eliza Burnet, Mrs Westcott (1851-1921) 174, 175
    Elsie Bridget (Westcott) Hamel (1877-1918) 174
    Family man 172, 174
    Finished with Illuminati 10th October 1902, 42
    Freemasonry memberships 175
    George Wynn Westcott (1883-1906) 175
    Hand written translation 15
    Hermetic Society of Eight 177
    History and Mysteries 20, 26, 28, 30
    Home Office 33
    Ida Grace Westcott 174
    Illuminati Regent for Great Britain 66

Initiator 44, 72, 180, 198, 216
Letter to Theodore Reuss in Berlin 30-33
Lilian Margret Westcott (1880-1924) 174
Made a Minerval 180
Martinist (BO) 180
Member of the Illuminati Order 30
No papers written on Illuminati 24
Non-masonic memberships 178
Not a member Ancient & Primitive Rite 43
Numbered papers 182
Ordre Martinist and Kabbalistic de la Rose-Croix 43
Publishing 181
Quatuor Coronati Lodge Papers 182
Secretary of Metropolitan College in 1885, 172
Setting up the illuminati 171
South Africa 24, 83, 174-176
S.R.I.A. 169, 171, 172
Steel trunk (archives) 24, 83
Stella Matutina 178-179, 186
Summer holiday 33
This enormous mistake 40-42
Two letters from Papus 17, 30, 33, 40, 42
Westcott and the S.R.I.A. 172
Westcott Illuminati letters 45
Wooden trunk (Westcott's papers) 23, 172, 181, 182
What, no images 26
White table lodges 195
William and Mary University in Virginia 96
William de Irwin Lodge, No. 162, 176
Wisdom schools 20, 108, 159
Women 34,165, 200, 203, 209,
Women and children 19, 116
Women members 20, 58, 116, 125, 154, 163,171, ,210,232
Women's Freemasonry 204, 209
Women's only Lodges 203
Wonderful bookshop 196, 204, 206, 209
Woodman, Dr William George Robert Woodman (1828-1891)
    169, 170, 172, 178, 179, 218
Woodman, W.G.R. (Imperator) 178
Word of the Grades
    Andreas Knight, Gabaon 140
    Andreas Knight, Notuma 139, 140, 141, 145, 154
    Minerval P.M.C.V., Per Me Coeci Vident 133- 136, 156
    Regents grade, REDEMTIS 161, 166
    Rose-Croix, I am that I am 166
    Synod/Epopt, I.N.R.I. and Mizpah 120, 144, 145, 146, 149,
    150, 154, 155, 156
Worshipped in spirit, God 110

Yale University 96
Yarker, John (1833-1913) 15, 30, 213
    6° as Supreme Grand Master of the Swedenborg Rite. 41
    A list of Yarker's writings 224
    Ancient & Primitive Rite of Masonry 40
    Conclusion 221
    English Martinist 40
    Freemasonry 217
    Initiated Baron Adolf Franz Leonhardi von Platz 34
    Is this to which Brother Reuss eludes 42
    John Yarker letters 45
    L'ancienne Maconnerie et le chevalier Ramsay 36
    Martinist Sovereign Delegate for Great Britain 34-35
    Non-masonic memberships 214
    Not blameless in this mistake 42
    Placates Westcott with Grand Senior Warden role 42
    Quatuor Coronati Research Lodge 223

Zelator on the 15 April 1880, 172
Zwack 95
ч ◊ Γ ◊ Μ 27, 28, 50, 57, 64, 69, 122, 124
ч ◊ Γ ◊ Μ or Z.O.Γ.O.M. not Z.O.T.O.M. 27